Fodor's 2014

CHICAGO

WELCOME TO CHICAGO

Chicago is a city with an appetite—for food, of course, but also for design, history, and culture. Come here to marvel at the cutting-edge architecture or take in the gorgeous views of Lake Michigan; to spend a day cheering with baseball fans and a night laughing at a comedy show; to shop, to visit renowned institutions like the Field Museum and the Adler Planetarium, and to experience the legendary blues scene. To do all this, you'll need nourishment: taste deep-dish pizza, piled-high hot dogs, Italian beef sandwiches, and more.

TOP REASONS TO GO

★ **Architecture:** The skyline dazzles with some of the country's most iconic buildings.

★ **Local Eats:** Cheap ethnic bites and gourmet chefs make Chicago a great food town.

★ **Art:** See everything from old masters at the Art Institute to outdoor sculptures in Millennium Park.

★ **Jazz and Blues:** Music venues are filled with both big-name legends and up-and-comers.

★ **Shopping:** Stop at designer shops on the Magnificent Mile or funky Wicker Park boutiques.

★ **Comedy:** Chicago improv venues are well-known training grounds for comedy superstars.

Fodor's CHICAGO 2014

Publisher: Amanda D'Acierno, *Senior Vice President*

Editorial: Arabella Bowen, *Executive Editorial Director*; Linda Cabasin, *Editorial Director*

Design: Fabrizio La Rocca, *Vice President, Creative Director*; Tina Malaney, *Associate Art Director*; Chie Ushio, *Senior Designer*; Ann McBride, *Production Designer*

Photography: Melanie Marin, *Associate Director of Photography*; Jessica Parkhill and Jennifer Romains, *Researchers*

Maps: Rebecca Baer, *Senior Map Editor*; Mark Stroud (Moon Street Cartography), David Lindroth, *Cartographers*

Production: Linda Schmidt, *Managing Editor*; Evangelos Vasilakis, *Associate Managing Editor*; Angela L. McLean, *Senior Production Manager*

Sales: Jacqueline Lebow, *Sales Director*

Marketing & Publicity: Heather Dalton, *Marketing Director*; Katherine Fleming, *Senior Publicist*

Business & Operations: Susan Livingston, *Vice President, Strategic Business Planning*; Sue Daulton, *Vice President, Operations*

Fodors.com: Megan Bell, *Executive Director, Revenue & Business Development*; Yasmin Marinaro, *Senior Director, Marketing & Partnerships*

Copyright © 2014 by Fodor's Travel, a division of Random House LLC.

Writers: Terri Colby, Carly Fisher, Jessica Herman, Heidi Moore, Roberta Sotonoff

Lead Editors: Amanda Sadlowski and Caroline Trefler

Editors: Heidi Johansen, Andrea Lehman, John Rambow

Production Editor: Elyse Rozelle

ISBN 978-0-7704-3268-3

ISSN 0743-9326

All details in this book are based on information supplied to us at press time. Always confirm information when it matters, especially if you're making a detour to visit a specific place. Fodor's expressly disclaims any liability, loss, or risk, personal or otherwise, that is incurred as a consequence of the use of any of the contents of this book.

SPECIAL SALES

This book is available at special discounts for bulk purchases for sales promotions or premiums. For more information, e-mail specialmarkets@randomhouse.com

PRINTED IN CHINA

10 9 8 7 6 5 4 3 2 1

CONTENTS

Fodor's Features

MAPS

ABOUT
THIS GUIDE

Fodor's Recommendations

Everything in this guide is worth doing—we don't cover what isn't—but exceptional sights, hotels, and restaurants are recognized with additional accolades. **Fodor's Choice★** indicates our top recommendations; and **Best Bets** calls attention to notable hotels and restaurants in various categories. Care to nominate a new place? Visit Fodors.com/contact-us.

Trip Costs

We list prices wherever possible to help you budget well. Hotel and restaurant price categories from **$** to **$$$$** are noted alongside each recommendation. For hotels, we include the lowest cost of a standard double room in high season. For restaurants, we cite the average price of a main course at dinner or, if dinner isn't served, at lunch. For attractions, we always list adult admission fees; discounts are usually available for children, students, and senior citizens.

Hotels

Our local writers vet every hotel to recommend the best overnights in each price category, from budget to expensive. Unless otherwise specified, you can expect private bath, phone, and TV in your room. For expanded hotel reviews, facilities, and deals, visit Fodors.com.

Restaurants

Unless we state otherwise, restaurants are open for lunch and dinner daily. We mention dress code only when there's a specific requirement and reservations only when they're essential or not accepted. To make restaurant reservations, visit Fodors.com.

Credit Cards

The hotels and restaurants in this guide typically accept credit cards. If not, we'll say so.

Top Picks		Hotels & Restaurants	
★	**Fodor's** Choice	⌂	Hotel
		⇆	Number of rooms
Listings		⦿⦿	Meal plans
⊠	Address	✕	Restaurant
⊠	Branch address	⚭	Reservations
☏	Telephone	🏛	Dress code
📠	Fax	▭	No credit cards
⊕	Website	$	Price
✉	E-mail		
🎫	Admission fee	**Other**	
☉	Open/closed times	⇨	See also
Ⓜ	Subway	☞	Take note
✛	Directions or Map coordinates	🏌	Golf facilities

1

EXPERIENCE CHICAGO

CHICAGO TODAY

A century ago, poet Carl Sandburg called Chicago "stormy, husky, brawling/city of the Big Shoulders" in an eponymous poem that still echoes city life today. Indeed, Chicago is stormier and huskier than ever, with political scandals breaking more frequently than the El train circles the Loop. But it's also cleaner, greener, and more urbane than expected—with bold new architecture, abundant green space, and a vibrant dining scene. So what will you find when you visit: a rough-and-tumble Midwestern town or a sophisticated metropolis? The answer is both, and much, much more.

Today's Chicago . . .

. . . is continually building and rebuilding. The iconic skyline dominates postcards and tourist snapshots—and for good reason. Architecture fans are excited to see the city that Daniel Burnham, Louis Sullivan, and Frank Lloyd Wright built, but modern development has also brought new energy. Recent years have seen the birth of the Millennium Park lakefront, the 92-story Trump Tower Chicago, and the innovative Aqua, an 82-story tower with balconies designed to look like waves. Development doesn't come without controversy, however. Some older buildings have been torn down to make way for the new, and preservationists decry each loss of a historic building to the wrecking ball.

. . . may have a little problem with corruption. Speaking of controversy, Chicago's political scene has witnessed the highest highs and the lowest lows in recent years. The high point: when about a quarter-million Chicagoans of every age, shape, and ethnicity gathered downtown to celebrate Illinois Senator Barack Obama's historic presidential election in 2008. The low point: pick one. Governor (and Chicago resident) Rod Blagojevich's 2011 conviction for trying to sell Obama's vacated Senate seat? Illinois Representative Jesse Jackson Jr.'s 2013 guilty plea to criminal charges of diverting campaign funds for personal use? Cook County Commissioner William Beavers's 2013 conviction for tax evasion? The Associated Press reported that there were 1,531 convictions for public corruption here between 1976 and 2010, the most of any district in the country.

. . . is a foodie's paradise. Visitors expecting deep-dish pizza and Italian beef sandwiches won't be disappointed, but they will have to elevate their expectations a

WHAT WE'RE TALKING ABOUT

If we're not waiting for the CTA (Chicago Transit Authority, that is), we're talking about it—complaining about the new high-capacity El cars or praising the Train Tracker estimated-arrivals app. We're uploading pics of the notable characters we encounter to the "People of the CTA" Facebook page. Equal measures funny, sad, and disgusting, the page had 109,000 "likes" at last count.

We rejoiced when the city finally lifted its ordinance banning onboard cooking on food trucks in July 2012. Although other restrictions have stopped some would-be operators from getting their mobile food vehicles rolling, there are still a slew of trucks offering already-prepared goodies. We track our favorites—like the Tamale Spaceship, Flirty Cupcakes, and the

hundredfold. Chicago is—dare we say it?—the most exciting city in the country for dining right now. It seems like there's a Food & Wine Best New Chef or *Top Chef* winner on every block. Sample cutting-edge cuisine from chef Grant Achatz at Next and Alinea, Homaro Cantu at Moto, and Graham Elliot at his eponymous restaurant. Gather for perfectly composed small plates at Stephanie Izard's Girl & the Goat, try to get reservations at Michael Carlson's notoriously always-booked Schwa, and venture north to Lincoln Square to the Michelin-starred Goosefoot (don't forget, it's BYOB). Or just spend your entire visit in Logan Square, where you'll have your pick of Lula Café, Telegraph Wine Bar, Longman & Eagle, and Revolution Brewing. Satisfied yet? We didn't even mention the hundreds of neighborhood ethnic eateries that let you dine across the globe without ever leaving the city.

. . . is in transition. Mayor Richard M. Daley's 22-year reign was a period of incredible resurgence for the city, complete with environmental development, sustainable building, and a failed Olympics bid. But it wasn't always diplomatic or even democratic, and the jury's still out on his replacement, another tough-talking Democrat—this time Obama's former chief of staff, Rahm Emanuel. His administration's hard-line tactics led to a highly contentious teachers' union strike in 2012, and kicked off 2013 with an unpopular decision to close 54 schools, the most in the city's history. The economy is still flailing, and devastating gun violence plagues the city's South and West sides.

. . . remains fiercely proud. Sure, Chicagoans like to complain—about the weather, about our sports teams, and especially about our politicians. But if an out-of-towner dares to diss our beloved city, you can bet there will be fireworks bigger than the ones over Navy Pier in summer. Sandburg was right again about Chicago when he wrote, "come and show me another city with lifted head singing/ so proud to be alive and coarse and strong and cunning."

Slide Ride (gourmet sliders)—on ChicagoFoodTruckFinder.com, RoamingHunger.com/Chi, and FoodTruckFreak.com, and we have our fingers crossed for a big food truck revolution any day now.

We're also big beer drinkers. If we're not busy home-brewing, we're heading to the local brewery to fill our growlers with the latest batch from Half Acre, Metropolitan Brewing, Piece, Haymarket, Revolution Brewing, and Finch's Beer Co.

Finally, we're huge on our sports teams. Whether we're bemoaning another Cubs' loss or celebrating the 2013 Stanley Cup victory of the Blackhawks, you can find our bars packed on game nights, cheering on the Bears, Cubs, White Sox, Blackhawks, and Bulls.

CHICAGO PLANNER

Visitor Centers

Chicago Cultural Center
✉ 77 E. Randolph St.
☎ 312/744–6630
🌐 www.cityofchicago.org
🕐 Mon.–Thurs. 9–7, Fri. and
Sat. 9–6, Sun. 10–5.

Chicago Water Works
✉ 163 E. Pearson St., at Michigan Ave. ☎ 312/742–8811
🌐 www.choosechicago.com
🕐 Jan.–Mar. 15, daily 10–5;
Mar. 16–June and Sept.–Dec.,
Mon.–Sat. 9:30–6, Sun. 10–5;
June–Sept., Mon.–Thurs. 9–7,
Fri. and Sat. 9–6, Sun. 10–6.

**Millennium Park Welcome
Center** ✉ 201 E. Randolph St.,
in the Northwest Exelon Pavilion, between Michigan Ave.,
and Columbus Ave.,
Loop ☎ 312/742–1168
🌐 www.millenniumpark.org
🕐 Daily 6 am–11 pm.

Getting Around

Chicago has an excellent network of buses and trains, which are collectively called the El (for "elevated," which many of them are). The combination should bring you within ¼ mile of any place you'd like to go. Those accustomed to cities will likely be comfortable on any train, anytime. Others may want to take extra caution after 11 pm. Buses are almost always safe; there are several express buses running from downtown to destinations like the Museum of Science and Industry.

As of this writing, the fare for the bus is $2, the train is $2.25, and a transfer is 25¢ with a Transit Card; if you're paying cash, all rides are $2.25. Travelers may want to get a Visitor Pass at their hotel, airport CTA stations, or any visitor center. These passes allow unlimited rides for a small fee, and are worth it as long as you take three trips a day.

For directions to specific places via public transportation, for public transportation maps, and for places to buy Transit Cards, see 🌐 www.transitchicago.com.

If you drive downtown, park in one of the giant city-owned parking lots underneath Millennium Park or by the Museum Campus, which charge a flat fee. Private lots usually cost double.

Street Smarts

Chicago is a city of about 2.8 million people, most of whom have good intentions. Still, it is a big city. It pays to be cautious and aware of your surroundings at all times.

Put down the cell phone and remove your earphones when strolling city streets or riding public transit. Hide valuables and flashy jewelry when you're out and about, or, better yet, leave them at home. Keep your purse or bags close to you and in clear view in restaurants and in bars. Never leave your belongings unattended, especially on trains or buses. Be polite but insistent with panhandlers. Legitimate vendors of *StreetWise*—the city's nonprofit magazine benefiting the homeless—should be able to provide an official badge. (The magazine sells for $2.)

Expect to have your bags and purses searched when entering sports stadiums, museums, and city buildings. You may be asked to show a photo ID at certain downtown buildings.

At night do what you would in any city: know your destination ahead of time, plan your route, and walk with confidence and purpose. Avoid dark or empty streets and skip those tempting shortcuts through the city's many alleys.

Saving Money

Chicago is a city of choices: you can splash out on the fanciest meals and pricey theater tickets or opt for fun activities that don't cost a dime.

If you plan to hit several major attractions, consider a **Chicago cityPASS** at participating locations or online (⊕ *www.citypass.com/chicago*). It will save you a combined total of about $80 on admission to these major attractions: Shedd Aquarium, the Field Museum, Skydeck Chicago at Willis (Sears) Tower, either the Museum of Science and Industry or John Hancock Center Observatory, and either Adler Planetarium or the Art Institute of Chicago. To save even more, time your museum visit for a day or time when admission is free. (⤳ *See "Free Things to Do" in this chapter for a comprehensive list of free museum days.)*

From spring to fall, neighborhood fests and free concerts abound. The most stunning place to catch a free concert is the Frank Gehry–designed Jay Pritzker Pavilion at Millennium Park. Daytime and evening concerts showcase everything from classical to jazz to punk rock.

When to Go

June, September, and October are mild and sunny. November through March the temperature ranges from crisp to bitter, April and May can fluctuate between cold/soggy and bright/warm, and July and August can either be perfect or serve up the deadly combo of high heat and high humidity. That said, the only thing certain about Chicago's weather, according to locals, is that it can change in an instant. If you head to Chicago in warmer months, you'll be able to catch some of the fantastic outdoor festivals; during the holiday season the city's decked out in lights.

Open Hours

Most businesses in Chicago are open 10–6. Some shops stay open as late as 9. Restaurants can be closed Monday, and usually stop serving around 10 pm on weeknights, 11 pm on weekends. There are a few 24-hour diners, but they are rarer than you might expect. Bars close at 2 am or 4 am.

Tickets

You can avoid the long lines at Chicago museums by buying tickets online at least a day in advance. The most popular architecture tour, led by the Chicago Architecture Foundation, always sells out—be sure to buy tickets in advance.

WHAT'S WHERE

Numbers refer to chapters.

2 The Loop, West Loop, and South Loop. Bounded by looping El tracks, the city's business center pulses with professionals scurrying between architectural landmarks. Restaurants and galleries dominate the West Loop; the once-desolate South Loop now teems with college students and condo dwellers.

3 Near North and River North. Shoppers stroll the Magnificent Mile between the John Hancock Center and the Chicago River, passing landmarks such as the Water Tower and Tribune Tower. Just north, stately mansions dominate the Gold Coast. Anchored by the Merchandise Mart, River North juxtaposes tourist traps with a thriving gallery scene.

4 Lincoln Park, Bucktown, Wicker Park, and Lincoln Square. Beyond the 1,200-acre park and the zoo, Lincoln Park boasts cafés and high-end boutiques. Starving artists used to call Wicker Park/ Bucktown home until skyrocketing rents killed the arty vibe. Most of the hipsters have decamped to Logan Square, where wide boulevards are lined with organic cafés, cocktail bars, and taquerias.

5 Lakeview and Far North Side. Baseball fans pilgrimage to Wrigley Field: just south of the ballpark, on Clark Street, are memorabilia shops and sports bars; a block east is Halsted Street, site of gay enclave Boystown. Farther north on Clark is Swedish-settled Andersonville, which has a quiet, residential feel.

6 Pilsen, Little Italy, and Chinatown. Mexican restaurants, mom-and-pop shops, and Spanish signage line 18th Street, the heart of Pilsen. Gone are many of the Near West Side's Italian groceries and shops, but you can still get a mean veal marsala on Taylor Street. In Chinatown skip the souvenir shops and head for the restaurants, teahouses, and bakeries.

7 Hyde Park. The main draw of this South Side neighborhood is the University of Chicago. Promontory Point has breathtaking lake and skyline views.

8 Outside Chicago. Just north of the city, Evanston is the site of Northwestern University and its leafy campus. West suburban Oak Park is best known for native sons Frank Lloyd Wright and Ernest Hemingway; Wright's home and studio are here, along with many notable examples of his architecture.

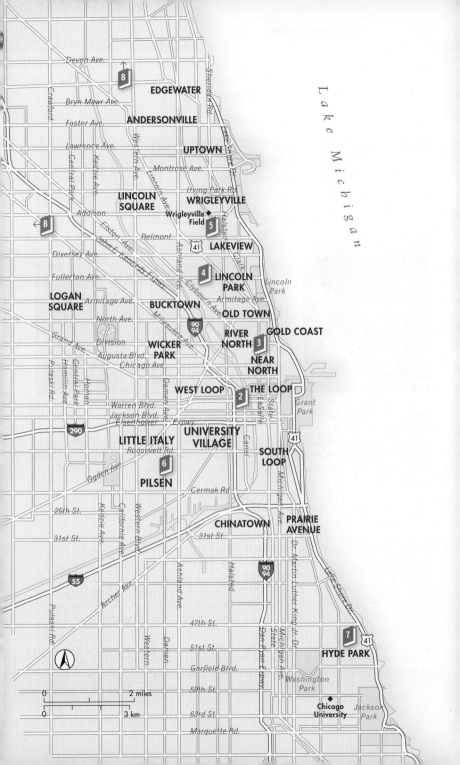

CHICAGO TOP ATTRACTIONS

Skydeck Chicago at Willis (Sears) Tower

(A) Take the ear-popping ride to the 103rd-floor observatory, where on a clear day you can see as far as Michigan, Wisconsin, and Indiana. At the top, interactive exhibits feature notable Chicagoans. Kids love Knee-High Chicago, a 4-foot-high exhibit that has cutouts of Chicago sports, history, and cultural icons at a child's eye-level. Fearless folks can step out onto the Ledge, twin glass boxes extending 4.3 feet from the Skydeck and suspended a dizzying 1,353 feet above the city. Security is very tight, so figure in a little extra time for your visit to the Skydeck.

John Hancock Center

(B) The third-tallest building in Chicago has the most impressive panoramic views of the lake and surrounding skyline—it's high enough to see the tops of neighboring buildings, but not so remote that you feel like you're looking out from a plane.

Skip the observatory and head to the bar that adjoins the Signature Room restaurant on the 95th floor—you'll spend your money on an exorbitantly priced cocktail instead of the entrance fee and enjoy the same view. Women can head to the 95th-floor ladies' room for the best view in the whole building.

The Magnificent Mile

(C) Exclusive shops, department stores, and boutiques line the northern half of swanky Michigan Avenue. Even better, the concentration of prestigious stores in vertical malls means you can get a lot of shopping done in winter without venturing into the bluster outside.

Navy Pier

(D) Yes, it's a little schlocky, but Navy Pier is fun, especially for families. Everyone can fan out to shop in the mall, play 18-hole minigolf in Pier Park in summer, see a movie at the IMAX Theatre, or explore the Chicago Children's Museum.

Plus, there's a stained-glass museum, a fun-house maze with scenes of Chicago landmarks, and an old-fashioned swing ride. Meet up later at the Ferris wheel for a photo op or just settle on the pier with a drink and enjoy the view.

Art Institute of Chicago

(E) This Chicago cultural gem has the country's best collection of Impressionist and Postimpressionist art, as well as the Renzo Piano–designed modern wing. It's also a great place to see all those paintings you've seen only on postcards, like *American Gothic* and *Nighthawks*.

Field Museum

(F) Say hello to Sue, the Field's beloved gigantic *T. rex,* before immersing yourself in this extraordinary museum's collection of anthropological and paleontological artifacts and animal dioramas. The dinosaurs are the thing here, but surprising collections of Tibetan Buddhist altars, mummies, and re-creations of famous gems may entice you to linger for hours.

Shedd Aquarium

(G) We find the experience of watching entire universities—not just schools—of fantastically colored fish, as well as dolphins and whales, completely mesmerizing. Don't miss the Wild Reef exhibit, where stingrays slide quietly under the Plexiglas at your feet.

Millennium Park

(H) Make a beeline for Frank Gehry's **Jay Pritzker Pavilion,** where an incredible sound system allows audiences to enjoy concert-hall sound in the great outdoors. The Bean, formally known as *Cloud Gate,* is a luminous polished-steel sculpture that plays tricks with the reflection of Chicago's skyline. In warmer months children of all ages can't resist a splash in the Crown Fountain, twin 50-foot towers that project close-up video images of Chicagoans "spitting" jets of water.

TOUR THE TOWN

Chicago Architecture Tours

Every great city has great buildings, but Chicago *is* its great buildings. Everything Chicagoans do is framed by some of the most remarkable architecture to be found anywhere. The best way to see the sky-scraping Loop towers or the horizontal sweep of the Prairie School is on one of these top tours.

Chicago Architecture Foundation. The foundation conducts excellent, docent-led boat, walking, and bus tours of the Loop and beyond. To get a panoramic view of Chicago's magnificent skyline, try the boat tours. The ArchiCenter, the foundation's home, also hosts exhibitions, lectures, and discussions. ⊠ *Santa Fe Bldg., 224 S. Michigan Ave.* ☎ *312/922–3432* ⊕ *www.architecture.org* ⊠ *$10 (and up) walking tours, $37.85 boat tour* ☉ *Walking tours run year-round; boat tours available April–Nov., daily.*

Chicago Greeter. Savvy local volunteers run free two- to four-hour walking tours of the city's neighborhoods and areas of interest, such as fashion, film, and public art. Tours run daily at 10 am and 1 pm; make your reservation 10 business days in advance. Those who don't sign up in advance for a Chicago Greeter tour can show up for an on-the-spot InstaGreeter tour, offered Friday through Sunday 10–4. Both Chicago Greeter and InstaGreeter tours depart from the Visitor Information Center at Chicago Cultural Center. ⊠ *77 E. Randolph St.* ☎ *312/744–8000* ⊕ *www.chicagogreeter.com.*

Chicago Trolley and Double Decker Co. This hop-on, hop-off ride takes visitors to many downtown and Loop highlights and allows you the flexibility to stop at attractions that catch your fancy. ☎ *773/648–5000* ⊕ *www.chicagotrolley.com* ⊠ *$35.*

TOUR ALTERNATIVES

Hop on a Shoreline water taxi and cruise down the river or on the lake. You won't get running narration, but it's not crowded and it's affordable—single rides range from $5 to $8 with stops at the Michigan Avenue Bridge, Union Station/Willis (Sears) Tower, Navy Pier, and the Museum Campus.

For a more adventurous spin down the river, rent a canoe or a kayak. Just beware of large boats and crew shells.

Kayak Chicago ⊠ *1501 N. Magnolia Ave.* ☎ *630/336–7245* ⊕ *www.kayakchicago.com.*

Wateriders ⊠ *Kingsbury Yacht Club, 950 N. Kingsbury St.* ☎ *312/953–9287* ⊕ *www.wateriders.com.*

River and Lakefront Tours

Hop into a boat and sail down the Chicago River for some of the prettiest views of the city. Some tours even head out to the lake for a skyscraper-studded panorama.

Mercury Chicago's Skyline Cruiseline. Mercury does Canine Cruises, where dogs are welcome, and a Chicago By Night tour at sunset. ⊠ *112 E. Wacker Dr.* ☎ *312/332–1353* ⊕ *mercuryskylinecruiseline.com* ⊠ *$28* ☉ *May–Oct., daily.*

Shoreline Sightseeing. Shoreline's been plying these waters since 1939 and has tours of both the river and Lake Michigan. ☎ *312/222–9328* ⊕ *www.shorelinesightseeing.com* ☉ *Apr.–Oct., daily; Nov., weekends only.*

Tall Ship Adventures of Chicago. Adventure and education meet on lake tours that illuminate Chicago's maritime history, the life of lake sailors, and environmentalism. In 2006 then-Mayor Richard M. Daley

declared the tall ship *Windy* the flagship of Chicago. ☎ *312/595–5555* ⊕ *www.tallshipadventuresofchicago.com.*

Wendella. See the city at dusk on the Chicago at Sunset tour. There's also a river architecture tour and a combined river and lake tour. ✉ *400 N. Michigan Ave., at the Wrigley Bldg.* ☎ *312/337–1446* ⊕ *www.wendellaboats.com* ☉ *Apr.–Nov., daily.*

Special-Interest Tours

Whether you're a foodie, a history buff, or a shopaholic, there's a custom tour for you.

Chicago Food Planet Food Tours. Sample local delicacies like deep-dish pizza, Polish pastries, Chicago-style hot dogs, and Szechuan cuisine on a Near North, Bucktown–Wicker Park, or Chinatown food-and-cultural tour. ☎ *312/445–9948* ⊕ *www.chicagofoodplanet.com.*

Chicago ShopWalk. Shop 'til you drop on one of these specialized trips focusing on local designers and boutiques. Personalized itineraries are available. ☎ *773/255–7866* ⊕ *www.chicagoshopwalk.com.*

Untouchable Tours: Chicago's Original Gangster Tour. Your guides, in character as Prohibition-era goons, take you on a bus tour through Chicago's checkered mafia past. Though the kitsch factor is high, the tours are stuffed with history and will take you to neighborhoods you might otherwise miss. ☎ *773/881–1195* ⊕ *www.gangstertour.com* ☒ *$30.*

Behind the Scenes

For a look at what (or who) makes the city tick, check out the following activities.

Federal Reserve Bank of Chicago. The facility processes currency and checks, scanning bills for counterfeits, destroying unfit currency, and repackaging fit currency. A visitor center in the lobby has permanent exhibits of old bills, counterfeit

money, and a million dollars in $1 bills. One-hour tours explain how money travels and show a high-speed currency-processing machine. Call in advance for reservations. ✉ *230 S. LaSalle St., Loop* ☎ *312/322–2400* ⊕ *www.chicagofed.org* ☒ *Free.*

Goose Island Brewery. Follow a brewer on a tour of this well-known Chicago brewery producing hand-crafted lagers, ales, and vintage ales. During the tour you'll sample six beers from the current rotation and receive a souvenir pint glass to take home. Reserve at least a week in advance. Tour participants must be 21 or older with valid ID. ✉ *1800 N. Clybourn Ave., Lincoln Park* ☎ *312/915–0071* ⊕ *www.gooseisland.com/pages/clybourn_brewpub* ☒ *$10* ☉ *Tours last 60–90 minutes and take place Sat. at 12:30, 2, and 3:30 and Sun. at 1 and 2:30.*

CITY ITINERARIES

Two Hours in Town

If you've got only a bit of time, go to a museum. Although you could spend days in any of the city's major museums, two hours will give you a quick taste of Chicago's cultural riches. Take a brisk walk around the **Art Institute** to see Grant Wood's *American Gothic*, Edward Hopper's *Nighthawks*, and one of the finest Impressionist collections in the country. Or check out the major dinosaur collection or the gorgeous Native American regalia at the **Field Museum**. Take a close look at the sharks at the **Shedd Aquarium.** If the weather's nice, stroll along the lakefront outside the **Adler Planetarium**—you'll see one of the nicest skyline views in the city. Wander down State Street or the Magnificent Mile or around Millennium Park. If you're hungry, indulge in one of Chicago's three famous culinary treats—deep-dish pizza (head to **Pizzeria Due** to avoid the lines at **Giordano's, Gino's,** and **Pizzeria Uno**); garden-style hot dogs; or Italian beef sandwiches. After dark? Hear some music at a local club. Catch some blues at **Blues Chicago** to get a taste of authentic Chicago.

■TIP→ Remember that many of the smaller museums are closed Monday.

A Perfect Afternoon

Do the zoo. Spend some time at the free **Lincoln Park Zoo and Conservatory** (the tropical plants will warm you up in winter), take a ride on the exotic animal–themed carousel, and then spend a couple of hours at the nearby **Chicago History Museum** for a quirky look at the city's past. If you'd like to stay in the Lincoln Park neighborhood a bit longer, have dinner at one of many great local restaurants and then head to **The Second City,** the sketch-comedy troupe that was the precursor to *Saturday Night Live.*

■TIP→ The Second City offers free improvisation after the last performance every night but Friday.

Sightseeing in the Loop

State Street, that Great Street, is home to the old **Marshall Field's,** which has been reborn as Macy's; Louis Sullivan's ornate iron entrance to the **Sullivan Center;** and a nascent theater district; as well as great people-watching. Start at Harold Washington Library at Van Buren and State streets and walk north, venturing a block east to the beautiful **Chicago Cultural Center** when you hit Randolph Street. Grab lunch at the Museum of Contemporary Art's serene Wolfgang Puck café, **Puck's at the MCA,** and then spend a couple of hours with in-your-face art. Go for steak at Morton's or the Palm before a night of Chicago theater. Broadway touring shows are on Randolph Street at the Ford Center for the Performing Arts Oriental Theatre or the Cadillac Palace, or head elsewhere for excellent local theater—the Goodman, Steppenwolf, Lookingglass, and Chicago Shakespeare will each give you a night to remember.

Get Outdoors

Begin with a long walk (or run) along the lakefront, or rent a bike or in-line skates and watch the waves on wheels. Then catch an El train north to **Wrigley Field** for Cubs baseball; grab a dog at the seventh-inning stretch, and sing your heart out to "Take Me Out to the Ball Game." Afterward, soak up a little beer and atmosphere on the patio at one of the local sports bars. Finish up with an outdoor concert in **Grant or Millennium Park.**

Family Time

Start at **Navy Pier**—or heck, spend all day there. The **Chicago Children's Museum** is a main attraction, but there's also an IMAX theater, a Ferris wheel, a swing ride, a fun house, a stained-glass museum, and, in summer, Chicago-themed miniature golf in Pier Park. If the crowds at the Pier get to be too much, walk to **Millennium Park**, where kids of all ages can ice-skate in winter and play in the fountain in summer, where giant digital portraits of Chicagoans spit streams of water to help cool you off. Whatever the weather, make sure to get your picture taken in the mirrored center of the Bean—the sculpture that's formally known as *Cloud Gate*. At night in summertime, take a stroll by Buckingham Fountain, where the dancing sprays jump to music and are illuminated by computer-controlled colored lights, or take a turn on the dance floor during Chicago's SummerDance celebration.

■■■**TIP→** Fireworks explode near Navy Pier every Wednesday at 9:30 pm and Saturday at 10:15 pm Memorial Day through Labor Day.

Cityscapes

Start at the top. Hit the heights of the **John Hancock Center** or **Skydeck Chicago** at the Willis (Sears) Tower for a grand view of the city and the lake. Then take a walking tour of downtown with a well-informed docent from the **Chicago Architecture Foundation**. In the afternoon, wander north to the **Michigan Avenue Bridge**, where you can take an informative boat tour of the Chicago River. Enjoy the architecture as you float by, resting your weary feet.

Shop Chicago

Grab your bankroll and stroll the **Magnificent Mile** in search of great buys and souvenirs. Walking north from around the Michigan Avenue Bridge, window-shop your way along the many upscale stores. Hang a left on **Oak Street** for the most elite boutiques. **Accent Chicago** (⌂ *875 N. Michigan Ave.*) is where serious souvenir hunters spend their cash. Dedicated shoppers will want to detour a little farther south to **State Street** in the Loop for a walk through the landmark Marshall Field's building, now Macy's. For a culture buzz, check out the **Museum of Contemporary Art** (closed Monday). After making a tough restaurant choice (prime rib at Smith & Wollensky's or Lawry's? or deep-dish pizza at Giordano's?), consider a nightcap at the **Signature Room** at the 95th-floor bar on top of the John Hancock Center—the city will be spread beneath your feet.

AUTHENTIC CHICAGO

So you've done the Art Institute and the Willis (Sears) Tower—now it's time to put away your tourist hat and make like a local. Luckily, it's not hard to figure out what Chicagoans like to do in their spare time. Here's how to follow in their footsteps.

Get Out of Downtown

Chicago is a city of neighborhoods, and in many of them you can see traces of each successive immigrant group. Each neighborhood in the city has its own flavor, reflected in its architecture, public art, restaurants, and businesses, and most have their own summer or holiday festivals. Here are a few standout 'hoods.

Andersonville. The charming diversity of the Swedish/Middle Eastern/gay mélange of Andersonville means you can have lingonberry pancakes for breakfast, hummus for lunch, and drinks at a gay-friendly bar after dinner.

Bronzeville. Bronzeville's famous local historic figures include Ida B. Wells—a women's-rights and African-American civil-rights crusader—the trumpeter Louis Armstrong, and Bessie Coleman, the first African-American woman pilot. The area has nine landmark buildings and is rapidly gentrifying.

Chinatown. The Chinese New Year dragon parade is just one reason to visit Chinatown, which has dozens of restaurants and shops and a quiet riverfront park.

Devon Avenue. Devon Avenue turns from Indian to Pakistani to Russian Orthodox to Jewish within a few blocks. Try on a sari, buy a bagel or electronics, or just people-watch—it's an excellent place to spend the afternoon.

Little Italy. Though most Italians moved to the West Side a couple of generations ago, Little Italy's Italian restaurants and lemonade stands still draw them back.

Pilsen/Little Village. The best Mexican restaurants are alongside Pilsen's famous murals. Be sure to stop into the National Museum of Mexican Art, which will give you an even deeper appreciation of the culture.

Brave the Cold

The city's brutal windy winters are infamous, but that doesn't keep Chicagoans from making the best out of the long cold months. Throw on lots of layers, lace up your ice skates, and show those city dwellers what you're made of.

The rink at **Millennium Park** (⊠ 55 N. Michigan Ave., Loop ☎ 312/742–1168 ⊕ www.millenniumpark.org) has free skating seven days a week from mid-November to mid-March and a dazzling view of the Chicago skyline. Skate rentals are $10 a session.

On the snowiest days some hardy souls **cross-country ski** and snowshoe on the lakeshore—bring your own equipment.

Loosen up by playing outdoor paddle tennis at **Midtown Tennis Club** (⊠ 2020 W. Fullerton Ave. ☎ 773/235–2300 ⊕ www.midtowntennisclub.com). If it's snowing, they turn on the heated floors.

Holiday-walk Chicago's windows during the **Magnificent Mile Lights Festival**, in November, the Saturday before Thanksgiving. The celebration includes music, ice-carving contests, and stage shows, and ends in a parade and the illumination of more than 1 million lights.

FREE THINGS TO DO

It's easy to spend money in Chicago, what with shopping, museum-entrance fees, restaurants, and theater, but if you'd like to put your wallet away for a while, here are some options. The Lincoln Park Zoo is also free.

Free Art

Chicago has some of the most famous public art in the country, including a **Picasso** in Daley Plaza, **Alexander Calder's** *Flamingo* in Federal Plaza, and the *Cloud Gate* sculpture in Millennium Park. For a fairly comprehensive list, see ⊕ *cityofchicago.org/publicart* or pick up a *Chicago Public Art* guide at a visitor center.

The **City Gallery** (⊠ *806 N. Michigan Ave.* ☎ *312/742–0808*) in the Historic Water Tower has rotating exhibits of Chicago-themed photography.

Five different galleries showcase contemporary visual art by local artists at the **Chicago Cultural Center** (⊠ *78 E. Washington St.* ☎ *312/744–6630* ⊕ *www. chicagoculturalcenter.org*).

Free Concerts

Grant Park and Millennium Park host regular classical and pop concerts in summer. For a schedule, pick up the *Chicago Reader* or visit the *TimeOut Chicago* website at *www.timeoutchicago.com*.

Chicago is a festival town, celebrating blues, jazz, and world music during the warm months. For a schedule, see ⊕ *www.explorechicago.org*.

Free concerts—from classic and jazz to electronica and world beat—are performed most weekdays at 12:15 in the **Chicago Cultural Center** (⊠ *78 E. Washington St.* ☎ *312/744–6630* ⊕ *www. chicagoculturalcenter.org*).

Free Movies

Local library branches and parks across the city show free movies throughout the summer—check the Chicago Park District website for details (⊕ *www. chicagoparkdistrict.com*).

Free Fireworks

Every Wednesday and Saturday night in summer Navy Pier puts on a showy display of colorful explosives. Watch from the pier or along the waterfront opposite Buckingham Fountain.

Free Improv

The world-famous Second City comedy troupe has a free improv set after the last performance every night but Friday. For more information, go to ⊕ *www. secondcity.com* or call ☎ *312/664–4032*.

Free Museum Days

Always Free: Jane Addams Hull-House Museum, Museum of Contemporary Photography, National Museum of Mexican Art, Oriental Institute Museum, Smart Museum of Art

Sunday: DuSable Museum of African-American History

Tuesday: Swedish American Museum Center (second Tuesday of each month)

Wednesday: Art Institute of Chicago (first and second Wednesday of each month)

Thursday: Chicago Children's Museum (5–8 pm only), Peggy Notebaert Nature Museum

∎ TIP→ The Shedd Aquarium, the Museum of Science and Industry, and the Field Museum, among others, offer free admission on certain weekdays in the winter; call the museums or visit their websites for specific dates.

CHICAGO WITH KIDS

Chicago sometimes seems to have been designed with kids in mind. There are many places to play and things to do, from building sand castles at one of the lakefront's many beaches to playing 18-hole minigolf at Navy Pier in summer. Here are some suggestions for ways to show kids the sights.

Museums

Several area museums are specifically designed for kids. At the **Chicago Children's Museum** (⌧ *700 E. Grand Ave., Navy Pier*) three floors of exhibits cast off with a play structure in the shape of a schooner, where kids can walk the gangplank and slide down to the lower level, and make a splash with a water playground, featuring a scaled-down river and a waterwheel.

Also at **Navy Pier** you'll find a Ferris wheel and Viennese swings (the kind that go around in a circle like a merry-go-round). In summer, crowds of kids make the most of Pier Park's 18-hole minigolf course, musical carousel, and remote-control boats.

Many other Chicago museums are also kid-friendly, especially the butterfly haven and the animal habitat exhibit with its climbable tree house at the **Peggy Notebaert Nature Museum,** the replica coal mine and hands-on Idea Factory at the **Museum of Science and Industry,** the dinosaur exhibits at the **Field Museum,** and the sharks and dolphins at the **John G. Shedd Aquarium.**

Parks, Zoos, and Outside Activities

Chicago's neighborhoods are dotted with area play lots that have playground equipment as well as several ice-skating rinks for winter months. On scorching days, visit the **63rd Street Beach House,** at 63rd Street and Lake Shore Drive in Woodlawn. The interactive spiral fountain in the courtyard jumps and splashes,

> **MORE IDEAS FROM FODORS.COM FORUMS**
>
> ■ Holiday Lights Festival on Michigan Avenue
>
> ■ Bulls, Cubs, or White Sox game
>
> ■ Day trip to Oak Park
>
> ■ Gospel Brunch at House of Blues (☏ *312/923–2000*)
>
> ■ Chicago Architecture Foundation Cruise (⊕ *www.architecture.org*)

leaving kids giggling and jumping. The **North Park Village Nature Center** on the far northwest side (on Pulaski Road north of Bryn Mawr Avenue) is a wilderness oasis, serving up 46 acres of trails and a kid-oriented Nature Center with hands-on activities and fun educational programs. Deer sightings are common here.

Millennium Park (⌧ *55 N. Michigan Ave.*) has a 16,000-square-foot ice-skating rink. Skaters have an unparalleled view of downtown as they whiz around the ice.

For more structured fun, there are two zoos: the free **Lincoln Park Zoo** (⌧ *2200 N. Cannon Dr., at Lake Shore Dr. and Fullerton Pkwy.*) and the large, suburban **Brookfield Zoo** (⌧ *1st Ave. and 31st St., Brookfield*), which has surprising exhibits such as a wall of pulsing jellyfish.

FABULOUS FESTIVALS

Chicago festivals range from local neighborhood get-togethers to citywide extravaganzas. Try to catch a neighborhood street fair for some great people-watching if you're in town between June and September. For details, see ⊕ *www.chicagoreader.com* or ⊕ *timeoutchicago.com*.

Chicago Air & Water Show. Thrill-seekers and families flock to the Chicago Air & Water Show, a lakefront spectacle featuring aerial acrobatics and daredevil water acts. See the U.S. Navy Blue Angels perform precision flying maneuvers at the two-day event in mid-August. ✉ *Lakeshore, Fullerton Ave. to Oak St.; focal point at North Ave. Beach* ☎ *312/744–3315* ⊕ *www.cityofchicago.org/city/en/depts/dca/supp_info/chicago_air_and_watershow.html*.

Chicago Blues Festival. The Chicago Blues Festival, in Grant Park, is a popular three-day, four-stage event in June starring blues greats from Chicago and around the country. If you see only one festival in Chicago, this is the one. ☎ *312/744–3315* ⊕ *www.cityofchicago.org/city/en/depts/dca/supp_info/chicago_blues_festival.html*.

Chicago Jazz Festival. The Chicago Jazz Festival holds sway for four days during Labor Day weekend in Millennium and Grant parks. ☎ *312/744–3315* ⊕ *www.cityofchicago.org/city/en/depts/dca/supp_info/chicago_jazz_festival.html*.

Magnificent Mile Lights Festival. The holiday season officially starts with the Magnificent Mile Lights Festival, a weekend-long event at the end of November with tons of family-friendly activities including musical performances, ice-carving contests, and stage shows. The fanfare culminates in a parade and the illumination of more than 1 million lights along Michigan Avenue. ⊕ *www.magnificentmilelightsfestival.com*.

St. Patrick's Day parade. The St. Patrick's Day parade turns the city on its head: the Chicago River is dyed green, shamrocks decorate the street, and the center stripe of Dearborn Street is painted the color of the Irish from Wacker Drive to Van Buren Street. This is your chance to get your fill of bagpipes, green beer, and green knee socks. It's more than four hours long, so you probably won't see the whole thing. ☎ *312/942–9188* ⊕ *www.chicagostpatsparade.com*.

Taste of Chicago. Taste of Chicago dishes out pizza, cheesecake, and other Chicago specialties to 3.5 million people over a 10-day period before the July Fourth holiday. ✉ *Grant Park, Columbus Dr. between Jackson and Randolph Sts.* ☎ *312/744–3315* ⊕ *www.cityofchicago.org/city/en/depts/dca/supp_info/taste_of_chicago.html*.

World Music Festival. At the weeklong World Music Festival, international artists play traditional and contemporary music at venues across the city in September. ⊕ *www.worldmusicfestivalchicago.org*.

Street fairs. Street fairs are held every week in summer, but two stand out as the best. **North Halsted Market Days,** in August, is the city's largest street festival. It's held in the heart of the gay community of Lakeview and has blocks and blocks of vendors as well as some wild entertainment, such as zany drag queens and radical cheerleaders. The **Taste of Randolph,** in June, is more sedate, featuring dishes from the fine restaurants lining the western end of Randolph Street. ⊕ *www.northalsted.com/pages/northalsted_market_days_/29.php* ⊕ *starevents.com/festivals/taste-of-randolph/*.

CHICAGO THEN AND NOW

The Early Days

Before Chicago was officially "discovered" by the team of Father Jacques Marquette, a French missionary, and Louis Jolliet, a French-Canadian mapmaker and trader, in 1673, the area served as a center of trade and seasonal hunting grounds for several Native American tribes, including the Miami, Illinois, and Pottawattomie. Villages kept close trading ties with the French, though scuffles with the Fox tribe kept the French influence at bay until 1779. That year, black French trader Jean Baptiste Point du Sable built a five-room "mansion" by the mouth of the Chicago River on the shore of Lake Michigan.

The Great Fire

The city grew until 1871, when a fire in the barn of Catherine and Patrick O'Leary spread across the city, killing hundreds. (Contrary to the legend, it was probably not started by a cow kicking over a lantern.) A recent drought coupled with crowded wooden buildings and wood-brick streets allowed the blaze to take hold quickly, destroying 18,000 structures within 36 hours.

Gangsters to the Great Migration

World War I (aka the Great War) changed the face of Chicago. Postwar—and especially during Prohibition (1920–33)—the Torrio–Capone organization expanded its gambling and liquor distribution operations, consolidating its power during the violent "beer wars" from 1924 to 1930. Hundreds of casualties include the seven victims of the infamous 1929 St. Valentine's Day Massacre. In 1934 the FBI gunned down bank robber and "Public Enemy No. 1" John Dillinger outside the Biograph Theater on the North Side, now a theater venue and a Chicago landmark.

The Great War also led to the Great Migration, when African-Americans from the South moved to the northern cities between 1916 and 1970. World War I slowed immigration from Europe, but increased jobs in Chicago's manufacturing industry. More than 500,000 African-Americans came to the city to find work, and by the mid-20th century African-Americans were a strong force in Chicago's political, economic, and cultural life.

IMPORTANT DATES IN CHICAGO HISTORY

1673	Chicago discovered by Marquette and Jolliet
1837	Chicago incorporated as a city
1860	First national political convention. Abraham Lincoln nominated as the Republican candidate for president
1871	Great Chicago Fire

The Notorious 1968 Democratic Convention

The Daley dynasty began when Richard J. Daley became mayor in 1955. He was reelected five times, and his son Richard M. Daley ran the city until recently.

The first Mayor Daley redrew Chicago's landscape, overseeing the construction of O'Hare International Airport, the expressway system, the University of Illinois at Chicago, and a towering skyline. He also helped John F. Kennedy get elected.

Despite these advances, Mayor Richard J. Daley is perhaps best known for his crackdown on student protesters during the 1968 Democratic National Convention. Americans watched on their televisions as the Chicago police beat the city's youth with sticks and blinded them with tear gas. That incident, plus his "shoot-to-kill" order during the riots that followed the assassination of Dr. Martin Luther King Jr., and his use of public funds to build giant, disastrous public housing projects like Cabrini–Green, eventually led to the temporary dissolution of the Democratic machine in Chicago. After Daley's death, Chicago's first black—and beloved—mayor, Harold Washington, took office in 1983.

Chicago Today

The thriving commercial and financial "City of Broad Shoulders" is spiked with gorgeous architecture and set with cultural and recreational gems, including the Art Institute, Millennium Park, 250 theater companies, and 30 miles of shoreline. Approximately 2.8 million residents live within the city limits, and tens of thousands commute from the ever-sprawling suburbs to work downtown.

The last Mayor Daley gave downtown a makeover, adding wrought-iron street furniture, planters of flowers, and Millennium Park. His focus on ecofriendly building initiatives led to a green roof installed on City Hall and brought new bike paths.

There are always controversies (former governor Rod Blagojevich was convicted of federal corruption charges in 2011 and current Mayor Rahm Emanuel is no stranger to contention), but most Chicagoans are fiercely proud to call the city home.

IMPORTANT DATES IN CHICAGO HISTORY

1886	Haymarket Riot
1893	World's Columbian Exposition
1968	Democratic National Convention
1973	Sears (now Willis) Tower, tallest building in North America, completed
2008	Then–Illinois Senator Barack Obama elected 44th president of the United States

FOR "DA FANS"

You can't talk about Chicago for long without hearing the name of at least one of its storied sports legends: Michael Jordan, Scottie Pippen, Walter "Sweetness" Payton, William "Refrigerator" Perry, Ernie Banks, "Slammin'" Sammy Sosa, "Shoeless" Joe Jackson. Sports fandom runs through the city's veins, win or lose. One of the best ways to experience the true spirit of Chicago is to join its fiercely loyal fans at a game.

Chicago Bears

Even people who don't know the gridiron from a nine-iron are familiar with "Da Bears," as immortalized in the famous *Saturday Night Live* skit. Chicago's hard-fought, smash-mouth brand of football has made the Monsters of the Midway the winningest franchise in NFL history; they won their 700th game in 2010. The team made it to the Super Bowl in 2006, eventually losing to the Colts, but after a disappointing 2011 season, general manager Jerry Angelo was fired and Phil Emery took over the reins. Despite a promising 7-1 start to the 2012 season, the Bears narrowly missed the playoffs with a final record of 10-6.

Where They Play: Soldier Field ⊠ *1410 South Museum Campus Drive, Near South Side*

Season: August–December

How to Buy Tickets: Ticketmaster ☎ *312/559–1212* ⊕ *www.chicagobears.com*

Most Notable Players: Dick Butkus, Mike Ditka, Sid Luckman, Bronko Nagurski, Walter Payton, Gale Sayers

Past Highlights: Jim McMahon's "statement" headbands and eventual Hall of Famer Richard Dent's stellar play helped the team shuffle right up to the Vince Lombardi Trophy after winning Super Bowl XX.

Chicago Bulls

Although the days of Air Jordan, three-peats, and Dennis Rodman in wedding dresses may be firmly in the rearview mirror, the legacy established by winning six championships in eight years has sustained the team's popularity, even through the leaner years that followed. Now, a new squad of fresh faces, led by consensus 2011 MVP Derrick Rose, is looking to put its stamp on the next Bulls dynasty. While Rose missed the entire 2012-2013 season due to an injury, the team still made the Eastern Conference Finals. They lost to the Miami Heat, but five consecutive years of playoff appearances indicate that the Bulls are back in the game for good.

Where They Play: United Center ⊠ *1901 W. Madison St., near West Side*

Season: October–April

How to Buy Tickets: Ticket office ☎ *312/455–4000* ⊕ *www.bulls.com*

Most Notable Players: Michael Jordan, Dennis Rodman, Scottie Pippen, Toni Kukoc

Past Highlights: The Bulls owned the 1990s, becoming the only team in NBA history to win more than 70 games in a season in 1995–96 with an incredible 72–10 record.

Note: Don't leave the game early to wander this area at night. There's no street parking, so plan to park in a nearby parking lot.

Chicago Cubs

Cubbies fans are certainly loyal, sticking by their "boys in blue" for 102 championship-free years. Some blame the record losing streak on a curse made by Billy Sianis, owner of the Billy Goat Tavern, after he and his ticket-holding goat were booted from Wrigley during Game 4 of the 1945 Cubs–Tigers World Series. The ensuing years have had their share of goats, but with new ownership, a new

manager in Mike Quade, and several promising young players, hope springs eternal for the Lovable Losers.

Where They Play: Wrigley Field ✉ *1060 W. Addison St., Lakeview*

Season: April–September

How to Buy Tickets: Ticket office ☎ *773/404-2827* ⊕ *www.chicago.cubs.mlb.com*

Most Notable Players: Ernie Banks, Ron Santo, Ryne Sandberg, Sammy Sosa

Past Highlights: "Slammin'" Sammy Sosa played a major role in reawakening Americans' interest in baseball in 1998 as he battled Mark McGwire in a historic chase for the home run record, finishing with 66 home runs.

Note: Take a 90-minute tour of the Friendly Confines for $25 per person.

Chicago White Sox

The South Side favorites won the World Series in 2005, sweeping the Astros in four games. Since then, though, the Sox have made the playoffs only once, when they won the AL Central in 2008. In 2011 manager Ozzie Guillen was replaced by former third baseman Robin Ventura, but so far performance has been uneven. The team spent much of 2012 in first place, only to slide downhill dramatically in the final weeks of the season.

Where They Play: U.S. Cellular Field ✉ *333 W. 35th St., South Side*

Season: April–September

How to Buy Tickets: Ticket office ☎ *312/674-1000* ⊕ *www.whitesox.mlb.com*

Most Notable Players: "Shoeless" Joe Jackson, Nellie Fox, Luis Aparicio, Harold Baines, Frank Thomas

Past Highlights: In July 2009 Mark Buehrle, a veteran pitcher who has spent his entire career with the White Sox, notched the second perfect game in the team's history, earning him a congratulatory phone call from President Obama (an avowed Sox fan).

Note: The area around the Cell is sketchy—don't leave valuables in your car, and be careful getting back to your car at night.

Chicago Blackhawks

Though the Hawks have led the NHL in attendance for the last three seasons, they too were hit by the seemingly citywide championship drought, having failed to win a Stanley Cup since 1961. But that's all changed: four straight years in the playoffs have seen two championships, with the Cup coming back to the Windy City in both 2010 and 2013. Owner Rocky Wirtz, the son of much-maligned owner William "Dollar Bill" Wirtz, deserves credit for changing ownership policies to attract elite talent—and fans—back to the United Center.

Where They Play: United Center ✉ *1901 W. Madison St., Near West Side*

Season: October–April

How to Buy Tickets: Ticket office ☎ *800/745-3000* ⊕ *www.blackhawks.nhl.com*

Most Notable Players: Stan Mikita, Pierre Pilote, Bobby Hull, Denis Savard, Tony Esposito

Past Highlights: The Hawks brought the Cup home to Chicago in 2010 on a thrilling sudden-death overtime goal by Patrick Kane to beat the Flyers in Game 6. Even the Chicago Picasso donned a hockey mask in celebration.

Note: There is no street parking near the United Center, so plan to park in a nearby parking lot.

A GOOD PUBLIC ART WALK

Chicago's museums house some of the most famous art anywhere, but don't forget the city's great outdoors. Some of the most impressive art here is outside, in plazas, parks, and other public spaces. The best part? It's all free.

Michigan Avenue and Millennium Park

Start your tour in front of the **Art Institute of Chicago** on Michigan Avenue at Adams Street, where you'll see the two iconic bronze lion statues that guard the entrance. Head north to the well-manicured paths of the museum's two public gardens, filled with fountains and sculptures, including Alexander Calder's **Flying Dragon.**

Exit at the south end of Millennium Park and check out the **Crown Fountain,** two 50-foot glass block towers separated by a granite reflecting pool. The towers project a collection of video images of the faces of 1,000 Chicagoans filmed by artist Jaume Plensa. From time to time, one of the faces sports pursed lips and "spits" water down, showering the shrieking crowd below. Don't miss Anish Kapoor's first public outdoor piece, **Cloud Gate** (affectionately called "the Bean" by locals). The shiny surface is like a giant fun-house mirror reflecting and distorting the skyline. Also of note is the Frank Gehry–designed **Jay Pritzker Pavilion,** an outdoor concert venue with curling ribbons of steel that frame the opening to the stage and connect to a trellis sound system.

Enter the Loop

Pass the Greek-inspired peristyle at the park's northwest corner to exit the park at Randolph Street. Head west on Randolph to **We Will,** a contemporary steel sculpture that's local artist Richard Hunt's ode to the city's diversity. Continue west until you reach the plaza of the James R. Thompson Center at LaSalle Street to see Jean DeBuffet's graffiti-inspired 1984 sculpture **Monument with Standing Beast.** Across LaSalle Street to the north, look up to see Richard Hunt's **Freeform** on the entrance of the State of Illinois building. The sculpture weighs 3 tons and is 2½ stories tall.

Daley Plaza

Next, head to Daley Plaza to see Picasso's **unnamed sculpture.** Opinions vary about whether the abstract installation represents a woman's head or one of the artist's Afghan hounds. Across the street is Joan Miró's **Chicago,** originally titled *The Sun, the Moon and One Star.* Stand behind the 39-foot mixed-media sculpture to see the blue mosaic work at its back.

Chase and Federal Plazas and the Federal Building

Walk east to Dearborn Street, then south to Chase Plaza to see **The Four Seasons** by Marc Chagall, a 70-foot-long mosaic/mural that depicts six Chicago-specific scenes. Continue two blocks south to Federal Plaza, where the **Flamingo** by Alexander Calder is a striking, 53-foot vermillion red contrast to the black and steel buildings around it. End your tour with a peek through the glass of the lobby of the Federal Building here to see the **Town-Ho's Story,** a crazy conglomeration of steel and aluminum that's part of Frank Stella's *Moby-Dick* series.

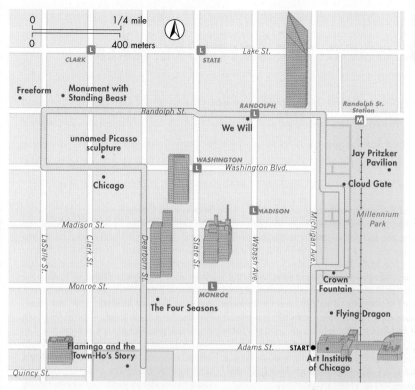

Highlights:	The Picasso, Joan Miró's Chicago, Cloud Gate, Crown Fountain.
Where to Start:	The Art Institute of Chicago (El Red and Blue lines at Jackson; Orange, Green, Pink, Brown, and Purple lines at Adams).
Length:	Two to four hours, depending on stopping times.
Where to Stop:	The Federal Building (El Red and Blue lines at Jackson; Brown, Orange, and Purple lines at LaSalle and Van Buren).
Best Time to Go:	A weekday morning in fall, when the weather is good and crowds tend to be light.
Worst Time to Go:	A frigid winter day or a busy summer weekend.
Good in the 'Hood:	The "Chicago Mix" of cheese and caramel popcorn at any of the handful of Garrett's Popcorn shops (✉ 26 W. Randolph St. at State St. and other locations) scattered around downtown. Just follow your nose.

A GOOD ARCHITECTURE WALK

The Great Fire of 1871 could have been the death of Chicago, but instead it proved to be a grand rebirth. Renowned architects treated the decimated urban landscape as a fresh palette for their innovative ideas, sparking a revolution that has never really ended. Chicago's skyline is one of the city's most precious attributes, ever-changing but always awe-inspiring.

Tall Buildings of Every Size

Chicago is the home of the modern skyscraper, so start your tour at Wacker Drive and Adams Street at the city's tallest building, the **Willis Tower** (aka the Sears Tower). The 1,454-foot giant was the tallest building in the world when it was finished in 1973. Then head to the famous **Rookery Building.** This 12-story stunner, completed in 1888 by Daniel Burnham and John Welborn Root, is the oldest standing highrise in town. On Jackson, check out the 45-story Art Deco **Chicago Board of Trade,** designed by Holabird & Root in 1930.

Chicago School and Modern Contrasts

Also on Jackson Street is Burnham and Root's 17-story **Monadnock Building.** Built in 1891, it's the last and tallest skyscraper built with masonry load-bearing walls. Head to Congress Parkway and Wabash Avenue to see Louis Sullivan and Dankmar Adler's **Auditorium Building,** a grand theater completed in 1889 that still hosts performances. These buildings are evidence of Chicago School architecture, which combined modern design practices of the time with traditional ideas like brick facades and ornamentation.

For a lesson in contrast, double back to Jackson and Dearborn streets to see the orderly, geometric 4.6-acre **Federal Center,** which was completed in the early 1970s by Mies van der Rohe. Don't miss the graceful slopes of **Chase Tower,** built in 1969 as the First National Bank of Chicago Building.

Stores and Centers

The **Sullivan Center,** at State and Madison streets, was Louis Sullivan's last major work in Chicago; note the elaborate cast-iron entryway ornamentation and three-part "Chicago Window," allowing plenty of light. Walk along State Street, past the **Reliance Building** (now the Hotel Burnham). This building is considered the first-ever glass-and-steel skyscraper. On the northeast corner of State and Washington streets, stop and admire **Macy's,** designed by Burnham in 1907 and most famous for the multistory atriums inside, one domed with a Tiffany mosaic.

Walk west on Randolph Street to reach the 648-foot **Richard J. Daley Center** at Clark Street, the tallest building in Chicago for four years until the John Hancock Center was built in 1969. Across Randolph is Helmut Jahn's dome-shape **James R. Thompson Center.**

Corncobs and High-Profile Towers

Head north on Clark Street, then east along the Chicago River to see **Marina City,** Bertrand Goldberg's pair of 61-story corncoblike apartment towers. Along the river at Kinzie Street is **Trump International Hotel & Tower,** a 1,389-foot skyscraper condo-hotel complex that was initially designed to be the world's tallest building before the events of 9/11.

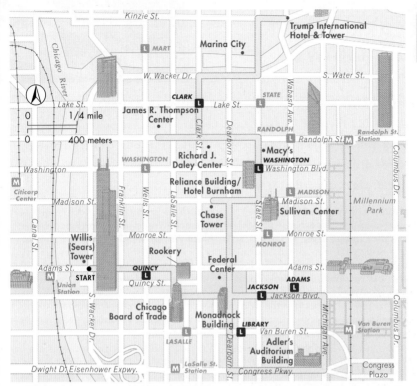

Highlights:	Willis Tower, Sullivan Center, Marina City.
Where to Start:	Willis Tower (El Brown, Orange, Pink, and Purple lines at Quincy).
Length:	Three to four hours, depending on stops.
Where to Stop:	Trump International Hotel & Tower (El Red Line at Grand).
Best Time to Go:	Late morning in the fall, when tourists are fewer and workers have settled in at their desks.
Worst Time to Go:	Summer weekends during one of the many downtown festivals.
Good in the 'Hood:	Browsing the shops on the ground floor of the Monadnock Building is like stepping back in time; eye vintage-inspired clothing and shoes at Florodora and Florodora Shoes, try on a fedora at Optimo Hats, or get a close shave at Frank's old-timey barbershop.

CLARK STREET PUB CRAWL

Once a Native American trail, Clark Street is one of Chicago's major arteries, running roughly 12 miles from Chinatown on the South Side to the border with Evanston at the north. A Clark Street pub crawl, with stops in three distinct neighborhoods, gives you a taste of this vibrant, diverse city that plays as hard as it works.

Downtown/River North

Begin your pub crawl where Clark Street meets the Chicago River. From the Clark Street Bridge, the city spreads out in all directions. On your left are the iconic corncob structures of Marina Towers, with Lake Michigan in the far distance, and a series of bridges spans the river on both sides.

If you're kicking off your walk during the day, head to **Fado** (⌧ *100 W. Grand Ave.* ☎ *312/836–0066*), an ornate Irish pub featuring decor imported from the Emerald Isle. Relax with a perfectly poured pint of Guinness and a hearty boxty. ■TIP➜ Blues fans should check the night's lineup at Blue Chicago just up the street at 536 N. Clark Street to see whether it's worth heading back downtown for music and a nightcap. After knocking back a pint or two, take a five-minute walk to the Grand Avenue Red Line station, where you'll hop on a northbound El train. You can also flag a cab or grab a northbound bus on Dearborn.

Lakeview/Wrigleyville

Exit the Red Line at Addison and walk to **Murphy's Bleachers** (⌧ *3655 N. Sheffield Ave.* ☎ *773/281–5356*), directly across from Wrigley Field's bleacher entrance. The historic sports bar's rooftop is the best place to watch a Cubs game outside of the Friendly Confines. With sports memorabilia lining the walls and

numerous brews on tap, it's the quintessential Wrigleyville experience. **Goose Island Wrigleyville** (⌧ *3535 N. Clark St.* ☎ *773/832–9040*) is a brewery/sports bar that pays homage to two local passions: beer and baseball, though it's less Cubs-centric than Murphy's. Finish getting your sports fix and head back to the Red Line stop at Addison.

Andersonville

Exit the Red Line at Berwyn and whet your thirst with a stroll through Andersonville. Beer aficionados flock to **The Hopleaf** (⌧ *5148 N. Clark St.* ☎ *773/334–9851*) for its mind-boggling selection of international drafts and bottled beers. Note that the bar area gets very crowded on weekends and there's almost always a wait for a table. Energy flagging by this point? Luckily it's just a quick stumble north to your last stop, **Simon's Tavern** (⌧ *5201 N. Clark St.* ☎ *773/878–0894*). Look for the neon sign depicting a fish hoisting a martini—a play on "pickled herring." This slightly divey bar is steeped in local history. The original owner, a bootlegger during Prohibition, used to cash paychecks in a bulletproof booth on the premises. When you're ready to call it a night, hail a cab or hike it back to the 24-hour Red Line.

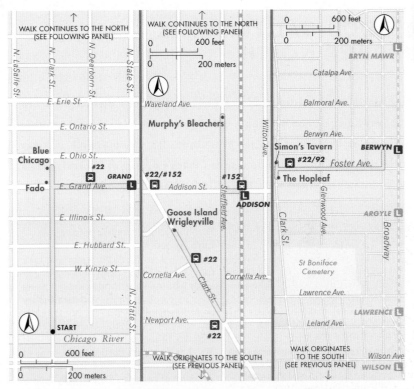

Highlights:	**River North**: View downtown in all its splendor from the Clark Street Bridge, memorialized in a Carl Sandburg poem of the same name. This neighborhood boasts boutiques, galleries, clubs, trendy restaurants, and businesses all concentrated within a few square blocks. **Wrigleyville**: Sports reign supreme in this North Side neighborhood, where Wrigley Field and sports bars surrounding it are the primary draw. **Andersonville**: Unpretentious bars, restaurants, and antiques shops line this stretch of Clark Street on the Far North Side, and side streets are quiet and tree-lined.
Where to Start:	Clark Street at the Chicago River (El Brown and Purple lines at the Merchandise Mart).
Length:	Three to four hours, depending on how long you mull over your beer (7 miles).
Where to Stop:	Simon's Tavern in Andersonville (El Red Line at Berwyn).
Best Time to Go:	Late afternoon or early evening.
Worst Time to Go:	Morning.

A GOOD GALLERY WALK IN RIVER NORTH

River North is the granddaddy of Chicago's gallery districts, a more established and refined neighborhood of art-centric businesses than other trendy areas like Pilsen and the West Loop. It's an easy walk to River North from most downtown hotels, and there's a bevy of hip restaurants and clubs interspersed with the galleries here, making it a one-stop destination for a great time out.

Superior Street: The Epicenter of It All

Start at the heart of the action, at the intersection of Superior and Wells streets. A walk in any direction from here can't go wrong if you're looking for galleries to browse, but we suggest heading west on pretty Superior Street to hit a huge cluster of galleries on this block right off the bat. The first among our favorites on this street is **Ann Nathan Gallery** (✉ *212 W. Superior St.* ☎ *312/664–6622*), which showcases both established and emerging sculptors and painters in a spacious, bright space with high ceilings and exposed wood beams. Just a few doors down is **ECHT Gallery** (✉ *222 W. Superior St.* ☎ *312/440–0288*), the go-to place for contemporary glass sculpture by artists including Dale Chihuly and Martin Blank.

At 300 West Superior Street you'll find several notable galleries, including **Catherine Edelman Gallery,** well known for its breathtaking collection of contemporary photography and mixed-media photo-based art, most in black and white. Vintage black-and-white photographs can be found directly across the street at **Stephen Daiter Gallery** (✉ *230 W. Superior St.* ☎ *312/787–3350*), which specializes in experimental works.

Franklin Street: Contemporary Curb Appeal

Head north to Franklin Street and take time to stop at the many shops and galleries with massive windows showcasing their wares. Don't miss **Architech Gallery of Architectural Art** (✉ *730 N. Franklin St.* ☎ *312/475–1290*); their collection includes lithographs from Frank Lloyd Wright's Wasmuth Portfolio and some of Daniel Burnham's original plans and construction documents. **Stephen Kelly Gallery** (✉ *750 N. Franklin St.* ☎ *312/867–1931*) showcases the colorful abstracts of the owner as well as a handful of other contemporary artists.

Wells Street: More Art and Tourist Hot Spots

Head back toward Wells Street, where you'll find a curious mix of sophisticated galleries and iconic restaurants (including '50s diner-style Ed Debevic's and Chicago-pizza classic Gino's East). Duck into **Roy Boyd Gallery** (✉ *739 N. Wells St.* ☎ *312/642–1606*), one of the oldest galleries in the neighborhood. Most of what you'll find here is abstract painting, drawing, and sculpture. Across the street is **Carl Hammer Gallery** (✉ *740 N. Wells St.* ☎ *312/266–8512*), known for its collection of outsider art by Chris Ware and Hollis Sigler, among others.

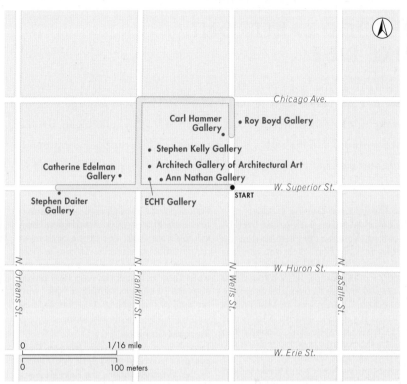

Highlights:	Ann Nathan Gallery, Architech Gallery of Architectural Art, Carl Hammer Gallery.
Where to Start:	Intersection of Superior and Wells (El Red and Brown lines at Chicago).
Length:	Two to three hours, depending on your browsing pace, and about half a mile.
Where to Stop:	Wells Street. The El Red and Brown lines at Chicago are a quick walk away.
Best Time to Go:	Friday evening, when new exhibitions open and area galleries stay open late.
Worst Time to Go:	Sunday or Monday, when most galleries are closed. Most galleries are open Tuesday through Saturday from noon to 5 pm. The crowd-averse should avoid this area in early May, when throngs of art lovers descend on galleries during the annual Expo Chicago fair.
Good in the 'Hood:	Pretty much everyone agrees that Rick Bayless's Xoco (⊠ 449 N. Clark St. ☎ 312/334–3688) is Mexican street food at its very finest, so be prepared for a wait (it's worth it).

A GOOD LAKEFRONT BIKE RIDE

There are few better ways to fall instantly in love with Chicago than by touring its lakefront path. You could do it on foot or by rollerblade, but the best way to take in the sights is by bicycle. You'll cover the most ground, get in some decent exercise, and—if you're lucky—get a nice tailwind to help you along courtesy of Lake Michigan.

First Things First: Getting a Bike

The entire lakefront path is just over 18 miles long. Your best bet is to start in the middle, at Navy Pier, where you can rent some wheels from **Bike and Roll Chicago** (✉ *600 E. Grand Ave.* ☎ *773/404–2500* ⊕ *www.bikechicago.com*); the company has additional locations at Millennium Park, the Riverwalk, and the 53rd Street Bike Center in Hyde Park. **Bobby's Bike Hike** (✉ *465 N. McClurg Ct.* ☎ *312/915–0995* ⊕ *www.bobbysbikehike.com*) is another option. Bobby's also books guided tours, including a kids' cycle and a historic Hyde Park tour. (⇨ *For more on Lakefront Activities, see Experience the Lakefront in this chapter.*)

North or South?

Either direction you head from Navy Pier will not disappoint. The north part of the trail hugs Lincoln Park and affords beautiful views, but it can be heavy with runners and skaters, and it might prove hard to navigate the traffic. Instead opt to head south. ▪TIP→ Addresses are painted on the pavement—"500S" for 500 South—so you can keep tabs on where you are.

Downtown Chicago

After five minutes or so, you'll be pedaling past downtown and the big and small boats bobbing in the bay at **Chicago Yacht Club,** which hosts the famous Race to Mackinac each July. At Randolph Street you can take a detour to check out **Millennium Park,** including the show-stopping Crown Fountain and *Cloud Gate* (Bean) sculpture. Just a few blocks south is **Buckingham Fountain** in Grant Park, one of the city's most recognizable landmarks. If you're here between April and October, wait to see the water show that happens every hour on the hour for 20 minutes starting at 9 am, with the final display ending at 11 pm; evening shows are set to lights and music.

Museum Campus

Less than a mile away is **Museum Campus,** a 57-acre lakefront park that's home to the **Shedd Aquarium, the Field Museum,** and **Adler Planetarium.** Solidarity Drive is a quiet, pretty detour with a promenade and access to **Northerly Island.** Actually a peninsula, it was home to Meigs Field airport until 2003, but is now a nature area with a small beach (12th Street Beach, a little-known downtown gem).

Soldier Field, Chinatown, and Beyond

Back on the path, you'll pass **Soldier Field,** home of the Chicago Bears football team, and **Burnham Skate Park,** a 20,000-square-foot expanse of ramps, rails, and straightaways for aspiring skateboarders, then **McCormick Place,** a massive exhibition center and trade show hall. Continue south on a much more serene trail. Stop for a quick dip at **Hyde Park,** home to the University of Chicago and the massive **Museum of Science and Industry,** or continue to the larger **63rd Street Beach** in Jackson Park, where you'll find the city's oldest beach house. The trail ends at 71st Street.

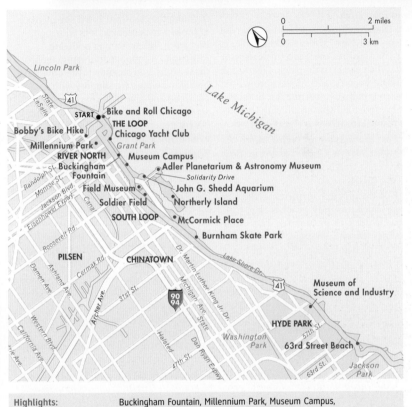

Highlights:	Buckingham Fountain, Millennium Park, Museum Campus, Northerly Island, Soldier Field, 63rd Street Beach.
Where to Start:	Navy Pier (El Red Line at Grand Ave.).
Length:	One to four hours, depending on stops.
Where to Stop:	71st Street (6 Jackson Park express bus has a bike rack).
Best Time to Go	A warm and sunny weekday morning, when the crowds are light and the lake is peaceful.
Worst Time to Go:	An unseasonably warm weekend when it will feel like the entire city decided to join you to take advantage of the weather.
Good in the 'Hood:	McDonald's Cycle Center in Millennium Park offers free bike parking, fee-based repairs, and lockers and showers for members.

EXPERIENCE THE LAKEFRONT

Enjoy the Lake

San Diego and Los Angeles may have the ocean, and New York its Central Park, but Chicago has the peaceful waters of Lake Michigan at its doorstep. Bikers, dog walkers, boaters, and runners crowd the lakefront paths on warm days; in winter the lake is equally beautiful, with icy towers formed from frozen sheets of water.

⇨ *For information on biking along the lakeshore, see A Good Lakefront Bike Ride in this chapter.*

Hit the Beach

One of the greatest surprises in the city is the miles of sandy beaches that Chicagoans flock to in summer. The water becomes warm enough to swim in toward the end of June, though the brave will take an icy dip through the end of October. Chicago has about 30 miles of shoreline, most of it sand or rock beach. Beaches are open to the public daily from 11 am (a handful at 9:30 am) to 7 pm, Memorial Day through Labor Day, and many beaches have changing facilities; all are wheelchair-accessible.

The **Chicago Park District** (☎ *312/742–7529* ⊕ *www.chicagoparkdistrict.com*) provides lifeguard protection during daylight hours throughout the swimming season.

All references to north and south in beach listings refer to how far north or south of the Loop each beach is. In other words, 1600 to 2400 North means the beach begins 16 blocks north of the Loop (at Madison Street, which is the 100 block) and extends for eight blocks.

⚠ Along the lakefront you'll see plenty of broken-rock breakwaters with signs that warn "No swimming or diving." Although Chicagoans frequently ignore these signs, you shouldn't. The boulders below the water are slippery with seaweed and may hide sharp, rusty scraps of metal, and the water beyond is very deep. It can be dangerous even if you know the territory.

Boating

Nothing beats the view of the Chicago skyline from the water, especially when the sun sets behind the sparkling skyscrapers. Plenty of boats are available to rent or charter, though you might want to leave the skippering to others if you're not familiar with Great Lakes navigation.

Sailboat lessons, rentals, and charters are available from **Chicago Sailing** (⊠ *Belmont Harbor, Lakeview* ☎ *773/871–7245* ⊕ *www.chicagosailing.com*). Chicago Sailing focuses on sailing instruction for all levels and includes a program on keeping your boat in tip-top shape.

Sailboats, Inc. (⊠ *Monroe Harbor, Loop* ☎ *800/826–7010* ⊕ *www.sailboats-inc. com*), one of the oldest charter-certification schools in the country, prepares its students to charter any type of boat.

THE LOOP

Including South Loop and West Loop

GETTING ORIENTED

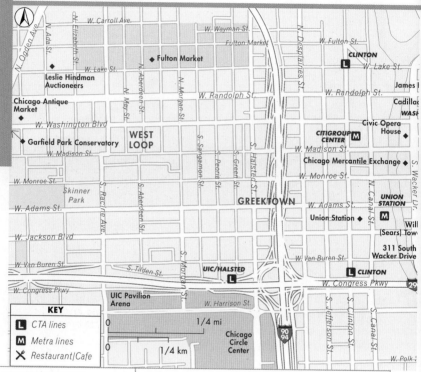

MAKING THE MOST OF YOUR TIME

Prepare for a long day in the Loop because of all the "must-sees," like the architectural boat tour (⇨ *Experience Chicago chapter*) and the Art Institute. Browse the shops on State Street, then take a trip out on the Ledge at Willis Tower and take a photo at Millennium Park's "Bean." Later, see a play or a Chicago Symphony concert. Designate another full day in the South Loop at Museum Campus: the Field Museum, Shedd Aquarium, and Adler Planetarium are all top-notch choices.

GETTING HERE

If you're driving, you'll probably be taking the expressways—Kennedy from the northwest, Edens/Kennedy from the north, Dan Ryan from the south, and Congress from the west. Lake Shore Drive runs north and south along Lake Michigan.

Or save on high parking fees and travel by CTA bus (☎ 312/836–7000 ⊕ www.transitchicago.com) or by El or rail. In the suburbs, hop on the Metra or South Shore Line and arrive at Union Station (Canal and Jackson streets). CTA's Red, Green, Blue, Yellow, Purple, Brown, and Pink lines link the city with the Loop.

SAFETY

Some parts of the South Loop feel sketchy, so stick to well-lighted streets at night. In the West Loop near Ashland Avenue and the United Center the gentrification comes to a halt; the streets around the Fulton Market area are deserted during off times. Exercise caution in both areas.

2

TOP REASONS TO GO

Get cultured: Spend an afternoon at the Art Institute.

Get spit on: Watch the faces screened onto the two towers of the Crown Fountain in Millennium Park spit at delighted onlookers.

Appreciate architecture: The Loop has some of the country's architectural gems.

Discover deep-dish: Eat deep-dish pizza at Pizzeria Uno, where it was invented.

Explore the world and beyond: See stars at the Adler Planetarium, spot your favorite fish at the John G. Shedd Aquarium, and stand next to Sue the *T. rex* at the Field Museum, all on the Museum Campus.

Ponder the Picasso: Make a visit to the Daley Center, named after the late mayor Richard J. Daley.

QUICK BITES

Caffè Baci. For breakfast, a quick snack, or pizza, this is a great find. Try the daily special, or a "Jojo," the bistro's signature sandwich. It's a *filone* (an Italian baguette) stuffed with prosciutto, mozzarella, artichoke hearts, basil, and plum tomatoes. Caffè Baci has four other locations in the Loop. ⊠ *20 N. Michigan Ave., Loop* ☎ *312/214–2224* ⊕ *www.caffebaci.com* ⊘ *Closed Sun.*

Garrett Popcorn. Lines form early and stay throughout the day. The popcorn is so popular that there are nine other Chicago locations and branches in Dubai, Hong Kong, Singapore, Japan, Kuwait, and Malaysia. ⊠ *26 W. Randolph St., Loop* ☎ *888/476–7267* ⊕ *www.garrettpopcorn.com* ⊠ *4 E. Madison St., Loop* ⊠ *27 W. Jackson Blvd., Loop.*

Heaven on Seven. This Loop legend is famous for casual Cajun breakfasts and lunches that have area office workers gladly lining up to be served. ⊠ *111 N. Wabash Ave., 7th fl., Loop* ☎ *312/263–6443* ⊕ *www.heavenonseven.com* ⊘ *Closed Sun.*

THE LOOP, INCLUDING WEST LOOP AND SOUTH LOOP

Sightseeing
★★★★☆
Dining
★★★☆☆
Lodging
★★★☆☆
Shopping
★★☆☆☆
Nightlife
★★★★☆

Defined by the El (the elevated train that makes a circuit around the area), the Loop is Chicago at its big-city best. Noisy and mesmerizing, it's a living architectural museum alongside shimmering Lake Michigan. Gleaming modern towers vie for space with late 19th- and early 20th-century buildings, and striking sculptures by Picasso, Miró, and Chagall watch over plazas alive with music and farmers' markets in summer.

THE LOOP

Updated by Roberta Sotonoff

Internationally known landmarks, including the Willis (formerly Sears) Tower, Millennium Park, and Buckingham Fountain, blanket the Loop landscape. Visitors and locals gush over the masterpieces at the Art Institute and the merchandise at State Street's stores. LaSalle Street, home of the thriving financial district, earned the moniker the Canyon (and it feels like one) because of the large buildings that flank either end of the relatively narrow street. The Loop oozes with charm and culture—it has an impressive symphony, top-rate theaters, fine restaurants, and swinging nightlife. (⇨ *The Good Architecture Walk in the Experience Chicago chapter for architecture highlights.*)

TOP ATTRACTIONS

150 North Michigan Avenue. Some wags have pointed out that this building, with its diamond-shape top, looks like a giant pencil sharpener. Built in 1984 as the Smurfit-Stone Building and later known as the Crain Communications Building, it has a slanted top that carves through the top 10 of its floors. In the plaza is Yaacov

Agam's *Communication X9,* a painted, folded-aluminum sculpture. You'll see different patterns in the sculpture depending on your vantage point. ⊠ *150 N. Michigan Ave., Loop.*

224 South Michigan Avenue. This structure, designed in 1904 by Daniel Burnham, who later moved his office here, was once known as the Railway Exchange Building and the Santa Fe Building, for a "Santa Fe" sign on its roof that has since been removed. ⊠ *224 S. Michigan Ave., Loop.*

GRID CITY

Getting around the Loop is easy. It's laid out like a grid. The intersection of State Street, which runs north–south, and Madison Street, which runs east–west, is the zero point from which the rest of the city fans out.

2

Chicago Architecture Foundation. The CAF uses the building's atrium for rotating exhibits about the changing landscape of Chicago and other cities and offers a variety of tours via foot, bus, and boat. ☎ *312/922–3432* ⊕ *www.architecture.org.*

FAMILY
Fodor's Choice
★

Art Institute of Chicago
⇨ *See highlighted feature in this chapter.*

Fodor's Choice
★

Chicago Board of Trade. Rising dramatically at the end of LaSalle Street— heart of the city's financial district—this 1930, 45-story streamlined giant (Holabird & Root) recalls the days when Art Deco was all the rage. The artfully lighted marble lobby soars three stories, and Ceres, the Roman goddess of agriculture, stands atop its roof. Trading is no longer done here, but it's worth a look at what was the city's tallest skyscraper until 1955, when the Prudential Center topped it. ⊠ *141 W. Jackson Blvd., Loop* ☎ *312/435–3590.*

Fodor's Choice
★

Chicago Cultural Center. Built in 1897 as the city's original public library, this huge building houses the Chicago Office of Tourism Visitor Information Center, as well as a gift shop, galleries, and a concert hall. Designed by the Boston firm Shepley, Rutan & Coolidge—the team behind the Art Institute of Chicago—it's a palatial affair of Carrara marble, mosaics, gold leaf, and the world's largest Tiffany glass dome. ⊠ *78 E. Washington St., Loop* ☎ *312/744–6630* ⊕ *www.chicagoculturalcenter.org* ⊗ *Daily 10–6; tours Wed., Fri., and Sat. at 1:15; concerts Sun. at 3.*

Chicago Theatre. When it opened in 1921, the grand and glitzy Chicago Theatre was tagged "the Wonder Theatre of the World." Its exterior has a shrunk-down version of the Arc de Triomphe, and inside, a grand lobby was patterned after the Royal Chapel at Versailles with a staircase copied from the Paris Opera House. Murals decorate the auditorium walls and ceiling. The seven-story, 3,600-seat space has served as a venue for films and such famous entertainers as John Philip Sousa, Duke Ellington, Jack Benny, Frank Sinatra, Prince, Ellen DeGeneres, Beyoncé, and Harry Connick Jr. Tours let you stand on the stage where they performed, go backstage, and peruse its autographed walls. ⊠ *175 N. State St., Loop* ☎ *312/443–1130* ⊕ *www.thechicagotheatre.com* 🎫 *$12 tours* ⊗ *Tours: May–Sept., Sun.–Fri. at noon, Sat. at 11 and noon; Oct.–Apr., Tues. and Thurs. at noon, Sat. at 11 and 12:30.*

LaSalle Street (the Cavern) is Chicago's financial hub.

Civic Opera House. The handsome home of the Lyric Opera of Chicago is grand indeed, with pink-and-gray Tennessee-marble floors, pillars with carved capitals, crystal chandeliers, and a sweeping staircase to the second floor. Designed by Graham, Anderson, Probst & White, the second-largest opera house in North America combines lavish Art Deco details with Art Nouveau touches. Tours are given a few times a year. ⊠ *20 N. Wacker Dr., Loop* ☎ *312/419–0033 Civic Opera House, 312/332–2244 Lyric Opera* ⊕ *www.civicoperahouse.com.*

Fine Arts Building. This creaky building was constructed in 1895 to house the showrooms of the Studebaker Company, then makers of carriages. Publishers, artists, and even architect Frank Lloyd Wright have used its spaces. Today the principal tenants are professional musicians. Take a look at the handsome exterior; then step inside the marble-and-woodwork lobby, noting the motto engraved in marble as you enter: "All passes—art alone endures." The building has an interior courtyard, across which strains of piano music and sopranos' voices compete with tenors' as they run through exercises. Visitors can get a peek at the studios and galleries and hear live music during Open Studios. ⊠ *410 S. Michigan Ave., Loop* ☎ *312/566–9800* ⊕ *www.fineartsbuilding.tv* ☯ *Weekdays 7 am–10 pm, Sat. 7 am–9 pm, Sun. 9–5.*

James R. Thompson Center. People either hate or love this state government building: former governor James Thompson, who selected the Helmut Jahn design, hailed it in his dedication speech in 1985 as "the first building of the 21st century." For others, it's a case of postmodernism run amok. A bowl-like form topped by a truncated cylinder, the 17-story building's sky-blue-and-salmon color scheme screams 1980s.

But the 17-story atrium, where exposed elevators zip up and down and sunlight casts dizzying patterns through the metal-and-glass skin, is one of the most animated interiors to be found anywhere in the city. The sculpture in the plaza is Jean Dubuffet's *Monument with Standing Beast.* It was once nearly as controversial as the building itself. The curved shapes, in white with black traceries, have led to its being nicknamed "Snoopy in a blender." The **Illinois Artisans Shop** (☎ *312/814–5321*), on the second level of the center, sells crafts, jewelry, and folk art by Illinois artists and is open weekdays 9–5. ✉ *100 W. Randolph St., Loop* ☎ *312/814–2141* ⊕ *www2.illinois.gov/cms/About/JRTC.*

> **DID YOU KNOW?**
>
> Terra-cotta, a baked clay that can be produced as tiles or shaped ornamentally, was commonly used by Chicago architects after the Great Fire of 1871.
>
> Heat resistant and malleable, the material proved an effective and attractive fireproofing agent for the metal-frame buildings that otherwise would melt and collapse. The facade of the Marquette Building at 140 South Dearborn Street is a particularly fine example.

Marquette Building. Like a slipcover over a sofa, the clean, geometric facade of the Marquette Building expresses what lies beneath: in this case, a structural steel frame. Sure, the base is marked with roughly cut stone and a fancy cornice crowns the top, but the bulk of the building mirrors the cage around which it is built. Inside is another story. The intimate lobby of this 1895 Holabird & Roche building is a jewel box of a space, where a single Doric column stands surrounded by a Tiffany glass mosaic depicting the exploits of French Jesuit missionary Jacques Marquette, an early explorer of Illinois and the Upper Midwest. The building is a clear example of the Chicago style, from the steel skeleton to the Chicago Windows to the terra-cotta ornamentation. ✉ *140 S. Dearborn St., Loop* ☎ *312/422–5500* ⊕ *www.marquette.macfound.org.*

FAMILY
Fodor's Choice
★
Millennium Park. "The Bean," the fountains, the Disney-esque music pavilion—all the pieces of this new park quickly stole the hearts of Chicagoans and visitors alike. The showstopper here is Frank Gehry's stunning **Jay Pritzker Pavilion.** Dramatic ribbons of stainless steel stretching 40 feet into the sky look like petals wrapping the music stage. The sound system, suspended by a trellis that spans the great lawn, provides concert-hall sound outside. So what can you see on this beautiful stage? Take your pick. There's the Grant Park Music Festival—a free classical-music series—as well as the city's popular free summer concerts, including the jam-packed Chicago Blues and Chicago Jazz festivals.

Hot town? Summer in the city? Cool off by letting a local resident spit on you. Okay, it's just a giant image of a Chicagoan's face—actually, dozens of Chicagoans' faces rotating through on two 50-foot-high glass block–tower fountains. The genius behind the **Crown Fountain,** Spanish sculptor Jaume Plensa, lined up the mouths on the digital photos with an opening in the fountain. When a face purses its lips, water shoots out its "mouth." Kids love it, and adults feel like kids watching it. It's at the southwest corner of the park.

BP BRIDGE

The *Cloud Gate* **sculpture,** otherwise known as "the Bean," awaits your delighted *ooohs* and *aaahs* as you stand beneath its gleaming seamless polished steel. Located between Washington and Madison streets, its curved reflective surface provides a fun-house mirror view of Chicago's storied skyline. The 2006 work is by the noted British artist Anish Kapoor.

> **FINDING FACTS**
>
> For information about the city's architectural treasures, contact the **Chicago Architecture Foundation** (☎ 312/922–3432 ⊕ www.architecture.org) or the **Chicago Convention and Tourism Bureau** (☎ 312/567–8500 ⊕ www.choosechicago.com).

In summer the carefully manicured plantings in the **Lurie Garden** bloom; in winter the **McCormick Tribune Ice Rink** is open for public skating. If you're feeling artsy, you can find out if there's a show playing at the indoor, underground **Harris Theater for Music and Dance,** behind the Jay Pritzker Pavilion. ⊠ *Between Michigan Ave. and Columbus Dr., Randolph and Monroe Sts., Loop* ☎ *312/742–1168* ⊕ *www.millenniumpark.org* ⊡ *Free* ☉ *Daily 6 am–11 pm.*

Monadnock Building. Built in two segments a few years apart, the Monadnock captures the turning point in high-rise construction. Its northern half, designed in 1891 by Burnham & Root, was erected with traditional load-bearing masonry walls (6 feet deep at the base). In 1893 Holabird & Roche designed its southern half, which rose around the soon-to-be-common steel skeleton. The building's stone-and-brick exterior, shockingly unornamented for its time, led one critic to liken it to a chimney. The lobby is equally spartan: lined on either side with windowed shops, it's essentially a corridor, but one well worth traveling. Walk it from end to end and you'll feel like you're stepping back in time. ⊠ *53 W. Jackson Blvd., at S. Dearborn St., Loop* ☎ *312/922–1890* ⊕ *www.monadnockbuilding.com.*

Prudential Plaza. There are two architecturally notable buildings at the plaza. Directly west of the Aon Center and across from Millennium Park is **One Prudential Plaza.** Designed by Alfonzo Lanelli and completed in 1955, this limestone and ridged aluminum structure was once the city's tallest building (barring the statue of Ceres atop the Board of Trade). At the time, it had the world's fastest elevators and an observation deck that became passé once some of the city's other behemoths were completed. Attached to One Prudential is its sibling **Two Prudential Plaza,** nicknamed "Two Pru," a towering glass-and-granite giant with an address of 180 North Stetson Avenue. Along with their neighbors they form a block-long business-oriented minicity. Two Prudential is the tallest reinforced concrete building in the city, and its blue detailing and beveled roof are instantly recognizable from afar. ⊠ *One Prudential, 130 E. Randolph St., Loop* ☎ *312/565–6700.*

Reliance Building. The clearly expressed, gleaming verticality that characterizes the modern skyscraper was first and most eloquently articulated in this trailblazing steel-frame tower, built by Burnham, Root, and Charles Atwood. Completed in 1895 and now home to the stylish Hotel

Burnham, at 1 West Washington Street, the building was a crumbling eyesore until the late 1990s, when the city initiated a major restoration. In the early and mid-1900s it was a mixed-use office building. Al Capone's dentist reportedly worked out of what's now Room 809. Don't be misled when you go looking for this masterpiece—a block away, at State and Randolph streets, a dormitory for the School of the Art Institute of Chicago shamelessly mimics it. Once you've found the real thing, don't miss the mosaic floor and ironwork in the reconstructed elevator lobby. The building boasts early examples of the Chicago Window, which define the entire building's facade by add-

> **DID YOU KNOW?**
>
> The Chicago Window, a popular window design used in buildings all over America (until air-conditioning made it obsolete), consists of a large fixed central pane with smaller movable windows on each side. The picture window offered light, and the double-hung windows let in the Lake Michigan breeze. Developed in Chicago by engineer and architect William Le Baron Jenney, who pioneered the use of metal-frame construction in the 1880s, the Chicago Window helps to define buildings across the city.

ing a shimmer and glimmer to the surrounding white terra-cotta. ⊠ *32 N. State St., Loop* ☎ *312/782–1111.*

Richard J. Daley Center. Named for late mayor Richard J. Daley, this boldly plain high-rise is the headquarters of the Cook County court system, but it's best known as the site of a sculpture by Picasso. Known simply as the *Picasso,* this monumental piece provoked an outcry when it was installed in 1967; baffled Chicagoans tried to determine whether it represented a woman or an Afghan hound. In the end, they gave up guessing and simply embraced it as a unique symbol of the city. The building was constructed in 1965 of Cor-Ten steel, which weathers naturally to an attractive bronze. In summer the building's plaza is the site of concerts, political rallies, and a farmers' market on Thursdays; during the holidays, the city's official Christmas tree is erected here, and Christkindlmarket, a traditional German market selling food and gifts, takes over the area. ⊠ *50 W. Washington St., Loop* ☎ *312/603–7980* ⊕ *www.thedaleycenter.com* ⊙ *Weekdays 8–5:30.*

Fodor's Choice **The Rookery.** This 11-story structure, with its eclectically ornamented
★ facade, got its name from the pigeons and politicians who roosted at the temporary city hall constructed on this site after the Great Chicago Fire of 1871; the structure didn't last long, and the Rookery replaced it. Designed in 1885 by Burnham & Root, who used both masonry and a more modern steel-frame construction, the Rookery was one of the first buildings in the country to feature a central court that brought sunlight into interior office spaces. Frank Lloyd Wright, who kept an office here for a short time, renovated the two-story lobby and light court, eliminating some of the ironwork and terra-cotta and adding marble scored with geometric patterns detailed in gold leaf. The interior endured some less tasteful alterations after that, but it has since been restored to the way it looked when Wright completed his work in 1907.

The Modern Wing of the Art Institute, which was designed by Renzo Piano and opened in 2009, is a stunning home for the renowned collection within.

The Frank Lloyd Wright Preservation Trust offers a 30-minute tour of the building on Monday, Tuesday, Thursday and Friday ($5). The Wednesday 45-minute tour includes the Burnham Library ($10). Tickets are available online at www.flwright.org. ⊠ *209 S. LaSalle St., Loop* ☎ *312/553–6100* ⊕ *therookerybuilding.com.*

Sullivan Center (*Carson Pirie Scott & Co.*). From 1899 to 2007 this was the flagship location for the department store Carson Pirie Scott. The work of one of Chicago's most renowned architects, it combines Louis H. Sullivan's visionary expression of modern design with intricate cast-iron ornamentation. The eye-catching rotunda and the 11 stories above it are actually an addition Sullivan made to his original building. In later years D.H. Burnham & Co. and Holabird & Root extended Sullivan's smooth, horizontal scheme farther down State Street. In 2012, the Sullivan Center became a shopping mall, with tenants that include Target and DSW. ⊠ *1 S. State St., Loop* ☎ *312/675–5500* ⊕ *www.thesullivancenter.com.*

Symphony Center. Now home to the acclaimed Chicago Symphony Orchestra (CSO), this complex includes Orchestra Hall, built in 1904 under the supervision of Daniel Burnham. The Georgian building has a symmetrical facade of pink brick with limestone quoins, lintels, and other decorative elements. An interior renovation, completed in 1997, added a seating area that is behind and above the stage, allowing patrons a unique vantage point. Backstage tours ($10) are available by appointment for groups of 10 or more; the Chicago Architecture Foundation offers tours for individuals. ⊠ *220 S. Michigan Ave., Loop* ☎ *312/294–3000* ⊕ *www.cso.org.*

FAMILY
Fodor's Choice
★

Willis Tower. At 110 stories and 1,730 feet tall, the former Sears Tower, designed by Skidmore, Owings & Merrill in 1974, was the world's tallest building until 1996. It may have lost the title and even changed its name, but the Willis Tower's 103rd-floor **Skydeck** and the Ledge remain hard to beat. Suspended 4.3 feet out from the building, this glass box offers thrills along with views; on a clear day, a whopping four states, Illinois, Michigan, Wisconsin, and Indiana, are visible. ■TIP➔ **Check the visibility ratings at the security desk before you decide to ride up and take in the view.** Interactive exhibits bring to life Chicago's dreamers, schemers, architects, musicians, and sports stars. Computer kiosks in six languages help international travelers key into Chicago hot spots. Knee-High Chicago is a 4-foot-high exhibit with cutouts of Chicago sports and history at a child's eye level. Enter on Jackson Boulevard to take the ear-popping ride to the 103rd-floor observatory. Video monitors turn the 70-second elevator ride into a fun-filled, thrilling trip. Before you leave, don't miss the spiraling Calder mobile sculpture *The Universe* in the ground-floor lobby on the Wacker Drive side. ✉ *233 S. Wacker Dr., Loop* ☎ *312/875–9696* ⊕ *www.theskydeck.com* ✉ *$18 Skydeck* ☉ *Skydeck Apr.–Sept., daily 9 am–10 pm; Oct.–Mar., daily 10–8.*

> **CHICAGO THEATER DISTRICT**
>
> On State, just north of Randolph Street, is the old theater district. The ornate 1921 Beaux Arts **Chicago Theatre**, a former movie palace, now hosts live performances and tours. Across the street is the **Gene Siskel Film Center**, which screens art, foreign, and classic movies. West on Randolph Street the **Ford Center for the Performing Arts–Oriental Theatre's** long, glitzy neon sign shines. The **Goodman Theatre**, on Dearborn, does new productions in the 1923 Art Deco landmark Harris & Selwyn Twin Theaters. One block west is the **Cadillac Palace Theatre.**

WORTH NOTING

311 South Wacker Drive. The first of three towers intended for the site, this pale pink building is the work of Kohn Pedersen Fox, who also designed 333 West Wacker Drive, a few blocks away. The 1990 building's most distinctive feature is its Gothic crown, blindingly lighted at night. During migration season so many birds crashed into the illuminated tower that the building management was forced to tone down the lighting. The building has an inviting atrium, with palm trees and a splashy, romantic fountain. ✉ *311 S. Wacker Dr., at W. Jackson Blvd., Loop* ☎ *312/692–8200* ⊕ *www.311southwacker.com.*

Bank of America Theatre. On Monroe, near State Street, the ornate Bank of America Theatre (formerly the LaSalle Bank Theatre and before that the Shubert Theatre) stages major Broadway plays and musicals. It was the tallest building in Chicago when it opened in 1906. ✉ *18 W. Monroe St., Loop* ☎ *800/775–2000.*

Continued on page 60

A GUIDE TO THE ART INSTITUTE

The Art Institute of Chicago, nestled between the contemporary public art showplace of Millennium Park and the Paris-inspired walk-ways of Grant Park, is both intimate and grand, a place where the rooms are human-scale and the art is transcendent.

Come for the sterling collection of Old Masters and Impressionists (an entire room is dedicated to Monet), linger over the extraordinary and comprehensive photography collection, take in a number of fine American works, and discover paintings, drawings, sculpture, design, and photography spanning the ages.

The Art Institute is more than just a museum; in fact, it was originally founded by a small group of artists in 1866 as a school with an adjoining exhibition space. Famous alumni include political cartoonist Herblock and artists Grant Wood and Ed Paschke. Walt Disney and Georgia O'Keeffe both took classes, but didn't graduate. The School of the Art Institute of Chicago, one of the finest art schools in the country, is across the street from the museum; occasionally there are lectures and discussions that are open to the public.

Top: Pose with one of the two bronze lions; Bottom: Millefiori paperweight, French, 1845/55

ORIENTATION TO THE MUSEUM

✉ 111 S. Michigan Ave., South Loop

☎ 312/443–3600

⊕ www.artic.edu/aic/

🎫 Adults $23; children, students, and seniors $17

🕙 daily 10:30–5, Thurs. 10:30–8

Take a breath in the gardens.

The Art Institute is a complicated jumble of four difficult-to-navigate buildings—you can only change buildings on the first level of the museum, and the map the museum gives out isn't very helpful. Here are some tips to help you find your way around:

■ On the lower level are textiles, decorative arts, the Thorne Miniature Room, and the Kraft Education Center. The first level includes the non-European galleries, and American art to 1890. The second level holds American art from 1900 to 1950 in the Rose Building, European art from all periods in the Allerton Building, and Impressionism.

Take in the museum's grandeur.

■ Pinpoint the five or six works you'd really like to see or pick two or three galleries and wander around after getting yourself there.

■ Guards expect visitors to ask for directions, so don't be shy.

■ Buy the audio tour ($7) by the coatroom as you enter—it provides descriptions for every gallery and work in the museum. All you do is key in the gallery number and the voices of curators will guide you around the room.

■ Don't miss the free rotating sculpture installations in the Bluhm Family Terrace, a 3,400-square-foot outdoor space on the West Pavilion's third floor, adjacent to the seasonally focused restaurant Terzo Piano (reservations recommended).

■ Before your visit, download and listen to free podcasts from the Art Institute Web site (⊕ www.artic. edu/aic)

FOR THE KIDS

Kids love the **Ryan Education Center**, on the first floor of the Modern Wing, which has five classrooms, three studios, a family orientation room, and a kids' shop. Computer learning centers allow kids to play interactive games and explore the collections virtually. In Gallery 10 of the Allerton Building is the Touch Gallery, which was originally designed for the blind. You can run your fingers over several bronze works.

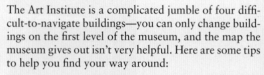

BEST PAINTINGS

AMERICAN GOTHIC (1930). GALLERY 263
Grant Wood won $300 for his iconic painting of a solemn farmer and his wife (really his sister and his dentist). Wood saw the work as a celebration of solid, work-based Midwestern values, a statement that rural America would survive the Depression and the massive migration to cities.

American Gothic (1930).

NIGHTHAWKS (1942). GALLERY 262
Edward Hopper's painting of four figures in a diner on the corner of a deserted New York street is a noir portrait of isolated lives and is one of the most recognized images of 20th-century art. The red-haired woman is the artist's wife, Jo.

THE CHILD'S BATH (1893). GALLERY 273
Mary Cassatt was the only American to become an established Impressionist and her work focused on the daily lives of women and children. In this, her most famous work, a woman gently bathes a child who is tucked up on her lap. The piece was unconventional when it was painted because the bold patterns and cropped forms it used were more often seen in Japanese prints at the time.

Nighthawks (1942).

SKY ABOVE CLOUDS IV (1965). GALLERY 249
(not pictured) Georgia O'Keeffe's massive painting, the largest canvas of her career, is of clouds seen from an airplane. The rows of white rectangles stretching toward the horizon look both solid and ethereal, as if they are stepping stones for angels.

The Child's Bath (1893).

THE OLD GUITARIST (1903/04). MODERN WING
(not pictured) One of the most important works of Pablo Picasso's Blue Period, this monochromatic painting is a study of the crooked figure of a blind and destitute street guitarist, singing sorrowfully. When he painted it, Picasso was feeling particularly empathetic toward the downtrodden—perhaps because of a friend's suicide—and the image of the guitarist is one of dignity amid poverty.

GRAINSTACK (1890/91). GALLERY 243
The Art Institute has the largest collection of Monet's Grainstacks in the world. The stacks rose 15 to 20 feet tall outside Monet's farmhouse in Giverny and were a symbol to the artist of sustenance and survival.

Grainstack (1890/91).

THE MODERN WING

The Modern Wing

In May 2009 the Art Institute unveiled its highly anticipated Modern Wing. Designed by Pritzker Prize–winning architect Renzo Piano, designer of Paris's Pompidou Center, the 264,000-square-foot addition is almost a separate museum unto itself, providing 65,000 square feet of display space for the museum's extensive collection of modern and contemporary art. With the addition, the Art Institute became the country's second largest art museum.

THE DESIGN

The rectangle of glass, steel, and limestone cost just under $300 million and took nearly four years to build. The airy, ultra-modern structure provides abundant natural light and dramatic views of Millennium Park through floor-to-ceiling windows. Green building features include a "flying carpet" canopy that filters sunlight through skylights in the third-floor galleries and a sophisticated lighting system that self-adjusts based on available light and temperature.

North facade of the Modern Wing

THE COLLECTION

View works from major art movements of the 20th and 21st centuries, ranging from painting and sculpture to video and installation art. Notable artists represented in the collection include Eva Hesse, David Hockney, Jasper Johns, Kerry James Marshall, Joan Mitchell, Jackson Pollock, Gerhard Richter, and Andy Warhol.

GRIFFIN COURT

The light-filled central corridor provides a dramatic passageway to the three-story pavilions flanking it on both sides and to the street-level Pritzker Garden. Griffin Court also houses a ticket area, gift shop, coat check, education center, garden café, and balcony café.

Griffin Court

NICHOLS BRIDGEWAY

A 625-foot pedestrian bridge soars over Monroe Street and the Lurie Gardens, connecting the third floor of the Modern Wing's West Pavilion to the southwest corner of Millennium Park—and providing stunning views of the park, skyline, and lake.

BLUHM FAMILY TERRACE

Rotating sculpture installations occupy the free, 3,400-square-foot outdoor space on the West Pavilion's third floor, adjacent to the seasonally focused restaurant Terzo Piano (reservations recommended).

A painting by Gerhard Richter

The lighting around Buckingham Fountain was designed to evoke soft moonlight.

Cadillac Palace Theatre. Opened in 1926 as a vaudeville venue, the theater was designed to evoke the Palace of Versailles. As time went on, its popularity waned. During the 1970s, it became a banquet hall, and in the '80s, a rock concert hall. Renovated in the '90s and reopened in 1999 as performing arts space for long-run Broadway shows, it has recaptured some of it former glory. ✉ *151 W. Randolph St., Loop* ☎ *312/977–1702.*

Carbide and Carbon Building (Hard Rock Hotel). Designed in 1929 by Daniel and Hubert Burnham, sons of the renowned architect Daniel Burnham, this is arguably the jazziest skyscraper in town. A deep-green terra-cotta tower rising from a black-granite base, its upper reaches are embellished with gold leaf. The original public spaces are a luxurious composition in marble and bronze. The story goes that the brothers Burnham got their inspiration from a gold-foiled bottle of champagne. So perhaps it's fitting that the building now houses the Hard Rock Hotel Chicago, party central for those who wouldn't be caught dead at the Four Seasons. ✉ *230 N. Michigan Ave., Loop.*

Chase Tower. This building's graceful swoop—a novelty when it went up—continues to offer an eye-pleasing respite from all the right angles surrounding it. And its spacious, sunken bi-level plaza, with Marc Chagall's mosaic *The Four Seasons,* is one of the most enjoyable public spaces in the neighborhood. Designed by Perkins & Will and C.F. Murphy Associates in 1969, the building has been home to a succession of financial institutions (its most recent name was Bank One Plaza). Names aside, it remains one of the more distinctive buildings around, not to mention one of the highest buildings in the heart of the Loop. ✉ *10 S. Dearborn St., Loop.*

2

Chicago Temple. The Gothic-inspired headquarters of the First United Methodist Church of Chicago was built in 1923 by Holabird & Roche, complete with a first-floor sanctuary, 21 floors of office space, a sky-high chapel (free tours available), and an eight-story spire (best viewed from the bridge across the Chicago River at Dearborn Street). Outside, along the building's east wall at ground level, stained-glass windows relate the history of Methodism in Chicago. Joan Miró's sculpture *Chicago* (1981) is in the small plaza just east of the church. ⊠ *77 W. Washington St., Loop* ☎ *312/236–4548* ⊕ *www.chicagotemple.org* ☾ *Tours: Mon.–Sat. at 2, Sun. after services.*

Federal Center and Plaza. The center is spread over three separate buildings: the Everett McKinley Dirksen Building; the John C. Kluczynski Building (230 S. Dearborn), which includes the Loop's post office; and the Metcalfe Building (77 W. Jackson). Designed in 1959 but not completed until 1974, this severe constellation of buildings around a sweeping plaza was Mies van der Rohe's first mixed-use urban project. Fans of the International Style will groove on this pocket of pure modernism, while others can take comfort in the presence of the Marquette Building, which marks the north side of the site. In contrast to this dark ensemble are the great red arches of Alexander Calder's *Flamingo*. The area is bounded by Dearborn, Clark, and Adams streets and Jackson Boulevard. ⊠ *Dirksen Building, 219 S. Dearborn St., Loop.*

Ford Center for the Performing Arts–Oriental Theatre. An opulent "hasheesh-dream decor" of Buddhas and elephant-type chairs made this a popular spot for viewing first-run movies starting in 1926. Though listed on the National Register of Historic Places in 1978, the building continued to crumble for some time after. In 1998 it was restored to its former splendor, and since that time has had a second life as a home to Broadway shows. ⊠ *24 W. Randolph St., Loop* ☎ *312/977–1702.*

Inland Steel Building. A runt compared to today's tall buildings, this crisp, sparkling 19-story high-rise from Skidmore, Owings & Merrill was a trailblazer when it was built in the late 1950s. It was the first skyscraper built with external supports (allowing for wide-open, unobstructed floors within), the first to employ steel pilings (driven 85 feet down to bedrock), the Loop's first fully air-conditioned building, and the first to feature underground parking. Frank Gehry is currently designing its renovation. ⊠ *30 W. Monroe St., Loop* ⊕ *www.inlandsteelbuilding.com.*

Macy's. This neoclassical building, designed by Daniel Burnham, opened in 1907 as one of the world's earliest department stores, Marshall Field's. Macy's acquired the chain in 2005 and changed the store's name. An uproar ensued, and many Chicagoans still refer to the flagship as Marshall Field's. A visit is as much an architectural experience as a consumer one. The building has distinct courtyards—one resembling an Italian palazzo—a striking Tiffany dome of mosaic glass, a calming fountain, and gilded pillars. Its green clock at the State and Randolph entrance is a Chicago landmark. For lunch, try the Walnut Room, and make sure to sample Frango mints. The store's specialty, they were once made on the 13th floor. ⊠ *111 N. State St., Loop* ☎ *312/781–1000* ⊕ *www.visitmacyschicago. com* ☾ *Mon. and Thurs.–Sat. 10–8, Tues. 9–9, Wed. 9–10, Sun. 11–6.*

SOUTH LOOP

The South Loop's main claim to fame is the Museum Campus—the Field Museum, Shedd Aquarium, and Adler Planetarium. Jutting out into the lake, it affords amazing skyline views. To the north, giant gargoyles (actually stylized owls signifying wisdom) loom atop the Harold Washington Library. East on Congress at Michigan Avenue is the Romanesque Revival–style Auditorium Theatre, designed by architects Sullivan and Adler. Farther south at Printers Row, lofts that once clattered with Linotype machines now hold condos. The South Loop begins more or less where the Loop itself ends, starting south of Van Buren, extending down to Chinatown, and including everything between Lake Michigan and the Chicago River.

TOP ATTRACTIONS

FAMILY **Adler Planetarium and Astronomy Museum.**

⇨ *See highlighted feature in this chapter.*

Fodor'sChoice **Auditorium Theatre.** Hunkered down across from Grant Park, this
★ 110,000-ton granite-and-limestone behemoth was an instant star when it debuted in 1890, and it didn't hurt the careers of its designers, Dankmar Adler and Louis H. Sullivan, either. Inside were offices, a 400-room hotel, and a 4,300-seat state-of-the-art theater with electric lighting and an air-cooling system that used 15 tons of ice per day. Adler managed the engineering—the theater's acoustics are renowned—and Sullivan ornamented the space using mosaics, cast iron, art glass, wood, and plaster. During World War II the building was used as a Servicemen's Center. Then Roosevelt University moved in and thanks to the school's Herculean restoration efforts, the theater is again one of the city's premiere performance venues. Tours are available. ⊠ *50 E. Congress Pkwy., South Loop* ☎ *312/922–2110* ⊕ *www.auditoriumtheatre.org* ▧ *$10 tour* ☉ *Tours: Mon. at 10:30 and noon, Thurs. at 10:30.*

Dearborn Station. Chicago's oldest standing passenger train station is now retail and office space. Designed in the Romanesque Revival style in 1885 by the New York architect Cyrus L.W. Eidlitz, it has a wonderful clock tower and a red-sandstone and redbrick facade ornamented with terra-cotta. Striking features inside are the marble floor, wraparound brass walkway, and arching wood-frame doorways. ⊠ *47 W. Polk St., South Loop* ☎ *312/554–8100* ⊕ *www.dearbornstation.com.*

FAMILY **Field Museum.**
Fodor'sChoice ⇨ *See highlighted feature in this chapter.*
★

FAMILY **Grant Park & Buckingham Fountain.** Two of Chicago's greatest treasures reside in Grant Park—the Art Institute and Buckingham Fountain. Bordered by Lake Michigan to the east, a spectacular skyline to the west, and the Museum Campus to the south, the ever-popular Grant Park serves as the city's front yard and unofficial gathering place. This pristine open space is decked out with walking paths, a stand of stately elm trees, and formal rose gardens, where Loop dwellers

ADLER PLANETARIUM

✉ *1300 S. Lake Shore Dr.,
South Loop* ☎ *312/922–7827*
⊕ *www.adlerplanetarium.
org* ⌨ *$12, $28 all-inclusive*
⊗ *Weekdays 9:30–4, week-
ends 9:30–4:30, plus 3rd
Thurs. of month 6–10 pm
ages 21 and up.*

TIPS

■ Additional charges apply
for the Grainger Sky Theater,
Definiti Space Theater, and
Samuel C. Johnson Family Star
Theater, but don't skip them—
they're the most important
reasons to go. Package prices
are available.

■ Take a quick ride in the
Atwood Sphere, the nation's
very first planetarium
experience.

■ Stop in at the Adler's café
for simple fare like panini
and salads, with breathtaking
views of the Chicago skyline.

Taking you on a journey through the stars to unlock
the mysteries of our galaxy and beyond, the Adler tells
amazing stories of space exploration through high-tech
exhibits and immersive theater experiences. Interactive
elements and real space artifacts bring these fascinating
tales of space and its pioneers down to earth.

Highlights

Feel like you are flying through the universe at the tech-
nologically advanced Grainger Sky Theater. You'll get
an up-close view of stunning space phenomena, whose
magnificent imagery is so realistic that it might only be
surpassed by actual space travel.

**Experience how the universe evolved more than 13.7
billion years ago**—from the Big Bang to modern day—
in the Adler's newest permanent exhibit, "The Universe:
A Walk Through Space and Time." A spectacular projection showcases the enormity of the universe, and
touch screens let you investigate diverse and beautiful
objects of deep space.

Turn your kids into modern-day space adventurers in
"Planet Explorers," which lets them feel what it's like
to climb, crawl, and fly through space.

See the restored *Gemini 12,* the spacecraft flown by
Captain Jim Lovell and Buzz Aldrin in 1966, in "Shoot
for the Moon." The exhibition also features rare objects
from Apollo and Gemini missions from Lovell's collection of personal space artifacts.

Journey into space in the Definiti Space Theater or don
3-D glasses to view celestial phenomena in the Adler's
new Samuel C. Johnson Family Star Theater.

FIELD MUSEUM

✉ 1400 S. Lake Shore Dr., South Loop ☎ 312/922–9410 ⊕ www.fieldmuseum.org 🎟 $15, $30 all-access pass ⊘ Daily 9–5; last admission at 4.

TIPS

■ Don't hesitate to take toddlers to the Field. In the Crown Family PlayLab, kids two to six years old can play house in a re-created pueblo and compare their footprints with a dinosaur's.

■ It's impossible to see the entire museum in one visit. Try to get tickets to the special exhibit of the season and then choose a couple of subjects you'd like to explore, like North American birds or Chinese jade.

■ The Sue Store sells a mind-boggling assortment of dinosaur-related merchandise.

■ Tucked in the back, the dining room comes with wonderful views of the lake and the Museum Campus.

More than 400,000 square feet of exhibit space fill this gigantic museum, which explores cultures and environments from around the world. Interactive exhibits examine such topics as the secrets of Egyptian mummies, the art and innovations of people living in the Ancient Americas, and the evolution of life on Earth. Originally funded by Chicago retailer Marshall Field, the museum was founded in 1893 to hold material gathered for the World's Columbian Exposition; its current neoclassical home opened in 1921.

Highlights

Explore one of the world's best dinosaur collections in the "Evolving Planet," an awe-inspiring journey through 4 billion years of life. And you can't miss the 65-million-year-old "Sue," the largest and most complete *Tyrannosaurus rex* fossil ever found. At the McDonald's Fossil Preparation Laboratory, you can watch paleontologists cleaning bones.

Shrink to the size of a bug to burrow beneath the soil in the "Underground Adventure" (additional fee). You'll come face-to-face with a giant, animatronic wolf spider and listen to the sounds of gnawing insects.

Travel to ancient Egypt via a working canal, a living marsh where papyrus is grown, a shrine to the cat goddess Bastet, burial-ceremony artifacts, and 23 mummies. Or spend a couple of hours taking in contemporary and ancient Africa. Dioramas reproduce the homes and lives of Africans from Senegal, Cameroon, and the Sahara.

Learn how museum scientists are preserving biodiversity at "Restoring Earth," in the Abbott Hall of Conservation.

Check out the 3-D theater, screening movies on dinosaurs, mummies, and Ice Age animals.

JOHN G. SHEDD AQUARIUM

⊠ *1200 S. Lake Shore Dr.,*
South Loop ☎ *312/939–2438*
⊕ *www.sheddaquarium.org*
⊒ *$8, $34.95 all-access pass*
⊗ *Memorial Day–Labor Day,*
daily 9–6; Tues. after Labor
Day–Sun. before Memorial
Day, weekdays 9–5,
weekends 9–6.

TIPS

■ Lines for the Shedd often extend all the way down the Neoclassical steps. Buy a ticket in advance to avoid the interminable wait, or spring for a cityPASS.

■ Soundings restaurant makes an elegant (albeit pricey) stop for lunch. The quiet tables look out over Lake Michigan—and there are very few Chicago eateries that can say that. The food court, Bubble Net, offers more moderately priced family fare, and Deep Ocean Café, in the Polar Play Zone, caters to kids. All restaurants are open daily from 11 am to 4 pm.

■ Catch live jazz on the Shedd's north terrace on Wednesday evenings from 5 to 10 June through early September. It coincides with Navy Pier's fireworks. A gorgeous view of the lake and skyline can make for a magical night.

One of the most popular aquariums in the country, the Shedd houses more than 32,500 creatures from around the world.

Highlights

Get an up-close look at piranhas, snakes, and stingrays. "Amazon Rising," an 8,600-square-foot exhibit that resembles a flooded forest, re-creates the rise and fall of floodwaters.

Shiver as sharks swim by in their 400,000-gallon tank as part of "Wild Reef," which explores the marine biodiversity and coral reefs in the Indo-Pacific. The exhibit also has colorful corals, stingrays that slide by under your feet, and other surprising creatures, all from the waters around the Philippines.

Stare down the knobby-headed beluga whales (they love to people-watch), observe Pacific white-sided dolphins at play, and explore the simulated Pacific Northwest nature trail in the spectacular Oceanarium, which has pools that seem to blend into Lake Michigan. The aquatic show here stars dancing belugas, leaping dolphins, and comical penguins. And be sure to get an underwater glimpse of the dolphins and whales through the viewing windows on the lower level, where you can also find a bunch of information-packed, hands-on activities.

Head to the 90,000-gallon "Caribbean Reef" exhibit to see sharks, stingrays, sea turtles, and other denizens of the deep dart around. It's most fun to observe when divers swim within, feeding the animals and talking to the crowd gathered outside. Kids have their own Polar Play Zone, where they can dress in penguin suits or explore Arctic waters in a miniature submarine.

and 9-to-5-ers take refuge from the concrete and steel. The park also hosts many of the city's largest outdoor events, including the annual Taste of Chicago, a vast picnic featuring foods from more than 70 restaurants.

The centerpiece of the park is the gorgeous, tiered **Buckingham Fountain** (✉ *Between Columbus and Lake Shore Drs. east of Congress Plaza*), which has intricate designs of pink-marble seashells, waterspouting fish, and bronze sculptures of sea horses. Built in 1927, it was patterned after a fountain at Versailles but is about twice the size. See it in all its glory between May 1 and October 1, when it's elaborately illuminated at night and sprays colorfully lighted waters. Linger long enough to experience the spectacular water display that takes place every hour on the hour, and you'll see the center jet of water shoot 150 feet into the air, not to mention some wonderful people-watching. ✉ *South Loop* ☎ *312/742–7529* ⊕ *www.chicagoparkdistrict.com/ parks/clarence-f-buckingham-memorial-fountain* ⊙ *Fountain: Apr.– mid-Oct., daily 8 am–10:45 pm.*

FAMILY **Harold Washington Library Center.** The library, which opened in 1991 and is named for the first African-American mayor of Chicago, was primarily designed by architect Thomas Beeby, of Hammond, Beeby & Babka. Gargantuan and almost goofy, this granite-and-brick edifice is a uniquely postmodern homage to Chicago's great architectural past. The heavy, rusticated ground level recalls the Rookery; the stepped-back, arched windows are a reference to the great arches in the Auditorium Theatre; the swirling terra-cotta design is pinched from the Marquette Building; and the glass curtain wall on the west side is a nod to 1950s modernism. The huge, gargoylelike sculptures atop the building include owls, a symbol of wisdom. The excellent **Children's Library** on the second floor, an 18,000-square-foot haven, has vibrant wall-mounted figures by Chicago imagist Karl Wirsum. Works by noted Chicago artists are displayed along a second-floor walkway above the main lobby. There's also an impressive Winter Garden with skylights on the ninth floor. Free programs and performances are offered regularly. ✉ *400 S. State St., South Loop* ☎ *312/747–4300* ⊕ *www.chipublib.org/branch/ details/library/harold-washington* ⊙ *Mon.–Thurs. 9–9, Fri. and Sat. 9–5, Sun. 1–5.*

FAMILY
Fodor'sChoice
★
John G. Shedd Aquarium.
⇨ *See highlighted feature in this chapter.*

Pontiac Building. An early Chicago School skyscraper—note its classic rectangular shape and flat roof—the simple, redbrick, 14-story Pontiac was designed by Holabird & Roche in 1891. It's their oldest existing building in Chicago. ✉ *542 S. Dearborn St., South Loop.*

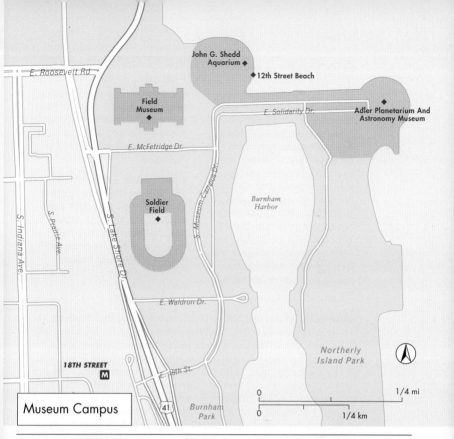

Museum Campus

Map labels:
E. Roosevelt Rd.
John G. Shedd Aquarium
12th Street Beach
Field Museum
E. Solidarity Dr.
Adler Planetarium And Astronomy Museum
E. McFetridge Dr.
S. Museum Campus Dr.
Burnham Harbor
Soldier Field
S. Indiana Ave.
S. Prairie Ave.
S. Lake Shore Dr.
E. Waldron Dr.
Northerly Island Park
18TH STREET
E. 18th St.
41
Burnham Park
0   1/4 mi
0   1/4 km

WORTH NOTING

Museum of Contemporary Photography. "Contemporary" is generally defined here as work made in the past two or three decades. Curators constantly seek out new talent and underappreciated established photographers, which means that there are artists here you probably won't see elsewhere. Rotating exhibits have included explorations of infrastructure, crime, and American identity. ✉ *600 S. Michigan Ave., South Loop* ☎ *312/663–5554* ⊕ *www.mocp.org* ⊠ *Free* ⊘ *Mon.–Wed., Fri., and Sat. 10–5; Thurs. 10–8; Sun. noon–5.*

Printers Row. Bounded by Congress Parkway on the north, Polk Street on the south, Plymouth Court to the east, and the Chicago River to the west, this district fell into disrepair in the 1960s, but a neighborhood resurgence began in the late 1970s. You can still see examples of buildings by the group that represented the First Chicago School of Architecture (including Louis Sullivan), as well as Dearborn Station, a Romanesque Revival–style structure that was once the city's main passenger train hub. These days this section of town is best known for the Printers Row Lit Fest, a weekend-long literary celebration held each June. ✉ *Between Congress Pkwy. and Polk St., Plymouth Ct. and the Chicago River, South Loop.*

MUSEUM CAMPUS TIPS

The 57-acre Museum Campus is home to the Big Three—the Field Museum, the John G. Shedd Aquarium, and the Adler Planetarium and Astronomy Museum—in a pedestrian-friendly, parklike setting. Park in one of the lots just past the Field Museum on McFetridge Drive, or ride the Chicago Trolley Hop On Hop Off Tour (☎ 773/648–5000). It connects the three museums with other downtown tourist attractions and train stations. Just east of the Field Museum is the Shedd Aquarium, on the lakefront, and farther

still, at the end of a peninsula jutting into Lake Michigan, is the Adler Planetarium, the Western Hemisphere's first modern planetarium. Look north from here for a fantastic view of the city skyline.

If you're visiting all three museums plus other big attractions, consider a Chicago cityPASS ($94). You'll avoid long lines and get access to the Field, the Shedd, and Willis Tower Skydeck, plus the Adler or the Art Institute, and the John Hancock Center Observatory or Museum of Science and Industry.

Soldier Field. Opened in 1924 as the Municipal Grant Park Stadium, the facility was renamed in 1925 to commemorate American soldiers who died during World War I. Just south of the Museum Campus, the building and its massive columns are reminiscent of ancient Greece. Since 1971 it's been the home of the Chicago Bears. A controversial modern glass expansion, which looks like a spaceship that landed on the arena, was completed in 2003. Behind-the-scenes tours feature the Doughboy Statue, Colonnades, field, South Courtyard, visitors' locker room, the suites, and the United Club. ✉ *1410 S. Museum Campus Dr., South Loop* ☎ *312/235–7000* ⊕ *www.soldierfield.net* ✍ *$15 tours.*

WEST LOOP

For an especially good meal, head to the West Loop, along the Chicago River. What was once skid row and meatpacking warehouses is now a vibrant community with trendy restaurants. Greektown, a five-block stretch of Halsted Street, serves up authentic *saganaki* (appetizers). A thriving art scene has emerged around Fulton Market.

TOP ATTRACTIONS

Chicago Antique Market. This famed indoor-outdoor flea market, held on the third Saturday and Sunday from April through November, is part of the Randolph Street Market Festival and is Chicago's answer to London's famed Portobello Road Market. Centered on Randolph Street and Ogden Avenue at Plumber's Hall, the market offers mid-century furniture, vintage handbags, ephemera, and much more. From May through September, free shuttles head back and forth between the Hall and Water Tower Place on the hour, from 10 to 4. ✉ *1340 W. Washington Blvd., West Loop* ☎ *322/666–1200* ⊕ *www.chicagoantiquemarket. com* ✍ *$8 online, $10 at gate* ۞ *Sat. 10–6, Sun. 10–5.*

Fulton Market. This stylish neighborhood is filled with chic restaurants, trendsetting galleries, shops, and showrooms for cutting-edge design and green living. Be aware, though, that the area remains a bustling commercial district. During the day the seafood, produce, and meat-packing plants swarm with heavy vehicles helmed by harried drivers. Exercise caution while driving or, better yet, take a cab. ⊠ *Along Fulton Market and Lake St. between Desplaines St. and Ashland Ave., West Loop* ⊕ *www.explorefultonmarket.com.*

Greektown. This small strip may as well be half a world away from the rest of the West Loop. Greek restaurants are the main draw here. Continue west on Madison, past the slew of new condo developments and vintage conversions in progress, and you'll come to one of Chicago's popular dining and nightlife destinations. On a stretch of Madison roughly between Sangamon and Elizabeth streets you'll find boutiques, trendy bars and lounges, and popular restaurants. The Hellenic Museum and Cultural Center, at 801 West Adams, explores the Greek immigrant experience and the influence of Greek culture. ⊠ *Halsted St. between Madison and W. Van Buren Sts., West Loop* ⊕ *www.chicagogreektown.com* ⊠ *Free.*

WORTH NOTING

Leslie Hindman Auctioneers. Antiques hunters with fat wallets may want to check the schedule at this fine-art auctioneer. It's the fifth-largest auction house in the country. Auctions include 20th-century decorative arts, American and European works of art, plus fine jewelry and timepieces. ⊠ *1338 W. Lake St., West Loop* ☎ *312/280–1212* ⊕ *www.lesliehindman.com.*

OFF THE
BEATEN
PATH

Garfield Park Conservatory. Escape winter's cold or revel in summer sunshine inside this huge "landscape art under glass" structure housing tropical palms, spiny cacti, and showy blooms. A children's garden is filled with climbable leaf sculptures and a tube slide that winds through trees. The "Sugar from the Sun" exhibit focuses on the elements of photosynthesis—sunlight, air, water, and sugar—in a full-sensory environment filled with spewing steam, trickling water, and chirping sounds. And don't miss the historic Jens Jensen–designed Fern Room with its lagoon, waterfalls, and profusion of ferns. Events include botanical-themed fashion shows, seasonal flower shows, and great educational programming. ■TIP→ **In 2011 hail damaged the Fern Room, Show House, and portions of the Desert House where the blooms are located. Repairs are scheduled for summer 2013.** ⊠ *300 N. Central Park Ave., Garfield Park* ☎ *312/746–5100* ⊕ *www.garfield-conservatory.org* ⊠ *Free* ☉ *Thurs.–Tues. 9–5, Wed. 9–8.*

3

NEAR NORTH AND RIVER NORTH

GETTING ORIENTED

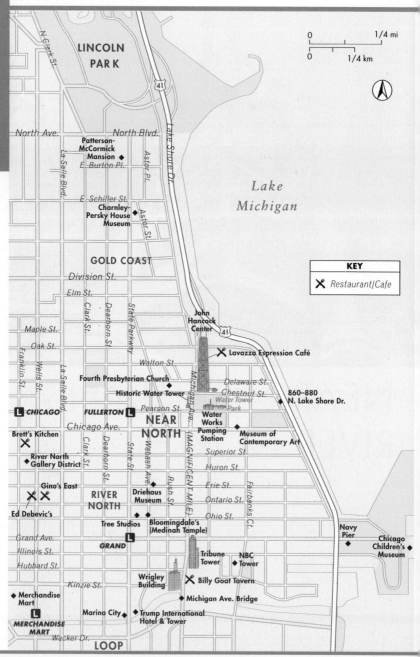

0 _____ 1/4 mi

0 _____ 1/4 km

LINCOLN PARK

41

North Ave.

North Blvd.

Patterson-McCormick Mansion ◆

E. Burton Pl.

Astor Pl.

La Salle Blvd.

E. Schiller St.

Charnley-Persky House Museum ◆

Astor St.

Lake Michigan

Lake Shore Dr.

GOLD COAST

Division St.

Elm St.

Clark St.

Dearborn St.

State Parkway

KEY

✗ Restaurant/Cafe

Maple St.

Oak St.

Franklin St.

Wells St.

La Salle Blvd.

John Hancock Center

41

Walton St.

✗ Lavazza Espression Café

Fourth Presbyterian Church ◆

Historic Water Tower ◆

Michigan Ave. (MAGNIFICENT MILE)

Delaware St.

Chestnut St.

Water Tower Park

860–880 N. Lake Shore Dr. ◆

L CHICAGO

FULLERTON L

Pearson St.

NEAR NORTH

Water Works

Chicago Ave.

Brett's Kitchen ✗

Clark St.

Dearborn St.

State St.

Wabash Ave.

Water Works Pumping Station

Museum of Contemporary Art ◆

River North Gallery District ◆

Superior St.

Huron St.

Gino's East ✗✗

Rush St.

Erie St.

Driehaus Museum

Ontario St.

Fairbanks Ct.

Ed Debevic's ✗

RIVER NORTH

◆

Ohio St.

Navy Pier

Tree Studios ◆

Bloomingdale's (Medinah Temple)

◆

Chicago Children's Museum ◆

Grand Ave.

Illinois St.

Hubbard St.

GRAND L

Tribune Tower

NBC Tower ◆

Kinzie St.

Wrigley Building

✗ Billy Goat Tavern

◆ Merchandise Mart

◆ Michigan Ave. Bridge

L

MERCHANDISE MART

Marina City ◆

◆ Trump International Hotel & Tower

Wacker Dr.

LOOP

GETTING HERE

Near North: If you're arriving from the north by car, take Lake Shore Drive south to the Michigan Avenue exit. From the south, exit at Grand Avenue for Navy Pier. The prepaid parking app SpotHero can save you money.

The 3, 4, 144, 145, 146, 167, and 151 buses run along Michigan Avenue. Buses 29, 65, and 66 all service Navy Pier. If you're using the El, take the Red Line to Chicago Avenue or Clark and Division.

River North: The Merchandise Mart has its own stop on the El's Brown and Purple lines. For drivers, there is a parking lot at 350 North Orleans Street. If you are heading to the northern tip of the neighborhood, take Wells Street to Chicago Avenue. You can also walk west from the Mag Mile a few blocks to get to the area.

MAKING THE MOST OF YOUR TIME

If you have kids, figure at least a day at Navy Pier for the Children's Museum and riding the Ferris wheel. Exercise your wallet and your people-watching skills on the Magnificent Mile, *the* Chicago shopping spot. Along the way, get a bird's-eye view of Chicago, including the Tribune Tower, Trump Tower, and Marina City, from the State Street Bridge. Art lovers can while away the day at the Museum of Contemporary Art or the galleries at River North.

TOP REASONS TO GO

Appreciate the views: Have a drink or a meal at the Signature Room at the John Hancock Center.

Enjoy art: Spend an afternoon perusing the art galleries.

Visit the Water Tower: It's one of the few structures that survived the Great Chicago Fire of 1871.

Shop: Browse the Mag Mile (North Michigan Avenue).

QUICK BITES

Billy Goat Tavern. Behind and a level down from the Wrigley Building is the inspiration for *Saturday Night Live*'s classic "cheezborger, cheezborger, cheezborger, cheeps, no fries, no Coke, Pepsi" skit. Grab a greasy burger at this no-frills grill, or just have a beer and absorb the comic undertones. ⊠ *430 N. Michigan Ave., Lower Level, Near North* ☎ *312/222–1525* ⊕ *www.billygoattavern.com.*

Brett's Kitchen. Under the El at Superior and Franklin, this is an excellent spot for a pastry, sandwich, or omelet, open until 4. ⊠ *233 W. Superior St., River North* ☎ *312/664–6354* ⊕ *www.brettskitchen.com* ◔ *Closed Sun.*

Ed Debevic's. The purposefully sassy waiters and waitresses at this touristy '50s-style diner keep the crowds entertained. ⊠ *640 N. Wells St., River North* ☎ *312/664–1707* ⊕ *www.eddebevics.com.*

Gino's East. Fill up on yummy Chicago deep-dish pizza at the graffiti-covered Gino's East. ⊠ *633 N. Wells St., River North* ☎ *312/988–4200* ⊕ *www.ginoseast.com.*

Lavazza Espression Café. This is the place to grab some Italian pastries, an espresso, or a quick drink. ⊠ *John Hancock Observatory, 875 N. Michigan Ave., Near North* ☎ *888/875–8439* ⊕ *www.jhochicago.com/en/plan-your-visit/espression-cafe.*

Sightseeing
★★★★★
Dining
★★★★☆
Lodging
★★★★☆
Shopping
★★★★☆
Nightlife
★★★★☆

With River North's art galleries and shopping, the Magnificent Mile, the Gold Coast, and upscale dining options, Near North holds some of the city's greatest attractions. Navy Pier and the Chicago Children's Museum are great family-friendly stops, and serious shoppers can seriously exercise their credit cards along Michigan Avenue's most famous stretch.

NEAR NORTH

Updated
by Roberta
Sotonoff

Chicago's Near North side begins north of the Chicago River and runs north on and around Michigan Avenue—including the neighborhoods of River North (west of Michigan Avenue and south of Chicago Avenue; *see separate section, below*), Streeterville, and the Gold Coast—all the way up to North Avenue and the verdant green of Lincoln Park.

Near North has some of the city's best shopping and most crowd-pleasing restaurants, as well as some of the city's most distinctive buildings. To get a taste, start at the beginning of the Mag Mile and check out the architecture of the Tribune Tower. Then browse the shops on Michigan Avenue as well as the upscale boutiques on Oak and many other side streets. The John Hancock Center offers one of the best sky-high views of the city. Instead of shelling out bucks at the observatory, get a drink at its Signature Lounge for about the same price; the view comes free.

Hugging the lakeshore north of Oak Street and east of Clark Street is the Gold Coast. Potter Palmer (the developer of State Street and the Palmer House Hotel) transformed the area when he built a mansion here, and his social-climbing friends followed his lead. The less fortunate residents thought the new arrivals must have pockets lined with gold. More recently, a different kind of mansion—Hugh Hefner's Playboy Mansion and its 50 bunnies—was at 1340 North State Street.

To the east of the Mag Mile on Grand Avenue, Navy Pier stretches a half mile into Lake Michigan. Packed with restaurants, souvenir stalls, and folks out for a stroll, this perpetually busy wonderland is adored by kids and adults alike. You'll find the Chicago Children's Museum, a 150-foot-high Ferris wheel, an IMAX theater, and the Chicago Shakespeare Theatre here. It is also the starting point for many lake cruises. Make sure to dedicate an evening to seeing and being seen at one of the chic local restaurants.

TOP ATTRACTIONS

Fodor's Choice ★ **860–880 N. Lake Shore Drive.** These twin apartment towers overlooking Lake Michigan were an early and eloquent realization of Mies van der Rohe's "less is more" credo, expressed in the high-rise. I-beams running up the facade underscore the building's verticality; inside, mechanical systems are housed in the center so as to leave the rest of each floor free and open to the spectacular views. Completed in 1951, the buildings are a prominent example of the International Style, which played a key role in transforming the look of American cities. ⊠ *860–880 N. Lake Shore Dr., at E. Chestnut St., Near North.*

FAMILY **Chicago Children's Museum.**
⇨ *See the feature later in this chapter.*

FAMILY Fodor's Choice ★ **John Hancock Observatory.** Designed by the same team (Skidmore, Owings & Merrill) that designed the Willis (formerly Sears) Tower, this multiuse skyscraper is distinguished by its tapering shape and enormous X braces, which help stabilize its 100 stories. Soon after it went up in 1970, it earned the nickname "Big John." No wonder: it's 1,127 feet tall, 1,502 feet counting its antennae. Packed with retail space, parking, offices, a restaurant, and residences, it has been likened to a city within a city. It's impressive from any angle and offers mind-boggling views from a 94th-floor observatory, where, like the Willis Tower, you can see to four states on clear days. Those with vertigo might prefer a seat in the Lavazza Espression Café or the bar of the 95th-floor Signature Room. The tab will be steep, but you don't pay the observatory fee and you'll be steady on your feet—*maybe.* ⊠ *875 N. Michigan Ave., Near North* ⊕ *www.jhochicago.com* ⊠ *Observatory $17.50* ⊗ *Daily 9 am–11 pm; last ticket sold at 10:30 pm.*

Fodor's Choice ★ **Magnificent Mile.** Originally designed by 19th-century architect Daniel Burnham, this famous section of Michigan Avenue is a potpourri of historic buildings, upscale boutiques, department stores, and posh hotels. Among its jewels are the Tribune Tower, the Wrigley Building, the John Hancock Center, the Drake Hotel, and the Historic Water Tower, one of the few structures that survived the Great Chicago Fire. ⊠ *Michigan Ave., between Chicago Ave. and Lakeshore Dr., Near North.*

CHICAGO CHILDREN'S MUSEUM

⊠ *Navy Pier, 700 E. Grand Ave., Near North* ☎ *312/527–1000* ⊕ *www. chicagochildrensmuseum. org* 🎫 *$14, free Thurs. 5–8 pm and 1st Sun. of month for children 15 and younger* ⊗ *Fri.–Wed. 10–5, Thurs. 10–8.*

TIPS

■ The museum issues read-mission bracelets that let you leave the museum and come back on the same day—a great idea for weary families who want to get a bite to eat or simply explore other parts of Navy Pier before coming back to the museum.

■ Stop for lunch at the nearby space-themed McDonald's or bring a picnic and grab a seat outside (in warm weather) or in the Crystal Ballroom (amid tropical plants and fountains).

■ Hour-long art workshops at Artabounds are free.

■ Most families spend an average of three hours visiting the museum.

■ The museum is designed for children 12 or younger. Adults may not enter the museum without a child.

Hands-on is the operative concept for this brightly colored Navy Pier anchor. Kids tinker with real tools in an open work space, climb through multilevel tunnels and the riggings of a ship, play at being a firefighter, dig for dinosaur fossils, and, if their parents allow it, get soaking wet.

Highlights

Oversize water tubs with waterwheels, pumps, brightly colored pipes, and fountains are all part of the splashy fun at "WaterWays," with raincoats for kids. If everyone pumps hard enough, water squirts 50 feet in the air.

The new "Tinkering Lab" lets children ask their own questions, play around with their own ideas, fail, and learn from their mistakes—all using real tools and materials.

A "garden" brimming with giant flowers and insects draws kids to the "Big Backyard" exhibit.

Kids can don authentic firefighter gear, operate a replica fire truck, slide down a pole, or practice escaping from a smoke-filled bedroom in "Play It Safe."

With real tools and wooden struts, kids can construct their own building in the "Skyline" exhibit.

Parents and children can scurry up a three-story-high rigging complete with crow's nest and gangplank on the "Kovler Family Climbing Schooner," reminiscent of boats that once sailed Lake Michigan. From the rope tunnels to the top, you can take in bird's-eye views of the museum, then slide back down to see tanks of fish.

"Dinosaur Expedition" lets families brush away dirt to discover the bones of a Suchomimus, a fish-eating dinosaur. The exhibit re-creates a trip to the Sahara led by University of Chicago paleontologist Paul Sereno.

MUSEUM OF CONTEMPORARY ART

✉ *220 E. Chicago Ave.,*
Near North ☎ *312/280–2660*
🌐 *www.mcachicago.org*
💲 *$12 suggested donation*
🕙 *Tues. 10–8, Wed.–Sun.*
10–5.

TIPS

■ Run by Wolfgang Puck, Puck's Café at the MCA has a tasty menu that makes it a good spot for lunch.

■ Try to catch one of the cutting-edge music and theater performances; one year, for example, the entire front of the museum was turned into a puppet theater.

■ In summer come for Tuesdays on the Terrace and be serenaded by local jazz bands. There's a cash bar evenings from 5:30 to 8 and a full menu at the café.

■ On the first Friday evening of every month the museum hosts a party ($18) with live music and hors d'oeuvres from 6 to 10.

■ A farmers' market sets up shop on Tuesday from mid-June through October. Pick up fresh snacks and enjoy a picnic in the museum's backyard sculpture garden (admission free).

A group of art patrons who felt the great Art Institute was unresponsive to modern work founded the MCA in 1967, and it has remained a renegade art museum ever since. It doesn't have any permanent exhibits; this gives it a feeling of freshness, but it also makes it impossible to predict what will be on display at any time. Special exhibits are devoted mostly to original shows you can't see anywhere else.

Highlights

The MCA building looks like a home for modern art— it's made of square metal plates with round bolts in each corner. These dramatic quarters were designed by Berlin architect Josef Paul Kleihues.

The 7,000-piece collection, still growing, includes work by René Magritte, Alexander Calder, Bruce Nauman, Sol LeWitt, Franz Kline, and June Leaf. This makes up about half the museum; the other half is dedicated to temporary exhibitions.

The museum showcases work in all mediums, including paintings, sculpture, works on paper, photography, video, film, and installations.

Guided "Exhibition Focus" tours, dedicated to short-run exhibits, happen daily. Highlights Tours, which provide a balanced sweep of the entire museum, are offered on weekends.

The MCA Store carries well-designed jewelry and quirky items for the home, from a porcelain eggshell from which a flower sprouts to goggles to be worn while chopping onions.

The John Hancock Center offers some of the best panoramic views of the city.

Michigan Avenue Bridge. Chicago is a city of bridges, and this is one of its most graceful. Completed in 1920, it features impressive sculptures on its four pylons representing major Chicago events: its exploration by Marquette and Joliet, its settlement by trader Jean Baptiste Point du Sable, the Fort Dearborn Massacre of 1812, and the rebuilding of the city after the Great Chicago Fire of 1871. The site of the fort, at the southeast end of the bridge, is marked by a commemorative plaque. As you stroll Michigan Avenue, be prepared for a possible delay; the bridge rises some hundred times between April and November to allow boat traffic to pass underneath.

McCormick Bridgehouse. Located in the southwest tower of the Michigan Avenue Bridge, this engaging museum provides a glimpse into the history of movable bridges—and some great city views in the process. Until the 1960s, the five-story bridgehouse housed the family of a man hired to tend the bridge. On lift days visitors can see the gears that still raise the bridge put to work. This is the only bridgehouse in Chicago that is open to the public. See the website for a lift schedule—reservations are a good idea. ⊠ *376 N. Michigan Ave., at Wacker Dr.* ⊕ *www.bridgehousemuseum. org* ⊠ *$4, $10 on bridge lift days* ☉ *Mid-May–Oct., Thurs.–Mon. 10–5.*

Fodor's Choice ★ **Museum of Contemporary Art.**
⇨ *See the feature in this chapter.*

FAMILY **Navy Pier.** No matter the season, Navy Pier is a fun place to spend a few hours, especially with kids in tow. Constructed in 1916 as a commercial-shipping pier and part of Daniel Burnham's Master Plan of Chicago, it stretches a half mile into Lake Michigan. Redesigned and re-opened in 1995, it's a major tourist draw. Outside, there's a landscaped area with gardens, a fountain, a carousel, a 15-story Ferris wheel, and a beer garden. Inside are Crystal Gardens, a six-story glass atrium that serves as an indoor event venue and botanical park; the Smith Museum of Stained Glass Windows; the Chicago Children's Museum; an IMAX theater; the Chicago Shakespeare Theatre; and a bevy of souvenir shops, restaurants, and bars. ⊠ *600 E. Grand Ave., Near North* ☎ *312/595–7437* ⊕ *www.navypier.com.*

Fodor's Choice ★ **Tribune Tower.** To create a home for his newspaper, *Chicago Tribune* publisher Colonel Robert McCormick held a design competition in which entrants were judged anonymously. After rejecting a slew of functional modern designs by such notables as Walter Gropius, Eliel Saarinen, and Adolf Loos, McCormick chose the work of architects Raymond Hood and John Mead Howells, who were inspired by the cathedral in Rouen, France. The result, which opened in 1925, was a soaring Gothic building with flying buttresses in its crown. Embedded in the exterior walls are chunks of material taken from famous sites, including the Taj Mahal. On the ground floor are the studios of WGN radio, part of the *Chicago Tribune* empire, which also includes WGN-TV, cable-television stations, and the Chicago Cubs. (Modesty was not one of Colonel McCormick's prime traits: WGN stands for the *Tribune*'s self-bestowed nickname: World's Greatest Newspaper.) ⊠ *435 N. Michigan Ave., Near North* ☎ *312/222–3232* ⊕ *www. tribune.com.*

Wrigley Building. The gleaming white landmark headquarters of the chewing-gum company—designed by Graham, Anderson, Probst & White—was instrumental in transforming Michigan Avenue from an area of warehouses to one of the most desirable spots in the city. Its two structures were built several years apart and later connected, and its clock tower was inspired by the bell tower of the grand cathedral in Seville, Spain. Be sure to check it out at night, when lamps bounce light off the building's terra-cotta facade. Its interior is undergoing a renovation. ⊠ *400–410 N. Michigan Ave., Near North* ⊕ *www.thewrigleybuilding.com.*

WORTH NOTING

Charnley-Persky House Museum. Designed by Frank Lloyd Wright with his mentor Louis Sullivan, this almost-austere residence represents one of Wright's first significant forays into residential design. Historians still squabble about who designed what here, but it's easy to imagine that the young go-getter had a hand in the cleanly rendered interior. Note how the geometric exterior looks unmistakably modern next to its fussy neighbors. Public tours of both the interior and exterior are available and last about one hour. Wednesday tours, which are free, are less comprehensive than Saturday tours; reservations are a good idea for large groups. ⊠ *1365 N. Astor St., Gold Coast* ☎ *312/573–1365* ⊕ *www.charnleyhouse.org* ▦ *Free Wed., $10 Sat.* ☉ *Wed. at noon, Sat. at 10 and noon.*

Continued on page 86

THE SKY'S THE LIMIT

Talk about baptism by fire. Although Chicago was incorporated in 1837, it wasn't until *after* the Great Fire of 1871 that the city really started to take shape. With four square miles gone up in flames, the town was a clean slate. The opportunity to make a mark on this metropolis drew a slew of architects, from Adler & Sullivan to H. H. Richardson and Daniel H. Burnham—names renowned in the annals of American architecture. A Windy City tradition was born: the city's continuously morphing skyline is graced with tall wonders designed by architecture's heavy hitters, including Mies van der Rohe; Skidmore, Owings & Merrill; and, most recently, Santiago Calatrava. In the next four pages, you'll find an eye-popping sampling of Chicago's great buildings and how they've pushed—and continue to push—the definition of even such a lofty term as "skyscraper."

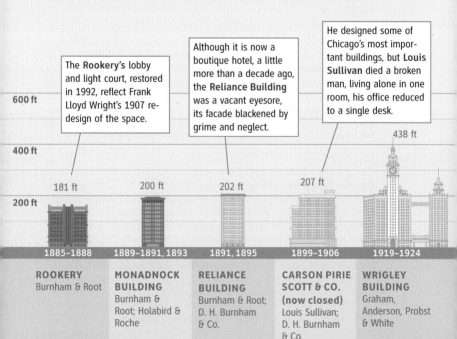

The **Rookery's** lobby and light court, restored in 1992, reflect Frank Lloyd Wright's 1907 re-design of the space.

Although it is now a boutique hotel, a little more than a decade ago, the **Reliance Building** was a vacant eyesore, its facade blackened by grime and neglect.

He designed some of Chicago's most important buildings, but **Louis Sullivan** died a broken man, living alone in one room, his office reduced to a single desk.

600 ft
400 ft
200 ft

181 ft
200 ft
202 ft
207 ft
438 ft

1885–1888	1889–1891, 1893	1891, 1895	1899–1906	1919–1924
ROOKERY Burnham & Root	**MONADNOCK BUILDING** Burnham & Root; Holabird & Roche	**RELIANCE BUILDING** Burnham & Root; D. H. Burnham & Co.	**CARSON PIRIE SCOTT & CO. (now closed)** Louis Sullivan; D. H. Burnham & Co.	**WRIGLEY BUILDING** Graham, Anderson, Probst & White

THE BIRTH OF THE SKYSCRAPER

Houses, churches, and commercial buildings of all sorts rose from the ashes after the blaze of 1871, but what truly put Chicago on the architectural map was the tall building. The earliest of these barely scrape the sky—especially when compared to what towers over us today—but in the late 19th century, structures such as William Le Baron Jenney's ten-story Home Insurance Building (1884) represented a bold push upward. Until then, the sheer weight of stone and cast-iron construction had limited how high a building could soar. But by using a lighter yet stronger steel frame and simply sheathing his building in a thin skin of masonry, Jenney blazed the way for ever taller buildings. And with only so much land available in the central business district, up was the way to go.

Although the Home Insurance Building was razed in 1931, Chicago's Loop remains a rich trove of early skyscraper design. Some of these survivors stand severe and solid as fortresses, while others manifest an almost ethereal quality. They—and their descendants along Wacker Drive, North Michigan Avenue, and Lake Shore Drive—reflect the technological, economic, and aesthetic forces that have made this city on the prairie one of the most dramatically vertical communities in the country.

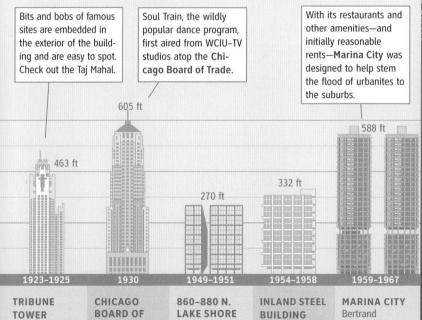

Bits and bobs of famous sites are embedded in the exterior of the building and are easy to spot. Check out the Taj Mahal.

Soul Train, the wildly popular dance program, first aired from WCIU–TV studios atop the **Chicago Board of Trade**.

With its restaurants and other amenities—and initially reasonable rents—**Marina City** was designed to help stem the flood of urbanites to the suburbs.

605 ft

463 ft

270 ft

332 ft

588 ft

1923–1925	1930	1949–1951	1954–1958	1959–1967
TRIBUNE TOWER Howells & Hood	**CHICAGO BOARD OF TRADE** Holabird & Root	**860–880 N. LAKE SHORE DRIVE** Ludwig Mies van der Rohe	**INLAND STEEL BUILDING** Skidmore, Owings & Merrill	**MARINA CITY** Bertrand Goldberg Associates

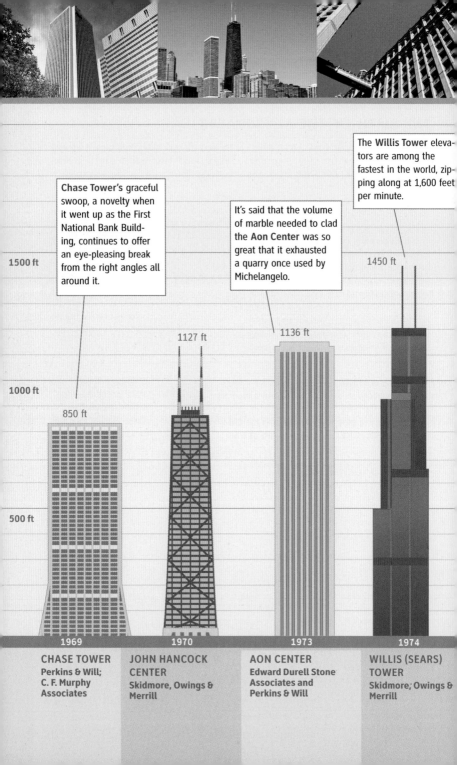

The **Willis Tower** elevators are among the fastest in the world, zipping along at 1,600 feet per minute.

Chase Tower's graceful swoop, a novelty when it went up as the First National Bank Building, continues to offer an eye-pleasing break from the right angles all around it.

It's said that the volume of marble needed to clad the **Aon Center** was so great that it exhausted a quarry once used by Michelangelo.

1500 ft

1450 ft

1136 ft

1127 ft

1000 ft

850 ft

500 ft

1969

1973

1974

1970

CHASE TOWER
Perkins & Will;
C. F. Murphy
Associates

**JOHN HANCOCK
CENTER**
Skidmore, Owings &
Merrill

AON CENTER
Edward Durell Stone
Associates and
Perkins & Will

**WILLIS (SEARS)
TOWER**
Skidmore; Owings &
Merrill

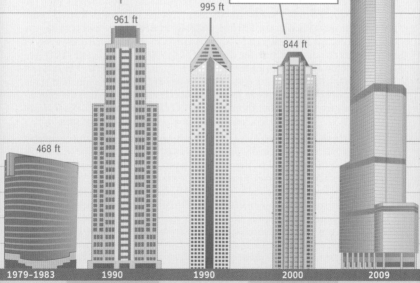

311 S. Wacker may not
be the tallest building in
town, but come dark, it's
one of the most visible,
lit by nearly 2,000 fluo-
rescent lights.

Although Park Tower
hovers over nearly ev-
erything around it, this
hotel/condo is consid-
ered a good neighbor,
thanks to its retro styl-
ing and warmly colored
facade.

1389 ft

995 ft

961 ft

844 ft

468 ft

1979–1983	1990	1990	2000	2009
333 W. WACKER DRIVE	311 S. WACKER DRIVE	2 PRUDENTIAL PLAZA	PARK TOWER	TRUMP TOWER
Kohn Pedersen Fox and Perkins & Will	Kohn Pedersen Fox	Loebl, Schlossman & Hackl	Lucien LaGrange Architects	Skidmore, Owens, and Merrill

Kids and kids-at-heart get their thrills at Navy Pier.

Fourth Presbyterian Church. A welcome visual and physical oasis amid the high-rise hubbub of North Michigan Avenue, this Gothic Revival house of worship was the first big building erected on the avenue after the Chicago fire. Designed by Ralph Adams Cram, the church drew many of its congregants from the city's elite. Local architect Howard van Doren Shaw devised the cloister and companion buildings. ■TIP➔ In July and August, concerts are given every Friday at 12:10 by the fountain in the courtyard off Michigan Avenue; concerts are performed in the sanctuary from September through June. ⊠ *126 E. Chestnut St., Near North* ☎ *312/787–4570* ⊕ *www.fourthchurch.org/about/architecture.html.*

Historic Water Tower. This famous Michigan Avenue structure, completed in 1867, was originally built to house a 137-foot standpipe that equalized the pressure of the water pumped by the similar pumping station across the street. Oscar Wilde uncharitably called it "a castellated monstrosity" studded with pepper shakers. One of the few buildings that survived the Great Chicago Fire of 1871, it remains a Chicago landmark and a symbol of the city's spirit. The small gallery inside has rotating art exhibitions of local interest. ⊠ *806 N. Michigan Ave., at Pearson St., Near North* ⊕ *www.explorechicago.org/city/en/things_see_ do/attractions/dca_tourism/water_tower.html* ▣ *Free* ⊙ *Daily 10–6:30.*

Water Works Pumping Station. Water is still pumped to some city residents at a rate of about 250 million gallons per day from this Gothic-style structure, which, along with the Water Tower across the street, survived the Great Chicago Fire of 1871. The **Lookingglass Theatre** calls this place home, as does one of the city's visitor centers. ⊠ *163 E. Pearson St., at Michigan Ave., Near North.*

A REVERED SCHOOL

The **Chicago School** had no classrooms and no curriculum. It didn't confer degrees. The Chicago School wasn't an institution at all, but a name given to the collection of architects whose work, beginning in the 1880s, helped free American architecture from the often rigid styles of the past. Nonetheless, a number of their buildings echoed a classical column, the lower floors functioning as the base, the middle floors as the shaft, and the cornice on top being the equivalent of a capital. In pioneering the "tall building," these architects used steel-frame construction; they also reduced ornamentation. Alumni include Daniel Burnham, William Le Baron Jenney, Louis Sullivan, Dankmar Adler, John Root, William Holabird, and Martin Roche.

NBC Tower. This 1989 limestone-and-granite edifice by Skidmore, Owings & Merrill looks back to the Art Deco days without becoming a victim of fashion's past. Four floors of the 38-story tower are dedicated to a radio and television broadcasting facility. ⊠ *455 N. Cityfront Plaza Dr., Near North* ☎ *312/222–9611* ⊕ *www.nbc-tower.com.*

Patterson-McCormick Mansion. On the northwest corner of Astor and Burton places in the swanky Gold Coast, you'll find this Georgian building, commissioned in 1891 by *Chicago Tribune* chief Joseph Medill and built by Stanford White. You cannot go inside the building, which has been converted into condos— it is said that Billy Corgan of the Smashing Pumpkins owns one of the units. ⊠ *20 E. Burton Pl., Gold Coast.*

RIVER NORTH

Once the warehouse district and for a time a place where many Chicago artists had their lofts, River North is now known for its large, often touristy restaurants, art galleries, and the enormous Merchandise Mart, which still serves as a neighborhood landmark. River North lies immediately north of the Loop and the Chicago River, south of Chicago Avenue, and west of the Mag Mile.

TOP ATTRACTIONS

Bloomingdale's (Medinah Temple). Built in 1912 for the Shriners, the former Medinah Temple is a Middle Eastern fantasy, with horseshoe-shape arches, stained-glass windows, and intricate geometric patterns around windows and doors (it once also held a 4,200-seat auditorium). It stood vacant for many years, but in 2003 a Bloomingdale's Home & Furniture Store opened in the space. ⊠ *600 N. Wabash Ave., River North* ⊗ *Mon.–Thurs. 10–7, Fri.–Sat. 10–8, Sun. noon–6.*

Driehaus Museum. Curious about how the wealthy built their urban palaces during America's Gilded Age? Steps away from the Magnificent Mile, the former Samuel Mayo Nickerson mansion has lavish interiors with 19th-century furniture and objets d'art, including pieces by Louis Comfort Tiffany and the Herter brothers. ⊠ *40 E. Erie St., River*

North ☎ *312/482–8933* ⊕ *www.driehausmuseum.org* ✉ *$20, tours $5 extra* ⊙ *Tues.–Sat. 10–5, Sun. noon–5; tours Tues.–Sat. at 11 and 2, Sun. at 1:30 and 3.*

The Merchandise Mart. The huge Merchandise Mart, on the river between Orleans and Wells streets, takes up nearly two square blocks. In fact, it was the largest building in the world when it opened in 1930, and it remains large enough to have its own stop on the El's Brown and Purple lines. Miles of corridors on its top floors are lined with trade-only furniture and home-design showrooms. LuxeHome, a collection of 30 or so upscale stores with an emphasis on home design and renovation, takes up the bottom two floors. ✉ *222 Merchandise Mart Plaza, River North* ☎ *800/677–6278* ⊕ *www.mmart.com* ⊙ *Showrooms weekdays 9–5; LuxeHome weekdays 9–5, Sat. 10–3.*

> ## GOLD COAST
>
> North of Oak Street, hugging Lake Shore Drive, is the Gold Coast neighborhood. Astor Street is the grande dame of Gold Coast promenades, and homes like the Patterson-McCormick Mansion and the Charnley-Persky House still impress. Where Dearborn Street meets Oak Street is the Gold Coast's famous shopping district. Past the former **Playboy Mansion** (✉ *1340 N. State St.*), all the way to North Boulevard, is a beautiful view of Lincoln Park.

River North Gallery District. North of the Merchandise Mart and south of Chicago Avenue, between Orleans and Dearborn streets, is a concentration of art galleries carrying just about every kind of work imaginable. In fact, virtually every building on Superior Street between Wells and Orleans houses at least one gallery. Visitors are welcome to stop in. On some Friday nights (check the *Chicago Gallery News* for dates), the galleries coordinate their exhibitions to showcase new works, and free art gallery tours leave from Chicago and Franklin on Saturday at 11. Although River North is still a good bet for great art, many artists have ditched the high-rent district for the cheaper, more industrial West Loop. ✉ *Between Chicago Ave. and Merchandise Mart, Orleans and Dearborn Sts., River North* ☎ *312/649–0064.*

WORTH NOTING

Marina City. Likened to everything from corncobs to the towers of Antonio Gaudí's Sagrada Familia in Barcelona, Bertrand Goldberg's twin towers were a bold departure from the severity of the International Style, which began to dominate high-rise architecture beginning in the 1950s. Completed in 1964, the towers house condominium apartments (all pie-shaped, with curving balconies); the bottom 19 stories of each tower are given over to exposed spiral parking garages. In addition to the apartments and marina, the complex has four restaurants, the House of Blues nightclub, the Hotel Sax Chicago, and a huge bowling alley. ✉ *300 N. State St., River North.*

Tree Studios. Built in 1894 with a courtyard and annexes constructed in 1911 and 1912, the nation's oldest surviving artist studios have been restored and designated a Chicago landmark. Shops, galleries, and event spaces now fill the studios. ✉ *4 E. Ohio St., at State St., River North.*

Trump International Hotel & Tower. The Chicago Sun-Times Building was torn down to make way for this 92-story tower, which was designed by Skidmore, Owings & Merrill and opened in 2009. A spire that elevates its height to a whopping 1,362 feet makes it the city's second-tallest building. The concrete-reinforced structure (Willis Tower and the John Hancock Center are reinforced by steel) is a glassy, tiered monolith whose biggest attribute is an idyllic location along the Chicago River. Although there's no viewing deck, the public can get picturesque views of downtown through the floor-to-ceiling windows of its 16th-floor restaurant, Sixteen, and bar, Rebar. ⊠ *401 N. Wabash Ave., River North.*

4

LINCOLN PARK, WICKER PARK, AND BUCKTOWN

With Logan Square

GETTING ORIENTED

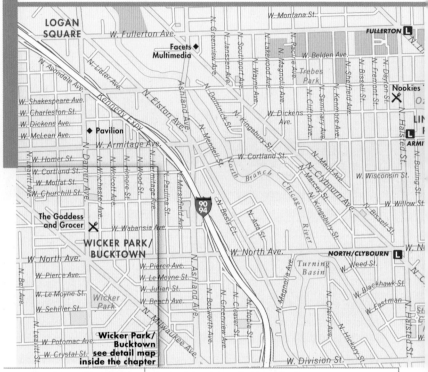

GETTING TO LINCOLN PARK	MAKING THE MOST OF YOUR TIME
Take the CTA Red Line or Brown Line train to either Armitage or Fullerton Avenue. Buses 11, 22, 36, and 151 take you through the area, too. If you're driving, take Lake Shore Drive to Fullerton Avenue and go west to Sheffield Avenue.	Lincoln Park can be done in two ways—with or without kids. For the kids, there is the Lincoln Park Zoo, the beach, and the Peggy Notebaert Nature Museum. Adults enjoy the area's shops, restaurants, and theaters. Lincoln Park's Steppenwolf Theatre and Old Town's Second City, the comedy club that launched endless comedians, are quintessential Chicago experiences. Wicker Park/Bucktown is good for funky shopping, people-watching, and cool restaurants.
GETTING TO LOGAN SQUARE	GETTING TO WICKER PARK/BUCKTOWN
Take the Kennedy Expressway to California Avenue (Exit 46A). By El, take the Blue Line toward O'Hare to Logan Square. From the Loop, take Bus 20 to Homan and Bus 82 north to Logan Square.	Take the Kennedy Expressway to North Avenue, and then head west to the triangular intersection of North, Milwaukee, and Damen avenues. Metered street parking is limited, and side-street parking is by resident permit only, so it's worth it to take advantage of restaurants' valet service. By El train, take the Blue Line to the Damen–North Avenue stop.

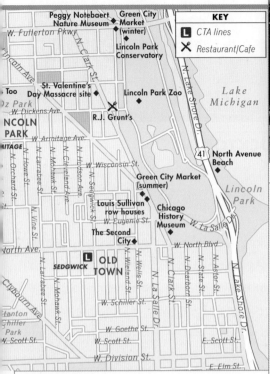

KEY

L CTA lines

✕ Restaurant/Cafe

Peggy Notebaert Nature Museum

W. Fullerton Pkwy

N. Clark St.

Lincoln Ave.

Green City Market (winter)

Lincoln Park Conservatory

Too

St. Valentine's Day Massacre site

Oz Park

W. Dickens Ave.

Lincoln Park Zoo

Lake Michigan

NCOLN PARK

W. Armitage Ave.

RITAGE

R.J. Grunt's

N. Howe St.

N. Larrabee St.

N. Cleveland Ave.

N. Mohawk St.

N. Hudson Ave.

N. Sedgwick St.

N. Orchard St.

N. Vine St.

W. Wisconsin St.

41 North Avenue Beach

Green City Market (summer)

Lincoln Park

Louis Sullivan row houses

W. Eugenie St.

Chicago History Museum

W. La Salle Dr.

The Second City

W. North Blvd.

North Ave.

L SEDGWICK

OLD TOWN

N. Wells St.

N. Wieland St.

N. La Salle Dr.

N. Clark St.

N. Dearborn St.

N. State St.

N. Aster St.

N. Lake Shore Dr.

N. Lake Shore Dr.

Clybourn Ave.

N. Larrabee St.

N. Mohawk St.

W. Schiller St.

Stanton Schiller Park

W. Scott St.

W. Goethe St.

W. Scott St.

E. Scott St.

W. Division St.

E. Elm St.

TOP REASONS TO GO

Enjoy the lakefront: Walk—or run, or bike—along the path heading south from North Avenue Beach, and take in the breathtaking views of the city along Lake Michigan.

Laugh: Catch the free improv after the show at the Second City every night except Friday.

Shop: Browse the boutiques along Lincoln Park's Armitage Avenue or shop for funky finds at the shops along Division Street, Milwaukee Avenue, and Damen Avenue.

Visit the animals: Say hello to the apes and other animals at the Lincoln Park Zoo. The added bonus is that it's free.

QUICK BITES

The Goddess and Grocer. The Goddess and Grocer serves tasty sandwiches and salads that please vegans and carnivores alike. ✉ 1646 N. Damen Ave., Bucktown ☎ 773/342–3200 ⊕ www.goddessandgrocer.com.

Nookies Too. The heaping breakfasts here, which are served anytime, make it a favorite with the neighborhood's late-night crowd. There are also branches of this long-running chain of diners in Old Town, Lakeview, and Edgewater. ✉ 2114 N. Halsted St., Lincoln Park ☎ 773/327–1400 ⊕ www.nookiesrestaurants.net.

R.J. Grunt's. Just outside Lincoln Park, R.J. Grunt's has been serving killer milk shakes and burgers since 1971. It's also known for its famous (and gargantuan) salad bar. ✉ 2056 N. Lincoln Park West, Lincoln Park ☎ 773/929–5363 ⊕ www.rjgruntschicago.com.

LINCOLN PARK, BUCKTOWN, AND WICKER PARK

Sightseeing
★★★★☆
Dining
★★★★☆
Lodging
★★★★☆
Shopping
★★☆☆☆
Nightlife
★★★★☆

In 1864 Lincoln Park—the *park,* which extends from North Avenue to Foster Avenue—became the city's first public playground. Its zoo is legendary. The area adjacent to it, bordered by Armitage Avenue, Diversey Parkway, the lake, and the Chicago River, took the same name. To the west, in Wicker Park and Bucktown, up-to-the-minute fashions mix with old-world memories and gorgeous Victorian-era architecture.

LINCOLN PARK

Updated by Roberta Sotonoff

Today Lincoln Park epitomizes all the things that people love—and love to hate—about yuppified urban areas: stratospheric housing prices, teeny boutiques with big-attitude salespeople, and plenty of fancy-schmancy coffee shops, wine bars, and cafés. It's also got some of the prettiest residential streets in the city, that gorgeous park, a great nature museum, a thriving arts scene, and the famous Steppenwolf Theatre.

Old Town, bordered by Division Street, Armitage Avenue, Clark Street, and Larrabee Street, began in the 1850s as a modest German working-class neighborhood. Now its diverse population resides in some of the oldest—and most expensive—real estate in Chicago. Its most renowned tenants are the comedy clubs the Second City and Zanies.

TOP ATTRACTIONS

Fodor'sChoice ★ **Chicago History Museum.** Seeking to bring Chicago's often complicated history to life, this museum has several strong permanent exhibits, including "Chicago: Crossroads of America," which demystifies tragedies like the Great Chicago Fire and the Haymarket Affair, in which a bomb thrown during a labor rally in 1884 led to eight anarchists being convicted of conspiracy. In "Sensing Chicago," kids can feel what the city was once like—they can catch a fly ball at Comiskey Park (now US Cellular Field), dress up like a Chicago-style hot dog, and "hear" the Great Chicago Fire. "Facing Freedom" takes a close look at what freedom means. Admission includes the audio tour. ⊠ *1601 N. Clark St., Lincoln Park* ☎ *312/642–4600* ⊕ *www.chicagohistory.org* ⊠ *$14* ⊙ *Mon.–Sat. 9:30–4:30, Sun. noon–5.*

> **DID YOU KNOW?**
>
> Begun in 1868 with a pair of swans donated by New York's Central Park, the Lincoln Park Zoo grew through donations of animals from wealthy Chicago residents and the purchase of a collection from the Barnum & Bailey Circus.

Facets Multimedia. Film buffs shouldn't leave Lincoln Park without visiting this movie theater, which presents an eclectic selection of films from around the world on its two screens. It also has a well-stocked DVD store that has more than 60,000 foreign, classic, and cult movies. ⊠ *1517 W. Fullerton Ave., Lincoln Park* ☎ *800/331–6197, 773/281–4114 showtimes* ⊕ *www.facets.org* ⊙ *DVD rental: Mon.–Sat. 10–10, Sun. noon–10.*

FAMILY Fodor'sChoice ★ **Lincoln Park Zoo.** At this urban enclave near Lake Michigan, you can face off with lions (separated by a window, of course) outside the Kovler Lion House; watch about two dozen gorillas and chimpanzees go ape in the sprawling Regenstein Center for African Apes, with three separate habitats featuring bamboo stands, 5,000 feet of swinging vines, and termite mounds for chimpanzee snacking; or watch some rare and endangered bear species, such as the spectacle bear (named for the eyeglasslike markings around its eyes).

Animals both slithery (pythons) and strange (sloths) reside in the glass-dome Regenstein Small Mammal and Reptile House, and the big guys (hippos, giraffes, and black rhinos) are in the Regenstein Animal Journey. Bird lovers should make a beeline to the McCormick Bird House, containing extremely rare birds, including the Bali mynah, Guam rail, and Micronesian kingfisher, some of which are extinct in the wild. The children's zoo, Farm-in-the-Zoo (farm animals and a learning center with films and demonstrations), and LPZoo Children's Train Ride appeal to youngsters. Be sure to leave time for a ride (or two) on the Endangered Species Carousel, featuring a menagerie of 48 rare and endangered animals. ⊠ *2001 N. Clark St., Lincoln Park* ☎ *312/742–2000* ⊕ *www.lpzoo.org* ⊠ *Free* ⊙ *Animal houses: Apr.–late May and early Sept.–Oct., daily 10–5; late May–early Sept., weekdays 10–5, weekends 10–6:30; Nov.–Mar., daily 10–4:30; gates open at 7.*

A lioness broods atop a rock at the Lincoln Park Zoo.

Old Town. A vibrant dining scene and lots of good bars and clubs make Old Town a top nightlife destination. ⊠ *Between Armitage Ave. and Division St., Clark and Larrabee Sts., Lincoln Park* ☎ *312/951–6106* ⊕ *www.oldtownchicago.org.*

The Second City. This legendary improv comedy club has served as a training ground for such stars as Alan Alda, Alan Arkin, John Belushi, Steve Carell, Tina Fey, Bonnie Hunt, Mike Myers, Bill Murray, and Amy Sedaris. Whether or not you go to a show, visit the lobby to check out the who's-who collection of photographs and caricatures of past troupe members. ⊠ *1616 N. Wells St., Old Town* ☎ *312/337–3992* ⊕ *www. secondcity.com* ⊙ *Shows Mon.–Thurs. at 8 pm, Fri. and Sat. at 8 and 11, Sun. at 7.*

WORTH NOTING

Green City Market. On Wednesday and Saturday mornings from May to October, the market takes over a large swath of grass at the south end of Lincoln Park. In addition to farm stands showcasing locally grown produce and sustainably raised meat, there are food booths and cooking demonstrations by local celebrity chefs. From November through April, an indoor incarnation of the market goes up every Saturday in the Peggy Notebaert Nature Museum's South Gallery, at 2430 North Cannon Drive. ⊠ *Summer market, 1750 N. Clark St., near N. Lincoln Ave., Lincoln Park* ☎ *773/880–1266* ⊕ *www.chicagogreencitymarket. org* ▦ *Free* ⊙ *Summer market 7–1; winter market 8:30–1.*

Lincoln Park Conservatory. Green grows on green in the lush tropical main room of this refreshing city greenhouse. Stroll through permanent displays in the Palm House, Fern Room, and Orchid House, or catch one of the special shows, like the fragrant Spring Flower Show in March or April and the festive Chrysanthemum Show in November. The peacefulness and abundant greenery inside the 1892 conservatory offer a refreshing respite in the heart of this bustling neighborhood. ✉ *2391 N. Stockton Dr., Lincoln Park* ☎ *312/742–7736* ⊕ *www.chicagoparkdistrict.com/parks/lincoln-park-conservatory* ⬚ *Free* ⊘ *Daily 9–5.*

> **DID YOU KNOW?**
>
> Another infamous Lincoln Park locale is the Biograph Theater (✉ *2433 N. Lincoln Ave., Lincoln Park* ☎ *773/871–3000*), now home to the Victory Gardens Theater. Notorious bank robber John Dillinger was shot and killed here by the FBI in 1934.

Louis Sullivan row houses. The love of geometric ornamentation that Sullivan eventually brought to such projects as the Carson Pirie Scott building (now the Sullivan Center) is already visible in these row houses, built in 1885. The terra-cotta cornices and decorative window tops are especially beautiful. ✉ *1826–1834 N. Lincoln Park West, Lincoln Park.*

FAMILY **North Avenue Beach.** The beautiful people strut their stuff along the lake at this beach. The beachhouse, which has concession stands, a restaurant, showers, and bike and volleyball rentals, resembles a steamship. There are about 50 volleyball courts, an outdoor fitness center, and lots of sand. ✉ *1600 N. Lake Shore Dr., Lincoln Park* ⊕ *www.chicagoparkdistrict.com/parks/north-avenue-beach.*

FAMILY **Oz Park.** Film fans—and younger visitors—love getting up close with Dorothy, Toto, and all the other beloved movie characters, which are here in sculpture form. The Wizard's author, L. Frank Baum, lived in Chicago at the turn of the 20th century. The park also has a play lot for pint-size visitors. It's between Webster and Dickens avenues and Burling and Larrabee streets. ✉ *2021 N. Burling St., Lincoln Park* ☎ *312/742–7898* ⊕ *www.chicagoparkdistrict.com/parks/Oz-Park* ⬚ *Free* ⊘ *Daily 6 am–11 pm.*

FAMILY **Peggy Notebaert Nature Museum.** Walk among hundreds of Midwest species of butterflies and learn about the impact of rivers and lakes on daily life at this modern museum washed in natural light. Like Chicago's other science museums, its primarily for kids, but even jaded adults may be excited when bright yellow butterflies land on their shoulders. The idea is to study nature inside without forgetting graceful Lincoln Park outside. Interesting temporary exhibits round out the offerings. ✉ *2430 N. Cannon Dr., Lincoln Park* ☎ *773/755–5100* ⊕ *www.naturemuseum.org* ⬚ *$9* ⊘ *Weekdays 9–5, weekends 10–5.*

DID YOU KNOW?

Lincoln Park faces a *Caddyshack-style* dilemma. In 2009 beavers colonized the North Pond area, and authorities worried about the destruction of nearby trees. Playing Carl Spackler (Bill Murray's role), the parks department tried unsuccessfully to relocate the intruders. Like their gopher counterpart in the movie, the beavers have so far evaded capture.

St. Valentine's Day Massacre site. On Clark Street near Dickens, there's a rather inconspicuous landscaped nursing home parking lot where the SMC Cartage Company once stood. There's no marker, but it's the site of the infamous St. Valentine's Day Massacre, when seven men were killed on the orders of Al Capone on February 14, 1929. The massacre targeted Capone's main rival in the illegal liquor trade, Bugs Moran. Though Moran wasn't in the warehouse that day, he was finished as a bootlegger. The event shocked the city and came to epitomize the violence of the Prohibition era. ⊠ *2122 N. Clark St., Lincoln Park.*

WICKER PARK

Wicker Park, the area south of North Avenue to Division Street, is inhabited by creative types, young families, university students, and older but hip professionals. Art galleries, coffeehouses, nightclubs, and funky shops line its streets—it's a far cry from the Mag Mile. Along Hoyne and Pierce avenues, near the park that gives the neighborhood its name, you'll find some of the biggest and best examples of Chicago's Victorian-era architecture. So many brewery owners built homes in this area that it was once dubbed Beer Baron Row. Farther south is the Ukrainian Village.

TOP ATTRACTIONS

Division Street. At the southern border of Wicker Park, Division Street has become a shopping and dining destination in its own right. Bars, boutiques, and trendy restaurants line the once-gritty thoroughfare, which lent its name to journalist Studs Terkel's 1967 book about urban life. To start your exploration, head west on the stretch of Division between Wolcott and Western avenues. ⊠ *Ukrainian Village/ Wicker Park.*

Wicker Park. South of the North Damen–Milwaukee intersection, this triangular park was donated to the city in 1870 by politician Charles Wicker. ⊠ *Between N. Damen and N. Wicker Park Aves. and W. Schiller St., Wicker Park.*

WORTH NOTING

Flatiron Arts Building. Opposite the Northwest Tower across the busy North Milwaukee–Damen intersection is this distinctive three-story, terra-cotta structure. Its upper floors have long served as a sort of informal arts colony, providing studio and gallery space for a number of visual artists. ⊠ *1579 N. Milwaukee Ave., Wicker Park* ☎ *312/335– 3000* ⊕ *www.flatiron.tv.*

North Avenue Baths Building. The beautiful facade is a clue to the building's past life, when it was a storied meeting spot for politicians who cut deals in the hot steam rooms, where it was difficult to plant wiretaps. ⊠ *2039 W. North Ave., Wicker Park.*

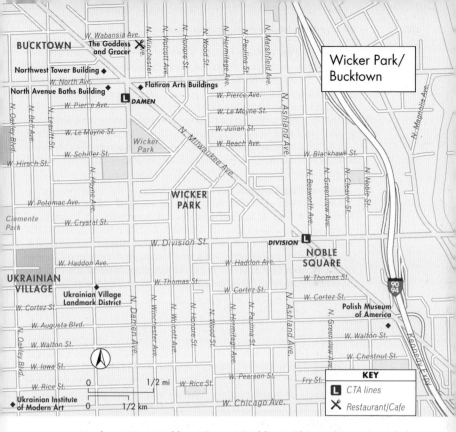

BUCKTOWN

The Goddess
and Grocer

Northwest Tower Building ◆

North Avenue Baths Building ◆

Flatiron Arts Buildings

L DAMEN

Wicker
Park

W. Wabansia Ave.

N. Winchester

N. Wolcott Ave.

N. Honore St.

N. Wood St.

N. Hermitage Ave.

N. Paulina Ave.

N. Marshfield Ave.

N. Ashland Ave.

N. Magnolia Ave.

W. North Ave.

W. Pierce Ave.

W. Pierce Ave.

W. Le Moyne St.

W. Le Moyne St.

W. Julian St.

N. Oakley Blvd.

N. Bell Ave.

N. Leavitt St.

W. Schiller St.

W. Beach Ave.

N. Milwaukee Ave.

W. Blackhawk St.

W. Hirsch St.

N. Hoyne Ave.

W. Potomac Ave.

**WICKER
PARK**

N. Bosworth Ave.

N. Greenview Ave.

N. Cleaver St.

N. Noble St.

Clemente
Park

W. Crystal St.

W. Division St.

DIVISION L

**NOBLE
SQUARE**

90
94

W. Haddon Ave.

W. Haddon Ave.

**UKRAINIAN
VILLAGE**

Ukrainian Village
Landmark District ◆

W. Thomas St.

W. Thomas St.

W. Thomas St.

W. Cortez St.

W. Cortez St.

W. Cortez St.

N. Damen Ave.

N. Winchester Ave.

N. Wolcott Ave.

N. Honore St.

N. Wood St.

N. Hermitage Ave.

N. Paulina Ave.

N. Ashland Ave.

**Polish Museum
of America** ◆

N. Oakley Blvd.

W. Augusta Blvd.

W. Walton St.

N. Green view Ave.

W. Walton St.

W. Chestnut St.

W. Iowa St.

W. Pearson St.

Fry St.

Kennedy Expy.

W. Rice St.

0   1/2 mi   W. Rice St.

Ukrainian Institute
of Modern Art ◆

0   1/2 km

W. Chicago Ave.

KEY	
L	CTA lines
✗	Restaurant/Cafe

Northwest Tower Building (*Coyote Building*). This striking triangular 12-story Art Deco office building, built in 1929, is the anchor of the North Milwaukee–Damen intersection and is used as a reference point from miles around. According to the *Chicago Tribune*, in the 1980s some artists dubbed it the Coyote Building, because they thought that the base attaching the flagpole to the rest of the tower "resembled a coyote howling at the moon." ⊠ *1600 N. Milwaukee Ave., Wicker Park.*

Polish Museum of America. The Chicago Metro area has the largest Polish population of any city outside Warsaw, and this museum celebrates that fact. Take a trip to the old country by strolling through exhibits of folk costumes, memorabilia from Pope John Paul II, American Revolutionary War heroes Tadeusz Kosciuszko and Casimir Pulaski, and pianist and composer Ignacy Paderewski. There's also Hussar armor and an 8-foot-long sleigh in the shape of a dolphin. A good place to catch up on your reading; the library has almost 100,000 volumes in Polish and English. ⊠ *984 N. Milwaukee Ave., Wicker Park* ☎ *773/384–3352* ⊕ *www.polishmuseumofamerica.org* ⊠ *$7* ⊙ *Fri.–Wed. 11–4.*

Ukrainian Institute of Modern Art. Modern and contemporary art fans head to this small museum at the far western edge of the Ukrainian Village. One of its two galleries is dedicated to changing exhibitions of mostly local Chicago and international artists. The second gallery features the museum's permanent collection of mixed media, sculpture, and painting from the 1950s to the present. Some of the most interesting works are kinetic steel wire sculptures by Konstantin Milonadis, the constructed reliefs of Ron Kostyniuk, and painted wood structures by Mychajlo Urban. ⊠ *2320 W. Chicago Ave., Ukrainian Village* ☎ *773/227–5522* ⊕ *www.uima-chicago.org* ✉ *Free* ☉ *Wed.–Sun. noon–4.*

Ukrainian Village Landmark District. For a glimpse of how the working class lived at the turn of the 20th century, head south of Wicker Park to the Ukrainian Village. In its center, on Haddon Avenue and on Thomas and Cortez streets between Damen Avenue and Leavitt Street, you'll find a well-preserved group of workers' cottages and apartments. (You can also glimpse similar brick and wood-frame houses north of here on Homer Street between Leavitt Street and Oakley Avenue.) ⊠ *Between Division St. and Chicago Ave., Western and Damen Aves., Ukrainian Village.*

BUCKTOWN

North of Wicker Park, Bucktown got its name from the goats kept by the area's original Polish and German immigrants. These days it's mostly residential with a fairly wealthy population of professionals who can afford the rents and the offerings in nearby boutiques, upscale bars, and restaurants, although evidence of ethnic roots remains strong.

TOP ATTRACTIONS

Damen Avenue. For some shopping—window or otherwise—with wares you won't likely find elsewhere, head to Damen Avenue. Fun restaurants and bars (some divey, others upscale) keep things busy at night, too. ⊠ *Between North and Fullerton Aves., Bucktown.*

LOGAN SQUARE

Spacious tree-lined boulevards are the dominant aspect of the Logan Square neighborhood, and many historic buildings still line the streets. This is one of Chicago's many ethnic neighborhoods, and a growing restaurant hot spot.

LAKEVIEW AND THE FAR NORTH SIDE

Visit Fodors.com for advice, updates, and bookings

GETTING ORIENTED

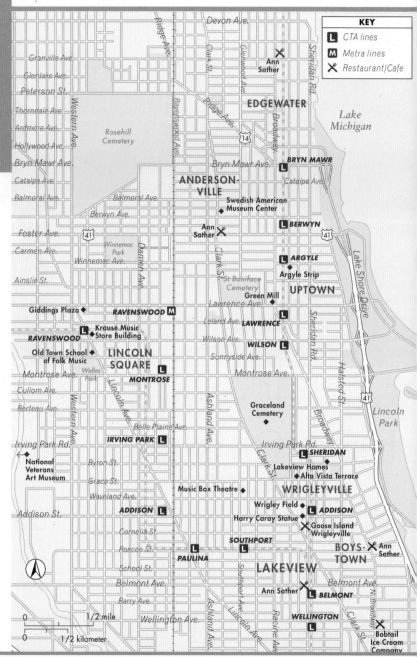

KEY

L CTA lines
M Metra lines
✕ Restaurant/Cafe

Devon Ave.

Granville Ave.

Glenlake Ave.

Peterson St.

Thorndale Ave.

Ardmore Ave.

Hollywood Ave.

Bryn Mawr Ave.

Catalpa Ave.

Balmoral Ave.

Foster Ave.

Carmen Ave.

Ainslie St.

Western Ave.

Rosehill Cemetery

Ravenswood Ave.

Ridge Ave.

Clark St.

Glenwood Ave.

Ann Sather ✕

EDGEWATER

Lake Michigan

14

Bryn Mawr Ave.

L BRYN MAWR

Catalpa Ave.

ANDERSON-VILLE

Swedish American Museum Center ◆

Berwyn Ave.

Balmoral Ave.

Ann Sather ✕

L BERWYN

41

Winnemac Park

Winnemac Ave.

41

Damen Ave.

Clark St.

St Boniface Cemetery

L ARGYLE

Argyle Strip ◆

Green Mill ◆

UPTOWN

Lawrence Ave.

Leland Ave.

LAWRENCE

L

Sheridan Rd.

Lake Shore Drive

Giddings Plaza ◆

RAVENSWOOD M

Krause Music ◆ Store Building

RAVENSWOOD L

Old Town School ◆ of Folk Music

LINCOLN SQUARE

Wilson Ave.

WILSON L

Sunnyside Ave.

Montrose Ave.

Wells Park

Montrose Ave.

MONTROSE L

Cullom Ave.

Berteau Ave.

Western Ave.

Lincoln Ave.

Belle Plaine Ave.

IRVING PARK L

National Veterans Art Museum ◆

Irving Park Rd.

Byron St.

Grace St.

Waveland Ave.

Addison St.

ADDISON L

Cornelia St.

Roscoe St.

PAULINA L

School St.

Belmont Ave.

Barry Ave.

Ashland Ave.

Graceland Cemetery ◆

Irving Park Rd.

L SHERIDAN

Lakeview Homes ◆ Alta Vista Terrace ◆

Music Box Theatre ◆

WRIGLEYVILLE

Wrigley Field ◆ L ADDISON

Harry Caray Statue ◆

✕ Goose Island Wrigleyville

SOUTHPORT

BOYS-TOWN ✕ Ann Sather

LAKEVIEW

Ann Sather ✕

L BELMONT

Belmont Ave.

Broadway

Clark St.

Halsted St.

41

Lincoln Park

Sheridan Rd.

Southport Ave.

Lincoln Ave.

Racine Ave.

Ashland Ave.

N. Broadway

Clark St.

0 ___ 1/2 mile

0 ___ 1/2 kilometer

Wellington Ave.

WELLINGTON L

✕ Bobtail Ice Cream Company

MAKING THE MOST OF YOUR TIME

A Wrigleyville and Lakeview stroll takes about an hour and a half, plus two more hours to browse the Southport shops. To experience the *real* Chicago, take in a Cubs game from Wrigley Field's bleachers.

To see all of the Far North's neighborhoods, allow a day. Visit Graceland Cemetery for an hour or two. Leave three hours for Andersonville's shops and Swedish American Museum Center, then another two for shopping on Devon Avenue. Later peek at the boutiques and do dinner in Lincoln Square.

GETTING HERE BY PUBLIC TRANSPORTATION

You may need to take a combination of bus and El. Buses 22 and 36 go to Lakeview from downtown, as do the Brown Line (Southport) and the Purple and Red lines (Belmont). Take the El's Red Line north toward Howard to Lawrence for Uptown, Wilson for Andersonville, and Loyola for Devon. The 155 bus from Devon reaches the Far North. The Brown Line El north toward Kimball to Western takes you to Lincoln Square.

QUICK BITES

Ann Sather. This nominally Swedish minichain serves breakfast until midafternoon, including legendary lingonberry pancakes and giant cinnamon buns. Other locations include Andersonville, Granville at Broadway, and Boystown. ⊠ *909 W. Belmont Ave., Lakeview* ☎ *773/348–2378* ⊕ *www.annsather.com.*

Bobtail Ice Cream Company. Head here for shakes, sundaes, and ice cream in flavors like Lakeview Barhopper, Cubby Crunch, and Daley Addiction. ⊠ *2951 N. Broadway, Lakeview* ☎ *773/880–7372* ⊕ *www.bobtailicecream.com.*

Goose Island Wrigleyville. This branch of the local microbrewery has a variety of its own beers and root beers on tap, plus good burgers. ⊠ *3535 N. Clark St., Wrigleyville* ☎ *773/832–9040* ⊕ *www.gooseisland.com.*

TOP REASONS TO GO

Take yourself out to the ball game: Sit in the bleachers with the locals at Wrigley Field, and be ready to throw the ball back onto the field if the opposing team hits a homer. When the Cubs are on the road, take a tour of the park.

Go to the movies: Catch a classic or indie flick at the vintage Music Box Theatre.

Tour Graceland Cemetery: Visit such famous "residents" as Marshall Field, George Pullman, and others at their final resting place.

Go Swedish: Check out the Swedish enclave Andersonville for authentic Swedish restaurants and bakeries.

GETTING HERE BY CAR

By car, take Lake Shore Drive north to Belmont (Lakeview), but keep in mind that parking can be scarce. When the Cubs play, take public transit. Head north up Western Avenue to between Montrose and Lawrence for Lincoln Square, Lawrence Avenue for Uptown, Foster Avenue for Andersonville, and Devon Avenue for the Far North.

LAKEVIEW AND THE FAR NORTH SIDE

Sightseeing
★★☆☆☆

Dining
★★★★☆

Lodging
★☆☆☆☆

Shopping
★★★★☆

Nightlife
★★★★☆

Running north in a rough row that runs parallel and close to the lake, the primarily residential neighborhoods in Lakeview and the Far North Side aren't the place for major museums or high-rises. Instead, they're best at giving you a feel for how local Chicagoans live. Whether you wander one of the many ethnic neighborhoods, contemplate the dignitaries (and scoundrels) buried in Graceland Cemetery, or celebrate a hard-won victory at Wrigley Field, this area is perfect for connecting with the sights and sounds that make Chicago the great city it is.

LAKEVIEW

Lakeview got its name from the 1850s-built Hotel Lake View, and by 1889 Chicago took the town for its own. Today it is a massive neighborhood made up of small enclaves, each with its own distinct personality. There's Wrigley Field surrounded by the beer-swilling, Cubby-blue-'til-we-die sports-bar fanaticism of Wrigleyville; the gay bars, shops, and clubs along Halsted Street in Boystown; and an air of urban chic along Southport Avenue, where young families stroll amid the trendy boutiques and ice-cream shops.

TOP ATTRACTIONS

Boystown. Just beyond Wrigleyville lies this section of Lakeview; it's been a major "gayborhood" since the 1970s, which also makes it one of the country's first. Although the area has become much more mixed in recent years, distinctive rainbow pylons still delineate Boystown—most of its gay-oriented shops, bars, and restaurants are concentrated on and around Halsted. In June the street becomes a sea of people, when Chicago's gay pride parade floats down the block. ⊠ *Between Broadway, Belmont Ave., and Halsted St., Boystown.*

Graceland Cemetery. Near Irving Park Road, this graveyard has crypts that are almost as strikingly designed as the city skyline. Some of Chicago's most prominent citizens, including Daniel Burnham and Marshall Field, are spending eternity here—the cemetery office

DID YOU KNOW?

The names on the grave sites at Graceland read like a who's who from a Chicago history book: Marshall Field, George Pullman, and Daniel Burnham are a few of the notables buried here. You can take a guided neighborhood tour or buy a walking-tour map at the entrance Monday through Saturday to explore on your own.

offers maps. Some of the elaborate crypts were designed by the architect Louis Sullivan (also a resident). ⊠ *4001 N. Clark St., Lakeview* ☎ *773/525–1105* ⊕ *www.gracelandcemetery.org* ☒ *Free* ☉ *Daily 8–4; office: Apr.–Nov., weekdays 9–4, Sat. 10–3, Dec.–Mar., Mon.–Sat., 9–1.*

Southport Avenue. Southport and other streets that travel north to Irving Park Road are lined with independent shops, many of which cater to well-dressed young women with money to burn. ⊠ *Southport Ave., between Grace St. and Belmont Ave., Wrigleyville* ⊕ *www. southportneighbors.com.*

Music Box Theatre. Southport's main claim to fame is this 1929 movie house, where you can still see twinkling stars and clouds on the ceiling and hear live organ music before the independent and classic films shown on its two screens. ⊠ *3733 N. Southport Ave., Wrigleyville* ☎ *773/871–6604* ⊕ *www.musicboxtheatre.com* ☒ *$9.25; check for Web specials.*

FAMILY

Fodor's Choice

★

Wrigley Field. With its first major league game played here on April 23, 1914, the venerable, ivy-covered home of the Chicago Cubs is the nation's second-oldest major league ballpark. The original scoreboard is still used. Score-by-innings, players' numbers, strikes, outs, hits, and errors are all posted manually. Die-hard fans opt for the bleachers, while the more gentrified prefer box seats along the first and third baselines. If you look up along Sheffield Avenue on the east side of the park, you can see the rooftop patios where baseball fans pay high prices to cheer for the home team. Ticketless fans sit in lawn chairs on Sheffield during the games, waiting for foul balls to fly their way. Also check out the **Harry Caray statue** commemorating the late Cubs announcer; in the bottom half of the seventh inning, fans sing "Take Me Out to the Ballgame" in his honor. Tours of the park and the dugouts are given from April to October when the Cubs are on the road. ⊠ *1060 W. Addison St., at Sheffield St., Wrigleyville* ☎ *773/404–2827* ⊕ *www.mlb.com/chc/ballpark* ☒ *Tours $25.*

Pay homage to the greats of Chicago's past at Graceland Cemetery.

WORTH NOTING

Lakeview Homes. On the side streets heading east and west of Boystown, two- and three-story gray-stone houses and other buildings line quiet, tree-lined streets. Wandering Lakeview's residential streets, you might even feel transported back in time to 1920s or '30s Chicago. In 2008 a stretch of Newport Avenue between Clark and Halsted was temporarily transformed into a cobblestone thoroughfare for the John Dillinger flick *Public Enemies* (starring Johnny Depp). ⊠ *Lakeview*.

FAR NORTH AND FAR NORTHWEST SIDES

The Far North and Far Northwest sides of Chicago are home to several of the city's most colorful neighborhoods. Just north of Lakeview, Uptown's beautiful architecture and striking old marquees are a testament to the time when it was a thriving entertainment district. Though it's been gritty for decades, it's now being redeveloped.

The area around Broadway and Argyle is known variously as Little Saigon, Little Chinatown, and North Chinatown. Andersonville was named for the Swedish community that settled near Foster Avenue and Clark Street in the 1960s, and it still maintains a huge concentration of Swedes.

Double street signs attest to Devon Avenue's diversity—in some places named for Gandhi, in others for Golda Meir, although much of the Jewish population has moved to Skokie. Whatever the name, the area is best explored on foot.

South of Devon via Western Avenue is the former German enclave of Lincoln Square, now a happening dining and shopping scene. One of the best ways to discover all these neighborhoods' cultural diversity is by sampling the food.

TOP ATTRACTIONS

FAMILY **Andersonville.** Just north of Uptown there's a neighborhood that feels like a small town and still shows signs of the Swedish settlers who founded it. It also has some great Swedish restaurants and bakeries, including Ann Sather. Helping anchor the area is the **Women & Children First** bookstore, at 5233 North Clark, which stocks an extensive selection of feminist and children's books. ⊠ *Between Glenwood, Foster, Ravenswood, and Bryn Mawr Aves., Andersonville* ☎ *773/728–2995* ⊕ *www.andersonville.org.*

Devon Avenue. Chicagoans flock here to satisfy cravings for Indian, Middle Eastern, and Asian fare, or, as the avenue moves west, a good Jewish challah. Indian restaurants and sari shops start popping up just west of Western Avenue. Though west of Talman Avenue was once an enclave for Orthodox Jews and Russian immigrants, many of the people, along with the shops, have migrated to the northern suburbs. ⊠ *Devon Ave., between Kedzie and Ridge Aves., Far North.*

Lincoln Square. Lincoln Square has long been known for its Teutonic heritage. It's home to two annual German fests—Mayfest in late May (held around a 30-foot-tall maypole) and German-American Fest in September—both with plenty of beer, brats, German-style pretzels, and folks dressed in lederhosen. Thursday evenings in summer bring concerts and a farmers' market. Since the 1990s this quiet North Side neighborhood, named for the Lincoln statue near Lawrence and Western avenues, has seen its currency with young professionals rise, and a spate of trendy new places is the result. Popular bars and restaurants line Lincoln Avenue between Montrose and Lawrence, and shopping is a draw, too. Many credit Lincoln Square's renaissance to the relocation of the **Old Town School of Folk Music** to a long-vacant Art Deco building on North Lincoln Avenue. In July, it sponsors the Square Roots festival. But those longing for a taste of Lincoln Square's ethnic roots shouldn't despair. There are still a handful of German restaurants and bars along Lincoln Avenue. Also still here is the 1922 **Krause Music Store building** (⊠ *4611 N. Lincoln Ave.*), the last work commissioned by architect Louis Sullivan, with its ornate green terra-cotta facade.

Pause for a rest in **Giddings Plaza** (⊠ *4731 N. Lincoln Ave.*), with a view of the bronze, tiered Giddings Square Fountain. From May to October the plaza holds frequent outdoor concerts. ⊠ *Between Foster, Montrose, and Damen Aves. and the Chicago River, Lincoln Square* ⊕ *www.LincolnSquareRavenswood.org.*

5

The ornate details on Andersonville buildings speak to the neighborhood's Swedish roots.

OFF THE BEATEN PATH

National Veterans Art Museum. This museum is now in Irving Park, southwest of Lincoln Square. Founded as the National Vietnam Veterans Art Museum, it showcased art by both allied soldiers and the Vietcong. Today the permanent exhibit features haunting works from all wars in which the United States has participated. ✉ *4041 W. Milwaukee Ave., Irving Park* ☎ *312/326–0270* ⊕ *www.nvvam.org* ✉ *Suggested donation $10* ☉ *Tues.–Sat. 10–5.*

Swedish American Museum Center. You don't have to be Swedish to find this tiny and welcoming museum interesting. On permanent display, for example, are trunks immigrants brought with them to Chicago and a map showing where in the city different immigrant groups settled. On the third floor, in the only children's museum in the country dedicated to immigration, kids can climb aboard a colorful Viking ship or "milk" a wooden cow, pulling rubber udders to collect streams of water in a bucket. ✉ *5211 N. Clark St., Andersonville* ☎ *773/728–8111* ⊕ *www.swedishamericanmuseum.org* ✉ *$4, free 2nd Tues. of month* ☉ *Weekdays 10–4, weekends 11–4; children's section Mon.–Thurs. 1–4, Fri. 10–4, weekends 11–4.*

WORTH NOTING

Argyle Strip. Also known as Little Saigon (and Little Chinatown and North Chinatown), this part of town is anchored by the El's Argyle Street stop's red pagoda. Home to many Vietnamese immigrants, the Strip teems with storefront noodle shops, bakeries, and pan-Asian grocery stores. Roasted ducks hang in shop windows and fish peer out from large tanks. ✉ *Between Foster, Lawrence, and Ravenswood Aves. and Lake Michigan, Uptown.*

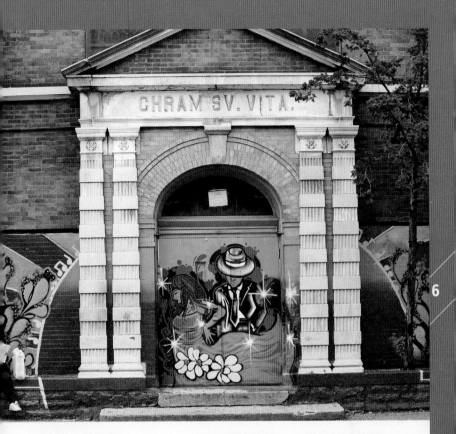

PILSEN, LITTLE ITALY, AND CHINATOWN

with University Village and Prairie Avenue

GETTING ORIENTED

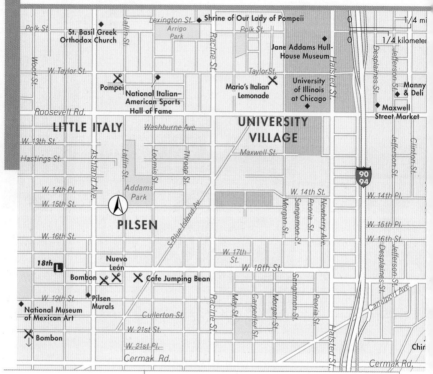

MAKING THE MOST OF YOUR TIME

Pilsen buzzes on weekends and during the Fiesta del Sol festival (at the end of July). On the second Friday of each month, neighborhood galleries stay open late for an art crawl. At night Little Italy's restaurants and bars bustle. On Sunday the Maxwell Street Market hums. Browse the shops and sample the goods along Wentworth Avenue or Chinatown Square. And don't forget to tour the nearby 19th-century Prairie Avenue homes, where many of the people who shaped Chicago lived.

GETTING HERE

By car: For Pilsen, take I–290 west to the Damen Avenue exit, and go south on Damen to 19th Street. There's parking at the National Museum of Mexican Art plus metered street parking. For Little Italy and University Village, take the Kennedy Expressway's Taylor Street exit and head west. Chinatown is west of Michigan Avenue via Cermak Road. There's a parking lot at Chinatown Gate, on Wentworth Avenue. Turn east off Michigan Avenue on East 21st Street to reach Prairie Avenue.

Public transportation: The El's Pink Line stops at the 18th Street station in the Pilsen area. Check out the station's colorful murals. Take the Blue Line to UIC/Halsted for University Village and the No. 9 Ashland bus to Little Italy. For Chinatown, take the El's Red Line south to Cermak.

TOP REASONS TO GO

Gallery-hop: On second Fridays in Pilsen the art galleries stay open late.

Shop: Haggle with the locals at the legendary Maxwell Street Market on Sunday.

Appreciate history: See where Chicago greats like Marshall Field and George Pullman lived in the Prairie Avenue Historic District.

SAFETY

The railway tracks and vacant lots between Pilsen and Little Italy make it unsafe to walk between the two neighborhoods. If possible, drive between these areas, or take the Blue Line to either UIC–Halsted or Racine to explore University Village and Little Italy. Then take the Pink Line to 18th Street for Pilsen. Chinatown and Prairie Avenue are a bit removed from the heart of the city and bordered by slowly gentrifying neighborhoods, so be cautious and aware. Limit your visit to well-lighted and well-populated main streets after dark.

QUICK BITES

Cafe Jumping Bean. At this cozy neighborhood coffee shop you'll find Mexican hot chocolate, focaccia pizzas, and fresh sandwiches. ✉ *1439 W. 18th St., Pilsen* ☎ *312/455–0019.*

Joy Yee's Noodles. From a massive menu, pan-Asian dishes arrive in a flash. The mouthwatering portions may be huge, but the prices aren't. ✉ *Chinatown Square Mall, 2159 S. China Pl., Chinatown* ☎ *312/842–8928* ⊕ *www.joyyee.com.*

Manny's Coffee Shop & Deli. The corned-beef sandwich here is the one that all the other delis in town aim to beat. ✉ *1141 S. Jefferson St., West Loop* ☎ *312/939–2855* ⊕ *www.mannysdeli.com.*

Pompei. Head to this branch of a local restaurant empire for salads, house-made pasta, and its famous thick, bready squares of pizza. ✉ *1531 W. Taylor St., Little Italy* ☎ *312/421–5179* ⊕ *www.pompeipizza.com.*

PILSEN, LITTLE ITALY, AND CHINATOWN

Sightseeing
★★★☆☆

Dining
★★★★☆

Lodging
★☆☆☆☆

Shopping
★★☆☆☆

Nightlife
★☆☆☆☆

A jumble of ethnic neighborhoods stretches west of the Loop and from the south branch of the Chicago River to the Eisenhower Expressway (I–290). Once home to myriad 20th-century immigrants, the area is now dominated by Pilsen's Mexican community, Little Italy, and the University of Illinois's Medical District and Circle Campus.

PILSEN

Updated
by Roberta
Sotonoff

Formerly full of Bohemian and Czech immigrants and now primarily Mexican, Pilsen is bounded on the east by 800 West Halsted Street, on the west by 2400 West Western Avenue, on the north by 16th Street, and on the south by the Chicago River. Keep an eye open for dramatic, colorful murals that showcase Mexican history, culture, and religion.

TOP ATTRACTIONS

Fodor'sChoice ★

National Museum of Mexican Art. As the largest Latino museum in the country, this is the one museum you shouldn't miss after you've done the big museums downtown. Galleries house impressive collections of contemporary, traditional, and Mesoamerican art from both sides of the border, as well as vivid exhibits that trace immigration woes and political fights. Its 5,500-object permanent collection includes pre-Cuauhtemoc artifacts, textiles, paintings, prints and drawings, and folk art. Every fall the giant "Day of the Dead" exhibit stuns Chicagoans with its altars from artists across the country. ⊠ 1852 W. 19th St., Pilsen ☎ 312/738–1503 ⊕ www.nationalmuseumofmexicanart.org ⊠ Free ☉ Tues.–Sun. 10–5.

Pilsen Murals. Murals give Pilsen its distinctive flair. You'll run into their bright colors and bold images at many turns during a walk through the neighborhood. At Ashland Avenue and 19th Street are two large murals illustrating Latino family life and Latinos at work. More murals created by community youth groups and local artists brighten up the

Bronzeville

Bronzeville lies between Douglas Boulevard (Cottage Grove Avenue) and Grand Boulevard (Martin Luther King Jr. Drive). History buffs can honor the neighborhood's numerous influential African-American inhabitants, and those interested in architecture should head to the Illinois Institute of Technology (IIT) campus to check out the Mies van der Rohe creations.

FOLLOW HISTORY'S TRAIL

After World War I, blacks began to move to Bronzeville to escape race restrictions prevalent in other parts of the city. Many famous African-Americans are associated with the area, including Andrew "Rube" Foster, founder of the Negro National Baseball League; civil rights activist Ida B. Wells; Bessie Coleman, the first African-American woman pilot; and jazz great Louis Armstrong. The symbolic entrance to the area is a tall statue at 26th Place and Martin Luther King Jr. Drive that depicts a new arrival from the South bearing a suitcase held together with string. There is a commemorative trail along Martin Luther King Jr. Drive between 25th and 35th streets, with more than 90 sidewalk plaques honoring the best and brightest of the community, including the late Gwendolyn Brooks,

whose first book of poetry was called *A Street in Bronzeville.*

ARCHITECTURE 101

"Less is more," claimed Mies van der Rohe, but for fans of the master's work, more is more at IIT. The campus has an array of the glass-and-steel structures for which he is most famous. Crown Hall, the jewel of the collection, has been designated a National Historic Landmark, but don't overlook the Robert F. Carr Memorial Chapel of St. Savior.

The McCormick Tribune Campus Center, designed by Dutch architect Rem Koolhaas, is fun to explore and pays homage to the Mies legacy. Its apparently opaque windows are actually see-through, as long as you stand head-on. Look at the glass walls near the entrance through a digital camera and you'll see depictions of IIT icons like Mies. In 2003 Helmut Jahn created the corrugated-steel, triple-glass student housing that runs alongside the El.

The campus is about 1 mile west of Lake Shore Drive on 31st Street. Both the El train's Green and Red line 35th Street stops are two blocks west of campus. ⊠ *S. State St. between 31st and 35th Sts.* ☎ *312/567–3000* ⊕ *www.iit.edu.*

6

blocks centered at 16th and Ashland; Aztec sun-god inserts decorate the sidewalk stones. ⊠ *Pilsen.*

WORTH NOTING

18th Street. Pilsen's main commercial strip is loaded with tempting restaurants, bakeries, and Mexican grocery stores. At 1515 W. 18th, past the *"Bienvenidos a Pilsen"* sign, is **Nuevo León**, a brightly painted family restaurant that has been an anchor in the neighborhood since the Gutiérrez family set up shop in 1962. Inhale deeply if the doors to the tortilla factory next door are open. ⊕ *www.eighteenthstreet.org.*

NEED A BREAK?

Bombon. If you like sweets or have kids in tow, keep an eye out for this bakery, which stocks a mind-boggling array of treats. ⊠ *1530 W. 18th St., Pilsen* ☎ *312/733-7788* ⊕ *www.chicagobestcakes.com* ⊠ *3748 W. 26th St., Little Village* ☎ *773/277-8777.*

Halsted Street. Since the late 1960s, Halsted Street near 18th Street has been home to a large number of artists living and working in the mixed-use artists' community known as the Chicago Arts District. Over the last 30 years, street-level art galleries and studios have put Pilsen on the map as a go-to art destination, and innovative spaces abound. On the second Friday of each month from 6 to 10 pm, 30 artists open their doors to the public and feature interpretive dance, installation, music, sculpture, visual displays, and performance art. Outside of 2nd Fridays, most studios have weekend hours or are available by appointment. ⊠ *Pilsen* ☎ *312/738-8000* ⊕ *www.chicagoartsdistrict.org.*

LITTLE ITALY

To the north of Pilsen is Little Italy, which, despite the encroachment by the University of Illinois at Chicago (UIC), still contains plenty of Italian restaurants, bakeries, groceries, and sandwich shops. The neighborhood is bordered by UIC (Morgan Street) on the east and Western Avenue on the west. Its north and south boundaries are Harrison and 12th streets (Roosevelt Road), respectively.

WORTH NOTING

National Italian-American Sports Hall of Fame. The NIASHF was founded by George Randazzo in 1978 to honor Italian-American athletes. Among the first to be honored was baseball player Joe DiMaggio. A sample of the other inductees include Rocky Marciano, Yogi Berra, Mary Lou Retton, and Phil Rizzuto. First housed in Elmwood Park, then Arlington Heights, the Hall of Fame came to Little Italy in 1994 with the help of the CEO of the Phoenix Suns, Chicago native Jerry Colangelo. If you are interested in relics like Rocky Marciano's first heavyweight championship belt, the last coat worn by Vince Lombardi as the legendary Green Bay Packers coach, or Mario Andretti's Indy 500 race car, this is your kind of place. ⊠ *1431 W. Taylor St., Little Italy* ☎ *312/226-5566* ⊕ *www.niashf.org* ☉ *Daily noon–4.*

St. Basil Greek Orthodox Church. Located near Polk Street, this gorgeous Greek Revival building, built in 1910, has an equally lavish interior. It was originally the Anshe Shalom Synagogue. ⊠ *733 S. Ashland Ave., Little Italy* ☎ *312/243-3738* ⊕ *www.stbasil.il.goarch.org.*

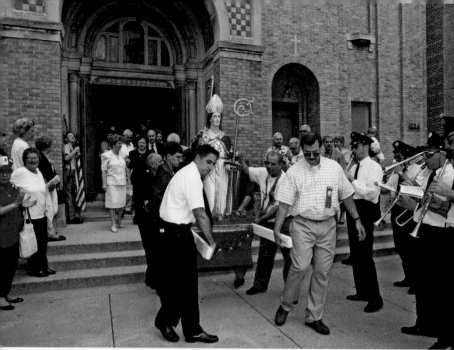

The Shrine of Our Lady of Pompeii keeps traditional Italian culture alive in Chicago.

Shrine of Our Lady of Pompeii. Completed in 1923 and built to accommodate the area's growing number of Italian immigrants, this church is the oldest continuously operating Italian-American church in Chicago. Its Romanesque Revival style was popular with the famous church architects Worthman and Steinbach, and its interior is filled with statues and striking stained-glass windows. At times, the church serves as a venue for concerts and theatrical productions. ⊠ *1224 W. Lexington St., Little Italy* ☎ *312/421–3757* ⊕ *www.ourladyofpompeii.org* ✉ *Free* ⊗ *Weekdays 9–4:30, Sun. mass at 8:30 and 11.*

Taylor Street. In the mid-19th century, when Italians started to migrate to Chicago, about one-third of them settled in and around Taylor Street, a 12-block stretch between Ashland and the University of Illinois at Chicago. It is best known for its Italian restaurants, though Thai food, tacos, and other ethnic options are here, too. ⊠ *Little Italy* ☎ *312/218–4044* ⊕ *www.taylorstreetarchives.com.*

NEED A BREAK?

Mario's Italian Lemonade. If you visit Taylor Street from May to early September, be sure to stop at Mario's Italian Lemonade, where everyone from politicians like Jesse Jackson to neighborhood families lines up for old-fashioned, slushy Italian ices. ⊠ *1066 W. Taylor St., Little Italy* ⊗ *May–Sept. 15, daily 11–midnight.*

Go back in time to the late 1800s at the opulent Glessner House.

UNIVERSITY VILLAGE

Little Italy blends into University Village at its northeast corner. The Village, UIC's booming residential area, is centered on Halsted Street south to 14th Street.

WORTH NOTING

Jane Addams Hull-House Museum. The redbrick Victorian Hull House was the birthplace of social work. Social-welfare pioneers and peace advocates Jane Addams and Ellen Gates Starr started the American settlement house movement in this house in 1889. They wrought near-miracles in the surrounding community, which was then a slum for new immigrants. Pictures and letters add context to the two museum buildings, which re-create the homey setting the residents experienced. The museum is located on the UIC campus. ⊠ *800 S. Halsted St., University Village* 🕾 *312/413–5353* ⊕ *www.hullhousemuseum.org* 📧 *Suggested donation $5* 🕗 *Tues.–Fri. 10–4, Sun. noon–4.*

Maxwell Street Market. Until 1967 this famous Sunday flea market, begun in the 1880s by Jewish immigrants, was the place to barter for bargains. Then UIC took most of the property to build university housing. The market limped along and finally closed in the 1990s, but a public uproar led to its relocation to South Desplaines Street between West Polk Street and West Roosevelt Road, about a half mile from the original site. Today more than 500 vendors sell clothing, power tools, and household items; blues musicians often play; and some of the best Mexican food in town is available. ⊠ *800 S. Desplaines St., University Village* 🕾 *312/745–4676* 🕗 *Sun. 7–3.*

PRAIRIE AVENUE

In the 1870s the **Prairie Avenue Historic District** served as Chicago's first Gold Coast. After the Chicago Fire of 1871, prominent Chicagoans, including George Pullman, Marshall Field, and the Armour family, had homes in the area two blocks east of Michigan Avenue, between 18th and 22nd streets. It's close to Chinatown, where Wentworth and Archer avenues are chockablock with Asian restaurants and shops.

> **DID YOU KNOW?**
>
> Clarke House Museum has been moved three times from its original location on Michigan Avenue between 16th and 17th streets. The last time, in 1977, it had to be hoisted above the nearby elevated train tracks.

TOP ATTRACTIONS

Clarke House Museum. This Greek Revival structure dates from 1836, making it Chicago's oldest surviving building. It's a clapboard house in a masonry city, built for Henry and Caroline Palmer Clarke to remind them of the East Coast they left behind. The Doric columns and pilasters were an attempt to civilize Chicago's frontier image. The everyday objects and furnishings inside evoke a typical 1850s–60s middle-class home. Tours begin at the Glessner House nearby. ⊠ *1827 S. Indiana Ave., Prairie Avenue* ☎ *312/326–1480* ⊕ *www.clarkehousemuseum. org* ⊠ *$10, $15 combo ticket with Glessner House, free Wed.* ☉ *Tours: Wed.–Sun. at noon and 2.*

Fodor's Choice ★ **Glessner House Museum.** This fortresslike, Romanesque Revival 1886 residence is the only surviving building in Chicago by architect H.H. Richardson, who also designed Boston's Trinity Church. Completed in 1887, the L-shape mansion's stone construction and short towers are characteristic of the Richardsonian Romanesque style. It's also one of the few great mansions left on Prairie Avenue, once home to such heavy hitters as retailer Marshall Field and meatpacking magnate Philip Armour. The area has lately seen the arrival of new, high-end construction, but nothing beats a tour of Glessner House, a remarkable relic of the days when merchant princes really lived like royalty. Enjoy the lavish interiors and the many artifacts, from silver pieces and art glass to antique ceramics and Isaac Scott carvings and furnishings. ⊠ *1800 S. Prairie Ave., Prairie Avenue* ☎ *312/326–1480* ⊕ *www.glessnerhouse. org* ⊠ *$10, $15 combo ticket with Clarke House, free Wed.* ☉ *Tours: Wed.–Sun. at 1 and 3.*

WORTH NOTING

Quinn Chapel. One of Chicago's African-American cornerstones, this church was founded in 1847 and served as an Underground Railroad stop. The present building, designed by Henry Starbuck, opened in 1891, and the rough-finished brick exterior is in keeping with the time. The interior has a tin ceiling and simple stained-glass windows. Many notable people have addressed the congregation, including President William B. McKinley, Booker T. Washington, and Dr. Martin Luther King Jr. ⊠ *2401 S. Wabash Ave., South Loop* ☎ *312/791–1846* ⊕ *www. quinnchicago.org* ⊠ *Free* ☉ *Daily 9:30–5.*

Second Presbyterian Church. This handsome Gothic Revival church was built in 1874 and designed by James Renwick, also the architect of the Smithsonian's Castle and New York City's St. Patrick's Cathedral. Inside this National Historic Landmark is one of the largest collections of Tiffany stained-glass windows anywhere. ✉ *1936 S. Michigan Ave., Prairie Avenue* ☎ *312/225–4951* ⊕ *www.2ndpresbyterian.org* ⊙ *Tues.–Fri. 9–1, services Sun. at 11.*

Wheeler Mansion. At the intersection of Calumet Avenue and Cullerton Street is another of the area's great mansions, which was nearly replaced by a parking lot before it was saved and painstakingly restored in the late 1990s. Today it's a boutique hotel. ✉ *2020 S. Calumet Ave., Prairie Avenue* ☎ *312/945–2020* ⊕ *www.wheelermansion.com.*

> ### PRAIRIE AVENUE AND CHINATOWN TOURS
>
> Package guided tours of both the Clarke House and the Glessner House museums are available Wednesday through Sunday (☎ *312/326–1480*). Wednesday tours are walk-in only and free and tend to fill up, so arrive early to guarantee a spot. The Chicago Chinese Cultural Institute (☎ *312/842–1988* ⊕ *www. chinatowntourchicago.com*) conducts 90-minute walking tours Friday to Sunday mornings in summer as well as food and dumpling-making tours. Reservations are necessary.

Willie Dixon's Blues Heaven Foundation. A cadre of music legends, including Etta James, Bo Diddley, Aretha Franklin, Koko Taylor, and John Lee Hooker, recorded here in the former Chess Records building. Guides regale visitors with tales of the famous stars, and you can check out the old recording studios, office, rehearsal rooms, and memorabilia. Call ahead. ✉ *2120 S. Michigan Ave., Prairie Avenue* ☎ *312/808–1286* ⊕ *www.bluesheaven.com* 🎟 *$10* ⊙ *Weekdays noon–4, Sat. noon–3.*

CHINATOWN

West of the Prairie Avenue district, this Chinese microcosm sits in the shadows of modern skyscrapers and 21st-century American life. The neighborhood is anchored by the **Chinatown Gate**, which spans West Cermak Road and South Wentworth Avenue. Referring to the tenacity of Chicago's first Chinese settlers, the gate's four gold characters proclaim, "The world belongs to the commonwealth." Also prominent are the enormous green-and-red pagoda towers of the **Pui Tak Center**, a church-based community center in the former On Leong Tong Building. Most visitors to Chinatown come only to eat, stock up on almond cookies, or scout out the gift and furniture shops for bargains on Wentworth Avenue. But Chinatown is more than that. Try also to take some time to wander the streets and check out the local grocery stores, where English is rarely heard, live fish and crabs fill vats, and hard-to-identify canned items and dried things bulge from the shelves.

Performers participate in a festival in Chinatown.

WORTH NOTING

Chinatown Square. Located on Princeton and Archer, this large square is punctuated by animal sculptures, each representing one of the 12 symbols of the Chinese zodiac. Below the sculptures is a plaque explaining the personalities of those born during each year. ⊠ *2133 S. China Pl., Chinatown.*

Nine Dragon Wall. One of three replicas outside China, the wall is modeled after the one in Beihai Park in Beijing. The red-and-gold wall with its nine large dragons and 500 smaller ones signifies good fortune. It is right next to the El's Red Line Cermak-Chinatown stop. ⊠ *W. Cermak Rd., Chinatown* ⊕ *www.chicagochinatown.org/?page_id=331.*

Ping Tom Memorial Park. Four pillars carved with dragon designs grace the entrance of this park, which is named for Chinatown's most renowned civic leader. The park's 12 beautifully landscaped acres are wedged within the shadows of railroad tracks, cranes, and highways. It is a serene place, with a children's playground and winding walking trails. On the shore of the Chicago River, a large yellow-and-red pagoda is a good place to see the boats float by and the looming Chicago skyline to the north. ⊠ *300 W. 19th St., Chinatown* ⊕ *www.chicagoparkdistrict. com/parks/Ping-Tom-Memorial-Park* ⊡ *Free* ⊙ *Daily 6 am–11 pm.*

HYDE PARK

GETTING ORIENTED

E. 46th St.
St. Gabriel
Catholic Church

Burnham
Park

Lake
Michigan

KEY

Ⓜ *Metra lines*
✕ *Restaurant/Cafe*

E. 47th St.

E. 48th St.

E. 49th St.

S. Cottage Grove Ave.

HYDE PARK

E. 50th St.

Heller House ◆ — Madison Park

Model Yacht
Basin

E. Hyde Park Ave.

S. Drexel Ave.
S. Ingleside Ave.
S. Greenwood Ave.
S. University Ave.
S. Woodlawn Ave.

E. 52nd St.

S. Dorchester Ave.
S. Blackstone Ave.
S. Harper Ave.
S. Lake Park Ave.

E. 53rd St.   E. 53rd St.

Nichols
Park

Ⓜ   S. Cornell Dr.

E. 54th St.

S. Kimbark Ave.
S. Kenwood Ct.
S. Ridgewood Ave.

E. 54th Ave.   E. 54th Ave.

Promontory
Point

Jimmy's:
The Woodlawn Tap
✕

S. Hyde Park Blvd.
S. Everett Ave.

E. 55th St.   E. 55th St.

E. 55th Pl.

Smart Museum of Art ◆

◆ DuSable Museum of
African American
History

Hyde Park
Historical
Society ◆

The Promontory ◆

Ⓜ

S. Cottage Grove Ave.

E. 56th St.

E. 57th St.   Medici
on 57th

Edwardo's ✕✕
Natural Pizza

Robie House ◆

S. Ellis Ave.

S. Dorchester Ave.
S. Blackstone Ave.
S. Harper Ave.

Museum of
Science and Industry

Oriental ◆
Institute

E. 58th St.

University
of Chicago ◆

E. 59th St.

Midway Plaisance

Midway Plaisance   *Midway Plaisance*

East
Lagoon

S. Stony Island Ave.

E. 60th St.

S. University Ave.

E. 61st St.

*Jackson
Park*

S. Cornell Ave.

West
Lagoon

0   600 feet
0   200 meters

S. Dorchester Ave.

South Shore
Cultural Center ◆

E. 62nd St.

GETTING HERE

By car, take Lake Shore Drive south to the 57th Street exit and turn left into the parking lot of the Museum of Science and Industry. You can also take the Metra Railroad train from Randolph Street and Michigan Avenue; get off at the 55th Street stop and walk east through the underpass two blocks, then south two blocks. From Indiana, take the South Shore Line to the 57th Street station. CTA buses 2, 6, X28, and 10 will also get you here from downtown.

MAKING THE MOST OF YOUR TIME

Visiting the Museum of Science and Industry will probably take most of a day. Go during the week to avoid crowds. Wind down by meandering through Jackson Park, the University of Chicago campus, or the Midway Plaisance, the main walkway for the 1893 World's Columbian Exposition.

QUICK BITES

Edwardo's Natural Pizza. The deep-dish pies at Edwardo's are some of the best in the city. ✉ *1321 E. 57th St., Hyde Park* ☎ *773/241–7960* ⊕ *www.edwardos.com.*

Jimmy's: The Woodlawn Tap. At this favored tavern, locals and university students gather for beer, hamburgers, Reuben sandwiches, and sausage. Accompanying the pub grub are Sunday-night jam sessions. ✉ *1172 E. 55th St., Hyde Park* ☎ *773/643–5516.*

Medici on 57th. Medici has served generations of University of Chicago students and faculty, many of whom carved their name on the tables and walls. The eatery is known for its pizzas and burgers. Just to the east is the Medici deli and bakery, which serves mouthwatering croissants. ✉ *1327 E. 57th St., Hyde Park* ☎ *773/667–7394* ⊕ *www.medici57.com.*

TOP REASONS TO GO

Get caught up in wonderment: Spend a few hours at the Museum of Science and Industry.

Enjoy Jackson Park: Do some exotic-bird-watching.

Appreciate Frank Lloyd Wright: Take a tour of the fantastic Robie House.

Enjoy the views: Pack a picnic for Promontory Point.

SAFETY

Hyde Park is bordered to the west, south, and north by some poor, and at times dangerous, areas. Use caution, especially in the evening.

KENWOOD

The Kenwood area of Hyde Park was once home to the city's elite; after many of the residents moved to the suburbs, the neighborhood became run-down—it has since rebounded to a large degree. The Swifts of meatpacking fame lived not far from President Barack Obama's house, which is off-limits. **St. Gabriel Church** (✉ *4522 S. Wallace St.* ☎ *773/268–9595*), designed in 1887 by Daniel Burnham and John Root, is marked by a tower, arched doorways, and a large round window. The parish was organized to serve Irish workers at the Union Stock Yards, once in operation nearby.

7

HYDE PARK

Sightseeing
★★★★☆

Dining
★★☆☆☆

Lodging
★☆☆☆☆

Shopping
★☆☆☆☆

Nightlife
★★☆☆☆

Hyde Park is something of a trek from downtown Chicago, but it's worth the extra effort. The community is rich in academic and cultural life, and it is also considered one of the country's most successfully integrated neighborhoods, which is reflected in everything from the people you'll meet on the street to the diverse cuisine available.

Updated
by Roberta
Sotonoff

Best known as the home of the University of Chicago, the neighborhood began to see significant growth only in the late 19th century, when the university opened in 1892 and the World's Columbian Exposition attracted an international influx a year later. The exposition spawned the Midway Plaisance and numerous Classical Revival buildings, including the behemoth Museum of Science and Industry. The Midway Plaisance still runs along the southern edge of the University of Chicago's original campus. Sprawling homes were soon erected for school faculty in neighboring Kenwood, and the area began to attract well-to-do types who commissioned famous architects to build them spectacular homes.

A number of architecturally riveting buildings are here, including two by Frank Lloyd Wright, the Robie House and Heller House, as different as night and day. There are also a thriving theater scene and several art and history museums. Most impressive, though, is the diverse population, with a strong sense of community pride and fondness for the neighborhood's pretty tree-lined streets, proximity to the lake, and slightly off-the-beaten-path vibe.

WORLD'S COLUMBIAN EXPOSITION

In 1893 the city of Chicago hosted the **World's Columbian Exposition.** The fair's mix of green spaces and Beaux Arts buildings offered the vision of a more pleasantly habitable metropolis than the crammed industrial center that rose from the ashes of the Great Fire. However, a ruffled Louis Sullivan prophesied that "the damage wrought to this country by the Chicago World's Fair will last half a century." He wasn't entirely wrong in his prediction—the neoclassical style vied sharply over the next decades with the native creations of the Chicago and Prairie schools, all the while incorporating their technical advances. One of Hyde Park's most popular destinations—the Museum of Science and Industry—was erected as the fair's Palace of Fine Arts. It's one of only three of the exposition's buildings still standing; the others are the Art Institute of Chicago building and a small ladies' "comfort station" behind the MSI.

TOP ATTRACTIONS

DuSable Museum of African American History. Sitting alongside the lagoons of Washington Park, the DuSable Museum offers an interesting—and haunting—exploration of the African-American experience. The most moving display is about slavery—the poignant, disturbing artifacts include rusted shackles used on slave ships. Other permanent exhibits include handwritten lyric sheets from Motown greats, letters and memorabilia of scholar W.E.B. DuBois and poet Langston Hughes, and a significant art collection. Rotating exhibits showcase African-American experiences, achievements, and contributions. ☒ *740 E. 56th Pl., Hyde Park* ☎ *773/947-0600* ⊕ *www.dusablemuseum.org* ⌦ *$10* ⊙ *Tues.–Sat. 10–5, Sun. noon–5.*

FAMILY **Museum of Science and Industry.**
Fodor'sChoice   ⇨ *See highlighted listing in this chapter.*
★

Oriental Institute. This gem began with artifacts collected by University of Chicago archaeologists in the 1930s (one is rumored to have been the model for Indiana Jones) and has expanded into an interesting, informative museum with a jaw-dropping collection from the ancient Near East, including the largest U.S. collection of Iraqi antiquities. There are amulets, mummies, limestone reliefs, gold jewelry, ivories, pottery, and bronzes from the 4th millennium BC through the 13th century AD. A 17-foot-tall statue of King Tut was excavated from the ruins of a temple in western Thebes in 1930. ☒ *1155 E. 58th St., Hyde Park* ☎ *773/702-9514* ⊕ *www.oi.uchicago.edu* ⌦ *Suggested donation $7* ⊙ *Tues. and Thurs.–Sat. 10–6, Wed. 10–8:30, Sun. noon–6.*

Promontory Point. This scenic, man-made peninsula, which projects into Lake Michigan, opened in 1937 as part of Burnham Park. Entry is by tunnel underneath Lake Shore Drive at 55th Street or the Lakefront Trail. The fawn-shaped David Wallach Memorial Fountain is located near the tunnel. The park's field house is a popular wedding venue, so you may catch a glimpse of a beaming bride during your visit. ☒ *5491 S. Shore Dr., Hyde Park* ☎ *312/747-1615* ⊕ *www.chicagoparkdistrict.com/parks/Burnham-Park* ⌦ *Free* ⊙ *Daily 6 am–11 pm.*

7

DID YOU KNOW?

The Laura Spelman Rocke-
feller Memorial Carillon at
the University of Chicago's
Rockefeller Chapel is the
largest instrument ever built,
with 72 bells and 100 tons
of bronze. Hear it ring after
Sunday services at 12:15, and
during the week at noon and
6 pm during the academic
year. In summer, check the
chapel's Bells of Summer
carillon festival schedule for
concert times.

MUSEUM OF SCIENCE AND INDUSTRY

✉ 5700 S. Lake Shore Dr., Hyde Park ☎ 773/684–1414
⊕ www.msichicago.org
🎫 $18, $26 with Omnimax
🕐 Late May–early Sept., daily 9:30–5:30; early Sept.–late May, daily 9:30–4.

TIPS

■ Use the museum map to plan out your visit. Your best bet is to hit a couple of highlights (the onboard U-boat tour will take about 20 minutes) and then see a couple of quirky exhibits.

■ If the kids get grouchy, bring them to the Idea Factory, a giant playroom where they can play with water cannons, blocks, and cranks. Limited to ages 10 and younger.

■ Relax with some ice cream in the old-fashioned ice-cream parlor, tucked away in a genteel re-creation of an Illinois main street.

■ On nice days, hordes of sunbathers and kite-flyers camp out on the giant lawn out front—it's almost as entertaining as the museum itself. Lake Michigan is across the street.

■ The museum has free-admission days, but the schedule changes often. Check the website for details.

The beloved MSI is one of the most-visited sites in Chicago, and for good reason. The sprawling open space has 2,000 exhibits on three floors, with new exhibits added constantly. The museum's high-tech interior is hidden by the Classical Revival exterior; it was designed in 1892 by D.H. Burnham & Company as a temporary structure to house the Palace of Fine Arts for the World's Columbian Exposition. (The MSI, the Art Institute, and a women's washroom are the fair's only surviving buildings.) The beautifully landscaped Jackson Park and its peaceful, Japanese-style Osaka Garden are behind the museum.

Highlights

Descend into the depths of a simulated coal mine on a "miner"-led tour that explores the technology behind digging energy out of the ground.

Get swallowed up by the opulent and detailed-as-a-film-set Fairy Castle (really a giant dollhouse), which has tiny chandeliers that flash with real diamonds and floors that are laid with intricate stone patterns.

Tour the cramped quarters of a U-505 German submarine—the only one captured during World War II (additional fee). Explore the free interactive exhibits surrounding the sub, which give stunning insight into the strategy behind the war at sea.

Discover how scientists can make frogs' eyes glow or watch baby chicks tap themselves out of their shells at the "Genetics–Decoding Life" exhibit.

Find out how your body works at "You! The Experience," with 50 fascinating interactive stations.

See giant bolts of lightning, make a rainbow, and manipulate an indoor tornado at "Science Storms."

Watch science- and space-related films on a giant screen at the Omnimax Theater.

7

The remarkable Robie House is a prime example of Frank Lloyd Wright's "open plan."

Fodor's Choice **Robie House.** Named one of the 10 most significant buildings of the 20th
★ century by the American Institute of Architects, the 9,000-square-foot
Robie House (1910) is long and low. Massive overhangs shoot out from
the low-pitched roof, and windows run along the facade in a glittering stretch. Inside, Wright's "open plan" echoes the great outdoors, as
one space flows into another, while sunlight streaming through decorative leaded windows bathes the rooms in patterns. The original dining
room had a table with lanterns at each corner, giving the illusion that
the table itself was a separate room. Other Wright innovations include
a three-car garage (now the gift shop), intercom, and central vacuum-
cleaner system. Check the website for tour options. It's a good idea to
make reservations in advance. ✉ *5757 S. Woodlawn Ave., Hyde Park*
☎ *312/994–4000* ⊕ *www.gowright.org/visit/robie-house.html* ✆ *$10–
$55, depending on tour* ☉ *Tours: Thurs.–Mon. at 11 and 3; museum
shop: Thurs.–Mon. 9–4.*

University of Chicago. Higher education dominates the physical and cultural landscape of Hyde Park and South Kenwood. Much of the original
campus was designed by Henry Ives Cobb. Its Gothic-style quadrangles
were meant to mimic Oxford and Cambridge. Especially of note are
the International House and the Rockefeller Memorial Chapel with
its 72-bell carillon, where regular concerts are performed. A departure from this architecture is the very modern-looking Booth School of
Business. Its horizontal accents imitate the Frank Lloyd Wright Robie
House (1910), located directly across the street. The university's Oriental Institute and the Smart Museum of Art are certainly worth a visit,
as is the university-run Court Theatre, which stages new and classic

MR. OBAMA'S NEIGHBORHOOD

Hyde Park's most famous family spends most of its time in Washington, D.C., these days, and the Secret Service prevents visitors from getting close to their Chicago home. Still, you can experience many of the First Family's favorite neighborhood haunts. Start at the **University of Chicago**, where Barack Obama taught law from 1992 to 2004. Make sure to look up: you'll see the university's iconic gargoyles on some buildings. From there, poke around at **57th Street Books** (⊠ *57th and Kimbark* ☎ *773/684–1300*), recommended by Michelle Obama for its extensive collection of fiction and nonfiction and its youth-oriented programs. The store bills itself as "the first stop for serious readers." With mind fed, it's time for some fresh air. Head east to Lake Shore Drive and walk to **Promontory Point** (⊠ *5491 S. Lake Shore Dr.*) for a stunning view of Lake Michigan. If you walk to the lake along East Hayes Drive, you'll pass by the basketball courts where President Obama likes to shoot hoops with his brother-in-law, Craig Robinson.

works. And a piece of trivia: the faculty, former faculty, and alumni of the University of Chicago have won 87 Nobel prizes, the most of any school in the country. Prizes have been awarded in every field; the most recent is President Barack Obama's Nobel Peace Prize in 2009. A self-guided tour of University of Chicago architecture, *A Walking Guide to the Campus*, is available for purchase in the University of Chicago Bookstore. ⊠ *Visitor Center: Reynolds Club, 5801 S. Ellis Ave., Hyde Park* ☎ *773/702–1234* ⊕ *www.uchicago.edu* ⊙ *Weekdays 8:30–5.*

WORTH NOTING

Heller House. When he designed this house in 1897, Frank Lloyd Wright was still moving toward the mature Prairie style achieved in the Robie House 13 years later. Unlike most of his long and low designs, it has three floors. The top floor has pillars and sculptured nymphs cavorting at the top. As was common with Wright—and very uncommon then and now—the entrance to the Heller House is on the side of the structure. The house is not open to the public. ⊠ *5132 S. Woodlawn Ave., Hyde Park.*

Hyde Park Historical Society. To get a good overview of the neighborhood, stop by the Hyde Park Historical Society, which sponsors lectures and tours. ⊠ *5529 S. Lake Park Ave., Hyde Park* ☎ *773/493–1893* ⊕ *www. hydeparkhistory.org* ✉ *Free* ⊙ *Weekends 2–4.*

Jackson Park. This Hyde Park gem was designed by Frederick Law Olmsted (co-designer of New York City's Central Park) for the World's Columbian Exposition of 1893. It has lagoons, a Japanese garden with authentic Japanese statuary, and the Wooded Island, a nature retreat with wildlife and 300 species of birds. Its 63rd Street Beach is a popular summer destination, and the state-of-the-art fitness center means there's entertainment rain or shine. ⊠ *Between E. 56th and 67th Sts., S. Stony Island Ave., and the lakefront, Hyde Park* ☎ *773/256–0903* ⊕ *www. chicagoparkdistrict.com/parks/jackson-park* ⊙ *Daily 6 am–11 pm.*

7

FOR THE BIRDS

Harold Washington Park and Jackson Park have a notable parakeet population. Rumor has it they escaped from a cage at O'Hare Airport and settled in area parks. Somehow these natives of the tropics have been able to survive the harsh Chicago winter and have become neighborhood fixtures.

DID YOU KNOW?

"The toasters," designed by I.M. Pei, are two U of C apartment buildings that sit on an island in the middle of the street. Fittingly enough, the blocky white buildings look like two pieces of toast.

The Promontory. The tan brick building, designed by Mies van der Rohe in 1949, was named for nearby Promontory Point, which juts out into the lake. Mies's first Chicago high-rise, it exemplifies the postwar trend toward a clean, simple style. Even from street level, the Lake Michigan views here are breathtaking. Note the skylines and belching smokestacks of Gary and Hammond, Indiana, to the southeast. ⊠ *5530–5532 S. Shore Dr., Hyde Park* ☎ *773/493–5599* ⊕ *www. miespromontoryapartments.com.*

Smart Museum of Art. If you want to see art masterpieces but don't want to spend a long day wandering one of the major art museums, the Smart may be just your speed. The diverse permanent collection of more than 12,000 pieces includes works by old masters; furniture by Frank Lloyd Wright; and sculptures by Degas, Matisse, Rodin, and Henry Moore. Temporary exhibits are a great way to see startlingly good art in a smaller, intimate space. ⊠ *5550 S. Greenwood Ave., Hyde Park* ☎ *773/702–0200* ⊕ *www.smartmuseum.uchicago.edu* ⊠ *Free* ☉ *Tues., Wed., and Fri.–Sun. 10–5; Thurs. 10–8.*

South Shore Cultural Center. Listed on the National Register of Historic Places, this opulent clubhouse on Lake Michigan is one of the last remaining Mediterranean resort–style buildings in the Midwest. The posh country club looks like something out of an F. Scott Fitzgerald novel. It boasts a 9-hole golf course, tennis courts, beach, horse stables, art gallery, and meeting rooms. With magnificent crystal chandeliers, balconies, pillars, and vaulted ceiling, its ballrooms and grand lobby wow visitors, including President Barack Obama and First Lady Michelle Obama, who chose the center for their wedding reception. It is also the home of the South Shore Cultural School of the Arts. ⊠ *7059 S. Shore Dr., Hyde Park* ☎ *773/256–0149* ⊕ *www.hydepark.org/parks/ southshore/aboutsscc.htm* ⊠ *Free* ☉ *Weekdays 9–6, Sat. 9–5.*

8

GETTING OUT
OF THE CITY

8

GETTING ORIENTED

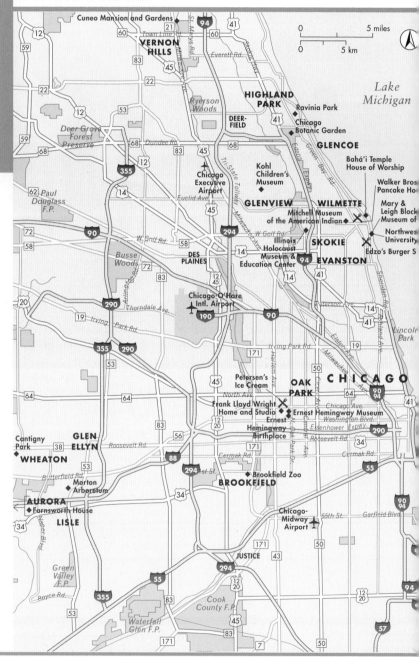

MAKING THE MOST OF YOUR TIME

A trip to Chicago shouldn't start and end within the city limits. There's a lot worth seeing and doing in the city's suburbs that makes the little added effort worthwhile. Spend at least half a day in historic Oak Park to learn about famous residents Ernest Hemingway and Frank Lloyd Wright. A second day to see points farther west can take you to the Brookfield Zoo or the Morton Arboretum. Chicago's picturesque North Shore won't disappoint either: spend a collegial day wandering Northwestern University's campus and downtown Evanston or take in a concert at Ravinia Park in Highland Park and the Chicago Botanic Garden in Glencoe.

QUICK BITES

Edzo's Burger Shop. From 10:30 to 4, Northwestern students and suits line up here for burgers (ground in-house), nine kinds of french fries (try the ones with truffle salt and Parmesan), and Nutella milk shakes. ⊠ *1571 Sherman Ave., Evanston* ☎ *847/864–3396* ⊕ *www.edzos.com* ☉ *Closed Mon.*

Petersen's Ice Cream. This old-fashioned ice cream parlor has been serving sundaes, shakes, malts, and cones of homemade ice cream for more than 90 years. ⊠ *1100 Chicago Ave., Oak Park* ☎ *708/386–6131* ⊕ *www.petersenicecream. com* ☉ *Closed Jan. and Feb.*

Walker Bros. Pancake House. Be prepared to stand in line for the mouthwatering apple cinnamon pancake, a massive disk loaded with apples, or the German pancake, a huge, puffy, oven-baked circle topped with powdered sugar. There are several branches, but the original Wilmette restaurant is where scenes from the 1980 movie *Ordinary People* were shot. ⊠ *153 Green Bay Rd., Wilmette* ☎ *847/251–6000* ⊕ *www.walkerbros.net.*

TOP REASONS TO GO

Expand your cultural knowledge: Take part in a tea ceremony or try your hand at calligraphy during weekend programs at the Mallott Japanese Garden inside the Chicago Botanic Garden.

See the animals: Get a fish's-eye view of polar bears swimming underwater at the belowground viewing area at the Brookfield Zoo's Great Bear Wilderness Habitat.

Get to know Frank Lloyd Wright: Take a trip back to 1909, the last year the famed architect lived and worked in his Oak Park Home and Studio.

Enjoy a picnic: Pack up a candelabra and some foie gras—or just a blanket and some bug spray—and head to the Ravinia Festival for a night of music under the summer stars.

Visit the Bahá'i Temple: Join creatures including chipmunks, deer, and red-tailed hawks, which often watch the sunset from the peaceful grounds of this majestic temple in Wilmette.

GETTING HERE

Via the El, take the Purple Line to Evanston and Wilmette, the Green Line to Oak Park, and the Yellow Line to Skokie. Many suburbs can also be reached by commuter rail: Metra (⊕ *www. metrarail.com*).

8

CHICAGO OUTSKIRTS

Updated
by Roberta
Sotonoff

Chicago's suburbs aren't just for commuters. The towns that lie to the north, west, and south of the city are rich in history, culture, museums, and outdoor activities. Add a day or two to your itinerary and get out of town for a concert, architecture tour, or zoo visit; the journey to the 'burbs is well worth those additional vacation days.

The closest suburbs to the city limits are homes to excellent theaters and museums that rival their city cousins. The farther out you go, the more likely you are to find wooded parks and wider streets that characterize the towns outside just about any major city. But Chicago's 'burbs are far from mirror images of others that dot the map. These bedroom communities are loaded with trip-worthy gems. Brookfield and Lisle, to the west, have top-notch zoos and exquisite gardens; along the North Shore, Highland Park and Evanston attract talented musicians and house internationally acclaimed art collections. And Oak Park is so rich in architectural history that you can't help but wish you had more time to just simply stay put.

Forget strip-mall fast food, too—it's not uncommon to find decidedly urban types doing a reverse commute to visit a trendy new restaurant or ethnic eatery outside the city limits. With Chicago's bus and train system reaching out to some of the nearer suburbs, the trips are painless. In short, don't overlook Chicago's suburbs when you plan a trip here. If you do, you'll surely be missing out on some of the very best things the metropolitan area has to offer.

WEST OF CHICAGO

OAK PARK

9 miles west of downtown Chicago.

⇨ *For information on the Frank Lloyd Wright houses of Oak Park, see "Frank Lloyd Wright" in this chapter.*

Ernest Hemingway Birthplace. Part of the literary legacy of Oak Park, this three-story, turreted Queen Anne Victorian, which stands in frilly contrast to the many streamlined Prairie-style homes elsewhere in the neighborhood, contains period-furnished rooms and many photos and artifacts pertaining to the writer's early life. Museum curators have restored rooms to faithfully depict the house as it looked at the turn of the 20th century. You can poke your head inside the room in which the author was born on July 21, 1899. ⊠ *339 N. Oak Park Ave., Oak Park* ☎ *708/848–2222* ⊕ *www.ehfop.org* ⌑ *$10 joint ticket with Hemingway Museum* ⊙ *Sun.–Fri. 1–5, Sat. 10–5; tours hourly.*

Ernest Hemingway Museum. How did the author's first 20 years in Oak Park affect his later work? Check out the exhibits and videos here to find out. Don't miss his first "book," a set of drawings with captions written by his mother, Grace. Holdings include reproduced manuscripts and letters. ⊠ *200 N. Oak Park Ave., Oak Park* ☎ *708/524–5383* ⊕ *www.ehfop.org* ⌑ *$10 joint ticket with Hemingway Birthplace* ⊙ *Sun.–Fri. 1–5, Sat. 10–5.*

BROOKFIELD

10 miles west of downtown Chicago.

FAMILY
Fodor's Choice
★

Brookfield Zoo. Spend the day among more than 2,000 animals at this gigantic zoo. The highlights? First, there's the 7½-acre **Great Bear Wilderness** exhibit, a sprawling replica of North American woodlands for the zoo's population of grizzlies, polar bears, bison, Mexican gray wolves, and bald eagles. It's the largest exhibit built in the zoo's history. Be sure to watch the polar bears from the popular underwater viewing area. Monkeys, otters, birds, and other rain-forest fauna cavort in the carefully constructed setting of rocks, trees, shrubs, pools, and waterfalls of **Tropic World.** At the **Living Coast** you can venture through passageways to see sharks, rays, and Humboldt penguins. Daily dolphin shows are a favorite even for adults. Harbor seals, grey seals, and sea lions inhabit a rocky seascape exhibit. Don't worry if you don't want to trek around the grounds—you can hop aboard a motorized safari tram ($4) in warm weather or the heated Snowball Express tram in the cold. During the winter holiday season, the evening **Holiday Magic** shows are a treat.

Continued on page 145

ERNEST HEMINGWAY: OAK PARK PROTÉGÉ

It seems unlikely that the rough-and-tumble writer and adventurer Ernest Hemingway was born in 1899 in the manicured suburb of Oak Park, Illinois, a town he described as having "wide lawns and narrow minds." He excelled at writing for the high-school paper—a skill that turned into his life's work. Hemingway later lived in Toronto and Chicago. Though his return visits to Oak Park were infrequent, the residents celebrate him there to this day.

8

FRANK LLOYD WRIGHT

1867–1959

The most famous American architect of the 20th century led a life that was as zany and scandalous as his architectural legacy was great. Behind the photo-op appearance and lordly pronouncements was a rebel visionary who left an unforgettable imprint on the world's notion of architecture. Nowhere else in the country can you experience Frank Lloyd Wright's genius as you can in Chicago and its surroundings.

Born two years after the Civil War ended, Wright did not live to see the completion of his late masterpiece, the Guggenheim Museum. His father preached and played (the Gospel and music) and dragged the family from the Midwest to New England and back before he up and left for good. Wright's Welsh-born mother, Anna Lloyd Jones, grew up in Wisconsin, and her son's roots would run deep there, too. Although his career began in Chicago and his work took him as far away as Japan, the home Wright built in Spring Green, Wisconsin—Taliesin—was his true center.

Despite all his dramas and financial instability (Wright was notoriously bad with money), the architect certainly produced. He was always ready to try something new—as long as it fit his notion of architecture as an expression of the human spirit and of human relationship with nature. By the time he died in 1959, Wright had designed over 1,000 projects, more than half of which were constructed.

Robie House, Chicago

WELCOME TO OAK PARK!

Oak Park is a leafy, quiet community just 10 miles west of downtown Chicago. When you arrive, head to the **Oak Park Visitors Center** (⊠ *1010 Lake St.* ☎ *708/524–7800* ⊕ *www.visitoakpark. com* ⊙ *Daily 10–5, until 4 in winter*) and get oriented with a free map.

Next, wander to the **Frank Lloyd Wright Home and Studio** (⊠ *951 Chicago Ave.* ☎ *708/848–1976* ⊕ *www.flwright.org* 🎟 *$15; walking tour $15; combined $25* ⊙ *Guided interior tours 11–4 daily; audio walking tours 10–3:30 daily. Tickets can be purchased in advance via the Web site*). From the outside, the shingle-clad structure may not appear all that innovative, but it's here that Wright

developed the architectural language that still has the world talking.

Financed with a $5,000 loan from his mentor, Louis Sullivan, Wright designed the home when he was only 22. The residence manifests some of the spatial and stylistic characteristics that became hallmarks of Wright's work: there's a central fireplace from which other spaces seem to radiate and an enticing flow to the rooms. In 1974, the local Frank Lloyd Wright Home and Studio Foundation, together with the National Trust for Historic Preservation, embarked on a 13-year restoration that returned the building to its 1909 appearance.

GETTING HERE

To get to the heart of Oak Park by car, take the Eisenhower Expressway (I-290) west to Harlem Avenue. Head north on Harlem and take a right on Lake Street to get to the Oak Park Visitors Center at Forest Avenue and Lake Street, where there's ample free parking. You can also take the Green Line of the El to the Harlem Avenue stop, or Metra's Union Pacific West Line from the Ogilvie Transportation Center in Citicorp Center downtown (500 W. Madison) to the Oak Park stop at Marion Street.

STROLLING OAK PARK

[Map showing: W. Augusta St., 7200 W, Frank Lloyd Wright Home and Studio, Ernest Hemingway Boyhood Home, W. Iowa St., 800 W, Kenilworth Ave., Moore-Dugal Home, Superior St., Marion St., Forest Ave., W. Chicago Ave., Ernest Hemingway Birthplace, W. Superior St., W. Erie St., Oak Park Visitors Center, W. Ontario St., Scoville Park, Ernest Hemingway Museum, W. Lake St., Unity Temple, W. North Blvd.]

WOMEN, FIRE, SCANDAL . . . AND OVER 1,000 DESIGNS

Dana Thomas House interior, 1904

1885 Wright briefly studies engineering at the University of Wisconsin.

1887 Wright strikes out for Chicago. He starts his career learning the basics with J. L. Silsbee, a residential architect.

1889 Wright marries Catherine Tobin; he builds her a home in suburban Oak Park, and they have six children together. In 1898 he adds a studio.

1893 Wright launches his own practice in downtown Chicago.

> "WHILE NEW YORK HAS REPRODUCED MUCH AND PRODUCED NOTHING, CHICAGO'S ACHIEVEMENTS IN ARCHITECTURE HAVE GAINED WORLD-WIDE RECOGNITION AS A DISTINCTIVELY AMERICAN ARCHITECTURE."

A leisurely stroll around the neighborhood will introduce you to plenty of **Frank Lloyd Wright houses.** All are privately owned, so you'll have to be content with what you can see from the outside. Check out 1019, 1027, and 1031 Chicago Avenue. These are typical Victorians that Wright designed on the sly while working for Sullivan.

For a look at the "real" Wright, don't miss the **Moore–Dugal Home** (1895) at 333 N. Forest Avenue, which reflects Wright's evolving architectural philosophy with its huge chimney and overhanging second story. Peek also at numbers 318, 313, 238, and 210, where you can follow his emerging modernism. Around the corner at 6 Elizabeth Court is the **Laura Gale House,** a 1909 project whose cantilevered profile foreshadows the thrusting planes Wright would create at Fallingwater decades later.

Between 1889 and 1913, Wright erected over two dozen buildings in Oak Park, so unless you're making an extended visit, don't expect to see everything. But don't leave town without a visit to his 1908 **Unity Temple** (⊠ *875 W. Lake*

A landmark profile: the eastern facade of the architect's home and studio, Oak Park.

St.☎ *708/848–6225),* a National Historic Landmark. Take a moment to appreciate Wright's fresh take on a place of worship; his bold strokes in creating a flowing interior; his unfailing attention to what was outside (note the skylights); and his dramatic use of concrete, which helps to protect the space from traffic noise.

Exterior, Unity Temple, Oak Park

1905 Wright begins designing the reinforced concrete Unity Temple.

1908 Construction begins on the Robie House in Chicago's Hyde Park neighborhood.

1909 Wright leaves for Europe with Mamah Cheney, the wife of a former client; Mrs. Wright does not consent to a divorce.

1911 Wright and Cheney settle at Taliesin, in Spring Green, Wisconsin.

GUIDED TOURS

A great way to get to know Oak Park is to take advantage of the guided tours. Well-informed local guides take small groups on tours throughout the day, discussing various architectural details, pointing out artifacts from the family's life, and often telling amusing stories of the rambunctious Wright clan. Reservations are required for groups of 10 or more for the home and studio tours. Note that you need to arrive as early as possible to be assured a spot. Tours begin at the **Ginkgo Tree Bookshop,** which is part of the home and studio. The shop carries architecture-related books and gifts. You can pick up a map ($3.95) to find other examples of Wright's work that are within easy walking or driving distance, or you can join a guided tour of the neighborhood led by volunteers.

THE HEMINGWAY CONNECTION

Frank Lloyd Wright wasn't the only creative giant to call Oak Park home. Ten years after Wright arrived, Ernest Hemingway was born here in 1899 in a proper Queen Anne, complete with turret. Wright was gone by the time Hemingway began to sow his literary oats. Good thing, too. It's doubtful the quiet village could have handled two such egos. ⇨ **See listings in this chapter for more information.**

Frank Lloyd Wright's distinctive take on a modern dining room.

TIPS

■ Tickets go on sale every October for the eagerly awaited annual **Wright Architectural Housewalk** in May, your chance to see the interiors of some of Oak Park's most architecturally notable homes. Check out ⊕ *www.gowright.org* for more details.

■ The Blue Line also stops in Oak Park, but we recommend sticking to the Green Line, as the Blue Line stop leaves you in a sketchy neighborhood.

Taliesin, Spring Green, Wisconsin

1914 Mrs. Cheney, her two children, and several other people are killed by a deranged employee, who also sets fire to Taliesin.

1915 With new mistress Miriam Noel in tow, the architect heads for Japan to oversee the building of the Imperial Hotel.

1922 Wright and his wife Catherine divorce.

1924 Wright marries Miriam Noel, but the marriage implodes three years later.

1928 Wright marries Olga (Olgivanna) Lazovich Milanoff. They have one daughter together.

PRAIRIE STYLE PRIMER

Primarily a residential mode, Wright's Prairie style is characterized by ground-hugging masses; low-pitched roofs with deep eaves; and ribbon windows. Generally, Prairie houses are two-story affairs, with single story wings and terraces that project into the landscape. Brick and stone, earth tones, and unpainted wood underscore the perception of a house as an extension of the natural world. Wright designed free-flowing living spaces defined by alternating ceiling heights, natural light, and architectural screens. Although a number of other Chicago architects pursued this emerging aesthetic, Wright became its

> "ALL FINE ARCHITECTURAL VALUES ARE HUMAN VALUES, ELSE NOT VALUABLE."

acknowledged master. Though Wright designed dozens of Prairie style homes, the most well-known is Robie House, in Chicago's Hyde Park neighborhood. A dynamic composition of overlapping planes, it seems both beautifully anchored to the ground and ready to sail off with the arrival of a sharp breeze.

IN FOCUS FRANK LLOYD WRIGHT

8

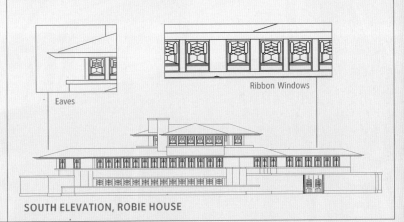

Eaves

Ribbon Windows

SOUTH ELEVATION, ROBIE HOUSE

Nathan G Moore-Dugal house, 1923

1930 The Taliesin Fellowship is launched; eager apprentices arrive to learn from the master.

1935 Fallingwater, the country home of Pittsburgh retailer Edgar J. Kaufmann, is completed at Bear Run, Pennsylvania.

1937 Wright begins construction of his winter getaway, Talesin West, in Scottsdale, Arizona.

1956 Wright designs the Guggenheim Museum in New York. It is completed in 1959.

1957 Wright joins preservationists in saving Robie House from demolition.

1959 Wright dies at the age of 91.

The two best educational exhibits are Habitat Africa and The Swamp. In **Habitat Africa** you can explore two very different environments. See such tiny animals as klipspringer antelope, which are only 22 inches tall, in the savanna exhibit, which also has a water hole, rock formations characteristic of the African savanna, and termite mounds. If you look closely in the dense forest exhibit, you might be able to find animals like the okapi. The **Swamp** is about as realistic as you would want an exhibit on swamps to be, with a springy floor and open habitats with low-flying birds vividly demonstrating the complex ecosystems of both Southern and Illinois wetlands. For hands-on family activities, check out the **Hamill Family Play Zoo** ($3.50), where kids can learn to care for nature by playing zookeeper, gardener, or veterinarian. ✉ *1st Ave. and 31st St., Brookfield* ☎ *708/688–8000, 800/468–6966* ⊕ *www.czs. org* ✉ *$15; free Tues. and Thurs. Oct.–Dec. and Sat., Sun., Tues., and Thurs. Jan.–Feb.; parking $10* ⊙ *Memorial Day–Labor Day, Mon.–Sat. 9:30–6, Sun. 9:30–7:30; Labor Day–Memorial Day, daily 10–5; indoor exhibits close 30 mins before closing time.*

LISLE

25 miles southwest of downtown Chicago.

Morton Arboretum. Enjoy the natural beauty of woodlands, wetlands, and prairie at this 1,700-acre outdoor oasis. Hike some of the 16 miles of manicured trails, or drive or bike along 9 miles of paved roads. Trees, shrubs, and vines bloom year-round, and every season is magnificent: spring's flowering trees, summer's canopy-covered trails, fall's dazzling foliage, and winter's serene beauty. Bike, snowshoe, and cross-country ski rentals are available. If you have kids, check out the award-winning 4-acre Children's Garden, which is stroller (as well as wheelchair) friendly. A one-acre maze garden will delight as you wind your way to the lookout platform. ✉ *4100 Illinois Rte. 53, Lisle* ☎ *630/968–0074* ⊕ *www.mortonarb.org* ✉ *$12, $8 Wed.; tram tours $6* ⊙ *Jan.–Feb., daily 9–4; Mar.–Apr. and Nov.–Dec., daily 9–5; May– Oct., daily 9–6.*

WHEATON

30 miles west of downtown Chicago.

Cantigny Park. The 500 acres of this estate offer multiple attractions: an impressive military history museum with immersive exhibits (including touch-screen videos and re-created battle scenes), sprawling grounds with formal gardens, and its own 27-hole public golf course with separate youth links. The centerpiece, however, is the Beaux Arts–style Col. Robert R. McCormick Museum. Built for the former *Chicago Tribune* owner, the 35-room mansion features the Joseph Medill Library, the stately wood-paneled Freedom Hall, and an Art Deco movie theater in the basement. The hidden Prohibition-era bar alone is worth a visit—we won't ruin the surprise by revealing where it is. ✉ *1S151 Winfield Rd., Wheaton* ☎ *630/668–5161* ⊕ *www.cantigny.org* ✉ *$5 per car when museums open, $2 when museums closed* ⊙ *Feb., Fri.– Sun. 9–sunset; Mar.–Apr. and Nov.–Dec., daily 9–sunset; May–Oct., daily 7–sunset.*

8

AURORA AND VICINITY

41 miles west of downtown Chicago.

The Aurora vicinity has overcome lean times as a tourist destination and now offers something for everyone. Rent a kayak from **Paddle and Trail** (⊕ *paddleandtrail.com*) and float on the Fox River. Explore the sunken gardens, hiking paths, and zoo at **Phillips Park** (⊕ *www.phillipsparkaurora. com*). Or check out the plethora of art galleries in downtown Aurora.

Farnsworth House. Just down the river from Aurora, near Plano, sits this minimalist dwelling of steel, wood, and travertine marble built by Ludwig Mies van der Rohe in 1951. The Farnsworth House appears to nearly float against a backdrop of serene river views and gardens. Brad Pitt chose the site for a Japanese jeans commercial he shot in 2007, raising $60,000 for the house's upkeep. The house, which the National Trust for Historic Preservation operates as a museum, may be seen only by guided tour (reservations highly recommended). ⊠ *14520 River Rd., Plano* ☎ *630/552–0052* ⊕ *www.farnsworthhouse.org* ⊠ *Tours: $20 in advance, $25 at door* ☉ *Apr.–Nov., Wed.–Sun. 9–4.*

NORTH OF CHICAGO

EVANSTON

10 miles north of downtown Chicago.

The home of Northwestern University is a pretty-as-can-be town in its own right, perched along the lake and studded with some magnificent homes and charming shops. There are also a number of cultural offerings here worth checking out.

Mary & Leigh Block Museum of Art. Among the most notable sights on the Northwestern University campus, this multiuse space comprising four galleries mounts exhibitions and hosts workshops, lectures, and symposia. Its Block Cinema screens classic and contemporary films. The impressive permanent collection includes prints, photographs, and other works on paper spanning the 16th to 21st centuries. An outdoor sculpture garden includes works by Joan Miró and Barbara Hepworth. ⊠ *Northwestern University, 40 Arts Circle Dr., Evanston* ☎ *847/491–4000* ⊕ *www.blockmuseum. northwestern.edu* ⊠ *Free* ☉ *Tues. and weekends 10–5, Wed.–Fri. 10–8.*

Mitchell Museum of the American Indian. Founded in 1977, the museum houses more than 10,000 Native American artifacts from the Paleo-Indian period through modern times. Permanent exhibits focus on tribes in the Plains, Southwest, Northwest Coast, Woodlands, and Arctic areas. Guided tours, lectures, and kids' craft mornings (weekends only) are a regular part of the programming here. ⊠ *3001 Central St., Evanston* ☎ *847/475–1030* ⊕ *www.mitchellmuseum.org* ⊠ *$5, free 1st Fri. of month* ☉ *Tues., Wed., Fri., and Sat. 10–5; Thurs. 10–8; Sun. noon–4.*

Northwestern University. The private university founded here in 1851 by town namesake John Evans sits on a sprawling, picturesque campus hugging Lake Michigan. Among its highly regarded undergraduate and graduate schools are the Medill School of Journalism and Kellogg School of Management. It's also home to the Mary and Leigh Block Museum of Art (see above), which houses more than 4,000 works

The three-island Japanese Garden at the Chicago Botanic Garden offers an oasis from the city.

in its permanent collection. Northwestern's Big Ten athletics program draws a mix of students and locals to games, especially to see the Wildcats football team play at Ryan Field. ✉ *633 Clark St., Evanston* ☏ *847/491–3741* ⊕ *www.northwestern.edu.*

GLENVIEW
17 miles north of downtown Chicago.

FAMILY **Kohl Children's Museum.** Adults are hard pressed to get youngsters to leave the 16 hands-on exhibits at this museum just west of Wilmette. Here toddlers to eight-year-olds can learn about solar power or how sounds make music. They can don a white jacket and be pretend doctors in a baby nursery or vets in an animal hospital. Kids really get into home construction in "Hands on House" and tire changing at "Car Care," and, of course, there is a spot to put on raincoats and play in the water. When weather permits, the 2-acre "Habitat Park," just outside, is a great place for bug hunting, wall painting, and wandering through a grass maze. ✉ *2100 Patriot Blvd., Glenview* ☏ *847/832–6600* ⊕ *www.kohlchildrensmuseum.org* ⊠ *$9.50* ☉ *Tues.–Sat. 9:30–5, Mon. 9:30 to noon (9:30–5, Jun.–Aug.).*

GLENCOE
19 miles north of downtown Chicago.

FAMILY **Chicago Botanic Garden.** Among the 26 different gardens here are the
Fodor's Choice three-island Malott Japanese Garden, the 5-acre Evening Island, and
★ the new Grunsfeld Children's Growing Garden. Three big greenhouses showcase desert, tropical, and semitropical climates with beautiful and fragrant flowers blooming year-round. Special summer exhibitions (admission fee) include the Model Railroad Garden, a 7,500-square-foot garden with 17 garden-scale trains traveling around nearly 50 models

of American landmarks, all made from natural materials, as well as Butterflies & Blooms, a 2,800-square-foot white mesh enclosure filled with hundreds of colorful butterflies interacting with plant life. ⊠ *1000 Lake Cook Rd., Glencoe* 🕾 *847/835–5440* ⊕ *www.chicagobotanic.org* 🖃 *Free; parking $20 per car* ⊙ *June–Aug., daily 7–9; Sept.–May, daily 8–sunset; 35-min tram tours: May–Oct., daily 10–4, weather permitting.*

HIGHLAND PARK
26 miles north of downtown Chicago.

Ravinia Park. If you enjoy music under the stars, the outdoor concerts at Ravinia are a stellar treat. The **Ravinia Festival,** a summerlong series of performances, is the hot-months' home of the Chicago Symphony Orchestra, but the festival also features popular jazz, chamber music, rock, pop, and dance acts. (There are also indoor concerts in cold months as part of the Rising Stars concert series.) Pack a picnic—and don't skimp, concertgoers do it up with everything from fine china to candelabras—and a blanket or chairs and sit on the lawn for a little more than the cost of a movie ($10 to $38). Large screens are placed on the lawn at some concerts so you won't miss anything. Seats are also available in the pavilion for a significantly higher price ($25 to $115). Restaurants and snack bars are on park grounds, so if you forget your goodies you still won't go hungry. Concerts usually start at 7:30 or 8 pm; the park usually opens three to four hours ahead to let everyone score spots and get settled. Weekend-morning concerts are aimed at kids, and families can take advantage of the park while it is slightly less crowded. ⊠ *Sheridan Rd. and Lincolnwood Rd., Highland Park* 🕾 *847/266–5100* ⊕ *www.ravinia.org* ⊙ *Outdoor concerts June–early Sept.*

SKOKIE
12 miles north of downtown Chicago.

Illinois Holocaust Museum & Education Center. In the 1970s a group of neo-Nazis planned a march in the predominantly Jewish suburb of Skokie, and local Holocaust survivors reacted by creating the Holocaust Memorial Foundation of Illinois, a group determined to educate the public about the atrocities of World War II. It took years of planning, but in 2009 the foundation finally unveiled a gem of a museum. The 65,000-square-foot building designed by architect Stanley Tigerman houses more than 11,000 Holocaust-related artifacts and exhibits about other modern genocides. An early 20th-century German rail car—of the type used by the Nazis during the Holocaust—serves as the Museum's central artifact. Other exhibitions include the Legacy of Absence Gallery, which features contemporary artistic responses to atrocities in Cambodia, Rwanda, Argentina, the Soviet Gulag, and elsewhere. The Make a Difference! Harvey L. Miller Youth Exhibition builds awareness of bullying and tolerance. ⊠ *9603 Woods Dr., Skokie* 🕾 *847/967–4800* ⊕ *www.ilholocaustmuseum. org* 🖃 *$12* ⊙ *Mon.–Wed. and Fri. 10–5, Thurs. 10–8, weekends 11–4.*

WILMETTE
14 miles north of downtown Chicago.

FodorśChoice ★ **Bahá'i Temple House of Worship.** Your mouth is sure to drop to the floor the first time you lay eyes on this stunning structure, a nine-sided building that incorporates architectural styles and symbols from many

The Bahá'i Temple's symmetrical architecture represents harmony.

of the world's religions. With its delicate lacelike details and massive dome, the Louis Bourgeois design emphasizes the 19th-century Persian origins of the Bahá'i religion. The formal gardens are as symmetrical and harmonious as the building they surround. The temple is the U.S. center of the Baha'i faith, which advocates spiritual unity, world peace, racial unity, and equality of the sexes. The visitor center has exhibits explaining the faith; here you can also ask for a guide to show you around. ■TIP➜ Go at night to see the striking 164-foot dome illuminated from within. ⊠ *100 Linden Ave., Wilmette* ☎ *847/853-2300* ⊕ *www.bahaitemple.org* 🖃 *Free* ⊗ *Visitor center: mid-May–mid-Sept., daily 10–8; mid-Sept.–mid-May, daily 10–5.*

VERNON HILLS
40 miles northwest of downtown Chicago.

Cuneo Mansion and Gardens. Samuel Insull, partner of Thomas Edison and founder of Commonwealth Edison, built a mansion in 1916 as a country home. After Insull lost his fortune, John Cuneo Sr., the printing-press magnate, bought the estate and fashioned it into something far more spectacular. The skylighted great hall in the main house resembles the open central courtyard of an Italian palazzo, the private family chapel has stained-glass windows, and a gilded grand piano graces the ballroom. The house is filled with antiques, porcelains, 17th-century Flemish tapestries, and Italian paintings. ⊠ *1350 N. Milwaukee Ave., Vernon Hills* ☎ *847/362-3042* ⊕ *www.luc.edu/cuneo* 🖃 *$10* ⊗ *Fri.–Sun. 11–4; tours at 11:30, 1, and 2:30.*

WHERE TO EAT

Updated by
Carly Fisher

Sure, this city has great architecture, museums, and sports venues. But at its heart, Chicago is really a food town. This is evident in the priority that good eating takes, no matter the occasion. Rain or shine, locals will wait in a line that snakes around the corner for dolled-up dogs at Hot Doug's. They'll reserve part of their paychecks to dine at inventive Alinea. And they love to talk about their most recent meal—just ask.

It's no wonder that outdoor festivals are often centered on food, from Taste of Chicago in summer, which packs the grounds at Grant Park, to smaller celebrations, like the German-American fest in Lincoln Square, a mini-Oktoberfest in fall.

Although the city has always had options on the extreme ends of the spectrum—from the hole-in-the wall Italian beef sandwich shops to the special-occasion spots—it's now easier to find eateries in the middle that serve seasonal menus with a farm-to-table mantra. For the budget conscious, it's also a great time to dine: some talented chefs aren't bothering to wait for a liquor license, opening BYOB spots turning out polished fare (just try Urban Belly in Logan Square).

Expect to see more Chicago chefs open casual concepts—Rick Bayless, Paul Kahan, and Michael Kornick have a head start with their respective sandwich, taco, and burger spots. Yet the goal remains the same: to feed a populace that knows good food and isn't willing to accept anything less than the best. In the following pages, you'll find our top picks, from quick bites to multicourse meals, in the city's best dining neighborhoods.

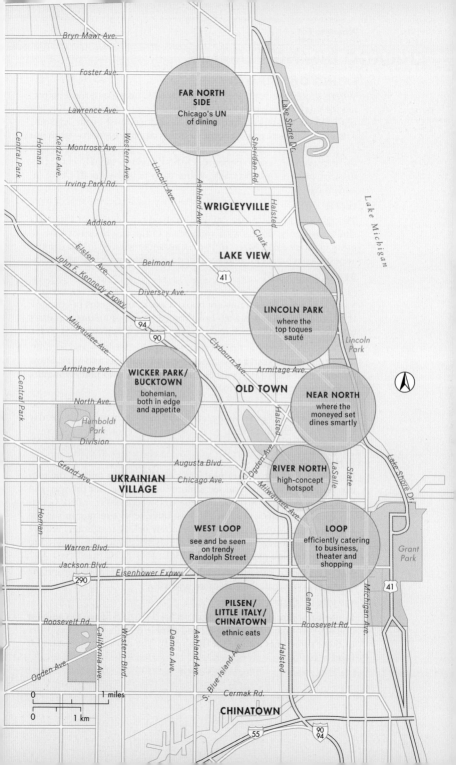

CHICAGO DINING PLANNER

EATING OUT STRATEGY

Where should we eat? With thousands of Chicago eateries competing for your attention, it may seem like a daunting question. But fret not—our expert writers and editors have done most of the legwork. The selections here represent the best this city has to offer—from hot dogs to haute cuisine. Search "Best Bets" for top recommendations by price, cuisine, and experience. Or find a review quickly in the listings, organized alphabetically within each neighborhood. Delve in, and enjoy!

WITH KIDS

Though it's unusual to see children in the dining rooms of Chicago's elite restaurants, dining with youngsters in the city does not have to mean culinary exile. Many of the restaurants reviewed in this chapter are excellent choices for families. They are marked with a FAMILY symbol.

RESERVATIONS

Plan ahead if you're determined to snag a sought-after reservation. Some renowned restaurants are booked weeks or months in advance. If you're a large group, always call ahead, as even restaurants that don't take reservations often will make exceptions for groups of six or larger.

But you can get lucky at the last minute if you're flexible—and friendly. Most restaurants keep a few tables open for walk-ins and VIPs. Show up for dinner early (5:30 pm) or late (after 9 pm) and politely inquire about any last-minute vacancies or cancellations.

If you're calling a few days ahead of time, ask whether you can be put on a waiting list. Occasionally, an eatery may ask you to call the day before your scheduled meal to reconfirm: don't forget, or you could lose out.

WHAT TO WEAR

In general, Chicagoans are neat but casual dressers; only at the top-notch dining rooms do you see a more formal style. But the way you look can influence how you're treated—and where you're seated. Generally speaking, jeans will suffice at most table-service restaurants in the $ to $$ range. Moving up from there, a few pricier restaurants require jackets. In reviews, we mention dress only when men are required to wear a jacket or a jacket and tie.

Note that shorts, sweatpants, and sports jerseys are rarely appropriate. When in doubt, call the restaurant and ask.

TIPPING AND TAXES

In most restaurants, tip the waiter 18%–20%. (To figure the amount quickly, just take 10% of the bill and double it.) Bills for parties of six or more sometimes include the tip already. The city's tax on restaurant food is 10.75%.

SMOKING

Smoking is prohibited in all enclosed public spaces in Chicago, including restaurants and bars.

WINE

Although some of the city's top restaurants still include historic French vintages, most sommeliers are now focusing on small-production, lesser-known new-world wineries. Some are even keeping their wine lists purposefully small, so that they can change them frequently to match the season and the menu. Half bottles are becoming more prevalent, and good wines by the glass are everywhere. Don't hesitate to ask for recommendations. Even restaurants without a sommelier on staff will appoint knowledgeable servers to lend a hand with wine selections.

PRICES

If you're watching your budget, be sure to ask the price of daily specials recited by the waiter or captain. The charge for specials at some restaurants is noticeably out of line with the other prices on the menu. Beware of the $10 bottle of water; ask for tap water instead. And always review your bill.

If you eat early or late, you may be able to take advantage of a prix-fixe deal not offered at peak hours. Most upscale restaurants offer great lunch deals, with special menus at cut-rate prices designed to give customers a true taste of the place.

Credit cards are widely accepted, but many restaurants (particularly smaller ones downtown) accept only cash. If you plan to use a credit card, it's a good idea to double-check its acceptability when making reservations or before sitting down to eat.

Prices in the reviews are the average cost of a main course at dinner or, if dinner is not served, at lunch.

USING THE MAPS

Throughout the chapter, you'll see mapping symbols and coordinates (✛) after property reviews. *To locate the property on a map, turn to the Chicago Dining and Lodging Atlas at the end of this chapter.* The first number after the (✛) symbol indicates the map number. Following that is the property's coordinate on the map grid.

BEST BETS FOR CHICAGO DINING

With thousands of restaurants to choose from, how will you decide where to eat? Fodor's writers and editors have selected their favorite restaurants by price, cuisine, and experience in the Best Bets lists below. In the first column, Fodor's Choice properties represent the "best of the best" in every price category. You can also search by neighborhood for excellent eats—just peruse the following pages.

Fodor's Choice ★

Alinea, $$$$, p. 189
Bar Toma, $$, p. 173
Big Star, $, p. 194
Blackbird, $$$$, p. 166
Boka, $$$, p. 190
Bristol, The, $$, p. 187
Frontera Grill, $$, p. 180
Girl & the Goat, $$$, p. 167
Hopleaf, $$, p. 199
Hot Doug's, $, p. 193
Little Goat, $$, p. 169
North Pond, $$$$, p. 191
Publican, The, $$$, p. 171
Purple Pig, $$, p. 183
Slurping Turtle, $$, p. 185
Spiaggia, $$$$, p. 177
Trenchermen, $$, p. 195
Urban Belly, $, p. 193
Yusho, $$, p. 193

Best by Price

$

Belly Shack, p. 192
Big Star, p. 194
Hot Doug's, p. 193
Manny's Coffee Shop and Deli, p. 165
Smoque BBQ, p. 199
Urban Belly, p. 193
Xoco, p. 187

$$

Au Cheval, p. 166
Avec, p. 166
Balena, p. 189
Bristol, The, p. 187
Frontera Grill, p. 180
Hopleaf, p. 199
Little Goat, p. 169
Nightwood, p. 201
Purple Pig, p. 183
Slurping Turtle, p. 185
Trenchermen, p. 195
Yusho, p. 193

$$$

Arun's, p. 198
Aria, p. 160
Boka, p. 190
Girl & the Goat, p. 167
Mercat a la Planxa, p. 165
mk, p. 182
NoMI Kitchen, p. 175
Publican, The, p. 171

$$$$

Alinea, p. 189
Blackbird, p. 166
Grace, p. 168
L2O, p. 191
North Pond, p. 191
Sixteen, p. 184
Spiaggia, p. 177
TRU, p. 177

Best by Cuisine

AMERICAN

DMK Burger Bar, p. 196
Hot Doug's, p. 193

BARBECUE

Honky Tonk Barbeque, p. 201
Smoke Daddy, p. 195
Smoque BBQ, p. 199

CHINESE

Han 202, p. 203
Lao Sze Chuan, p. 203
Phoenix, p. 203

FRENCH

Bistro Campagne, p. 199
Everest, p. 161
Henri, p. 162
Le Bouchon, p. 188

ITALIAN

Coco Pazzo, p. 179
Osteria via Stato, p. 182
Spiaggia, p. 177

JAPANESE

Kamehachi, p. 174
Slurping Turtle, p. 185
Takashi, p. 189
Yusho, p. 193

LATIN AMERICAN

Province, p. 171

MEXICAN

Big Star, p. 194
Frontera Grill, p. 180
Salpicon, p. 176
Xoco, p. 187

NEW AMERICAN

Bristol, The, p. 187
Lula Café, p. 193
mk, p. 182
Naha, p. 182

PIZZA

Bar Toma, p. 173
Piece, p. 195
Spacca Napoli Pizzeria, p. 200

SOUTHERN

Big Jones, p. 198
Table Fifty-Two, p. 177

SPANISH

Café Iberico, p. 179
Mercat a la Planxa, p. 165
Tavernita, p. 185
Vera, p. 172

STEAKHOUSE

David Burke's Primehouse, p. 179
Gibsons Bar & Steakhouse, p. 174
Keefer's, p. 181

THAI

Arun's, p. 198

VEGETARIAN

Green Zebra, p. 168
MANA Food Bar, p. 194
Native Foods Café, p. 194

Best by Experience

BAR FOOD

Hopleaf, p. 199
Publican, The, p. 171

BEST BREAKFAST

Ina's, p. 168
Lou Mitchell's, p. 169
Manny's Coffee Shop and Deli, p. 165

BEST BRUNCH

Ina's, p. 168
Lula Café, p. 193
Mindy's Hot Chocolate, p. 189
North Pond, p. 191

BEST HOTEL DINING

Café des Architectes, p. 173
L2O, p. 191
Sixteen, p. 184

BEST VIEWS

Everest, p. 161
NoMI Kitchen, p. 175
North Pond, p. 191
Plaza, The, p. 163
Sixteen, p. 184
Spiaggia, p. 177

BUSINESS DINING

NoMI Kitchen, p. 175
Sepia, p. 172
Spiaggia, p. 177
Tavern at the Park, p. 163

CAFÉ EATS

Café Selmarie, p. 199
Julius Meinl Café, p. 197
Milk & Honey, p. 194
Pierrot Gourmet, p. 175
Sweet Maple Café, p. 202

CHICAGO CLASSICS

Billy Goat Tavern, p. 178
Gene & Georgetti, p. 180
Mr. Beef, p. 182
Twin Anchors Restaurant & Tavern, p. 192

CHILD-FRIENDLY

Ann Sather, p. 196
Café Selmarie, p. 199
Ed Debevic's, p. 179
Eleven City Diner, p. 164
Scoozi!, p. 184
Smoque BBQ, p. 199

GASTROPUBS

Hopleaf, p. 199
Longman & Eagle, p. 193
Publican, The, p. 171

GOOD FOR GROUPS

Fogo de Chao, p. 180
Plaza, The, p. 163
Parthenon, The, p. 170

HOT SPOTS

Au Cheval, p. 166
Avec, p. 166
Big Star, p. 194
Blackbird, p. 166
Girl & the Goat, p. 167
Paris Club, p. 183
Trenchermen, p. 195
Yusho, p. 193

LATE-NIGHT DINING

Au Cheval, p. 166
Avec, p. 166
Big Star, p. 194
Hopleaf Bar, p. 199
Maude's Liquor Bar, p. 169
Purple Pig, The, p. 183

MOST INNOVATIVE

Alinea, p. 189
Graham Elliot, p. 180
Moto, p. 170

PRE-THEATER MEAL

312 Chicago, p. 160
Atwood Café, p. 160
Boka, p. 190
Henri, p. 162

QUIET MEAL

Arun's, p. 198
Les Nomades, p. 174

SPECIAL OCCASION

Everest, p. 161
L2O, p. 191
North Pond, p. 191
TRU, p. 177

9

HOW TO EAT LIKE A LOCAL

Many travelers head to Chicago with an epicurean checklist in mind, a must-eat of Chicago foodstuff. The truth of course is that it's impossible to truly taste Chicago in just one visit; even locals are constantly learning about new chefs and stumbling upon old eateries they just didn't notice before. Here are some Chicago foods to place at the top of your list.

PIZZA

The undisputed deep-dish king of the country, Chicago-style pizza is often imitated, but there's nothing like tasting the thick crust, mountains of cheese, and chunky tomato sauce in its birthplace. You'll see tourists flock to the big-name places, but these aren't tourist traps—they're the real deal. And if deep-dish isn't your thing, there are many pizza joints that offer Chicago-style thin-crust pizza, with a firm, crunchy crust that some locals will claim is just as good, if not better, than its deep-dish cousin.

HOT DOGS

Most cities have plenty of indiscriminate hot dog vendors, but in Chicago, the hot dog is an art. For traditional Chicagoans the condiment list is set in stone: yellow mustard, white onions, sweet pickle relish, sport peppers, and celery salt. Any requests for ketchup will not only mark you as a tourist, but might even garner a few scoffs. No need to get picky with a place—wander into any vendor with a proud "Vienna Beef" sign in the window and you'll be satisfied; be on the lookout for places that offer both classic recipes and other rarer meat combinations (antelope hot dogs anyone?).

THE STEAK HOUSE

For a slightly more upscale Chicago dining experience, you'll find a huge number of steak houses, all ready for you to sit back and indulge in a classic porterhouse and a glass of red wine. You can hardly walk a block in River North or the Gold Coast without spotting a dark, classy steak house inviting you to kick-it old school. Midwestern farms from neighboring states mean a constant influx of fresh, local beef to the city, making a steak dinner a perfect way to begin and/or end any trip.

MEXICAN FOOD

If you're in Chicago, you're a long way from Mexico, but that doesn't mean you have to eat like it. Mexican immigrants have been making Chicago their home for decades and bringing their culinary traditions with them. Pilsen is the neighborhood for tortilla factories, Hispanic grocery stores, and plenty of soulful, inexpensive Mexican cooking. For a hip Chicago spin on south-of-the-border cuisine, head to Near North, where you'll find an array of eclectic eateries that offer a bold and unforgettable taste of Mexico.

ASIAN FUSION

For a cheap and classic Asian meal, head to Chinatown, but more adventurous eaters should travel north for a taste of Bill Kim's "belly" empire. The chef currently has three restaurants all

over the city, each transforming standard Asian fare with unexpected and delicious twists. The original, Urban Belly (Avondale), offers casual Asian street food, while Belly Shack (Logan Square) meshes Kim's Korean roots with his wife's Puerto Rican heritage, and Belly Q (West Loop) goes the Korean-BBQ route.

ITALIAN BEEF

Yep, more meat. These delicious sandwiches are found wherever hot dogs are sold, but they certainly deserve some attention of their own. Slices of seasoned roast beef are layered with sweet peppers and onions on a long roll with varying amounts of meat sauce, creating a messy and classic Chicago meal. There's heated debate over where to get the best sandwich (every local has their opinion), but don't fret—your options are virtually endless and you'd have to try hard to find a place that doesn't deliver the goods.

9

(top left) Grilled sirloin served at Atwood Café, a Loop favorite; (top right) beer and a bratwurst, a classic Chicago combo; (bottom right) the namesake dish at Don Pedro Carnitas in Pilsen

RESTAURANT REVIEWS

Listed alphabetically within neighborhood.

THE LOOP, INCLUDING SOUTH LOOP AND WEST LOOP

Business, theater, and shopping converge in the Loop, the downtown district south of the Chicago River distinguished by the elevated train that circles it. Long the city's financial center, the Loop is commuter central for inbound office workers. It's also Chicago's historic home of retail, where the flagship Marshall Field's (now Macy's) once made State Street a great shopping destination. As a theater district, the Loop hosts the Tony-awarded Goodman Theater, which mounts its own productions, as well as the Oriental, Cadillac Palace, and Bank of America theaters, which generally run Broadway tours. In feeding these diverse audiences, Loop restaurants run the gamut from quick-service to high-volume and special-occasion. Beware noontime and pre-curtain surges (you'll need a reservation for the latter). It tends to clear out on weekends, and many restaurants close up shop.

A short trip to the West Loop—particularly Randolph Street—is where you'll find Chicago's restaurant row. Nearly every celebrity chef in town has set up post here, including Grant Achatz, Paul Kahan, Stephanie Izard, and Graham Elliot. Whether you're craving pizza and pasta or tapas and tacos, the flavors here are sure to satisfy any discerning foodie.

THE LOOP

$$ ITALIAN 🍴 **312 Chicago.** Part handy hotel restaurant, part Loop power diner, and all Italian down to its first-generation chef, Luca Corazzina, 312 Chicago earns its popularity with well-executed dishes that range from rigatoni Bolognese to Tuscan *bistecca*—grilled rib-eye steak with arugula and potato wedges. We're tempted to carbo-load on the house-baked bread alone but make sure to save room for Italian-inspired desserts like vanilla cheesecake with polenta cookies and Fabbri Amarena cherries. Note that upstairs tables are quieter. [$] *Average main: $25* ✉ *Hotel Allegro, 136 N. LaSalle St., Loop* ☎ *312/696–2420* 🌐 *www.312chicago.com* 🕒 *No lunch Sat.* ⊕ *1:C6.*

$$$ ASIAN FUSION 🍴 **Aria.** Can't decide between Korean, Chinese, or Indonesian? Take your globe-trotting taste buds to Aria, which roams the world's larder with abandon: tuna sashimi, free-range chicken breast seasoned with Indonesian spices, Thai-inspired Maryland striped sea bass, Mongolian lamb rib, and pork and shiitake dumplings with cognac hoisin. Among generous freebies, tandoori-baked naan bread with Indian-inspired dipping sauces arrives before the meal, and a trio of exotically spiced potatoes comes with the entrées. In the convivial lounge, a full sushi bar also caters to adventurous appetites. [$] *Average main: $31* ✉ *Fairmont Chicago, 200 N. Columbus Dr., Loop* ☎ *312/444–9494* 🌐 *www.ariachicago.com* ⊕ *1:F6.*

$$ AMERICAN 🍴 **Atwood Café.** The Loop can be all business, even after hours, but you'll find an enclave of personality at this restaurant in the Hotel Burnham. Mahogany columns, cherrywood floors, gold café curtains, and curvy

The annual Taste of Chicago draws crowds.

banquettes provide color, and floor-to-ceiling windows let in the light, which is especially welcome at breakfast. The mostly American menu includes reliables like pan-roasted chicken breast, roasted brisket, and thick pork chops, peppered by contemporary fare such as seared scallops with saffron emulsion, and root-beer braised duck leg. $ *Average main: $25* ⊠ *Hotel Burnham, 1 W. Washington St., Loop* ☎ *312/368–1900* ⊕ *www.atwoodcafe.com* ✛ *4:F1*.

$$$$
SEAFOOD
✕ **Chicago Catch 35.** You can eavesdrop on advertising types who do the after-five mix-and-mingle at this spot on the ground floor of the Leo Burnett Building. When it comes to the menu, there's no shortage of choices: fish and shellfish entrées come in various preparations, from grilled to seared to baked. Classic seafood appetizers are delivered with a twist, such as coconut- and beer-battered shrimp, giant surf clams with ginger-chili aioli, and seared scallop pot stickers. The restaurant, with its marble, granite, and beautifully set woodwork, is an inviting space to relax, and the multilevel dining room provides plenty of eye candy, plus glimpses of the Chicago River beyond. There is a local jazz trio on Tuesday through Saturday evenings. $ *Average main: $42* ⊠ *35 W. Wacker Dr., Loop* ☎ *312/346–3500* ⊕ *www.catch35.com* ⊘ *No lunch weekends* ✛ *1:D6*.

$$$$
FRENCH
✕ **Everest.** No one expects romance at the top of the Chicago Stock Exchange, but Everest does its best to throw you a curve wherever and whenever. Consider the trip: two separate elevators whisk you 40 stories up, where there are sweeping views of the city's sprawl westward. Then there's the food. It's French, but with an Alsatian bent—a nod to chef Jean Joho's roots. He just might add Alsace Riesling to his risotto. And finally, there's the space, where modern sculpture

melds with art nouveau. The whole experience, from the polished waiters to the massive wine list, screams "special occasion!" It's prix fixe only. [$] *Average main: $145* ✉ *440 S. LaSalle St., 40th Floor, Loop* ☎ *312/663–8920* 🌐 *www.everestrestaurant.com* ✍ *Reservations essential* 👔 *Jacket required* 🕒 *Closed Sun. and Mon. No lunch* ✥ *4:F2.*

$$ STEAKHOUSE 🍴 **The Grillroom Chophouse & Winebar.** If you're going to see a performance at the Bank of America Theatre across the street, you're close enough to dash over here for a drink at intermission (we love the lengthy by-the-glass wine selections). Pre- and post-curtain, the clubby confines fill with show-goers big on beef, though there are also ample raw bar, seafood, and pasta choices. For the most relaxing experience, plan to come after the theatergoers have left for Act I. [$] *Average main: $25* ✉ *33 W. Monroe St., Loop* ☎ *312/960–0000* 🌐 *www.grillroom-chicago.com* 🕒 *No lunch weekends* ✥ *4:F2.*

$ SOUTHERN 🍴 **Heaven on Seven.** Every day is Mardi Gras at Heaven on Seven, which pursues a good time all the time. The restaurant, with two locations in the city, has a menu centered around a daring collection of hot sauces, and the food is plentiful and filling. Some guests find the menu too spicy for their kids, but would go back for the well-priced Mardi Gras jambalaya, fried oyster po'boy, cheese grits, and chicory coffee. Cheddar-jalapeño biscuits and chocolate peanut-butter pie are great menu bookends. [$] *Average main: $12* ✉ *111 N. Wabash Ave., 7th Floor, Loop* ☎ *312/263–6443* 🌐 *www.heavenonseven.com* 🕒 *Closed Sun. No dinner except on 3rd Fri. of month* [$] *Average main: $12* ✉ *600 N. Michigan Ave., 2nd Floor, Near North* ☎ *312/280–7774* 🌐 *www.heavenonseven.com* ✥ *1:E6.*

$$$$ FRENCH 🍴 **Henri.** A little French decadence never hurt anyone, so prepare to get the white-tablecloth treatment at this elegant French-American fine dining restaurant overlooking Millennium Park. Inspired by architect Louis Henri Sullivan, the spacious salon is accented with refined turn-of-the-20th-century European touches like seafoam-green silk drapes and crystal chandeliers. Indulge in opulent starters like raw oysters or smoked steak tartare before moving on to heartier classics like Dover sole with braised leek, salsify, and brown butter, and bouillabaisse packed with lobster, shrimp, clams, mussels, saffron broth, and rouille. Oenophiles will appreciate the exclusive and biodynamic wine list, with plenty of wines by the glass. [$] *Average main: $40* ✉ *18 S. Michigan Ave., Loop* ☎ *312/578–0763* 🌐 *www.henrichicago.com* ✥ *1:E6.*

$$$$ STEAKHOUSE 🍴 **Morton's, The Steakhouse.** Morton's in the Gold Coast neighborhood can be more fun, but this location, a spin-off of the Gold Coast original, is one of Chicago's best steak houses. Excellent service and a good wine list add to the principal attraction: beautiful, hefty steaks cooked to perfection. A kitschy tradition mandates that everything on the menu, from gargantuan Idahos to massive slabs of beef, is brought to the table for your approval before you order. White tablecloths create a classy feel. It's no place for the budget conscious, but for steak lovers it's a 16-ounce (or more) taste of heaven. [$] *Average main: $42* ✉ *65 E. Wacker Pl., Loop* ☎ *312/201–0410* 🌐 *www.mortons.com* 🕒 *No lunch Sat. or Sun.* ✥ *1:E6.*

$$ 🍴 **The Plaza.** Location trumps service at The Plaza, where a seat outside
AMERICAN in summer, in full view of Millennium Park, is among the best in the
FAMILY city. The waitstaff is not always on top of things—grin and bear it with another drink from the outdoor bar. The menu includes small plates, soups and salads, and main courses, with a something-for-everyone selection. The burgers are first-rate, as is the more ambitious seasonal fare such as duck tacos and American Kobe beef sliders. A grab-and-go window supplies park picnics. In winter, the restaurant shuts down to make way for the ice-skaters warming up in the rink right outside the picture windows. [$] *Average main: $25* ✉ *Millennium Park, 11 N. Michigan Ave., Loop* ☎ *312/521–7275* 🌐 *www.parkgrillchicago.com* ⏲ *Closed Nov.–May* ✥ *1:F6.*

$$ 🍴 **Petterino's.** Theatergoers to the Goodman, the Palace, and the Ori-
ITALIAN ental pack Petterino's (next door to the Goodman lobby) nightly. Not that the Italian supper club with framed caricatures of celebs past and present couldn't stand on its own merits. The deep, red-velvet booths make a cozy stage for old-school classics like steak Diane, shrimp *de jonghe* (covered in garlicky bread crumbs then baked), tomato bisque, chicken vesuvio, as well as prime steaks, seafood, and pastas. Although the show is usually next door, on Monday nights Petterino's hosts live open-mike cabaret. [$] *Average main: $20* ✉ *150 N. Dearborn St., Loop* ☎ *312/422–0150* 🌐 *www.petterinos.com* ✥ *1:D6.*

$$ 🍴 **Russian Tea Time.** Exotica is on the menu and in the air at this spot
RUSSIAN that's favored by visitors to the nearby Art Institute and the Symphony Center. Mahogany trim, samovars, and balalaika music set the stage for dishes from Russia and neighboring republics (the owners hail from Uzbekistan), including Ukrainian borscht, *blinis* (small, savory pancakes) with salmon caviar, Moldavian meatballs, and classic beef Stroganoff. Chilled vodka flights (three shots) certainly do help the herring go down. [$] *Average main: $15* ✉ *77 E. Adams St., Loop* ☎ *312/360–0000* 🌐 *www.russianteatime.com* ✥ *4:G2.*

$$ 🍴 **Tavern at the Park.** Given its unique take on American and Italian
AMERICAN classics and the splendid view of Chicago's Millennium Park, it would be a mistake to pass up this near–Michigan Avenue gem. Noise from the bar carries up to the second floor, giving this spacious restaurant a lively feel. The prime-rib sliders and expertly fried calamari are perfect starters; mains run the gamut from seared scallops to butternut squash ravioli or the slow-roasted prime rib. Though many favor the warm blueberry-apple bread pudding for dessert, the chocolate-chip ice-cream sandwich (big enough for four to share) shouldn't be missed. Don't plan on a weekday lunch without a reservation—local businesspeople have made this their hangout. [$] *Average main: $25* ✉ *130 E. Randolph St., Loop* ☎ *312/552–0070* 🌐 *www.tavernatthepark.com* ⏲ *Closed Sun.* ✥ *1:F6.*

$$ 🍴 **Trattoria No. 10.** It's hard to camouflage a basement location, but
ITALIAN Trattoria No. 10 gives it a good go with terra-cotta colors, arched entryways, and quarry-tile floors, all of which evoke Italy. Pre-theater diners crowd in for the house specialties such as ravioli filled with seasonal stuffings like asparagus and provolone, classic antipasti selections like caprese salad with vine-ripened tomatoes and *bufala* mozzarella,

Chef Paul Kahan works his magic in the kitchen at Blackbird.

and substantial *secondi piatti* like grass-fed New York strip steak with artichoke-gorgonzola risotto. Meanwhile, cheap chowsters elbow into the bar for the $15 nibbles buffet served 5–7:30 pm Tuesday through Friday with a $6 drink minimum. [$] *Average main: $24* ✉ *10 N. Dearborn St., Loop* ☎ *312/984–1718* 🌐 *www.trattoriaten.com* 🕓 *Closed Sun. No lunch Sat.* ✥ *4:F1.*

SOUTH LOOP

$ AMERICAN FAMILY 🍴 **Eleven City Diner.** For all its great food, Chicago is not a big deli town, which endears Eleven City Diner, an old-school deli and family restaurant in the South Loop, to the locals. You can get breakfast all day (latkes and lox are popular, as is the "hoppel poppel": scrambled eggs with salami, potatoes, onions, and peppers) but deli staples like matzo-ball soup and pastrami and corned-beef sandwiches shouldn't be missed. There are also classic diner options including burgers, and soda-fountain floats and malts from the staff soda jerk. Breaking from the deli tradition, Eleven City also sells beer, wine, and cocktails. In keeping with its theme, there's an old-fashioned candy counter on your way out. [$] *Average main: $10* ✉ *1112 S. Wabash Ave., South Loop* ☎ *312/212–1112* 🌐 *www.elevencitydiner.com* ✥ *4:G3.*

$ AMERICAN 🍴 **Epic Burger.** After walking through exhibits at the Art Institute, follow the local college crowd to this order-at-the-counter eatery. While the ambience is kitschy (think bright orange walls and televisions broadcasting cartoons), the food is, as owner David Friedman describes it, "more mindful." Friedman sources fresh, natural beef for Epic's burgers, which are shaped by hand, cooked to order, and served atop fresh buns on non-petroleum-based plates. Burger add-ons include Wisconsin cheese, nitrate-free bacon, and an organic fried egg. While this might mean the meal costs more than other counter-service spots, it all goes back to Friedman's goal of building a greener burger joint—and it all just seems to taste extra good. [$] *Average main: $9* ✉ *517 S. State St., South Loop* ☎ *312/913–1373* 🌐 *www.epicburger.com* ✥ *4:G3.*

$$ ITALIAN

🍴 **Gioco.** The name means "game" in Italian, and the restaurant fulfills the promise not with venison, but in the spirit of having fun. The decor is distressed-urban, with brick walls and well-worn hardwood floors—the space is said to have been used by the Chicago gangsters of the early 1900s as a gambling house—but the menu is comfort-Italian, with rustic fare like homemade linguine with Manila clams, grilled lamb chops, and roasted sea bass with puttanesca sauce. It's a cozy, neighborhoody spot that keeps the regulars coming back. [$] *Average main: $25* ✉ *1312 S. Wabash Ave., South Loop* ☎ *312/939–3870* 🌐 *www.giocorestaurant.com* 🕒 *No lunch Sat.* ✥ *4:G4.*

$ AMERICAN

🍴 **Manny's Coffee Shop and Deli.** Kibitzing counter cooks provide commentary as they sling chow—thick corned-beef and pastrami sandwiches, soul-nurturing matzo-ball soup, and piping-hot potato pancakes—at this classic Near South Side cafeteria. Though they occasionally bark at dawdlers, it's all in good fun—though looking for seating in two teeming, fluorescent-lighted rooms is not, so you're best off coming at off hours. Don't try to pay the hash-slingers; settle up as you leave. [$] *Average main: $12* ✉ *1141 S. Jefferson St., South Loop* ☎ *312/939–2855* 🌐 *www.mannysdeli.com* ✍ *Reservations not accepted* 🕒 *Closed Sun.* ✥ *4:E4.*

$$$ SPANISH

🍴 **Mercat a la Planxa.** Inside the Blackstone Hotel, this Catalan-inspired restaurant offers a stylish respite from Michigan Avenue. Philadelphia-based chef Jose Garces returned to his native Chicago for Mercat, where he created a menu of small and midsize plates of Catalan *sopas* (soup), cured meats, *fideos* (Spanish pasta), and a variety of vegetable sides, all of which are great for sharing. Be sure to try the *cocas*, flat breads topped with a range of ingredients, from bean purée, shrimp, and chorizo to short ribs and horseradish. Don't let the small, cramped bar at the entrance fool you; once you walk up the stairs, you'll encounter an airy dining room with a view of Grant Park. [$] *Average main: $29* ✉ *638 S. Michigan Ave., South Loop* ☎ *312/765–0524* 🌐 *www.mercatchicago.com* ✥ *4:G3.*

WEST LOOP

$$ MODERN AMERICAN

🍴 **694 Wine & Spirits.** This smart wine bar is proof that you don't need more than a minimal kitchen (limited to what will fit behind the bar's counter) to thrill foodies. Simple snacks, such as a flight of various butters accompanied by artisan bread and slices of salami from Armandino Batali (Mario's pop) complement the real draw: hand-picked wines from around the world. The two-story, cork-lined space really comes into its own later in the evening. For a more low-key experience, come on a weeknight as a precursor to dinner at a nearby West Loop restaurant. [$] *Average main: $19* ✉ *694 N. Milwaukee Ave., West Loop* ☎ *312/492–6620* 🌐 *www.694wineandspirits.com* 🕒 *No lunch. Closed Sun.* ✥ *3:E6.*

$$ DINER 🍴 **Au Cheval.** A menu packed with burgers, fries, and chopped liver might sound like your classic dive, but Au Cheval is no greasy spoon. Exposed brick, dim lighting, and antique-inspired fixtures give off a sultry feel, and rich takes on classic American diner dishes like crispy fries with Mornay sauce, garlic aioli, and fried farm egg, and griddled bratwurst with smashed potatoes and roasted-garlic gravy satisfy your cravings. Don't be fooled by the $10 price tag on the single cheeseburger—it's gigantic, and totally delicious. Like a good diner, the restaurant is open late, but with the added bonus of a solid craft beer and cocktail list to carry you through the night. [$] *Average main: $16* ✉ *800 W. Randolph St., West Loop* ☎ *312/929–4580* 🌐 *www.auchevalchicago.com* ✍ *Reservations not accepted* ✥ *4:D1.*

$$ MEDITERRANEAN 🍴 **Avec.** Go to this Euro-style wine bar when you're feeling gregarious; the rather stark space has seating for only 48 people, and it's a tight fit. The results are loud and lively, though happily the shareable fare—a mix of small and large Mediterranean plates, such as chorizo-stuffed dates and whole roasted fish from a wood-burning oven—is reasonably priced. Avec is as popular as its next-door neighbor Blackbird (and run by the same people), and only early birds are guaranteed tables. The doors open at 3:30 pm. [$] *Average main: $18* ✉ *615 W. Randolph St., West Loop* ☎ *312/377–2002* 🌐 *www.avecrestaurant.com* ✍ *Reservations not accepted* ⏲ *No lunch* ✥ *1:A6.*

$$ KOREAN BARBECUE 🍴 **Belly Q.** Chef-owner Bill Kim expands his Belly empire (Urban Belly, Belly Shack) with this third iteration: a trendy Korean barbecue house on the edge of Randolph's restaurant row. Secure a seat at one of the six grill tables—if you can—to engage in the authentic live fire action of DIY grilling over an open flame, with meats like short ribs and spicy lemongrass chicken. But bystanders can still order grilled meats safely on the sidelines, along with dishes like tea-smoked duck breast, steamed Chinese barbecue buns with hoisin sauce, and savory Asian pancakes stuffed with seafood or goat cheese. If you have the courage, warm up with a few drinks and head to the restaurant's karaoke lounge to belt out a few songs post-meal. [$] *Average main: $25* ✉ *1400 W. Randolph St., West Loop* ☎ *312/563–1010* 🌐 *www.bellyqchicago.com* ⏲ *No lunch Sat.* ✥ *4:B1.*

$$$$ MODERN AMERICAN Fodor's Choice ★ 🍴 **Blackbird.** Being cramped next to your neighbor has never been as fun as it is at this hot spot run by award winning chef Paul Kahan. Celebs pepper the sleek see-and-be-seen crowd that comes for the creative dishes and exceptional cocktail list. While the menu changes constantly, you'll always find choices that highlight seasonal ingredients, such as rack of lamb with leeks and *spigarello* (wild broccoli) in spring, or grilled sturgeon with mustard spaetzle in winter. It all plays out against a minimalist backdrop of white walls, blue-gray banquettes, and aluminum chairs. Reservations aren't required, but they might as well be; the dining room is typically booked solid on Saturday night. [$] *Average main: $38* ✉ *619 W. Randolph St., West Loop* ☎ *312/715–0708* 🌐 *www.blackbirdrestaurant.com* ✍ *Reservations essential* ⏲ *Closed Sun. No lunch Sat.* ✥ *1:A6.*

$$$$ STEAKHOUSE 🍴 **Carmichael's Chicago Steak House.** The look here is old-time Chicago—oak and brass, black-and-white photographs, and waiters wearing black vests and ties—though the true vintage is late 1990s. We forgive them the

The dining room at Atwood Café

ruse because of the well-priced (under $40) Angus steaks, which make this one of the more reasonable top-tier steak houses in town (and one of the most popular for basketball fans heading to the United Center for a game). Orange-sesame glazed salmon or pan-seared scallops are good non-beef options. Live music lures diners to the lush garden in summer. $ *Average main: $38* ⊠ *1052 W. Monroe St., West Loop* ☏ *312/433–0025* ⊕ *www.carmichaelsteakhouse.com* ⊘ *No lunch weekends* ✛ *4:C2.*

$$ ✕ **De Cero Taqueria.** Sometimes you want celebrity chef–made regional
MEXICAN Mexican, and sometimes you just want a really good taco. For the latter, as well as zesty margaritas, a convivial setting, and lick-the-mortar-clean guacamole, grab a table at De Cero, the Mexican standout on Randolph Street's restaurant row. The highlight of the menu is the taco list. Each of 15 tacos is priced individually and made to order for a mix-and-match meal. Top choices include chipotle chicken, duck confit with corn salsa, and braised lamb with queso fresco, cucumber crema, and mint. The restaurant is wood-tables-and-benches casual and can get loud; beat the crowds by phoning ahead for reservations, especially on weekends. $ *Average main: $15* ⊠ *814 W. Randolph St., West Loop* ☏ *312/455–8114* ⊕ *www.decerotaqueria.com* ⊘ *Closed Sun. and Mon. No lunch Sat.* ✛ *4:D1.*

$$$ ✕ **Girl & the Goat.** Bravo's *Top Chef* Season 4 champion Stephanie
MEDITERRANEAN Izard's highly anticipated restaurant lives up to the hype, serving shar-
Fodor's Choice able plates of seasonal Mediterranean fare. The antithesis of fussy,
★ Girl & the Goat's rustic decor features communal butcher tables, dark antique fixtures, and an open kitchen. Dishes are grouped into straightforward categories—vegetable, fish, and meat—and range from marinated English pea pods with buttermilk-balsamic vinaigrette

to roasted pig's face with tamarind and cilantro sauces. Not surprisingly, goat-centric plates take prominence, including a goat-liver mousse with pickled rhubarb and blackberry mostarda. Desserts are also inventive, like the indulgent goat cheese cake with hazelnut crunch, candied beets, and cajeta. $ *Average main: $32* ✉ *809 W. Randolph St., West Loop* ☎ *312/492–6262* ⊕ *www.girlandthegoat. com* ⌖ *Reservations essential* ⊘ *No lunch* ✛ *4:D1.*

$$$$
ECLECTIC

✕ **Grace.** Breakout culinary star Curtis Duffy (veteran of Avenues and Alinea) makes a home for his inventive white-tablecloth cuisine at this West Loop stunner. Duffy artfully plates delicate, hyper-seasonal dishes on two tasting menus—flora and fauna themed—for $185 each. For a fine dining institution, the menu is refreshingly vegetable heavy, where parsnip with dried pineapple, tarragon ice, and fennel mingle alongside poached chestnut, Perigord truffle, roasted-almond milk, and red sorrel. If you can spare the extra cash, opt for the wine pairings—though the nonalcoholic pairings are just as exceptional. $ *Average main: $185* ✉ *652 W. Randolph St., West Loop* ☎ *312/234–9494* ⊕ *www.grace-restaurant.com* ⊘ *Closed Sun. and Mon.* ✛ *1:A6.*

$
VEGETARIAN

✕ **Green Zebra.** Chef Shawn McClain took the vegetable side dish and ran it up the marquee, earning raves nationwide for giving vegetables the gourmet treatment. But don't call it vegetarian, McClain says—it's "flexitarian," mostly veggie but not strictly so. The result gives good-for-you vegetables the starring role in a sleek shop suave enough to seduce the most ardent meat lovers. Chef de cuisine Jon DuBois changes the menu seasonally with dishes such as roast beets with horseradish foam, Burrata cheese with smoked radicchio, or sunchoke ravioli with melted goat cheese and hazelnuts. The occasional fish dish—like pan-seared trout—makes do for carnivores. $ *Average main: $12* ✉ *1460 W. Chicago Ave., West Loop* ☎ *312/243–7100* ⊕ *www.greenzebrachicago.com* ✛ *3:C5.*

$
DINER

✕ **Ina's.** Locals don't call owner Ina Pinkney Chicago's "Breakfast Queen" for nothing. Dishes like vegetable hash, "scrapple" (polenta mixed with cheddar and black beans, fried into a disk, and served with eggs and chorizo), and Southern fried chicken and waffles at breakfast, and warm goat-cheese salads, chicken potpie, and homemade meatloaf at lunch offer something for everyone, with a homey warmth that keeps the regulars coming back for more. It's extra convenient for the Randolph Street loft dwellers, so Ina's regularly generates a queue, especially on weekends. $ *Average main: $9* ✉ *1235 W. Randolph St., West Loop* ☎ *312/226–8227* ⊕ *www.breakfastqueen.com* ⊘ *No dinner* ✛ *4:C1.*

$$
BISTRO

✕ **La Sardine.** We don't know if the sardine reference was meant to telegraph the seating arrangements, but, yes, it's snug here. Still, the solid menu of traditional French bistro favorites—including warm goat-cheese salad, bouillabaisse, and roasted chicken with potato purée—seems to put everyone in a convivial mood. Save room for decadent desserts like crème brûlée and warm apple tart, which are bound to evoke envious looks from adjacent diners. $ *Average main: $22* ✉ *111 N. Carpenter St., West Loop* ☎ *312/421–2800* ⊕ *www.lasardine.com* ⊘ *Closed Sun. No lunch Sat.* ✛ *4:C1.*

Friends chat over wine and snacks at Pierrot Gourmet.

$$
ECLECTIC
FAMILY
Fodor's Choice
★

✕ **Little Goat.** Following the wild success of her flagship restaurant, the Girl & the Goat, *Top Chef* alum Stephanie Izard switches gears with this all-day counterpart. The diner/bakery/bar is open from early morning until late night, serving up comfort foods like fresh pastries, soups and sandwiches, burgers, and classic supper-club entrées. Expect a rotating seasonal menu heavy on Americana nostalgia with a splash of Izard's eclectic touches, such as brandade and pork belly Benedict with kimchi-topped biscuits, and a sloppy joe made from goat with rosemary slaw on a squish-squash roll. One of the bonuses of having an in-house bakery is a killer dessert menu, so save room for sweets. $ *Average main: $20* ✉ 820 W. Randolph St., West Loop 🕾 312/888–3455 ⊕ *www.littlegoatchicago.com* ⌕ *Reservations not accepted* ✛ 4:D1.

$
DINER

✕ **Lou Mitchell's Restaurant.** Shelve your calorie and cholesterol concerns; Lou Mitchell's heeds no modern health warnings. The diner, a destination close to Union Station since 1923, specializes in high-fat breakfasts and comfort-food lunches. You can start the day with eggs and home-made hash browns by the skillet; later in the day this is the place to take a break for meatloaf and mashed potatoes. Though you'll almost certainly have to have deal with out-the-door waits, staffers dole out doughnut holes and Milk Duds to pacify hunger pangs. $ *Average main: $8* ✉ 565 W. Jackson Blvd., West Loop 🕾 312/939–3111 ⊕ *www. loumitchellsrestaurant.com* ▭ *No credit cards* ☉ *No dinner* ✛ 4:E2.

$$
BISTRO

✕ **Maude's Liquor Bar.** A classic French menu of dishes like chicken liver mousse and French onion fondue is the only thing traditional about this sexy Randolph Street hotspot. Dim lighting, reclaimed vintage touches, and an indie soundtrack set the mood for sipping on cocktails like the Smokey Violet Smash and snacking on small plates like warm marinated mushrooms with swiss chard. If your table is feeling particularly indulgent, spoil yourselves with the towering Maude's Plateaux seafood platter for $155, filled with a ridiculous sampling of lobster, crab, mussels, oysters, shrimp, and ceviche large enough to share among a party of four. $ *Average main: $25* ✉ *840 W. Randolph St., West Loop* ☎ 312/243-9712 ⊕ *www.maudesliquorbar.com* ☾ No lunch ✢ 4:D1.

$$$$
ECLECTIC

✕ **Moto Restaurant.** Mad-scientist chef Homaro Cantu has become a cult figure in the Windy City. His restaurant-cum-laboratory is sequestered in the city's still-working meatpacking district. Many of the techniques perfected in the basement kitchen have been put to use in the chef's work with NASA and corporate America. Inside the minimalist dining room patrons pay for the privilege of being guinea pigs. The spectacle begins with the menu—daily changing multicourse menus are available in 10- and 20-course options—which is printed on edible paper. Flavors are seared into wine glasses by an industrial laser, rigatoni is fashioned from lychee puree, and frozen flapjacks are "cooked" table-side on a liquid-nitrogen-filled box. The awe-factor is big but the portions are small. $ *Average main: $175* ✉ *945 W. Fulton Market, West Loop* ☎ 312/491–0058 ⊕ *www.motorestaurant.com* ☖ *Reservations essential* 👔 *Jacket and tie* ✢ 4:D1.

$$
MODERN
EUROPEAN

✕ **Nellcôte.** Inspired by the French Riviera mansion where the Rolling Stones recorded "Exile on Main Street," Nellcôte blends European opulence with raw bohemian chic. Most of the menu is driven by the restaurant's in-house flour mill, which is used to make everything from pizzas (topped with ingredients like fennel sausage, local ramps, and burrata) and pastas (hand-cut taglioni and orecchiette) to desserts (baba au rhum and apple pound cake). For a quieter dining experience, avoid Friday and Saturday nights, when the restaurant transforms into a sceney club with loud thumping music. $ *Average main: $19* ✉ *833 W. Randolph St., West Loop* ☎ 312/432–0500 ⊕ *www.nellcoterestaurant.com* ✢ 4:D1.

$$$$
ECLECTIC

✕ **Next Restaurant.** Grant Achatz's buzzworthy sophomore effort is big on concept: the restaurant completely transforms itself every three months to focus on a unique theme. The opening menu, Paris 1906, paid homage to famed chef Auguste Escoffier's tenure at the Ritz Paris. Subsequent incarnations have transported guests to Kyoto in autumn or explored the adult interpretation of childhood. The tasting menu ranges in price from $65 to $365, depending on the date and time you book; tickets are paid for in advance, nonrefundable, and available only online—or via resale markets at highly inflated prices against season ticket holders. Tables accommodate two to four guests, with the exception of the six-person kitchen table. $ *Average main: $110* ✉ *953 W. Fulton Market, West Loop* ☎ 312/226–0858 ⊕ *www.nextrestaurant.com* ☖ *Reservations essential* ☾ *Closed Mon. and Tues. No lunch* ✢ 4:D1.

$
GREEK
FAMILY

✕ **The Parthenon.** The claim to fame here is the *saganaki*, the Greek flaming-cheese dish, which the Parthenon says it invented in 1968, thereby introducing "*opa!* " to the American vocabulary. So, ordering the flaming cheese here is a rite of passage for any first-time visitors, and it's delicious, but the regulars return to this Greektown hot spot for lamb and chicken preparations, often skewered on sticks. In fact, the restaurant also takes credit for being the first to serve gyros stateside.

Smoked golden trout at The Publican

True or not, indulge the legends and stick to these classics. Be sure to ask for pita bread and a side of *tzatziki*, a yogurt-and-cucumber-based dipping sauce. The food is cheap and the atmosphere is festive and family-friendly. [$] *Average main: $13* ✉ *314 S. Halsted St., West Loop* ☎ *312/726–2407* 🌐 *www.theparthenon.com* ✣ *4:D2.*

$$ MODERN AMERICAN

🍴 **Province.** Many restaurants source local ingredients and recycle, but chef-owner Randy Zweiban takes sustainability a step further by housing his restaurant in a gold LEED-certified building; the dining space itself shows its natural side discreetly, with cork-top tables and floors and a petrified-wood installation. Expect seasonal menus that spotlight Latin and Spanish flavors alongside contemporary American dishes, like rotisserie chicken with ancho mole, chorizo with romesco, or seviche with preserved lemons and olives. There are a variety of small and medium-size plates, and entrées come in full and half sizes. [$] *Average main: $23* ✉ *161 N. Jefferson St., West Loop* ☎ *312/669–9900* 🌐 *www.provincerestaurant.com* 🕒 *Closed Sun. No lunch Sat.* ✣ *4:E1.*

$$$ AMERICAN Fodor's Choice ★

🍴 **Publican Restaurant.** Don't call this beer-focused hot spot a gastropub—chef Paul Kahan (of Blackbird fame) prefers "beer hall" (though wine is available, too). Certainly the long communal tables, at which beer connoisseurs sample from a selection hovering around 100 brews, give the bustling space the air of an Oktoberfest celebration. Chef de cuisine Brian Huston's seafood- and pork-focused menu does give an elevated nod to pub fare, though, and diners share shucked oysters and just-fried pork rinds before tucking into grilled, smoky country ribs, fried perch, and beef-heart tartare. Arrive early or call for a reservation—seating fills up fast. [$] *Average main: $35* ✉ *837 W. Fulton Market, West Loop* ☎ *312/733–9555* 🌐 *www.thepublicanrestaurant.com* ✣ *4:D1.*

$$$ MODERN AMERICAN 🍴 **Sepia.** The name may evoke nostalgia for the building's gritty past as a print shop, but Sepia is thoroughly forward-thinking in both its design (glassed-in chandeliers and leather-topped tables) and its simple, seasonal dishes created by chef Andrew Zimmerman. Order some country pâté for the table while you review the menu, which includes appetizers like seared scallops and entrées such as skate served with cauliflower and a raisin-caper sauce. A well-chosen, international wine list and thoughtfully prepared classic cocktails satisfy oenophiles and mixologists alike. Though reservations can be hard to come by for dinner, seats at the communal tables are first-come, first-served. [$] *Average main: $30* ✉ *123 N. Jefferson St., West Loop* ☎ *312/441–1920* 🌐 *www.sepiachicago.com* ✥ *4:E1.*

$$ SPANISH 🍴 **Vera.** Food and wine go hand-in-hand at this Spanish wine bar run by husband-and-wife team Mark and Elizabeth Mendez. Championing for what she calls a "sherry revolution," Elizabeth curates a progressive wine list, including a flowing tap system that pours three rotating varietals to complement Mark's Latin-inspired cuisine. Naturally, a wine bar demands charcuterie and cheese, but Vera's personality truly shines in small plates like lamb and beef *albondigas* (meatballs) with whipped ricotta, and anchovies with pickled garlic and celery leaves. Vegetarians will also feel at home with thoughtful dishes like fried artichokes with Idiazabal cheese and beer garlic vinaigrette. [$] *Average main: $22* ✉ *1023 W. Lake St., West Loop* ☎ *312/243–9770* 🌐 *www.verachicago.com* ⏲ *Closed Mon.* ✥ *4:C1.*

$$ ITALIAN 🍴 **Vivo.** Vivo was trendy on this west-of-the-Loop stretch long before Randolph Street's restaurant row got hot, and it still draws a crowd. It may be slightly more about the scene—brick walls, black ceiling, open wine racks, and lots of pretty people—than the cuisine, but you'll find reliable Italian fare as well as a fun evening. You can't go wrong with bruschetta, osso buco, house-made ravioli, and free-range lamb chops. [$] *Average main: $25* ✉ *838 W. Randolph St., West Loop* ☎ *312/733–3379* 🌐 *www.vivo-chicago.com* ⏲ *No lunch weekends* ✥ *4:D1.*

$$ MODERN AMERICAN 🍴 **West Town Tavern.** While it's a little off the beaten path, you can trust that your cabbie will know how to get you here, and it's worth the trip. The handsome wood bar and brick walls may be tavern staples, but the open kitchen and oversize dining-room mirror give the (correct) impression that you'll find more than just cheeseburgers. The menu delivers with a mix of upscale comfort foods (try the house-made potato chips with balsamic syrup and Parmesan cheese—and pizza-style flat breads) and gussied-up fare like duck confit and pepper-crusted beef tenderloin in a zinfandel sauce. The focused wine list globe-trots for value. [$] *Average main: $21* ✉ *1329 W. Chicago Ave., West Loop* ☎ *312/666–6175* 🌐 *www.westtowntavern.com* ⏲ *Closed Sun. No lunch* ✥ *3:D5.*

NEAR NORTH AND RIVER NORTH

A couple of decades ago, when Rick Bayless and his wife, Deann, opened Frontera Grill, River North was still seen as a dicey part of town. In fact, anything west of Michigan Avenue was suspect. How times change. Now the mammoth Chicago Merchandise Mart anchors River North, where art and design trades patronize the area's hot spots, including Slurping Turtle, Tavernita, and Paris Club, as well as its refined restaurants, such as mk, Naha, and Topolobampo. Meanwhile the nearby Near North district, home to shopping's Magnificent Mile and the residential Gold Coast, specializes in upscale restaurants that suit the clientele like a bespoke suit. The Magnificent Mile is the land of posh hotels (Sofitel and Park Hyatt) and their sleek dining rooms (Café des Architectes and NoMI Kitchen, respectively), as well as stand-alone stars like TRU, Spiaggia, and Les Nomades. Head north on Wells Street to Old Town, or expect to spend a fair bit on dinner.

NEAR NORTH

$$ ✕ **Allium.** Believe it or not, one of Chicago's finest hot dogs is hiding
AMERICAN at luxury hotel Four Seasons. Long heralded as a fine dining destination (formerly Seasons), the hotel recently gave its restaurant a much-needed face-lift and a new, casual backdrop. Seasonal ingredients drive the comfort-heavy menu, which includes dishes like bison tartare with waffle chips and beer mustard, Wagyu short-rib sliders, and the famed Chicago-style hot dog with "housemade everything." End with nostalgic sweets like blood-orange "Dreamsicle" cupcakes, s'mores, or a bag of apple fritters. The white-tablecloth vibe may have dropped, but be wary of your wallet—prices tend to add up quickly here. $ *Average main: $22* ⊠ *The Four Seasons Hotel, 120 E. Delaware Pl., Near North* ☎ *312/799–4900* ⊕ *www.alliumchicago.com* ✛ *1:E2.*

$$ ✕ **Bar Toma.** Italian culinary master Tony Mantuano (of Spiaggia and
ITALIAN Terzo Piano) has reclaimed the Water Tower tourist trap area as Chi-
FAMILY cago's landmark piazza with his neighborhood pizzeria, Bar Toma.
Fodor'sChoice Visitors stroll in throughout the day to snack on Roman-style *fritti*
★ (fried appetizers) and hand-rolled mozzarella, sip imported wines, and feast on artisanal wood-fired pizzas made with premium ingredients like house-cured *guanciale* (Italian bacon) and rapini. If your schedule only allots for a grab-and-go bite, stop in for a quick gelato or *mamaluchi* (Italian doughnuts stuffed with lemon marmalade). $ *Average main: $21* ⊠ *110 E. Pearson St., Near North* ☎ *312/266–3110* ⊕ *www. bartomachicago.com* ✛ *1:E2.*

$$ ✕ **Bistrot Margot.** We love this Old Town bistro for its faithfully executed
BISTRO menu, budget-friendly prices, and Parisian Art Nouveau interior, even if we do have to sit rather close to our neighbors. Chef-owner Joe Doppes whips up silky chicken-liver mousse, succulent *moules marinières* (mussels in white wine), escargots simmered in rich garlic butter, and expertly seared fish in amandine sauce. The additional seating on the second floor has more of an intimate French country-home feel. Bistrot Margot continues to draw the crowds, so come early or make a reservation. $ *Average main: $23* ⊠ *1437 N. Wells St., Near North* ☎ *312/587–3660* ⊕ *www.bistrotmargot.com* ✛ *3:G3.*

$$$ ✕ **Café des Architectes.** French cuisine sometimes gets knocked for being
FRENCH too rich, heavy, and expensive, but this is an image that Southern-born chef Greg Biggers is doing his best to prove wrong at this stylish restaurant on the ground floor of the Sofitel hotel. Biggers serves guinea hen with a black garlic confit and maitake mushrooms and pairs Alaskan halibut with baby spinach and fingerling potatoes, highlighting seasonal ingredients sourced from local farmers. Standout sweets, such as the sampler of miniature Parisian desserts or the Meyer lemon

panna cotta, are worth the indulgence. Try the three-course prix-fixe market selection menu for $39; it's a steal. $ *Average main: $29* ✉ *Sofitel Chicago, 20 E. Chestnut St., Near North* ☎ *312/324–4000* ⊕ *www.cafedesarchitectes.com* ✛ *1:E2.*

$$$ ✕ **Ditka's.** NFL Hall-of-Famer Mike Ditka was one of only two coaches
STEAKHOUSE to take the Bears to the Super Bowl. Sure, it was back in 1985, but Bears fans have long memories, and they still love "Da Coach" as well as his clubby, sports-themed restaurant where local performer John Vincent does dead-on impressions of Frank Sinatra, Tuesday through Saturday. The dark-wood interior and sports memorabilia are predictable, but the menu clearly aims to please a large and diverse audience. Café staples (salads, fish) and bar food (burgers, pot roast) join steak-house fare (steaks, chops) and a few unexpected indulgences (sustainably sourced seafood dishes). $ *Average main: $31* ✉ *Tremont Hotel, 100 E. Chestnut St., Near North* ☎ *312/587–8989* ⊕ *www.mikeditkaschicago.com* ✛ *1:E2.*

$ ✕ **Fox & Obel.** Skip the tourist-trap funnel-cake fare at Navy Pier and opt
CAFÉ instead for this riverside gourmet market just a block away. The prepared fine and organic foodstuffs are treated with reverence, and although service is cafeteria-style, selections are decidedly more sophisticated. The signature club with applewood-smoked bacon and basil-pesto mayo is a winner, as are the salmon burger and pretty much everything else we've tried. The adjacent market bistro has table service and is open for dinner daily and brunch on the weekend. $ *Average main: $12* ✉ *401 E. Illinois St., Near North* ☎ *312/410–7301* ⊕ *www.fox-obel.com* ✛ *1:G4.*

$$$$ ✕ **Gibsons Bar & Steakhouse.** Chicago movers and shakers mingle with
STEAKHOUSE conventioneers at Gibsons, a lively, homegrown, Gold Coast steak house renowned for overwhelming portions, good service, and celebrity spotting. Generous prime steaks and chops are the focus of the menu, but there are plenty of fish options, too, including planked whitefish and massive Australian lobster tails. Desserts are huge: the gargantuan slice of carrot cake could feed a table of four. $ *Average main: $45* ✉ *1028 N. Rush St., Near North* ☎ *312/266-8999* ⊕ *www.gibsonssteakhouse. com* ☖ *Reservations essential* ✛ *1:D1.*

$$ ✕ **Kamehachi.** It seems like there's a sushi spot on practically every cor-
JAPANESE ner in Chicago, but when Kamehachi opened in Old Town in 1967 it was the first, though the restaurant has since moved down the block to a loftier space complete with sushi bar, upstairs lounge, and flowering garden (in season). Quality fish, updated decor, and eager-to-please hospitality keep fans returning. Behind the busy sushi bar, chefs manage both restaurant orders and the many take-out calls from neighbors. Combination sushi meals, which include maki rolls, nigiri sushi, and miso soup, are a relative bargain, running from $16 to $30. $ *Average main: $14* ✉ *1531 N. Wells St., Near North* ☎ *312/664–3663* ⊕ *www. kamehachi.com* ✛ *3:G3.*

$$$$ ✕ **Les Nomades.** Intimate and elegant doesn't make headlines, but Les
FRENCH Nomades holds a torch for tender refinements. Wood-burning fireplaces and original art warm the dining rooms of this Streeterville brownstone, and the carefully composed menu of French food includes the usual suspects, such as duck consommé, but also more contemporary fare, such as warm asparagus with crispy poached egg, and earthy indulgences

Fanciful desserts at Pierrot Gourmet

like roasted squab breast with crispy sweetbreads. You can compose your own prix-fixe dinner from the menu; four courses cost $115; five courses cost $130. [$] *Average main: $115* ✉ *222 E. Ontario St., Near North* ☎ *312/649–9010* 🌐 *www.lesnomades.net* ✍ *Reservations essential* 👔 *Jacket required* ⏰ *Closed Sun. and Mon. No lunch* ✣ *1:F4.*

$$$ MODERN AMERICAN

🍴 **NoMI Kitchen.** Suits and ties are no longer de rigueur at the Park Hyatt's NoMI Kitchen, a seventh-floor lifestyle-focused concept that goes along with NoMI Lounge, NoMI Garden, and NoMI Spa. The warm space includes wood tables with leather accents, an open kitchen, and a locally sourced, approachable menu rooted in French techniques. Dessert is not to be missed, with seasonally changing sweets that range from house-made ice creams and sorbets to delectable cookies and tarts. Fans of Isamu Noguchi's *Wintry Branches* will be relieved to find that the sculpture now resides in the main dining room. [$] *Average main: $35* ✉ *Park Hyatt Hotel, 800 N. Michigan Ave., Near North* ☎ *312/239–4030* 🌐 *www.hyatt.com/gallery/nomi/kitchen.html* ✣ *1:E3.*

$$ FRENCH

🍴 **Pierrot Gourmet.** Despite the legions of shoppers on Michigan Avenue, there are few casual cafés to quell their collective hunger, making this bakery-patisserie-café a welcome neighbor. Lunches center on upscale greens like herb salad with olives and Parmesan, along with open-face *tartine* sandwiches on crusty, house-made sourdough. Break mid-afternoon for a *tarte flambé*—an Alsatian flatbread with bacon and onions—accompanied by a glass of Riesling. Solo diners are accommodated at the magazine-strewn communal table. Meals are served all day long. The upscale Peninsula Hotel runs Pierrot, accounting for both the high quality and the high cost. [$] *Average main: $15* ✉ *Peninsula Hotel, 108 E. Superior St., Near North* ☎ *312/573–6749* 🌐 *www.peninsula.com/chicago* ✣ *1:E3.*

$$ ✕ **Pump Room.** Once famous for its star-studded clientele like Frank
MODERN Sinatra and Humphrey Bogart, the iconic Pump Room was on the verge
AMERICAN of extinction before world class chef Jean-Georges Vongerichten and
legendary hotelier Ian Schrager revived the Chicago landmark with a
glitzy redesign and concept overhaul. The result is a sceney enclave
mirroring Vongerichten's award-winning New York restaurant, ABC
Kitchen. Diners can dig into whole-wheat flatbreads and homemade
pastas topped with seasonally-driven ingredients like Meyer lemon
cream and asparagus pesto, while keeping an eye out for the celebri-
ties that are often spotted at the bar. $ *Average main: $24* ⊠ *Public
Chicago, 1301 N. State Pkwy., Near North* ☎ 312/229-6740 ⊕ *www.
pumproom.com* ✛ *3:H4.*

$$$ ✕ **RL.** Power brokers, moneyed locals, and Michigan Avenue shoppers
AMERICAN keep the revolving doors spinning at RL, the initials of designer Ralph
Lauren who lent his name and signature *soigné* style to the eatery that
adjoins his Polo/Ralph Lauren store. Inside, cozy leather banquettes are
clustered under hunt-club-style art hung on wood-paneled walls. The
menu of American classics, including crab Louis, Dover sole in lemon
butter, and steak Diane flamed in the dining room, perfectly suits the
country-club-in-the-city setting. $ *Average main: $30* ⊠ *115 E. Chicago
Ave., Near North* ☎ 312/475-1100 ⊕ *www.rlrestaurant.com* ✛ *1:E3.*

$$ ✕ **Salpicón.** Anyone who does authentic Mexican in Chicago operates
MODERN in the shadow of Frontera Grill's Rick Bayless—which makes it easier
MEXICAN for those in the know to snag a table at Salpicón. Chef Priscila Sat-
koff grew up in Mexico City, and her renditions of mole poblano and
grilled fish with salsa fresca have unforced flair. Wash 'em down with
a belt of one of 100 tequilas or choose from the extensive selection of
vintage wines. Once you try the Mexican-style Sunday brunch, with
dishes like skirt steak and eggs, you'll have a hard time going back to
eggs Benedict. $ *Average main: $24* ⊠ *1252 N. Wells St., Near North*
☎ *312/988-7811* ⊕ *www.salpicon.com* ☾ *No lunch* ✛ *1:G4.*

$$$ ✕ **Shanghai Terrace.** As precious as a jewel box, and often as pricey, this
CANTONESE red, lacquer-trimmed 70-seat restaurant hidden away in the Peninsula
Hotel reveals the hotelier's Asian roots. Come for upscale dim sum, styl-
ishly presented, and luxury-laden dishes such as steamed fish, XO duck,
miso-braised pork belly, and lobster consommé. A patio that seats up to
60 during warmer months lets you revel in a relaxing meal four stories
above the madding crowds of Michigan Avenue. Though fans admire
the attentive, professional service, some warn that diners with larger
appetites might leave feeling unsatisfied. $ *Average main: $29* ⊠ *Peninsula Hotel, 108 E. Superior St., 4th fl., Near North* ☎ 312/573-6744
⊕ *www.peninsula.com/chicago* ☾ *Closed Mon.* ✛ *1:E3.*

$$$ ✕ **Signature Room at the 95th.** When you've got the best view in town and
AMERICAN a lock on special-occasion dining, do you need to be daring with the
food? The Signature Room keeps it simple, making a formal affair of
dishes such as rack of lamb and sautéed salmon while everyone ogles
the skyline views from the John Hancock's 95th floor. If you come at
lunch, the daytime light lets you see Lake Michigan; the $20 lunch
buffet is a steal, but only available on Fridays and Saturdays. Sunday
brunch is lavish—and pricey. $ *Average main: $34* ⊠ *John Hancock*

Center, 875 N. Michigan Ave., 95th fl., Near North ☎ 312/787–9596 🌐 www.signatureroom.com ⊕ 1:E2.

$$$$ ITALIAN Fodor's Choice ★ 🍴 **Spiaggia.** Refined Italian cooking dished alongside three-story picture-window views of Lake Michigan make Spiaggia one of the city's top eateries. The tiered dining room guarantees good sight lines from each table. Chef Tony Mantuano prepares elegant, seasonal dishes such as housemade gnocchi with black truffles, wood-roasted veal tenderloin, or cabbage-wrapped black cod with scallops. Oenophiles consider the wine list to be scholarly. For Spiaggia fare minus the luxury price tag, try lunch or dinner at the casual Cafe Spiaggia next door. [$] *Average main: $40 ✉ 980 N. Michigan Ave., Near North ☎ 312/280–2750 🌐 www.spiaggiarestaurant.com ✍ Reservations essential 👔 Jacket and tie ⏲ No lunch ⊕ 1:E2.*

$$$ SOUTHERN 🍴 **Table Fifty-Two.** If it feels like everyone is a regular at chef Art Smith's Gold Coast restaurant, they very well might be. Oprah's former personal chef is not short on friends and admirers, yet newcomers who score a reservation feel just as welcome in the cozy, country-home environs, particularly when the complimentary cheese biscuits arrive. While the menu strays to Asia and Europe, at its core is a formidable Southern lineup of dishes such as Lowcountry shrimp with stone-ground grits, a fried-green-tomato napoleon, and fried chicken (a Sunday- and Monday-only special). Save room for Smith's hummingbird cake, a homey banana-and-pineapple concoction topped with cream-cheese frosting. If you're in the neighborhood without a reservation, walk in and see whether the chef's counter is available: the restaurant keeps five seats open in front of the pizza oven. [$] *Average main: $29 ✉ 52 W. Elm St., Near North ☎ 312/573–4000 🌐 www.tablefifty-two.com ✍ Reservations essential ⏲ No lunch ⊕ 3:G4.*

$$$$ FRENCH 🍴 **TRU.** More than a decade after Tru opened under the direction of former chef/partners Rick Tramonto and Gale Gand, the award-winning progressive French restaurant still retains its critical acclaim under the helm of new executive chef Anthony Martin. Expect stylish, contemporary dishes such as truffled lobster and rib eye with grilled foie gras, which complement the dining room's gallery-like feel (an Andy Warhol hangs on the wall). The caviar platter is served on a stunning coral display and the 14-course prix-fixe menu, priced at $158, is enough luxury to make anyone feel like royalty. Several of those courses are dessert, so save space. [$] *Average main: $158 ✉ 676 N. St. Clair St., Near North ☎ 312/202–0001 🌐 www.trurestaurant.com ✍ Reservations essential 👔 Jacket required ⏲ Closed Sun. No lunch ⊕ 1:F3.*

$$ AMERICAN 🍴 **Viand.** Ebullient chef-owner Steve Chiappetti's personality is written all over Viand, a lively restaurant and bar that's a breath of fresh air after designer-centric Michigan Avenue, just a half block away. Expect Midwestern flavors prepared with contemporary flair, like free range roasted chicken with crispy red potatoes and lemon garlic, and seared pork chop with chili spiced potatoes and fire- roasted sweet peppers. Don't miss the grilled lamb, the four-cheese ravioli with truffle sauce, and a chat with the friendly chef. Adjacent to a Courtyard by Marriott, the restaurant serves breakfast, lunch, and dinner, and the bar is a busy meeting spot. [$] *Average main: $22 ✉ 155 E. Ontario St., Near North ☎ 312/255–8505 🌐 www.viandchicago.com ⊕ 1:F4.*

9

The Signature Room on the 95th floor in the John Hancock building offers unparalleled views.

RIVER NORTH

$ AMERICAN 🍴 **Billy Goat Tavern.** The late comedian John Belushi immortalized the Goat's short-order cooks on *Saturday Night Live* for barking, "No Coke! Pepsi!" and "No fries! Cheeps!" at customers. And you can still hear the shtick at this subterranean hole-in-the-wall favored by reporters from the nearby *Tribune* and the *Sun-Times*. Griddle-fried "cheezborgers" are the featured chow at this super-cheap, friendly spot, and people-watching is a favorite sport. [$] *Average main: $4* ✉ *430 N. Michigan Ave., Lower Level, River North* ☎ *312/222–1525* 🌐 *www.billygoattavern.com* 💳 *No credit cards* ✣ *1:E5.*

$$ WINE BAR 🍴 **Bin 36.** This hip hybrid—a fine-dining establishment, a lively wine bar, and an excellent cheese purveyor—serves wine and cheese pretty much any way you want it. For wine, you can choose by the bottle, glass, half glass, and as flights of multiple 2½-ounce tastings. For cheese, options are by individual sample or multiples—or as an ingredient, as in the lamb meatballs stuffed with Manchego cheese, romesco, and mint. The menu similarly encourages sampling, with lots of small-plate grazing choices. Entrées, such as roasted whole duck and ahi tuna carpaccio, are helpfully listed with wine recommendations. An all-glass west wall and 35-foot ceilings lend a lofty look to the sprawling space, which can be noisy. Since it's open all day, it's also a good choice for between-standard-mealtime nibbles. [$] *Average main: $27* ✉ *339 N. Dearborn St., River North* ☎ *312/755–9463* 🌐 *www.bin36.com* ✣ *1:D5.*

$$$ WINE BAR 🍴 **The Boarding House.** If the stunning 4,000 wine bottle installation on the ceiling of the dining room isn't a dead giveaway, this Old Town newcomer belongs to Master Sommelier and former *Check, Please!* host Alpana Singh. Wine is obviously a big deal here; a 30-page catalog

presents varietals from around the globe. Start in the first-floor wine bar, snacking on artisanal pizzas, charcuterie boards, and oysters on the half shell, before heading to the second-floor dining room to feast on a sumptuous menu of hazelnut-crusted short rib with five-spice sweet potato; Maine lobster poutine; and Strauss veal chop with citrus-braised endive, foie gras sauce, and watercress. $ *Average main: $32* ✉ *720 N. Wells St., Near North* ☎ *312/280-0720* ⊕ *www.boardinghousechicago. com* ⊘ *No lunch* ✛ *1:C3.*

$$
TAPAS ✗ **Cafe Iberico.** A Spanish expat from Galicia runs this tapas restaurant hailed by visiting Spaniards and local families, dating couples, and cheap chowhounds. It's easy to build a meal from the selection of small plates, which range from baked goat cheese to Spanish ham, grilled squid, skewered beef, and the classic *pulpo a la plancha* (grilled octopus with potatoes and olive oil)—most for under $10. This is a loud and boisterous spot, so be prepared for conviviality—but on weekends waits can stretch to hours. $ *Average main: $15* ✉ *737 N. LaSalle Blvd., River North* ☎ *312/573–1510* ⊕ *www.cafeiberico.com* ✛ *1:C3.*

$$$
TUSCAN ✗ **Coco Pazzo.** The spread of antipasti that greets you upon entrance into this Tuscan-inspired restaurant is a sign of good things to come. Coco Pazzo serves lusty, aggressively seasoned fare, such as homemade pasta with rabbit ragu, venison with pine nuts and currants, and wood-grilled Florentine steaks. Stop in at lunch for pizzas fresh from the wood-fired oven. The discreet but professional service goes far toward softening the open loft setting of exposed-brick walls and wood floors, but the scene is rather formal. The well-rounded, exclusively Italian wine list is impressive: *Wine Spectator* has lauded its selection ranging from popular to boutique producers. $ *Average main: $30* ✉ *300 W. Hubbard St., River North* ☎ *312/836–0900* ⊕ *www.cocopazzochicago.com* ⊘ *No lunch weekends* ✛ *1:C5.*

$$$$
STEAKHOUSE ✗ **David Burke's Primehouse.** New York celebrity chef David Burke runs Primehouse in the boutique James hotel, and though local reception was initially cautious—after all, what could a New Yorker teach a Chicagoan about steak?—the restaurant has been roundly embraced for its convivial setting and sense of playfulness—note the fill-your-own doughnuts for dessert. Cuts of meat include a 28-day, dry-aged rib eye and the bone-in filet mignon. The best seats are the red-leather booths along the walls. $ *Average main: $47* ✉ *The James Hotel, 616 N. Rush St., River North* ☎ *312/660–6000* ⊕ *www.davidburke.com/ restaurant_primehouse.html* ✛ *1:E4.*

$
AMERICAN
FAMILY ✗ **Ed Debevic's.** Gum-snapping waiters in garish costumes trade quips and snide remarks with customers at this tongue-in-cheek re-creation of a 1950s diner, but it's all good, clean fun (except perhaps when they dance on the counter without removing their shoes). The menu is deep and cheap with 10 different hamburgers, six chili preparations, four types of hot dogs, a large sandwich selection, and "deluxe plates" such as meatloaf, pot roast, and chicken-fried steak. Kids love it here; unlike a real 1950s diner, however, Ed's has a selection of cocktails and wines for their parents. $ *Average main: $10* ✉ *640 N. Wells St., River North* ☎ *312/664–1707* ⊕ *www.eddebevics.com* ⌨ *Reservations not accepted* ✛ *1:C4.*

$$$$ BRAZILIAN

🍴 **Fogo de Chão.** Gaucho-clad servers parade through the dining room brandishing carved-to-order skewered and grilled meats at this all-you-can-eat Brazilian churrascaria. First stop for diners is the lavish salad bar, then, using a plate-side chip, you signal green for "go" to bring on lamb, pork loin, ribs, and several beef cuts, stopped only by flipping your chip to red, for "stop." You can restart as often as you like. If that's not enough, there are starchy sides and desserts included in the $51.50 price as well; only drinks are extra. Compared to traditional steak houses, this carnivorous all-inclusive feast is somewhat of a bargain. Go on a busy night (Thursday, Friday, or Saturday) to ensure that the meat is tender and not dried out from reheating—this is also when the restaurant is the most fun and liveliest. [$] *Average main: $51* ✉ *661 N. LaSalle Blvd., River North* ☎ *312/932–9330* 🌐 *www.fogodechao.com* 🕑 *No lunch weekends* ✥ *1:C3.*

$$ MEXICAN

Fodor's Choice ★

🍴 **Frontera.** Devotees of chef-owner Rick Bayless queue up for the bold flavors of his distinct fare at this casual restaurant brightly trimmed in Mexican folk art. The menu changes monthly, but you can count on the freshest ingredients and options that include several varieties of guacamole, seafood, and ceviche, smaller "street food" options like soft or crispy tacos, and a variety of main courses typified by dishes like trout in cilantro sauce, red chili–marinated pork, and black-bean tamales filled with goat cheese. Bayless visits Mexico annually, updating his already extensive knowledge of regional food and cooking techniques, and he frequently takes his staff with him, ensuring that even the servers have an encyclopedic knowledge about the food. There are a limited number of reservations available, but most seats are first-come, first-serve—expect a wait. [$] *Average main: $24* ✉ *445 N. Clark St., River North* ☎ *312/661–1434* 🌐 *www.rickbayless.com/restaurants/grill.html* 🕑 *Closed Sun. and Mon.* ✥ *1:D5.*

$$$$ STEAKHOUSE

🍴 **Gene & Georgetti.** This old-school steak house, in business since 1941, is a Chicago institution. It thrives on the buddy network of high-powered regulars and celebrities who pop into the historic River North joint to carve up massive steaks, quality chops, and the famed "garbage salad"—a kitchen-sink creation of greens with vegetables and meats. The menu also includes Italian-American classics such as eggplant parmigiana and veal Vesuvio, along with simple seafood dishes like lobster tail, salmon, and whitefish. Service can be brusque if you're not connected, and prices can be steep, but the vibe is Chicago to the core. [$] *Average main: $40* ✉ *500 N. Franklin St., River North* ☎ *312/527–3718* 🌐 *www.geneandgeorgetti.com* 🕑 *Closed Sun.* ✥ *1:C4.*

$$$$ ECLECTIC

🍴 **Graham Elliot.** No chef gets to host his own food competition show without knowing how to throw some punches in the kitchen. The flagship restaurant of *MasterChef* host Graham Elliot puts contemporary fine dining in a sleek restaurant, with tunes of Wilco and the Police adding to the backdrop. Inventive market-fresh dishes such as scallop almondine and Wagyu beef make cameos on one of the two tasting menus ($125 and $165). The boisterous space with exposed-brick walls succeeds in combining a casual vibe with fine-dining flourish. Elliot calls it "bistronomic"; his fans simply call it good eating. [$] *Average main: $165* ✉ *217 W. Huron St., River North* ☎ *312/624–9975* 🌐 *www.grahamelliot.com* ✍ *Reservations essential* 🕑 *Closed Mon. and Tues.* ✥ *3:G5.*

$$ SEAFOOD 🍴 **GT Fish & Oyster.** The "GT" here stands for chef-partner Giuseppe Tentori, whose latest restaurant coup reinterprets the classic seafood shack as a refined, contemporary eatery, decorated with a few well-placed nautical details: think mounted shark jaws and rope buoy chandeliers. With an oyster bar spanning East and West coasts and dishes like smoked sunfish ceviche and a lobster roll stuffed with a full pound of chunky, sweet lobster, GT Fish & Oyster seems out to prove that this Chicago spot can tackle seafood as well as any coastal city. [$] *Average main: $23* ✉ *531 N. Wells St., River North* ☎ *312/929–3501* 🌐 *www.gtoyster.com* ✥ *1:C4.*

$$$ STEAKHOUSE 🍴 **Harry Caray's Italian Steakhouse.** Famed Cubs announcer Harry Caray died in 1998, but his legend lives on as fans continue to pour into the namesake restaurant where Harry frequently held court. Italian-American specialties including pastas and chicken Vesuvio share menu space with top-quality prime steaks and chops. The wine list has won a number of national awards. If you're looking for a classic Chicago spot to catch a game, the generally thronged bar serves items off the restaurant menu. Or follow the summer crowds to Navy Pier to the Harry Caray's outpost there. [$] *Average main: $30* ✉ *33 W. Kinzie St., River North* ☎ *312/828–0966* 🌐 *www.harrycarays.com* ✥ *1:D5.*

$$$$ JAPANESE 🍴 **Japonais.** Style and substance come together at sleek, chic Japonais. If the lengthy menu looks intimidating, you should feel free to trust the servers to direct you to savories such as lobster spring rolls, sweet-vinegar-seaweed salad, and a raft of winning maki-roll combinations including octopus with spicy tuna. A traditional seating area with tables is supplemented by a couch-filled lounge, where you can also order from the entire menu, and the indoor-outdoor bar downstairs has seasonal seating along the Chicago River—the latter, not surprisingly, gets super-crowded on weekends. [$] *Average main: $46* ✉ *600 W. Chicago Ave., River North* ☎ *312/822–9600* 🌐 *www.japonaischicago.com* ⏲ *No lunch weekends* ✥ *1:A3.*

$$$ SEAFOOD 🍴 **Joe's Seafood, Prime Steaks & Stone Crab.** Joe's may be far from the ocean, but the winning combination of stone crabs and other seafood, as well as prime steaks, has made this outpost of the original South Florida restaurant a continued success since it opened in 2000. The signature stone crabs are in season October to May, and the simple preparation—chilled with mustard sauce for dipping—suits the delicate meat best; they're served already cracked, but be prepared to get your hands dirty. There's plenty else on the menu all year-round, too, but the stone crabs are undeniably a star. The restaurant is almost as popular as the Miami original, so be sure to make reservations or expect a wait. [$] *Average main: $33* ✉ *60 E. Grand Ave., River North* ☎ *312/379–5637* 🌐 *www.joes.net/chicago* ✥ *1:E4.*

$$$ STEAKHOUSE 🍴 **Keefer's.** It's definitely a steak house, but acclaimed chef John Hogan's definition of a steak-house menu breaks convention by including his signature bistro fare, inventive daily specials (pray for the seafood-rich potpie), and plenty of fish offerings, as well as New York strips and hefty porterhouses. The circular room drops the he-man pose, too. All of which explains why Keefer's pulls the most diverse and gender-balanced crowd of the meat market. It's a good choice for all

types of occasions. [$] *Average main: $38* ✉ *20 W. Kinzie St., River North* ☎ *312/467–9525* 🌐 *www.keefersrestaurant.com* ⏲ *Closed Sun. No lunch Sat.* ✥ *1:D5.*

$$$ MODERN AMERICAN 🍴 **mk.** Foodies and fashionistas flock to owner-chef Michael Kornick's ultrahip spot for its sleek look and elegant menu. In a renovated former commercial paint facility, mk pairs its brick walls and soaring ceilings with fine linens, expensive flatware, and designer wine stems. Menus change with the season, and mains tend to hew to two or three dominant flavors—à la halibut with braised baby fennel and kalamata olives, and rabbit with glazed onions and stone-ground grits—rather than getting overcomplicated. It's not cheap, but it is special. [$] *Average main: $35* ✉ *868 N. Franklin St., River North* ☎ *312/482–9179* 🌐 *www.mkchicago.com* ⏲ *No lunch* ✥ *1:C2.*

$ AMERICAN 🍴 **Mr. Beef.** A Chicago institution for two-fisted Italian beef sandwiches piled with green peppers and provolone cheese, Mr. Beef garners citywide fans from area hard hats to restaurateurs and TV personalities. Service and setting—two indoor picnic tables and a dining rail—are fast-food no-nonsense, and the fare is inexpensive. This workingman's favorite is, go figure, located near River North's art galleries. [$] *Average main: $7* ✉ *666 N. Orleans St., River North* ☎ *312/337–8500* 💳 *No credit cards* ⏲ *Closed Sun. No dinner* ✥ *1:B3.*

$$ LATIN AMERICAN 🍴 **Nacional 27.** Named after the 27 nations south of the U.S. border, this pan-Latin restaurant serves a smattering of cross-cultural dishes from the Caribbean, Costa Rica, Mexico, Brazil, and Argentina. The menu is designed for sharing, with tapas like *tostones* (crispy plantains) and roasted corn fundido alongside seviches, tacos, and empanadas. It's best to come with a group if you want to order the slow-cooked pork Cubano with coconut rice, black beans, and plantains. The circular bar has its own following, independent of the food, if you're looking for innovative cocktails. And after 11 pm on weekends, the floor in the middle of the dining room is cleared for salsa and merengue dancing. [$] *Average main: $20* ✉ *325 W. Huron St., River North* ☎ *312/664–2727* 🌐 *www.nacional27chicago.com* ⏲ *Closed Sun. No lunch* ✥ *1:B3.*

$$$ MEDITERRANEAN 🍴 **Naha.** Cousins Carrie and Michael Nahabedian lend their name (well, the first two syllables, anyway) and considerable culinary and hospitality skills to this upscale venture. The clean space is done in shades of cream and sage, and the menu focuses on sophisticated and eye-catching dishes such as whole-roasted squab, honey-lacquered duck breast, or vanilla bean-roasted scallops. Wine is treated with reverence, from the well-chosen selection of vintages to the high-quality stemware. Solos and social-seekers can sit at the convivial bar and order from the main menu. [$] *Average main: $43* ✉ *500 N. Clark St., River North* ☎ *312/321–6242* 🌐 *www.naha-chicago.com* ⏲ *Closed Sun. No lunch Sat.* ✥ *1:D4.*

$$ ITALIAN 🍴 **Osteria via Stato.** It's no-brainer Italian here, where the shtick is to feed you without asking too many questions. If you opt for the $38.95 prix-fixe, you pick an entrée and waiters do the rest, working the room with several rounds of communal platters of antipasti, then pasta, followed by your entrée, and dessert. There's even a "just bring me wine"

program for $30 that delivers preselected Italian vino to your table throughout your meal. The results are savory enough, but Osteria shines brightest at making you feel comfortable. For a faster meal, dine in the pizza bar, which is also open for lunch. $ *Average main: $18* ✉ *620 N. State St., River North* ☎ *312/642–8450* ⊕ *www.osteriaviastato.com* ⊘ *No lunch* ✛ *1:D4.*

$$
MODERN FRENCH

✕ **Paris Club.** A stuffy French bistro this is not: lighting is low, music is loud, and space is usually tight, but that's what attracts the well-heeled diners to this see-and-be-seen restaurant, downstairs from the velvet-rope Studio Paris rooftop club. The restaurant feels clubby, too, but it takes food seriously, courtesy of acclaimed chef Jean Joho (Everest). Parisian favorites like coq au vin, country pâté, and steak frites mingle among modernized dishes like macaroni gratinée with ham, and lobster crostini with truffled scrambled egg. $ *Average main: $22* ✉ *59 W. Hubbard St., River North* ☎ *312/595–0800* ⊕ *www.parisclubchicago. com* ⊘ *No lunch* ✛ *1:D5.*

$$
PIZZA

✕ **Pizzeria Due.** Serving inch-thick pizzas in a comfortable, though well-worn dining room, Pizzeria Due is where everyone goes when they've found out that Uno, the original home of Chicago's deep-dish pizza up the street, has an hour-plus wait. Those in the know, though, say that Due is the place to order thin-crust pizza, while Uno is the traditional deep dish (both restaurants serve both styles). Regardless, Due quickly builds its own waiting list, and it's not unusual to wait for more than an hour here as well. The best strategy for dining out at either spot is to arrive early or opt to come at lunch. $ *Average main: $17* ✉ *619 N. Wabash Ave., River North* ☎ *312/943–2400* ⊕ *www. unos.com* ✛ *1:E4.*

$$
PIZZA

✕ **Pizzeria Uno.** Chicago deep-dish pizza got its start here in 1943, and both local and out-of-town fans continue to pack this Victorian brownstone for the filling pies—and the dim paneled rooms with reproduction light fixtures make the setting a slice of Old Chicago. Spin-off Due down the street handles the overflow. Plan on two thick, cheesy slices or less as a full meal. This is no quick-to-your-table pie, so do order salads and be prepared to entertain the kids during the inevitable wait. $ *Average main: $17* ✉ *29 E. Ohio St., River North* ☎ *312/321–1000* ⊕ *www.unos.com* ✛ *1:E4.*

$$
MEDITERRANEAN
Fodor's Choice
★

✕ **The Purple Pig.** The Magnificent Mile is known for many things—stunning architecture, historical landmarks, world-class shopping—but dining isn't usually one of them. An anomaly on the strip that both locals and tourists enjoy is Mediterranean wine bar the Purple Pig. Adventurous eaters will revel in the offal-centric dishes like pig's ear with crispy kale, pickled peppers, and fried egg, and roasted bone marrow with herbs, but vegetarians also get excited about dishes like salt-roasted beets with whipped goat cheeses and pistachio vinaigrette. This is a wine bar, and it's definitely worth exploring the hefty international wine list, which includes many affordable wines by the glass. $ *Average main: $18* ✉ *500 N. Michigan Ave, River North* ☎ *312/464–1744* ⊕ *www.thepurplepigchicago.com* ⌦ *Reservations not accepted* ⊘ *No breakfast* ✛ *1:E4.*

9

$$ AMERICAN 🍴 **Rockit Bar & Grill.** A classic tavern for the clubby set, Rockit Bar & Grill serves upscale bar food, pours creative cocktails, and aims to please everyone from celebrity visitors (who generally get the VIP treatment in the barroom upstairs) to picky kids. The extensive menu spans salads, sandwiches, and burgers (try the Kobe version), as well as comfort-food entrées like barbecue pulled pork and jerk seasoned mahi-mahi. Designer Nate Berkus gained a reputation working for Oprah; here he went rustic-chic, with tree-stump cocktail tables and antler chandeliers. After dinner, head upstairs to shoot some pool and check out the singles scene. Or move uptown and head to the Rockit Burger Bar offshoot in Wrigleyville, at 3700 N. Clark Street. [$] *Average main: $15* ✉ *22 W. Hubbard St., River North* ☎ *312/645–6000* 🌐 *www.rockitbarandgrill.com* ✥ *1:D5.*

$$ MODERN AMERICAN 🍴 **Sable Kitchen + Bar.** Sleek, stylish, and boasting one of the city's most accomplished mixology programs, it's almost hard to believe that Sable Kitchen + Bar is a hotel restaurant. This is definitely a dining destination in itself though, thanks to chef Heather Terhune—a "Top Chef: Texas" contestant—who serves contemporary American dishes like short-rib sliders with root-beer glaze, and lovingly crafted cocktails from seasoned mixologist Mike Ryan. Can't wait for dinner to dig into mini lamb burgers or duck confit flatbread? The restaurant offers all-day dining, so you can order dinner for breakfast. [$] *Average main: $22* ✉ *Hotel Palomar, 505 N. State St., River North* ☎ *312/755–9704* 🌐 *www.sablechicago.com* ✥ *1:E4.*

$$ ITALIAN FAMILY 🍴 **Scoozi!.** This ever-popular trattoria continues to attract a yuppie crowd after 5 pm and plenty of wandering suburbanites on the weekend. You'll recognize the restaurant by the gigantic tomato over the front door; inside, a sprawling, two-level dining room presents loft-chic looks of exposed-brick walls, open-truss ceiling, and steel garage doors. This place is nothing if not chameleon; groups love the shareable antipasti and pizzas, families with kids meld right into the cacophony, and couples find the energy relieves the focus on a boring date. [$] *Average main: $19* ✉ *410 W. Huron St., River North* ☎ *312/943–5900* 🌐 *www.leye.com* 🕒 *No lunch* ✥ *1:B3.*

$$$ SEAFOOD 🍴 **Shaw's Crab House.** Shaw's is, hands down, one of the city's best seafood spots, and though it's held an exalted position for years, the restaurant doesn't rest on its laurels. The kitchen stays on track, turning out famed classics like silky crab cakes and rich halibut from a menu that's been updated to also include sushi, maki, and fresh sashimi selections. The seafood salad served at lunch is big enough for two. Lunch, by the way, is rather a bargain, with well-priced entrées and $1 desserts. The restaurant does have something of a split personality, with a clubby main dining room in nautically themed loft digs as well as a lively exposed-brick bar where shell shuckers work extra hard. [$] *Average main: $29* ✉ *21 E. Hubbard St., River North* ☎ *312/527–2722* 🌐 *www.shawscrabhouse.com* ✥ *1:E5.*

$$$$ MODERN AMERICAN 🍴 **Sixteen.** Uninterrupted views of the landmark Wrigley Building, Lake Michigan, and the Chicago River make it easy to overlook the food at Sixteen—but you shouldn't. Located on the 16th floor (hence the name) of the sleek Trump International Hotel & Tower, the restaurant

serves chef Thomas Lents's unique take on modern American cuisine. Each tasting menu (4, 8, or 16 courses for $105, $150, or $210) tells a seasonal tale, with dishes such as pickled foie gras with hearth spices and borscht, and sturgeon with fennel, oyster, and caviar, followed by innovative desserts from pastry chef Patrick Fahy. Power lunching is still popular here, with the potato-leek soup remaining a menu staple. Breakfast, with house-made crumpets, jumbo lump crab omelet, and freshly squeezed juices, are an indulgent accompaniment to early-morning views over the lake. [$] *Average main: $210* ✉ *Trump International Hotel & Tower, 401 N. Wabash Ave., River North* ☎ *312/588–8000* 🌐 *www.trumpchicagohotel.com* ✥ *3:H6.*

$$ RAMEN Fodor's Choice ★ 🍴 **Slurping Turtle.** Slurping is not only allowed at this casual River North noodle shop—it's encouraged. Chef Takashi Yagihashi's ramen gained a cult following at his eponymous Bucktown restaurant—but it was available only on weekends for lunch; now the all-star ramen has a permanent home at Slurping Turtle. Bursting with umami, the ramen is almost a religious experience here—particularly the Shoyu ramen with egg noodle, classic Tokyo-style soy broth, braised pork shoulder, naruto, and bamboo shoots. Ramen portions are extremely generous, but it's worth making room for the *bincho* (white charcoal) grilled meats and yakitori snacks like duck-fat fried chicken. [$] *Average main: $18* ✉ *116 W. Hubbard St., River North* ☎ *312/464–0466* 🌐 *www.slurpingturtle.com* ✥ *1:C5.*

$$ ASIAN 🍴 **Sunda.** Named for the Sunda Shelf, an ancient Southeast Asian landmass, this trendy spot scours Asia for riotously flavorful fare. There's a full sushi bar, of course, but we're more impressed by dishes such as the oxtail pot stickers, garlicky lump crab noodles, and Australian Wagyu rib-eye with yuzu-chili-stuffed bone marrow. Well-executed cocktails complement the sweet, sour, and spicy dishes. The buzzing and expansive space cobbles together communal tables, traditional and lounge seating, and Asian antiques. [$] *Average main: $24* ✉ *110 W. Illinois St., River North* ☎ *312/644–0500* 🌐 *www.sundachicago.com* ✥ *1:D4.*

9

$$ JAPANESE FUSION 🍴 **SushiSamba.** It's been more than 10 years since the first SushiSamba opened in New York, serving a unique blend of Japanese, Peruvian, and Brazilian food and cocktails, and the Chicago outpost is still a happening scene. The trendy hot spot combines a nightclub vibe—dramatic multilevel design, freely flowing cocktails, the coed bathroom—with an inventive menu: all the usual sushi suspects are here, as well as miso-marinated Chilean sea bass, premium-grade Japanese Wagyu beef, and sashimi seviche such as salmon with blood orange and tomato. An all-weather rooftop lounge, popular with the late-night crowd, serves cocktails (including an impressive sake list) and the full menu. [$] *Average main: $24* ✉ *504 N. Wells St., River North* ☎ *312/595–2300* 🌐 *www.sushisamba.com* ✥ *1:C4.*

$$ SPANISH 🍴 **Tavernita.** Inspired by the bustling culture of San Sebastián, Tavernita is actually two spaces: a sleek contemporary Spanish restaurant and a buzzing corner bodega called Barcito. Tavernita has been drawing rave reviews since it opened. The main restaurant draws sceney crowds with club music and signature kegged cocktails, and chef Ryan Poli's menu entertains foodies with dishes like ceviche with celery, tomatoes,

Creative cuisine at Alinea

ginger, cilantro, and orange, and pork-belly *bocadillos* (sandwiches) with apple jam and pickled red onions on a brioche bun. If you just want a quick bite, though, you can sidestep to Barcito for stand-and-eat *pinxtos* (bar snacks) like *croquetas* with Iberico ham and saffron aioli, and marinated olives. If you get lost in translation, the menu has a handy glossary of Spanish food terminology to help you find your way. [$] *Average main: $26* ✉ *151 W. Erie St., River North* ☎ *312/274–1111* 🌐 *www.tavernita.com* ⊕ *1:C4.*

$$$ MEXICAN 🍴 **Topolobampo.** Chef-owner Rick Bayless wrote the book on regional Mexican cuisine—several books, actually—and here he takes his faithfully regional food upscale. Next door to the more casual Frontera Grill, Topolobampo is the higher-end room, with a more subdued mood and luxury menu, though it shares Frontera's address, phone, and dedication to quality. The ever-changing offerings showcase game, seasonal fruits and vegetables, and exotic preparations: adobo-marinated lamb and rock hen in a sauce of almonds and tomatoes are two examples. [$] *Average main: $34* ✉ *445 N. Clark St., River North* ☎ *312/661–1434* 🌐 *www.rickbayless.com* ✍ *Reservations essential* 🕒 *Closed Sun. and Mon. No lunch Sat.* ⊕ *1:D5.*

$$ ECLECTIC 🍴 **Vermilion.** Vermilion touts itself as a Latin–Indian fusion restaurant, but the best dishes here are the Eastern ones, such as artichoke pakoras and tamarind-glazed ribs. Lots of small-plate options—led by the lamb chops and scallops—encourage sampling. Despite cool fashion photography on the walls and techno music in the air, the welcome here is warm. Late-night dining hours on weekends draw a club-going crowd. [$] *Average main: $28* ✉ *10 W. Hubbard St., River North* ☎ *312/527–4060* 🌐 *www.thevermilionrestaurant.com* 🕒 *No lunch weekends* ⊕ *1:D5.*

$$ AMERICAN 🍴 **Wildfire.** This is as close as you can get to the grill without staying home and firing up the barbie, but the atmosphere here is a bit more refined than your backyard, and the menu isn't your average burgers and hot dogs. The Wildfire kitchen's wood-burning oven is visible from the dining room at this cozy supper club–style joint that plays a sound track of vintage jazz. No culinary innovations here, just exceptional chopped salad, roasted prime rib, and salmon roasted on a cedar plank, along with wood-fired, whole-wheat pizzas and fried calamari. Top taste: the roasted prime rib. [$] *Average main: $26* ✉ *159 W. Erie St., River North* ☎ *312/787–9000* 🌐 *www.wildfirerestaurant.com* 🕐 *No lunch* ⊕ *1:C4.*

$ MEXICAN 🍴 **Xoco.** By opening a third restaurant next door to perennial favorites Frontera Grill and Topolobampo, celeb chef Rick Bayless has taken control of this River North block. With Xoco, he's given the city the ultimate place for *tortas* (Mexican sandwiches) filled with spiced-up fare such as *cochinita pibil* (suckling pig with pickled red onions, black beans, and searing habanero salsa) and *caldos,* generous bowls of pozole and other Latin-inspired soups served after 3 pm. First timers shouldn't pass up the hot chocolate (available at breakfast, lunch, and dinner) made from cacao beans that are roasted and ground on the premises; a steaming cup is as rich as a chocolate bar and best consumed with a plate of hot churros. Enter around the corner on Illinois Street and join the (often long) line; orders are taken at the counter. [$] *Average main: $11* ✉ *449 N. Clark St., River North* ☎ *312/334–3688* 🌐 *www.rickbayless.com* ✍ *Reservations not accepted* 🕐 *Closed Sun. and Mon.* ⊕ *1:D5.*

LINCOLN PARK, WICKER PARK, BUCKTOWN, AND LOGAN SQUARE

River North captures most of the expense-account diners, but the neighborhoods to the west of downtown—Bucktown, Wicker Park, and Logan Square—are where some of the city's most innovative dining occurs. With concepts like the vegetarian-friendly MANA, the pork-heavy Bristol, cult favorite Hot Doug's, and dessert-focused Mindy's Hot Chocolate, West Side restaurateurs serve great food without looking like they're trying too hard. Pick a 'hood and wander on foot—good eating won't be hard to find.

To the east lies Lincon Park, named for the lakefront park it borders. Often a first stop for recent Chicago transplants moving to the city as well as the permanent residence of families inhabiting pricey brownstones, the popular neighborhood is definitely worth exploring. From a food perspective, it's host to several of Chicago's best restaurants, including Alinea and Boka. On commercial thoroughfares such as Clark, Halsted, and Armitage, you can spend an afternoon bouncing back and forth from great restaurants and cafés to hip shops.

BUCKTOWN

$$ AMERICAN Fodor's Choice ★ 🍴 **The Bristol.** While Bucktown isn't wanting for dining options, this self-proclaimed "eatery and bar" sets itself apart by focusing intently on the food. Chef Chris Pandel sources local produce and features meat from sustainably raised animals. As a consequence, it isn't rare to find braised goat on the frequently changing menu. He also offers playful

The Bristol burger with cheddar and pickles

takes on more familiar fare, turning out popular small plates such as chicken wings stuffed with chorizo, baked-to-order monkey bread, and the raviolo, a plate-size stuffed pasta filled with ricotta and egg yolk. Make reservations or plan to arrive early; the boisterous dining room gets busy. The upstairs lounge, though, is a pleasant place to wait for a table to free up. [$] *Average main: $24* ✉ *2152 N. Damen Ave., Bucktown* ☎ *773/862–5555* 🌐 *www.thebristolchicago.com* ✍ *Reservations essential* 👔 *Jacket and tie* 🕓 *No lunch Mon.–Sat.* ✥ *3:B1.*

$$ ECLECTIC 🍴 **Feast.** The cozy fireplace and sofa-filled lounge create a fittingly social, casual setting for the arty Bucktown locals who dine here regularly. If you can't find something to eat here, you're not hungry: world cuisines from Cuba to India mingle freely on the expansive, bold menu. Standouts include the maple-glazed pork chop, barbecue salmon over corn buttermilk hot cakes, and the chimichurri skirt steak. Or snag a table at brunch for breakfast burritos and challah French toast. [$] *Average main: $18* ✉ *1616 N. Damen Ave., Bucktown* ☎ *773/772–7100* 🌐 *www.feastrestaurant.com* ✥ *3:B3.*

$$ BISTRO 🍴 **Le Bouchon.** The French comfort food at this charming-but-cramped bistro in Bucktown is in a league of its own. The onion tart has been a signature dish of owner Jean-Claude Poilevey for years; he also does a succulent sautéed rabbit and a definitive *salade Lyonnaise* (mixed greens topped with bacon croutons and a poached egg). Save room for the fruit tarts. And don't attempt Le Bouchon on a Saturday night without a reservation. [$] *Average main: $21* ✉ *1958 N. Damen Ave., Bucktown* ☎ *773/862–6600* 🌐 *www.lebouchonofchicago.com* 🕓 *Closed Sun.* ✥ *3:B2.*

$$ AMERICAN 🍴 **Mindy's Hot Chocolate.** The city's most celebrated pastry chef, Mindy Segal, goes solo at Hot Chocolate, and as you might expect, it's a hit for a really great dessert selection ranging from a creative soufflé tart with salted caramel ice cream and homemade pretzels to warm brioche doughnuts and hot chocolate with homemade marshmallows. How sweet it is—and how busy it is. The savory menu is well crafted, too, with choices such as a pork chop with sausage and spaetzle and a tuna melt made with tuna poached in olive oil, wild capers, and Havarti cheese. [$] *Average main: $23* ✉ *1747 N. Damen Ave., Bucktown* ☎ *773/489–1747* 🌐 *www.hotchocolatechicago.com* ⏲ *Closed Mon.* ✧ *3:B3.*

$$ JAPANESE 🍴 **Takashi.** It's not often that a chef who has made a name for himself in Las Vegas retreats to a neighborhood restaurant, but that's exactly what Takashi Yagihashi did when he left his post as executive chef of Okada at Wynn Las Vegas. At his intimate, dinner-only restaurant in Bucktown, Yagihashi serves French- and American-inspired small and large plates with Japanese accents, such as duck with quince compote and a ginger-orange glaze, and soy- and ginger-braised caramel pork belly with pickled daikon. The upstairs room is quiet and relaxed; request a seat downstairs to peek at the action in the glassed-in kitchen. [$] *Average main: $27* ✉ *1952 N. Damen Ave., Bucktown* ☎ *773/772–6170* 🌐 *www.takashichicago.com* ⏲ *Closed Mon. No lunch Tues.–Sat.* ✧ *3:B2.*

LINCOLN PARK

$$$$ MODERN AMERICAN Fodor's Choice ★ 🍴 **Alinea.** Believe the hype and secure tickets—yes, tickets— well in advance. Chicago's most exciting restaurant demands an adventurous spirit and a serious commitment of time and money. If you have four hours and $265 to spare, the 18-course tasting menu that showcases Grant Achatz's stunning, cutting-edge food is a fantastic experience. The gastronomic roller coaster takes you on a journey through intriguing aromas, visuals, flavors, and textures. The menu changes frequently, but you might find green beans perched on a pillow that emits nutmeg-scented air, sweetbreads served with burnt bread and toasted hay, and Earl Grey paired with caramelized white chocolate. Though some dishes—they range in size from one to four bites—may look like science projects, there's nothing gimmicky about the procession of bold and elegant tastes. The hours fly by in the windowless bi-level dining room, aided by the effortless service and muted decor. [$] *Average main: $265* ✉ *1723 N. Halsted St., Lincoln Park* ☎ *312/867–0110* 🌐 *www.alinea-restaurant.com* ✍ *Reservations essential* 🧥 *Jacket required* ⏲ *Closed Mon. and Tues. No lunch* ✧ *3:E3.*

$$ MODERN ITALIAN 🍴 **Balena.** Lincoln Park newcomer Balena busted onto the scene with a lot of winning points: the support of culinary powerhouses the Boka Group (Boka, Girl and the Goat, GT Fish & Oyster, Perennial Virant) and the Bristol, a prime location across from Steppenwolf Theater, and a sexy Italian-inspired design that draws a respectable crowd. Be prepared to order plenty, from airy housemade pastas and crispy wood-fired pizzas to Mediterranean coastal fare like prawns with grapes and finger chiles, or Tuscan kale with tonnato and sardines. Dessert is not to be missed, particularly elevated classics like tiramisu with chocolate

North Pond chef Bruce Sherman shops for fresh ingredients.

sauce and coffee steusel, and the *affogato* (vanilla gelato with a shot of espresso) served with cinnamon sugar doughnuts for dipping. $ *Average main: $22* ✉ *1633 N. Halsted St., Lincoln Park* ☎ *312/867–3888* ⊕ *www.balenachicago.com* ⊗ *No lunch* ✛ *3:E3.*

$$$
MODERN AMERICAN
Fodor's Choice
★

✗ **Boka.** If you're doing Steppenwolf pre-theater dinner on North Halsted Street, this upscale spot gets the foodie stamp of approval, especially with Charlie Trotter alumnus chef Giuseppe Tentori in the kitchen. The seasonally driven menu is constantly changing, offering creative fare such as squid with spicy pineapple, Faroe Island salmon with razor clams and black rice, and venison with apple bacon sauce, beer-braised collard greens, and confit baby turnips. The slick lounge and outdoor patio both serve food, so this is a big draw even for those not watching curtain time. $ *Average main: $35* ✉ *1729 N. Halsted St., Lincoln Park* ☎ *312/337–6070* ⊕ *www.bokachicago.com* ⌕ *Reservations essential* ⊗ *No lunch* ✛ *3:E3.*

$$
SPANISH

✗ **Cafe Ba-Ba-Reeba!.** The name is kitschy cute, and it's jammed with partying Lincoln Parkers, so you might not think the food is a sell point—but you'd be wrong: expat Spaniards swear this is one of the best Spanish restaurants in town, and the colorful Mediterranean-style interiors encourage the fiesta feel. The large assortment of cold and warm tapas ranges from goat cheese *croquetas* to spicy potatoes with tomato aioli. It's worth checking out the entrée menu, too, for paella and skewered meats. In warm weather six different flavors of sangria flow freely on the outdoor patio. $ *Average main: $20* ✉ *2024 N. Halsted St., Lincoln Park* ☎ *773/935–5000* ⊕ *www.cafebabareeba.com* ⊗ *No lunch Mon.–Thurs.* ✛ *3:E2.*

$$$$ SEAFOOD 🍴 **L2O.** Expect to fork over some serious cash for L2O's three-course prix-fixe menu and seven-course tasting menus—but if it's opulence you're after, this luxury restaurant won't disappoint. L2O sources only the finest specialty ingredients for delicacies like premium caviar paired with langoustine tartare and Meyer lemon or Maine lobster with foie gras torchon. A four-course prix-fixe menu for $140 and a lengthy 13-course menu for $210 are also exciting choices. Deciphering the menu may take some assistance, but the serene, earth-tone dining room and professional staff help soothe any worries. Tradition, in the form of delicate soufflés and macaroons, return at the end of the meal for a sweet send-off. [$] *Average main: $140* ✉ *2300 N. Lincoln Park W, Lincoln Park* ☎ *773/868–0002* 🌐 *www.l2orestaurant.com* ✍ *Reservations essential* 👔 *Jacket required* 🕒 *Closed Tues.* ✥ *3:G1.*

$$ BISTRO 🍴 **Mon Ami Gabi.** Although there are now satellite restaurants in the Chicago suburbs and across the country, the original Mon Ami Gabi has not lost its charm. This little piece of Paris re-creates a classic bistro with views of Lincoln Park that could pass—with the help of a couple of glasses of *vin* from the wine cart—for the Tuileries. Park-front windows let in ample natural light, warming the wood-trimmed interior. Best bites include several versions of steak frites, as well as bistro essentials such as steamed mussels and skate with crispy garlic chips. The menu features a rotating list of specials, such as cassoulet and pan-seared sea bass. [$] *Average main: $21* ✉ *2300 N. Lincoln Park W, Lincoln Park* ☎ *773/348–8886* 🌐 *www.monamigabi.com* 🕒 *No lunch* ✥ *3:G1.*

$$$$ AMERICAN Fodor's Choice ★ 🍴 **North Pond.** A former Arts and Crafts–style warming house for ice-skaters at Lincoln Park's North Pond, this gem in the woods fittingly champions an uncluttered culinary style. Talented chef Bruce Sherman emphasizes organic ingredients, wild-caught fish, and artisanal farm products. Menus change seasonally, but order the Midwestern favorite walleye pike if available. Like the food, the wine list seeks out boutique producers. The food remains top-notch at brunch but the scene, dense with strollers and high chairs, is far from serene. [$] *Average main: $36* ✉ *2610 N. Cannon Dr., Lincoln Park* ☎ *773/477–5845* 🌐 *www.northpondrestaurant.com* 🕒 *Closed Mon. and Tues. Jan.–Apr. No lunch Oct.–May* ✥ *2:H6.*

$$ ECLECTIC 🍴 **Perennial Virant.** Locavore obsessives should look no further than this farm-to-table gem facing Lincoln Park's seasonal farmers market, the Green City Market. The fourth of Boka Restaurant Group's trendy restaurant empire (Boka, Girl & the Goat, GT Fish & Oyster) teams up with sustainability poster boy chef Paul Virant (also of the suburban restaurant Vie) to create a rotating menu of beautiful, locally driven dishes like caramelized egg and sweet pea ravioli, and pan-seared Great Lakes whitefish. The restaurant's motto is "eat what you can, and can what you can't"—hence the shelves of house-made preserves that grace the walls and are incorporated into the menu in everything from the pickled celery in the smoked ham hock beignets, to the jams and sauces, and the bitters used in the cocktails. [$] *Average main: $27* ✉ *1800 N. Lincoln Ave., Lincoln Park* ☎ *312/981-7070* 🌐 *www.perennialchicago.com* 🕒 *No lunch* ✥ *3:G2.*

Hot Doug's famous offerings

$$ ✕ **Twin Anchors Restaurant & Tavern.** For a taste of classic Chicago, stop
AMERICAN   into Twin Anchors, which has been dishing out baby back ribs since
1932. The nautically themed brick tavern was a favorite of Frank
Sinatra, who still croons nightly on the jukebox. If you're not in the
mood for a messy slab of mild or zesty ribs—they're the main draw
on the menu—order the battered codfish fry or the roasted chicken.
In truth, dinner here is really less about cuisine and more about the
scene—local and touring celebs often visit—but lovers of barrooms
with personality don't mind the typically long waits during prime
time. $ *Average main: $21* ✉ *1655 N. Sedgwick St., Lincoln Park*
☎ *312/266–1616* ⊕ *www.twinanchorsribs.com* ⚏ *Reservations not
accepted* ⊗ *No lunch weekdays* ✛ *3:G3.*

LOGAN SQUARE

$ ✕ **Belly Shack.** Chef Bill Kim affectionately refers to Belly Shack—the
ECLECTIC   sequel to his acclaimed Logan Square noodle house Urban Belly—as
his "love story," because the menu fuses his Korean roots and his
wife's Puerto Rican background. Not to be missed are the Belly Dog
topped with egg noodles, pickled green papaya, togarashi-spiced fries,
and the Boricua, a *jibarito* (fried plantain sandwich) with marinated
tofu, hoisin sauce, and brown rice. Much like Urban Belly, space is
tight at this casual-yet-hip BYOB, so it's best to show up early to
avoid a wait. $ *Average main: $9* ✉ *1912 N. Western Ave., Logan
Square* ☎ *773/252–1414* ⊕ *www.bellyshack.com* ⚏ *Reservations not
accepted* ⊗ *Closed Mon.* ✛ *3:A2.*

$ AMERICAN FAMILY Fodor's Choice ★

🍴 **Hot Doug's.** Don't tell the zealots who have made Hot Doug's famous that these are *just* hot dogs—these "encased meats" go beyond your standard hot dog. Expect gourmet options like chipotle chicken sausage, smoked crawfish and pork sausage with spicy remoulade, lamb sausage with raita, and even, sometimes, antelope sausage—there are about 10 specials every day, in addition to the regular menu. Come on a Friday or Saturday, when the indulgent (and locally infamous) duck-fat fries are available. The clientele is a curious mix of hungry hard hats and serious foodies, neither of whom care about the lack of frills or inevitable long line. Hot Doug's is open only until 4 pm, so plan accordingly. [$] *Average main: $8* ✉ *3324 N. California Ave., Logan Square* ☎ *773/279–9550* 🌐 *www.hotdougs.com* ✍ *Reservations not accepted* 💳 *No credit cards* 🕒 *Closed Sun. No dinner* ✥ *2:A4.*

$$ MODERN AMERICAN

🍴 **Longman & Eagle.** Chef Jared Wentworth adheres to a farm-to-table aesthetic, so the menu at this hip gastropub changes often. Look for dishes such as roasted bone marrow with red-onion jam and sourdough crostini, or pork-belly confit with squash risotto and soy caramel. Options range from bar snacks and small plates to substantial entrées, so mix and match as you please—as long as you chase your meal with one of nearly 150 whiskeys on offer. Wine and beer lovers won't go thirsty either; the beer selection is large and well chosen, and the well-edited wine list leans toward biodynamic and small-batch producers. [$] *Average main: $24* ✉ *2657 N. Kedzie Ave., Logan Square* ☎ *773/276–7110* 🌐 *www.longmanandeagle.com* ✍ *Reservations not accepted* ✥ *3:A1.*

$$ AMERICAN

🍴 **Lula Café.** Locals worship Lula Café, a neighborhood favorite that's a quick walk from the Logan Square El stop. A bohemian storefront splits a spacious café with counter seating and an intimate dining room with closely set wooden tables and chairs. The food is stellar: expect modern dishes like wild bass with blood orange and olives, or maple-scented rabbit with rosemary sweet potatoes. Menus are seasonal, change frequently, and champion farm sources; in fact the restaurant holds prix-fixe farm dinners every Monday. Lula is open for breakfast and lunch, and diners come from far and wide for brunch, when hour-long waits are common. [$] *Average main: $32* ✉ *2537 N. Kedzie Blvd., Logan Square* ☎ *773/489–9554* 🌐 *www.lulacafe.com* 🕒 *Closed Tues.* ✥ *3:A1.*

$ KOREAN Fodor's Choice ★

🍴 **Urban Belly.** It's easy to strike up a conversation with local foodies at this casual BYOB Asian street-food spot. And there's a lot to discuss: should you go for a bowl of udon noodles swimming in a chili-lime broth or the pho-spiced duck dumplings and "phat rice" (fried rice with diced pork belly and short rib)? Either way, it's hard to go wrong with anything chef Bill Kim creates in his tiny kitchen. But come early: despite the restaurant's out-of-the-way location in the residential Avondale neighborhood, seating at the four long communal tables is first-come, first-served, and spots fill up quickly. [$] *Average main: $12* ✉ *3053 N. California Ave., Logan Square* ☎ *773/583–0500* 🌐 *www.urbanbellychicago.com* ✍ *Reservations not accepted* 🕒 *Closed Mon.* ✥ *2:A6.*

$$ JAPANESE Fodor's Choice ★

🍴 **Yusho.** Yes, it's Japanese, but a standard sushi-teriyaki spot this is not. Charlie Trotter's veteran Matthias Merges gives diners a cheffed-up look at contemporary Japanese cuisine with this hip Avondale yakitori joint. Most dishes are modestly priced and portioned to encourage sharing, including *okonomiyaki* (a savory omelet stuffed with blue prawn, cabbage, and chickpea) and twice-fried chicken with *matcha* (green tea) and lime, along with plenty of vegetarian-friendly dishes. Score a deal on Sunday with the Sunday Noodles special for $20, which includes a ramen, soba, or somen noodle dish, soft-serve ice cream, and beverage. [$] *Average main: $20* ✉ *2853 N. Kedzie Ave., Logan Square* ☎ *773/904–8558* 🌐 *www.yusho-chicago.com* ✍ *Reservations not accepted* ⏲ *No lunch Mon.–Sat.* ✥ *3:A1.*

WICKER PARK

$ MEXICAN Fodor's Choice ★

🍴 **Big Star.** It's cramped and noisy, and the service is often ambivalent, but most locals are willing to bear the substantial waits at Big Star because the tacos are some of the best in the city. Most of this honky-tonk taqueria's star power comes from chef Paul Kahan (of Blackbird, Avec, and The Publican), who serves up tasty tacos like spit-roasted pork shoulder with grilled pineapple and beer-battered tilapia with spicy chipotle slaw. If it's a taco emergency, skip the line for a table and head to the takeout window, taking your tacos to the spacious park across the street. [$] *Average main: $12* ✉ *1531 N. Damen Ave., Wicker Park* ☎ *773/235–4039* 🌐 *www.bigstarchicago.com* ✍ *Reservations not accepted* 💳 *No credit cards* ✥ *3:B3.*

$$ VEGETARIAN

🍴 **MANA Food Bar.** It's easy to miss this slim, stylish restaurant amid the clothing boutiques and bars along Division Street, but those in the know squeeze in for globally inspired vegetarian and vegan fare. Dishes are small, so plan to order a few to share. The health-conscious among you will delight in chef Jill Barron's dishes of red quinoa salad and curried cauliflower with brown rice, but carnivores won't miss their meat with mushroom sliders and hearty, sweet-potato pancakes served with chutney. Apart from the food, the list of sake-based cocktails fills the seats along the long wooden bar: try the refreshing cucumber "sakerita" when it's available. [$] *Average main: $16* ✉ *1742 W. Division St., Wicker Park* ☎ *773/342–1742* 🌐 *www.manafoodbar.com* ✍ *Reservations not accepted* ⏲ *No lunch Sun.–Thurs.* ✥ *3:C4.*

$ CAFÉ

🍴 **Milk & Honey Café.** Division Street has long been a prowl of night owls but with the growing number of spas and boutiques in the area, not to mention the many work-from-home locals, this boho neighborhood needed a good breakfast and lunch spot. Milk & Honey exceeds expectations with hearty (eggs) and healthful (granola) breakfasts, and creative sandwiches (the avocado with smoked Gouda is delicious) at lunch. Choice seats change with the season: out on the sidewalk café in warm weather; in near the fireplace in cooler temperatures. [$] *Average main: $8* ✉ *1920 W. Division St., Wicker Park* ☎ *773/395–9434* 🌐 *www.milkandhoneycafe.com* ⏲ *No dinner* ✥ *3:B4.*

$ VEGETARIAN FAMILY

🍴 **Native Foods Cafe.** When Wicker Park's veggie-centric Earwax Café closed after 21 years, vegans and vegetarians decamped to this new California transplant. Even devoted carnivores scarf down the café's satisfying vegan dishes featuring house-made tempeh, seitan, and other faux meats. Don't miss the decadent-tasting desserts, made without refined sugar. Additional locations in Lakeview and the Loop. [$] *Average main: $9* ✉ *1484 N. Milwaukee Ave., Wicker Park* ☎ *773/489–8480* 🌐 *www.nativefoods.com* [$] *Average main: $9* ✉ *1023 W. Belmont Ave., Lakeview*

The dining room at Urban Belly

☎ 773/549–4904 🌐 *www.nativefoods.com* [$] *Average main: $9* ✉ *218 S. Clark St., Loop* ☎ *312/332–6332* 🌐 *www.nativefoods.com* ✥ *3:B3.*

$$ PIZZA 🍴 **Piece Brewery & Pizzeria.** The antithesis of Chicago-style deep-dish pizza, Piece's flat pies mimic those made famous in New Haven, Connecticut. The somewhat free-form, eat-off-the-baking-sheet pizzas come in plain (tomato sauce, Parmesan, and garlic), white (olive oil, garlic, and mozzarella), or traditional red, with lots of topping options. Salads like the greens with Gorgonzola and pears are more stylish than expected, and house-brewed beers pair perfectly with the chow. It's good enough that multipierced Wicker Parkers are willing to risk dining alongside local families (with kids in tow) in this former garage space. [$] *Average main: $15* ✉ *1927 W. North Ave., Wicker Park* ☎ *773/772–4422* 🌐 *www.piecechicago.com* ✥ *3:B3.*

$$ BARBECUE 🍴 **Smoke Daddy.** A rib-and-blues emporium in the gentrified though still funky Wicker Park neighborhood, Smoke Daddy serves up tangy barbecued ribs—with generously supplied napkins for swabbing stray sauce. Fans pack the bar and the booths for the chow, which includes richly flavored smoked pulled pork and homemade fries, as well as for the no-cover R&B and jazz bands that play nightly after 9:30. It's a short walk from the Division Street El stop, making this barbecue spot an ideal point from which to explore the neighborhood's hipster scene. [$] *Average main: $19* ✉ *1804 W. Division St., Wicker Park* ☎ *773/772–6656* 🌐 *www.thesmokedaddy.com* ✥ *3:B4.*

$$ ECLECTIC Fodor's Choice ★ 🍴 **Trenchermen.** When most people think of "adventurous dining," the first thought usually turns to offal. But this new Wicker Park hot spot is full of unusual flavors beyond pork-centric dishes that are bound to be a first for most. Brothers and chef-owners Michael and Pat Sheerin serve

up original dishes with white-tablecloth interpretations like organic Scottish salmon with braised red cabbage, pumpernickel dumplings, and candied quinoa, and aged Peking duck with pastrami sausage, rye spaetzle, and parsnip. The dining room is often booked, but seating in the sleek, antique-inspired bar is first come, first served. Grab a stool and a drink, and order the pickle tots with red-onion yogurt and chicken bresaola as a dinner primer. ⓢ *Average main: $25* ⊠ *2039 W. North Ave., Wicker Park* ☎ *773/661–1540* ⊕ *www.trenchermen.com* ⊗ *No lunch Mon.–Sat.* ⊹ *3:B3.*

LAKEVIEW AND FAR NORTH SIDE

Some of Chicago's best ethnic food is found on the Far North Side, a vast catchall district north of Irving Park Road running all the way to suburban Evanston. Lakeview includes the subdistricts of Wrigleyville (buffering Wrigley Field) and Boystown. Restaurants that cluster around neighborhood hubs, like Lincoln Square and Andersonville, tend to take on similar characteristics—they're approachable, but also unique. Ethnic hole-in-the-wall restaurants such as German beer bars Chicago Brauhaus and Huettenbar share the same strip as romantic enclaves such as Bistro Campagne, so that every picky diner can find something to satisfy his or her craving. Both are pedestrian-friendly; Lincoln Square lies on the Brown Line El, though Andersonville is better reached via cab.

LAKEVIEW

$ | SCANDINAVIAN | FAMILY ✕ **Ann Sather.** This Scandinavian mini-chain, open since 1945, is a Chicago institution for good reason: the aroma of fresh cinnamon rolls, Swedish pancakes with lingonberries, and waffles put this place on the map. It still draws a mob—at this location and at the handful of other spots on the city's North Side—where hungry diners line up along the block for weekend breakfasts. Sure, you can order a familiar brunch dish like eggs Benedict, but why not try the stellar potato pancakes with applesauce instead? There are a handful of Scandinavian specialties at lunch, as well as standard café sandwiches and salads. ⓢ *Average main: $10* ⊠ *909 W. Belmont Ave., Lakeview* ☎ *773/348–2378* ⊕ *www. annsather.com* ⊗ *No dinner* ⊹ *2:F4.*

$ | AMERICAN ✕ **DMK Burger Bar.** Chef-owner Michael Kornick, of the restaurant mk, knows fine dining, but he is also a longtime fan of the simple burger. The two worlds commingle at DMK Burger Bar, where patties from grass-fed beef come topped with green chilies or caramelized onions and chipotle ketchup, and fries are adorned with truffle aioli. Yet the place is anything but fussy: the burgers, which are $9 each, are listed on the menu by number, and any of them can be made into a turkey burger on request. (There are also lamb and veggie options.) Diners used to thick burgers should consider ordering a double, since the patties here are purposely on the flat side. Come during the week to avoid the hour-long weekend waits, or be prepared to spend some time with a locally brewed beer at the bar. ⓢ *Average main: $10* ⊠ *2954 N. Sheffield Ave., Lakeview* ☎ *773/360–8686* ⊕ *www.dmkburgerbar.com* ⌔ *Reservations not accepted* ⊹ *2:F5.*

Pastry display at Milk & Honey Café

$ CAFÉ 🍴 **Julius Meinl Café.** Viennese coffee roaster Julius Meinl operates this very European café in an unexpected location at the intersection of Addison and Southport, just a few blocks from Wrigley Field. Comfortable banquettes and a supply of international newspapers entice coffee sippers to stick around, and vegetable focaccia and pear-and-Brie sandwiches, hazelnut-and-blue-cheese salads, *Frittaten* (Austrian beef broth with crepe noodles), and loads of European pastries feed the peckish. The Austrian breakfast of soft-boiled egg, ham, and Emmentaler cheese is a gem. Classical and jazz combos entertain on Friday and Saturday. [$] *Average main: $8* ✉ *3601 N. Southport Ave., Lakeview* ☎ *773/868–1857* 🌐 *northamerica.meinl.com* ✥ *2:D3.*

$ AMERICAN FAMILY 🍴 **Kitsch'n on Roscoe.** If you love all things '70s, you'll love Kitsch'n as much as the regulars. It's a diner in retro garb, with lava lamps and vintage appliances that have been turned into table lamps. The menu is full of fun options like pesto-dyed "green eggs and ham" and Twinkies tiramisu but there are also straight shooters like a hefty tuna melt or chicken and waffles. Weekends are jammed; midweek is better for relaxing. [$] *Average main: $11* ✉ *2005 W. Roscoe St., Lakeview* ☎ *773/248–7372* 🌐 *www.kitschn.com* 🕘 *No dinner* ✥ *2:B4.*

$$ ITALIAN 🍴 **Mia Francesca.** Moderate prices and a smart, urbane style drive ceaseless crowds to this Lakeview storefront. Enlightened Italian dishes like classic bruschetta, *quattro formaggi* (four-cheese) pizza, artichoke and prosciutto pasta, and roast chicken are made with fresh ingredients and avoid stereotypical heaviness. The limited meat options keep the menu prices low. While you wait for one of the small, tightly spaced tables—and you *will* wait—you can have a drink at the bar. There are more than 20 other Francesca's locations around town, including Francesca's Forno in Wicker Park, Francesca's on Taylor in Little Italy, and Francesca's on Chestnut in the Gold Coast. [$] *Average main: $15* ✉ *3311 N. Clark St., Lakeview* ☎ *773/281–3310* 🌐 *www.miafrancesca.com* 🕒 *No lunch weekdays* [$] *Average main: $15* ✉ *1576, N. Milwaukee Ave., Wicker Park* ☎ *773/770-0184* 🌐 *www.miafrancesca.com* 🕒 *No breakfast Mon.-Fri.* [$] *Average main: $15* ✉ *1400, W. Taylor St., Little Italy* ☎ *312/829-2828* 🌐 *www.miafrancesca.com* 🕒 *No lunch Sunday* ✥ *2:F4.*

$$ TURKISH 🍴 **Turquoise Restaurant and Café.** This bustling Turkish-owned café attempts to please every palate with a mixed menu of Continental and Turkish foods, but it's the latter that star here. Don't-miss items include lamb *begendi* (braised lamb shoulder with cherry tomatoes, red bell peppers, and eggplant), *sogurme* (a smoked eggplant, yogurt, and walnut dip), and homemade *lahmacun* (flatbread topped with ground beef). Vested waiters, white tablecloths, and wood-trimmed surroundings outclass the neighborhood lot. [$] *Average main: $20* ✉ *2147 W. Roscoe St., Lakeview* ☎ *773/549–3523* 🌐 *www.turquoisedining.com* ✥ *2:B4.*

$$ ASIAN 🍴 **Yoshi's Café.** Decades ago Yoshi's was launched as a pricey fine-dining restaurant in the Lakeview neighborhood. We offer this history lesson to say that while the atmosphere went jeans-casual and the prices became more reasonable, the cooking quality remained, and remains, high. Yoshi Katsumura turns out informal French-Asian cuisine, like duck breast with baked quail egg in brioche or roasted Japanese pumpkin filled with tofu (it's good enough to convert a carnivore). Sunday brunch includes the expected eggs along with a Japanese-inspired breakfast (fish, miso soup, vegetables, and steamed rice). [$] *Average main: $19* ✉ *3257 N. Halsted St., Lakeview* ☎ *773/248–6160* 🌐 *www.yoshiscafe.com* 🕒 *Closed Mon.* ✥ *2:F4.*

FAR NORTH SIDE

$$$$ THAI 🍴 **Arun's.** One of the finest Thai restaurants in Chicago—some say in the country—is also one of the most expensive, featuring only 12-course tasting menus for a flat $85. The kitchen artfully composes six appetizers, four entrées, and two desserts nightly, using the freshest ingredients. Results might include shrimp-filled golden pastry baskets, whole tamarind snapper, and veal medallions with ginger-lemongrass sauce. Arun's out-of-the-way location in a residential neighborhood on the northwest side doesn't discourage a strong following among locals and visiting foodies. [$] *Average main: $85* ✉ *4156 N. Kedzie Ave., Irving Park* ☎ *773/539–1909* 🌐 *www.arunsthai.com* ✍ *Reservations essential* 🕒 *Closed Mon. No lunch* ✥ *2:A1.*

$$ SOUTHERN 🍴 **Big Jones.** Even if you weren't raised by a Southern grandmother, the heirloom cooking at this Andersonville restaurant will make you feel right at home. A parlorlike backdrop sets the scene for chef-owner Paul Fehribach's contemporary American takes on classic Southern dishes. The menu revives century-old recipes scrupulously sourced from historical cookbooks from New Orleans to Appalachia and re-creates them with high-quality, sustainable ingredients. Brunch is particularly special here, served with complimentary beignets for an extra touch of Southern hospitality. [$] *Average main: $20* ✉ *5347 N. Clark St., Far North Side* ☎ *773/275–5725* 🌐 *www.bigjoneschicago.com* ✥ *2:D1.*

$$ ✕ **Bistro Campagne.** If you're looking for rustic French fare on the North
FRENCH Side, this is the place to come: crispy roast chicken with mushroom
ragout, steak piled with frites, goat cheese salad, and ale-steamed mus-
sels are top-notch, while the lovely, wood-trimmed Arts and Crafts
interior is the perfect complement to a relaxing meal. In warmer
weather, ask for a table in the torch-lighted garden. Prices are reason-
able, including those for the French-centric wine list. $ *Average main:*
$24 ✉ *4518 N. Lincoln Ave., Lincoln Square* ☎ *773/271–6100* ⊕ *www.*
bistrocampagne.com ☾ *No lunch Mon.–Sat.* ✚ *2:B1.*

$$ ✕ **Café Selmarie.** For a light meal in Lincoln Square, line up at this
CAFÉ bakery-turned-café, a longstanding favorite among locals—especially
during warmer months, when the outdoor patio beckons. Breakfast
means brioche French toast and vegetarian breakfast sandwiches; lunch
ranges from goat cheese salads to turkey and Brie sandwiches; and dinner runs to pan-seared salmon and herb-roasted chicken. Don't miss the
fabulous pastries (you can also buy them to go at the front counter).
Pass summer waits pleasantly in the neighboring plaza; other seasons,
you're out in the cold. $ *Average main: $16* ✉ *4729 N. Lincoln Ave.,*
Lincoln Square ☎ *773/989–5595* ⊕ *www.cafeselmarie.com* ☾ *No din-*
ner Mon. ✚ *2:B1.*

$$ ✕ **Chicago Brauhaus.** The German immigrants who settled in Lincoln
GERMAN Square have mostly moved on, making room for a generation of urban
FAMILY families, but they left behind the Brauhaus, an Oktoberfest of a restau-
rant featuring a live band playing nightly polkas and waltzes that bring
old-timers and new converts to the dance floor. Though the atmosphere
is the draw over the food, you can't go wrong with the bratwurst and
sauerkraut or the schnitzel. Large tables add to the convivial atmo-
sphere; you may make some new friends. As expected, there is a good
selection of German beer. $ *Average main: $15* ✉ *4732 N. Lincoln*
Ave., Lincoln Square ☎ *773/784–4444* ⊕ *www.chicagobrauhaus.com*
☾ *Closed Tues.* ✚ *2:B1.*

$$ ✕ **Hopleaf.** When hops devotee Michael Roper added a dining room
AMERICAN onto the back of his beloved tavern, swillers were thrilled with the
Fodor's Choice opportunity to sop their suds with delectable specialties such as Belgian-
★ style mussels steamed in white ale with herbs, Montreal-style brisket
(it's slow roasted and briefly smoked, and less sweet than New York–
style brisket) with coleslaw and Stilton mac and cheese, and duck Reuben sandwiches on marble rye. Even with the expansion of a second
full dining room and upstairs space, it's still best to arrive early to avoid
waiting in the bar for a table. But don't bring the kids; Roper insists
that only those of legal drinking age can eat here. $ *Average main: $18*
✉ *5148 N. Clark St., Far North Side* ☎ *773/334–9851* ⊕ *www.hopleaf.*
com ⟝ *Reservations not accepted* ✚ *2:D1.*

$ ✕ **Smoque BBQ.** The sweet smoky aroma wafting out of this casual bar-
BARBECUE becue spot always attracts a crowd, and while the line to order at the
FAMILY counter extends out the door on weekends, it moves quickly. If you can't
make up your mind between brisket or shredded pork shoulder (both
are tender and cooked for about 14 hours), order the half-and-half—a
sandwich with half of each. Or try a slab of ribs. Sides of vinegar-spiked
slaw, rich baked beans, and corn bread round out the meal, and kids

9

Bustling Hopleaf Bar

love the creamy mac and cheese. Smoque is BYOB, so pick up a beer or two before arriving if desired. $ *Average main: $14* ✉ *3800 N. Pulaski Rd., Irving Park* ☎ *773/545–7427* ⊕ *www.smoquebbq.com* ⬥ *Reservations not accepted* ⊘ *Closed Mon.* ✛ *2:A2.*

$$ ✗ **Sola Restaurant.** While you can dine very well in Chicago's neigh-
MODERN borhoods, most local joints aren't as ambitious as Sola, which would
AMERICAN be right at home downtown and probably far more expensive there. Now North Siders don't have to travel far for ginger-glazed salmon, bacon-wrapped pork tenderloin, and barramundi with black rice. Chef-owner-surfer Carol Wallack's affinity for Hawaii shows in Pacific Rim fare like "Kalua" pot stickers and Kauai prawns. Proving its affection for the neighborhood, the restaurant is fronted by a wall of windows and is warm within, thanks to a gas fireplace. Go around the corner to Byron Street to find the front door. $ *Average main: $27* ✉ *3868 N. Lincoln Ave., North Center* ☎ *773/327–3868* ⊕ *www. sola-restaurant.com* ✛ *2:C2.*

$$ ✗ **Spacca Napoli Pizzeria.** Despite Chicago's renown for deep-dish pizza,
PIZZA locals are swept away by the thin-crust Neapolitan pies at this bright
FAMILY Ravenswood gem. Finely ground Italian flour, imported buffalo mozzarella, hand-stretched dough, and a brick, wood-fired oven built by Italian craftsmen are credited for producing the bubbling, chewy crusts of these pies, which diners eat with a fork. Antipasti, a well-priced Italian wine and beer selection, and desserts like tiramisu round out the menu. The proprietors shun takeout and turn up the lights a little too high, but the food wins out, accounting for out-the-door waits, even on weekdays. In summer, angle for a table on the large pleasant sidewalk patio. Reservations can be made for Friday and Saturday only. $ *Average main:*

$16 ✉ 1769 W. Sunnyside Ave., Ravenswood ☎ 773/878–2420 🌐 www.spaccanapolipizzeria.com ⏲ Closed Mon. No lunch Tues. ✥ 2:C1.

$ SCANDINAVIAN FAMILY 🍴 **Svea.** The North Side's Andersonville neighborhood, once a haven for Swedes, plays host to the humble Svea, a Swedish version of an American diner. There are Swedish pancakes with lingonberries and Swedish rye *limpa* bread with eggs in the morning; lunch means Swedish meatballs and open-face sandwiches. The digs are no-frills, but the service is almost unvariably friendly. The locals love it. [$] *Average main: $6 ✉ 5236 N. Clark St., Andersonville ☎ 773/275–7738 ▭ No credit cards ⏲ No dinner ✥ 2:D1.*

PILSEN, LITTLE ITALY, AND CHINATOWN

If there ever were a need to convince someone of Chicago's culinary diversity, a progressive dinner through Chinatown, Little Italy, and Pilsen would be the way to go. Pilsen, Chicago's vibrant Mexican neighborhood; Chinatown, a confluence of tea shops, dim-sum spots, and hardware stores; and Little Italy, which runs through Chicago's medical district, make for a fun day's adventure that's off the beaten tourist path. Expect to eat cheaply and well in both Pilsen and Chinatown. And although Little Italy is no longer a truly living and breathing Italian neighborhood, the main drag, Taylor Street, makes for pleasant strolling and casual grazing (and stay tuned for new Italian restaurants on their way).

PILSEN

$$ BARBECUE 🍴 **Honky Tonk Barbeque.** The twang of country meets the tang of barbecue sauce at this Pilsen spot known for award-winning barbecue. There's definitely plenty of meat on the menu—from ribs and brisket to whole-smoked chicken—but the tender pulled pork might be the standout; try it first with a dab of regular sauce, then try the spicy. Setting the scene for the down-home meal are dining rooms decked out in vintage Americana (including a pink fridge) accompanied by live honky-tonk music on weekends and the occasional weekday evening. As for the address, it's easy to spot the restaurant: look for the flames painted alongside the entrance. [$] *Average main: $15 ✉ 1800 S. Racine Ave., Pilsen ☎ 312/226–7427 🌐 www.honkytonkbbqchicago.com ✍ Reservations not accepted ⏲ Closed Mon. ✥ 4:C5.*

$$ MODERN AMERICAN 🍴 **Nightwood.** It's almost as if a piece of Brooklyn touched down here on the southern border of the Pilsen neighborhood. Everyone who works here appears to double as an artist or musician, which seems appropriate given the artful, understated dishes. Like its sister restaurant, Lula Café in Logan Square, local and seasonal rule the menu. There is usually at least one spit-roasted entrée, perhaps chicken, pork loin, or duck leg, along with a vegetarian main and a fish option, as well as house-made pastas, and appetizers that make use of the freshest produce. You can see the open kitchen from the bar, but to be close to the flames, snag a seat next to the fireplace on the enclosed patio, complete with a living wall. Nightwood draws a crowd at brunch, and the maple-bacon doughnut is unforgettable. [$] *Average main: $26 ✉ 2119 S. Halsted St., Pilsen ☎ 312/526–3385 🌐 www.nightwoodrestaurant.com ⏲ No lunch Mon.–Sat. No dinner Sun. ✥ 4:D6.*

9

$ MEXICAN 🍴 **Nuevo León.** Fill up on the exotic (tripe soup) or the familiar (tacos) at this bustling, family-run restaurant in the heart of Pilsen, Chicago's Mexican neighborhood. Big tables are often filled with large groups, lending a fiesta feel to the scene. Fans love the authentic food, including *chilaquiles* (tortillas with salsa and scrambled eggs) for breakfast and dinners of shrimp fajitas, chiles rellenos, and *barbacoa* (braised beef served with refried beans). Brush up your Spanglish; not all servers are fluent in English, though all are welcoming to newcomers. To wash it all down, order a tall glass of *horchata*, a milky, cinnamon-flecked rice beverage, or bring a couple of beers; Nuevo León is BYOB. [$] *Average main: $10* ✉ *1515 W. 18th St., Pilsen* ☎ *312/421–1517* 🌐 *www.nuevoleonrestaurant.com* ✍ *Reservations not accepted* 💳 *No credit cards* ✥ *4:B5.*

LITTLE ITALY

$$ FRENCH 🍴 **Chez Joël Bistro Français.** Unlike the rest of Taylor Street, which is predominantly Italian in allegiance, Chez Joël waves the flag for France. The sunny, cozy bistro, run by brothers Joël and Amed Kazouini, serves well-prepared classics like steak frites, coq au vin, escargots, and bouillabaisse. It's a favorite with the locals thanks to its authentic bistro feel. There is a full bar and a reasonably priced wine list favoring French and Californian selections. On a warm Chicago day, ask for a seat outside on the patio. [$] *Average main: $21* ✉ *1119 W. Taylor St., Little Italy* ☎ *312/226–6479* 🌐 *www.chezjoelbistro.com* 🕒 *Closed Mon. No lunch Sat.* ✥ *4:C3.*

$$ PIZZA 🍴 **Pompei Little Italy.** Cheap, cheerful, and fast—what's not to love about Pompei? Little Italy's only casual café with a strong kitchen specializes in square slices of pizza, each under $4, with toppings ranging from shredded onions and sausage to basil and tomato. One to two easily makes a meal. Between the University of Illinois Chicago students and the Rush University Medical Center workers, Pompei is jammed at lunch. If you can tolerate the self-serve system at dinner, the evening hours are more relaxing. If pizza's not your thing, salad, generous sandwiches, and handmade pastas are also on the menu. And keep your eye out for Pompei's Near North and Lakeview locations. [$] *Average main: $21* ✉ *1531 W. Taylor St., Little Italy* ☎ *312/421–5179* 🌐 *www.pompeipizza.com* ✥ *4:B4.*

$ AMERICAN FAMILY 🍴 **Sweet Maple Cafe.** On a Sunday morning, this breakfast-all-day spot is easy to find on Taylor Street: just look for the line out the door. In fact, expect a line on most days as customers ranging from students to police officers and politicians wait for a table in anticipation of warm, buttery biscuits and a side of generous hospitality. Laurene Hynson's menu has something for everyone: buttermilk pancakes and hefty omelets for those who prefer American classics, as well as dishes such as the Dias and Noches Scramble—eggs cooked with grilled chicken and jalapenos and served with a side of freshly made salsa. Not to be overlooked are the home fries, which come in any combination of peppers, cheese, and bacon. For non–breakfast eaters, well-executed salads and soups are available after 11:30 on weekdays. [$] *Average main: $9* ✉ *1339 W. Taylor St., Little Italy* ☎ *312/243–8908* 🌐 *www.sweetmaplecafe.com* ✍ *Reservations not accepted* 🕒 *No dinner* ✥ *4:B4.*

\$\$ ✕**Three Aces.** The rustic menu here, heavy on pasta and pizza, fits
PIZZA nicely among the Little Italy neighbors, but the grittier rock 'n' roll
vibe and free-flowing craft beer makes Three Aces stand out among
the other classic mom-and-pop restaurants. Expect less eggplant Parm
and more farmhouse Italian: there's grilled rapini with blood sausage,
wheat berry, celery heart, radish, and satsuma, and pappardelle Bolog-
nese with seasoned mascarpone, mint, and Parmesan. Desserts are
never without a splash of healthy booze, like cake doughnuts with coffee glaze and stout punch during winter and St-Germain elderflower
liqueur–spiked Italian ice in the summer. $ *Average main: $12* ⊠ *1321
W. Taylor St., Little Italy* ☎ *312/243–1577* ⊕ *www.threeaceschicago.
com* ✛ *4:C4.*

CHINATOWN

\$ ✕**Emperor's Choice.** This sophisticated restaurant sets out to prove
CHINESE that Chinese specialties can get beyond deep-fried prawns and Kung
Pao chicken, and it succeeds with strong seafood offerings, such as
baked clams, Peking-style lobster, or Dungeness crab, fried and served
whole, and seasoned with salt. There is also a separate menu of "delicacies," which includes items like shark's fin soup and pork belly. Diners come for the good food, decent prices, and friendly service—not
for the atmosphere, which is cramped and bustling. $ *Average main:
$13* ⊠ *2238 S. Wentworth Ave., Chinatown* ☎ *312/225–8800* ⊕ *www.
emperorschoicechicago.com* ✛ *4:F6.*

\$\$ ✕**Han 202.** Tasting menus tend to come with sky-high prices, but that's
CHINESE not the case at this BYOB spot in Chicago's Bridgeport neighborhood,
just south of Chinatown. For a flat $25 you get five courses, which
can progress from a small cup of spicy snow crab soup to Shanghai
dumplings, sweet walnut shrimp, and spicy-sweet Chilean sea bass,
ending with a small sweet bite, like a chocolate truffle. While portions
aren't overwhelming, they are satisfying. Compared with the low-key
entrance, the dining room is sleeker—and more comfortable—than
you'd expect, making the southward trek all the more worthwhile.
$ *Average main: $25* ⊠ *605 W 31st St., Chinatown* ☎ *312/949–1314*
⊕ *www.han202.com* ☾ *No lunch* ✛ *4:F6.*

\$ ✕**Lao Sze Chuan.** If you're looking for spicy, filling food and great prices
CHINESE in Chinatown, check out this Szechuan kitchen from Tony Hu, the
neighborhood's most prolific restaurateur. Chilies, garlic, and ginger
seem to go into every dish, whether it's chicken, green beans, eggplant, or dumplings. The digs are nothing to write a postcard home
about, but you'll feel smug for choosing it once the feast is finished
and you're sipping your tea with a happy tummy. $ *Average main:
$14* ⊠ *2172 S. Archer Ave., Chinatown* ☎ *312/326–5040* ⊕ *www.
tonygourmetgroup.com* ✛ *4:F6.*

\$\$ ✕**Phoenix Restaurant.** This bustling dim sum house can feel overwhelm-
CHINESE ing with the hordes of diners who flock here on weekends, and service
can be brusque, but even so, it delivers. First Phoenix softens you up
with second-floor picture-window views that frame the Loop skyline.
Then, just when you're most vulnerable, it develops the food punch—
and it's a pretty good one, too. The dim sum, dispensed from rolling
carts all day long on weekends, is a big draw; don't miss the barbecue

9

pork buns (*char siu bao*) or the shrimp dumplings (*shumai*). Arrive before noon on weekends or stew as you wait—and wait. $ *Average main: $20* ✉ *2131 S. Archer Ave., Chinatown* ☎ *312/328–0848* ⊕ *www.chinatownphoenix.com* ✛ *4:F6.*

HYDE PARK

A 20-minute drive from downtown is historic Hyde Park, one of the city's most self-contained enclaves, and where residents are steadfastly loyal to their local businesses. Restaurants in intellectual Hyde Park have a welcoming "come as you are" air about them that's a pleasant surprise for a neighborhood that houses a top-tier university and the country's highest-profile couple. Perhaps the area's proximity to downtown has made flashy eateries and big-name chefs unnecessary. It might be for the best, since visitors tend to feel comfortable in any restaurant, regardless of how much foodie cred they bring to the table. In the compact heart of the area, expect to find a little of everything, from Thai eats to pizza spots, bakeries, and coffee shops.

$$

ASIAN

FAMILY

✗ **Chant.** Asian-cuisine purists might raise their eyebrows at dishes such as Peking duck flautas or Asian ratatouille strudel, but Chant's Asian-inspired global cuisine has plenty of fans. Those who crave familiar Thai takeout can order the pleasantly chewy wide-egg noodle *pad se-eu* while non-meat eaters appreciate the broad selection available (several dishes, even the pad Thai, can be prepared vegan). There's even a kids' menu. A full bar, with cocktails, wine, and several bottled Asian beers, distinguishes this pan-Asian eatery from restaurants with similar menus, making it a hangout on weekend nights and at Sunday brunch when live music draws a crowd ready to groove. $ *Average main: $20* ✉ *1509 E. 53rd St., Hyde Park* ☎ *773/324–1999* ⊕ *www. chantchicago.com* ✛ *4:H5.*

WHERE TO EAT AND STAY IN CHICAGO

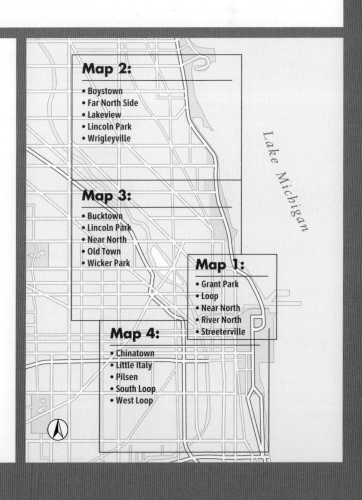

Map 2:
- Boystown
- Far North Side
- Lakeview
- Lincoln Park
- Wrigleyville

Map 3:
- Bucktown
- Lincoln Park
- Near North
- Old Town
- Wicker Park

Map 1:
- Grant Park
- Loop
- Near North
- River North
- Streeterville

Map 4:
- Chinatown
- Little Italy
- Pilsen
- South Loop
- West Loop

Lake Michigan

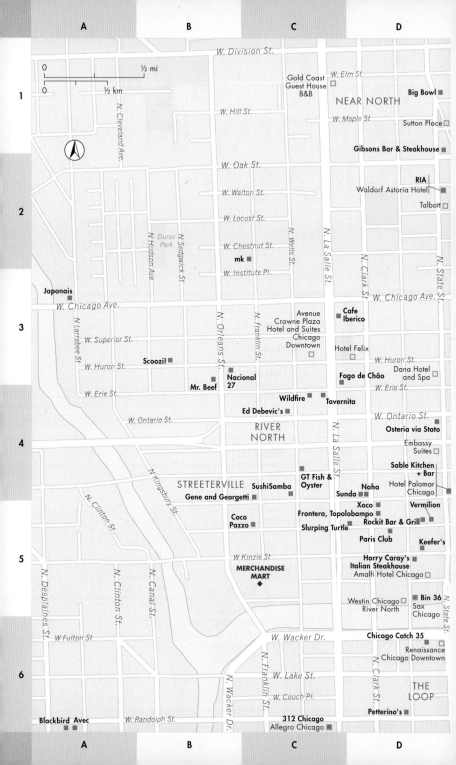

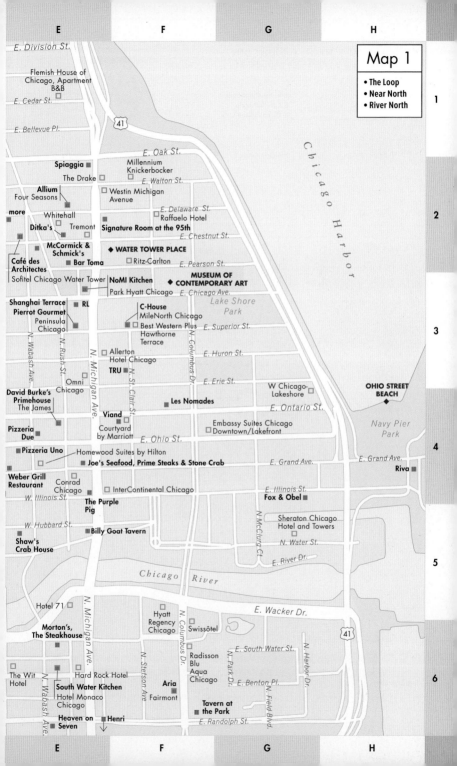

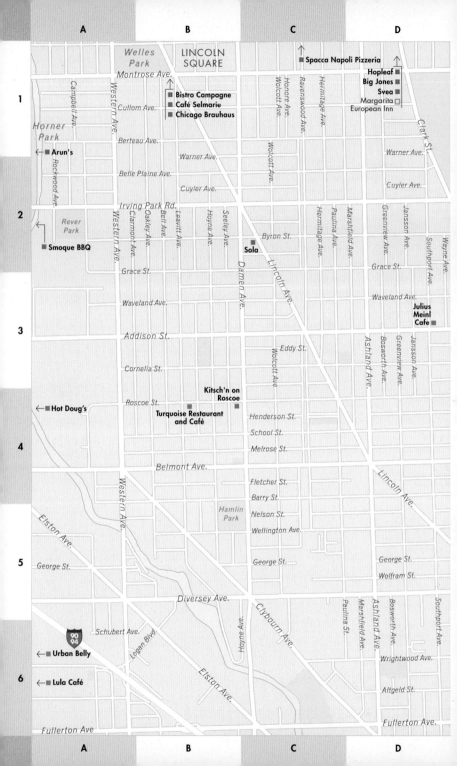

Welles Park

LINCOLN SQUARE

Montrose Ave.

■ Spacca Napoli Pizzeria

Hopleaf ■
Big Jones ■
Svea ■
Margarita □
European Inn

Campbell Ave.

Western Ave.

Cullum Ave.

■ Bistro Campagne
■ Café Selmarie
■ Chicago Brauhaus

Honore Ave.
Wolcott Ave.
Ravenswood Ave.
Hermitage Ave.

Clark St.

Horner Park

Berteau Ave.

Warner Ave.

Warner Ave.

Rockwood Ave.

← ■ Arun's

Belle Plaine Ave.

Cuyler Ave.

Cuyler Ave.

Irving Park Rd.

Rever Park

Clarmont Ave.
Oakley Ave.
Bell Ave.
Leavitt Ave.
Hoyne Ave.
Seeley Ave.

Byron St.

Hermitage Ave.
Paulina Ave.
Marshfield Ave.
Greenview Ave.
Jansson Ave.
Southport Ave.
Warne Ave.

■ Smoque BBQ

Sola ■

Grace St.

Grace St.

Waveland Ave.

Damen Ave.

Lincoln Ave.

Waveland Ave.

Julius Meinl Cafe ■

Addison St.

Cornelia St.

Eddy St.

Wolcott Ave.

Ashland Ave.
Bosworth Ave.
Greenview Ave.
Jansson Ave.

Roscoe St.

Kitsch'n on Roscoe
■

← ■ Hot Doug's

Turquoise Restaurant and Café ■

Henderson St.

School St.

Melrose St.

Belmont Ave.

Fletcher St.

Barry St.

Hamlin Park

Nelson St.

Wellington Ave.

Lincoln Ave.

Western Ave.

Elston Ave.

George St.

George St.

George St.

Wolfram St.

Diversey Ave.

Clybourn Ave.

Hoyne Ave.

Paulina St.
Marshfield Ave.
Ashland Ave.
Bosworth Ave.
Southport Ave.

90 94

Schubert Ave.

← ■ Urban Belly

Logan Blvd.

Wrightwood Ave.

← ■ Lula Café

Altgeld St.

Elston Ave.

Fullerton Ave.

Fullerton Ave.

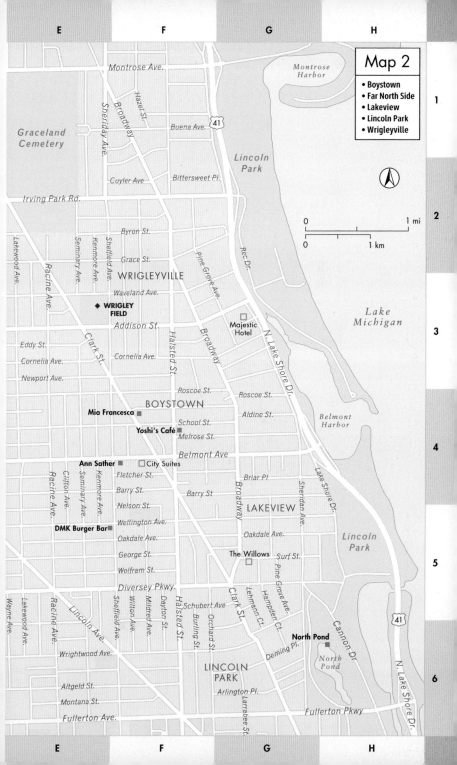

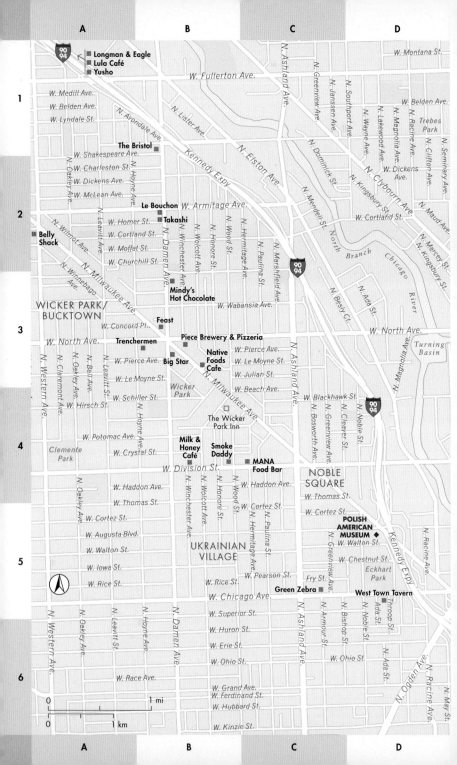

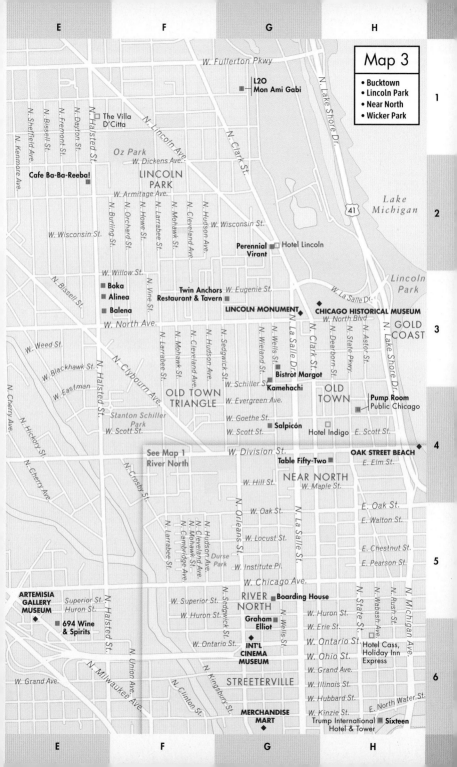

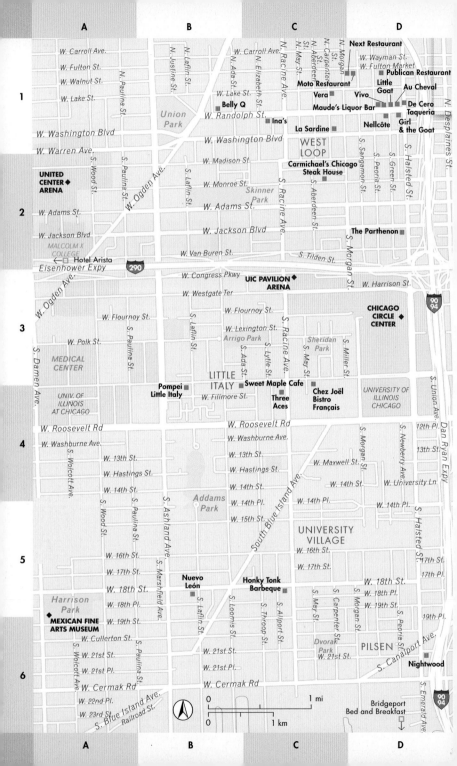

Map 4

- Chinatown
- Little Italy
- Hyde Park
- Pilsen
- South Loop
- West Loop

E. Wacker Dr.

W. Fulton St.
W. Wacker Dr.
E. Wacker Dr.

Province
See Map 1
River North
W. Lake St.
W. Randolph St.

Sepia
CITY HALL ◆
Atwood Café
Hotel Burnham
W. Washington St.
W. Calhoun Pl.
Trattoria No. 10
LOOP
Park Grill

W. Madison St.
The Silversmith Hotel & Suites
W. Monroe St.
The Grillroom
Chophouse & Winebar
Hampton
Majestic
Henri
E. Monroe St.
CHICAGO YACHT CLUB ◆

W Chicago City Center
Palmer
House
Hilton
Terzo
Piano
THE ART INSTITUTE OF CHICAGO ◆

W. Adams St.
UNION STATION ◆
JW Marriott
Chicago
Everest
Russian Tea Time
E. Jackson Blvd
Chicago Harbor

Lou Mitchell's
Pritzger Park
E. Van Buren St.
Grant Park

W. Van Buren St.
W. Congress Pkwy
290
E. Congress Dr.
BUCKINGHAM FOUNTAIN ◆

Wyndham Blake
Epic Burger
Mercat a la Planxa

Holiday Inn & Suites
Chicago-Downtown
W. Harrison St.
E. Harrison St.
Renaissance
Blackstone
Chicago

PRINTER'S ROW
SPERTUS MUSEUM ◆
E. Balbo Ave.

W. Polk St.
W. Polk St.
E. Balbo Dr.
Hilton Chicago
Essex Inn
E. 8th St.

LOGAN MONUMENT ◆

W. Taylor St.
S. E. 9th St.

COLUMBIA COLLEGE ART MUSEUM ◆
11th St.
SHEDD AQUARIUM ◆

Manny's Coffee Shop and Deli
Roosevelt
Road Park
Eleven City Diner
E. Roosevelt Rd

SITE OF CHICAGO FIRE (1871) ◆
SOUTH LOOP
13th St.
Gioco
FIELD MUSEUM OF NATURAL HISTORY ◆
E. McFetridge Dr.

SOLDIER FIELD STADIUM ◆
Burnham Harbor

W. 14th Pl.
E. 14th Pl.

Hyde Park

E. 50th St.

W. 15th St.
HELLER HOUSE ◆
Madison Park

0 ——— 600 feet
E. Hyde Park Ave.
0 ——— 200 meters
E. 52nd St.

W. 16th St.
AMERICAN POLICE CENTER & MUSEUM ◆
E. 53rd St.
Nichols
Park
Chant

W. 18th St.
W. 19th St.
E. 54th St.

E. 54th Ave.

20th St.
20th Pl.
E. 55th St.
E. 55th Pl.

CHINATOWN
Lao Sze Chuan
Phoenix Restaurant
W. Cermak Rd
DAVID AND ALFRED SMART MUSEUM OF ART ◆
E. 56th St.
HYDE PARK HISTORICAL SOCIETY ◆

For Hyde Park and South Chicago see inset to the right
Emperor's Choice
W. 23rd St.
E. 57th St.
Jackson Park

Han 202

WHERE TO STAY

Updated by
Terri Colby

Chicago hotel rates are as temperamental as the city's climate. And just as snow in April and 70-degree weather in November are not uncommon, it is widely accepted that a hotel's room rates may drop $50 to $100 overnight—and rise again the next day. It all depends on the season and what festivals, conferences, and other events are happening around town.

Even so, it's wise to shop around. Focus on a neighborhood of interest, such as the Magnificent Mile area and the rest of the Near North side, and you'll find budget chains such as Embassy Suites and luxury properties such as the Four Seasons Hotel Chicago within a few blocks of each other.

Or ask yourself whether you'd rather be surrounded by the sedately dressed—think Trump International Hotel—or tattooed hipsters, à la the James Chicago. Is it romance you're seeking—try the Dana—or a quick weekend escape with the kids in tow (they can splash around the pool at the Radisson Blu, then walk a block to Millennium Park)?

On the lower end, expect well-maintained, but often boxy and sparsely decorated rooms. The good news is that free Wi-Fi is now a feature of most budget-friendly hotels, such as the Best Western and Holiday Inn chains, or local outfits such as the Essex Inn.

Top-tier hotels have no problem filling their rooms: in some cases, this has little to do with amenities. Instead, their vibrant bar scenes are the draw, as is the case at the W Chicago Lakeshore, W Chicago–City Center, theWit, and the James Hotel. Rooms at these hot spots usually don't go for less than $250, but the "it" factor is huge, with attractive crowds queuing at the bar and lounging in the restaurants. That said, the roughly 1,500 new hotel rooms that came on the scene in 2013 may help lower prices and increase quality, though it's too early to tell for sure.

WHERE SHOULD I STAY?

Neighborhood	Vibe	Pros	Cons
The Loop	Mostly historic hotels of architectural interest in an area filled with businesspeople on weekdays and shoppers on weekends. The scene has become increasingly hip over the years.	Accessible public transportation and abundant cabs; a business district with decent nightlife.	El train noise; construction common; streets can sometimes be bare in late evening. It draws an older, more established crowd.
West Loop and South Loop	Mixed residential and business neighborhoods that are gentrifying, although empty buildings and storefronts are not uncommon.	Hotels are cheaper; streets are quieter; Museum Campus and McCormick Place are within easy reach; family-friendly; lots of new lounges and restaurants.	Sometimes long walks to public transportation; minimal shopping; quiet at night with many darkened streets. If you're looking for entertainment, it might require a quick drive or a long walk.
Near North	The pulse of the city, on and around North Michigan Avenue, has ritzy high-rise hotels and plenty of shopping and restaurants. As you go farther north, streets become residential.	Many lodging options, including some of the city's most luxurious hotels. Lively streets abuzz until late night; safe. The shopping couldn't be better for those with deep pockets.	Some hotels on the pricey side; crowded sidewalks; lots of tourists. And don't expect to find many bargains here.
River North	Lots of chains, from hotels to restaurants to shops, patronized mostly by travelers. Though this is a tourist haven, the area also has many art galleries and antiques stores.	Affordable lodging; easy access to public transportation; attractions nearby are family-friendly, especially during the day; high concentration of nightclubs.	Area might be too touristy for some. This is Chicago's home for chain restaurants; parking is a drag.
Lincoln Park	Small, boutique hotels tucked on quiet, tree-lined streets with many independent shops and restaurants. Pedestrian-friendly area; you don't need a car to find a restaurant, bar, or bank.	Low crime; great paths for walks; lots of parkland. From hot dogs to sushi, this place has it all; eclectic collection of shops and restaurants, ranging from superaffordable to the ultrapricey.	Limited hotel selection; long walks to El train. Parking is almost impossible in some spots, and garages don't come cheap; very young and trendy crowd.
Lakeview and Far North Side	Especially busy around Wrigley Field, where both Chicagoans and travelers congregate in summertime; the area's lodging is midsize boutique hotels and B&Bs.	Low crime; moderately priced hotels; shopping and dining options at all price ranges, including many vintage-clothing boutiques; a plethora of sports-themed bars.	Congested traffic; panhandlers common, especially around El stations and Wrigley Field. Parking is a nightmare when the Cubs are playing in town.

10

CHICAGO LODGING PLANNER

LODGING STRATEGY

Where should we stay? With hundreds of Chicago hotels, it may seem like a daunting question. But don't worry—our expert writers and editors have done most of the legwork. The selections here represent the best this city has to offer—from the best budget motels to the sleekest designer hotels. Scan "Best Bets" on the following pages for top recommendations by price and experience. Or find a review quickly in the listings. Search by neighborhood, then alphabetically. Happy hunting!

FACILITIES

Unless otherwise noted in the individual descriptions, all the hotels listed have private baths, central heating, and private phones. Almost all hotels have Internet and phones with voice mail, as well as valet service. Many now have wireless Internet (Wi-Fi) available, although it's not always free.

RESERVATIONS

Hotel reservations are an absolute necessity when planning your trip to Chicago—hotels often fill up with convention traffic, so book your room in advance.

WITH KIDS

In the listings, look for the word "family," which indicates the property is particularly good for kids.

PRICES

Prices in the reviews are the lowest cost of a standard double room in high season; they do not take into account discounts or package deals you may find on consolidator websites.

USING THE MAPS

Throughout the chapter, you'll see mapping symbols and coordinates (✢ 3:F2) after property names or reviews. *To locate the property on a map, turn to the Chicago Dining and Lodging Atlas at the end of the Where to Eat chapter.* The first number after the ✢ symbol indicates the map number. Following that is the property's coordinate on the map grid.

BEST BETS FOR CHICAGO LODGING

Fodor's offers a selective listing of high-quality lodging experiences at every price range, from the city's best budget motel to its most sophisticated luxury hotel. Here we've compiled our top recommendations by price and experience. The best properties—those that provide a remarkable experience in their price range—are designated in the listings with the Fodor's Choice logo.

Fodor'sChoice★

Bridgeport Bed and Breakfast, $, p. 224
Essex Inn, $, p. 222
Flemish House of Chicago, $$, p. 226
Four Seasons Hotel Chicago, $$$$, p. 226
Hotel Burnham, $$, p. 221
Hotel Lincoln, $$, p. 237
James Chicago, $, p. 228
Park Hyatt Chicago, $$$, p. 229
The Peninsula Chicago, $$$$, p. 229
Public Chicago, $, p. 229
Radisson Blu Aqua, $$, p. 222
Ritz-Carlton Chicago, $$$$, p. 229
Sofitel Chicago Water Tower, $$$, p. 231

Trump International Hotel & Tower Chicago, $$$$, p. 234
Waldorf Astoria Chicago, $$$$, p. 231

Best by Price

$

Best Western Hawthorne Terrace, p. 237
Bridgeport Bed and Breakfast, p. 224
City Suites Hotel, p. 238
Essex Inn, p. 222
Hampton Majestic, p. 220
James Chicago, p. 228
Margarita European Inn, p. 238
Millennium Knickerbocker Hotel, p. 228
Public Chicago, p. 229

$$

Flemish House of Chicago, p. 226
Hilton Chicago, p. 222

Hotel Burnham, p. 221
Hotel Lincoln, p. 237
Radisson Blu Aqua, p. 222
theWit, p. 222

$$$

Park Hyatt Chicago, p. 229
JW Marriott Chicago, p. 221
Renaissance Blackstone Chicago Hotel, p. 224
Sofitel Chicago Water Tower, p. 231

$$$$

Four Seasons Hotel Chicago, p. 226
The Peninsula Chicago, p. 229
Ritz-Carlton Chicago, p. 229
Trump International Hotel & Tower Chicago, p. 234
Waldorf Astoria Chicago, p. 231

Best by Experience

BEST CONCIERGE

Fairmont Chicago, p. 220
Hotel Monaco Chicago, p. 221

BEST POOL

Essex Inn, p. 222
Hilton Chicago, p. 222
InterContinental Chicago, p. 228
Peninsula Chicago, p. 229
Trump International Hotel & Tower Chicago, p. 234

BEST SPA

Four Seasons Hotel Chicago, p. 226
James Chicago, p. 228
Trump International Hotel & Tower Chicago, p. 234
Valeo Spa at JW Marriott Hotel, p. 221

MOST KID-FRIENDLY

Essex Inn, p. 222
Holiday Inn & Suites Chicago-Downtown, p. 224
Hotel Allegro Chicago, p. 220
Hotel Monaco Chicago, p. 221
Radisson Blu Aqua Chicago, p. 222
Ritz-Carlton Chicago, p. 229

10

HOTEL REVIEWS

Listed alphabetically within neighborhood. The following reviews have been condensed for this book. Please go to Fodors.com for full reviews of each property.

THE LOOP, INCLUDING SOUTH LOOP AND WEST LOOP

Chicago's business district, laced with the overhead train tracks of the El, is a desirable—if slightly noisy—place to stay. Hotels here tend to be fairly priced; many are housed in historic buildings, giving them a charm you won't find along glitzier North Michigan Avenue. Easy access to the Art Institute and Millennium Park is a plus.

In the South Loop, the spots of gentrification—most apparent in the new restaurants popping up along South Michigan Avenue—have made this area increasingly popular. A hotel boom has not occurred here yet, so lodging choices are limited to a few old reliables. Many hotels offer package deals with the nearby Museum Campus.

THE LOOP

$$ HOTEL 🏨 **Fairmont Chicago.** On a quiet block near both Michigan Avenue and Lake Michigan, this 45-story pink-granite building has suites with stunning views of Millennium Park. **Pros:** spacious rooms; a short walk from the heart of the city. **Cons:** no pool; not child-friendly. [$] *Rooms from: $289* ✉ *200 N. Columbus Dr., Loop* ☎ *312/565–8000* 🌐 *www.fairmont.com* 🛏 *622 guest rooms, 65 suites* 🍴 *No meals* ⊕ *1:F6.*

$ HOTEL 🏨 **Hampton Majestic, Chicago Theatre District.** The Hampton Majestic is in one of the most high-traffic areas of town; it offers stunning and quiet guest rooms with rust-colored walls and chocolate-brown furnishings. **Pros:** steps from the Art Institute and downtown theaters; unique style; great complimentary breakfast. **Cons:** a hike to the Magnificent Mile; the lobby can seem too crowded with furniture. [$] *Rooms from: $199* ✉ *22 W. Monroe, Loop* ☎ *312/332–5052, 800/548–8690* 🌐 *www.hamptonmajestic.com* 🛏 *135 rooms* 🍴 *Breakfast* ⊕ *4:F2.*

$$ HOTEL 🏨 **Hard Rock Hotel Chicago.** The restaurant chain may not be that wonderful, but the hotel—flashy, loud, and packed with plasma TVs—has our approval; set within the glitzy, Art Deco 40-story Carbide and Carbon Building, it has modern rooms adorned with rock-and-roll paraphernalia and a busy bar, Angels & Kings. **Pros:** well-appointed rooms with great views; good location; Aveda bath products. **Cons:** the dim lighting can get old. [$] *Rooms from: $260* ✉ *230 N. Michigan Ave., Loop* ☎ *312/345–1000, 866/966–5166* 🌐 *www.hardrockhotelchicago.com* 🛏 *361 rooms, 20 suites* 🍴 *No meals* ⊕ *1:E3.*

$ HOTEL FAMILY 🏨 **Hotel Allegro Chicago.** Theater lovers will relish an opportunity to stay at this Art Deco–themed hot spot; the eclectic decor—including pop art–inspired chairs and sofas—is a hit, and the lobby's black-and-gray wallpaper looks super sharp. **Pros:** C.O. Bigelow products in the bathrooms; yoga equipment available upon request; complimentary 24/7 fitness center. **Cons:** small bathrooms and closets. [$] *Rooms from: $209* ✉ *171 W. Randolph St., Loop* ☎ *312/236–0123, 800/643–1500* 🌐 *www.allegrochicago.com* 🛏 *452 rooms, 31 suites* 🍴 *No meals* ⊕ *1:C6.*

$$ **Hotel Burnham.** This historic
HOTEL property, built in 1895 by D. H.
Fodor's Choice Burnham and Co. as one of the
★ first skyscrapers, retains original
details that include Carrara marble wainscoting, terrazzo floors, and large windows in the very heart of the Loop. **Pros:** beautifully restored building; good location right on corner of State Street; free

WORD OF MOUTH

"Chicago is a big convention destination, so hotel rates are very sensitive to supply and demand. If your dates are flexible, you'll be able to find a better deal."
—Citylights

wine hour; steps to public transportation. **Cons:** you can hear the El from some rooms. $ *Rooms from: $239* ✉ *1 W. Washington St., Loop* ☎ *312/782–1111, 866/690–1986* ⊕ *www.burnhamhotel.com* ⤳ *103 rooms, 19 suites* ❑ *No meals* ✛ *4:F1.*

$$ **Hotel Monaco Chicago.** A renovated lobby featuring pops of color and
HOTEL texture (check out the high-gloss red alligator fabric on the registra-
FAMILY tion desk), as well as redesigned meeting rooms named for international destinations such as Tokyo and Paris, inspire wanderlust here; guest rooms reflect the hotel's global-chic aesthetic, with steamer-trunk nightstands and Moroccan lamps. **Pros:** comfortable beds; no extra charge for pets. **Cons:** small gym for a hotel of this size and splendor. $ *Rooms from: $239* ✉ *225 N. Wabash Ave., Loop* ☎ *312/960–8500, 866/610–0081* ⊕ *www.monaco-chicago.com* ⤳ *171 rooms, 20 suites* ❑ *No meals* ✛ *1:E6.*

$$ **Hyatt Regency Chicago.** A massive, light-filled lobby—part of a $168
HOTEL million renovation—is the centerpiece of the Hyatt Regency Chicago, the city's largest hotel with 2,018 rooms in a prime downtown locale. **Pros:** great winter rates; excellent location. **Cons:** there's always a lot of activity in a hotel of this size; not designed for families. $ *Rooms from: $289* ✉ *151 E. Wacker Dr., Loop* ☎ *312/565–8000* ⊕ *www. chicagoregency.hyatt.com* ⤳ *2,018 rooms* ❑ *No meals* ✛ *1:F5.*

$$$ **JW Marriott Chicago.** Mixing architectural elegance with a sleek mod-
HOTEL ern style, this historic property has lots of gorgeous areas, from a light-filled and welcoming lobby bar to elegantly styled and spacious rooms with high ceilings and marble baths. **Pros:** friendly staff; super-comfy beds; blocks from Art Institute and Millennium Park; use of 24-hour fitness center and pool included in rates. **Cons:** lackluster views; not a good option for families. $ *Rooms from: $329* ✉ *151 W. Adams St., Loop* ☎ *312/660–8200, 888/238–2427* ⊕ *www.jwmarriottchicago.com* ⤳ *581 rooms, 29 suites* ❑ *No meals* ✛ *4:F2.*

$$ **The Palmer House Hilton.** The epitome of a grande dame, this bustling
HOTEL and massive property in the center of the Loop has a lobby ceiling mural that wows and lots of gold, marble, and tapestry; the rooms aren't as glitzy, but the location's hard to beat. **Pros:** within walking distance of almost everything most visitors want to do. **Cons:** some rooms are quite small; steep parking fees and daily charges for fitness center; you can hear the El train from some rooms. $ *Rooms from: $259* ✉ *17 E. Monroe St., Loop* ☎ *312/726–7500, 800/445–8667* ⊕ *www.palmerhousehiltonhotel.com* ⤳ *1,639 rooms, 40 suites* ❑ *No meals* ✛ *4:F2.*

10

$$ 🏨 **Radisson Blu Aqua.** With design savvy inside as well as out, this
HOTEL gem has generously sized rooms and so many amenities and so much
FAMILY outdoor space that it feels like an upscale resort in the heart of
Fodor'sChoice downtown. **Pros:** great location; unique design; friendly. **Cons:** room
★ keycards need to be swiped quickly in the elevator, or you're sent off
to the lobby. **$** *Rooms from: $249* ⊠ *221 N. Columbus Dr., Loop*
☎ *312/565–5258, 800/333–3333* ⊕ *www.radissonblu.com* ↻ *334
rooms, 18 suites* ❂| *No meals* ⊹ *1:F6.*

$ 🏨 **The Silversmith Hotel and Suites.** Don't be fooled by the tiny front
HOTEL entrance under the El; the oak-covered lobby is enormous, one of the
largest in the city. **Pros:** convenient to public transportation. **Cons:** the
entrance can be hard to find; some guests complain about outside noise.
$ *Rooms from: $159* ⊠ *10 S. Wabash Ave., Loop* ☎ *312/795–6500,
800/979–0084* ⊕ *www.silversmithhotel.com* ↻ *143 rooms, 63 suites*
❂| *No meals* ⊹ *4:G2.*

$$ 🏨 **Swissôtel Chicago.** The Swissôtel's triangular Harry Weese design
HOTEL allows for panoramic vistas of the city, lake, or river—and the com-
fortable, contemporary rooms feel like condos, with marble bathrooms.
Pros: guests love the view, the pool, and the location. **Cons:** pricey
parking. **$** *Rooms from: $279* ⊠ *323 E. Wacker Dr., Loop* ☎ *312/565–
0565, 888/737–9477* ⊕ *www.swissotelchicago.com* ↻ *621 rooms, 40
suites* ❂| *Multiple meal plans* ⊹ *1:F6.*

$$$ 🏨 **W Chicago City Center.** With a lobby that feels like a club and spa-
HOTEL cious high-tech rooms done up in graphite and cream, this financial
district hotel welcomes a lively crowd along with business travelers.
Pros: sleek, modern design; great location. **Cons:** no free in-room Wi-Fi;
you can hear the El from some rooms. **$** *Rooms from: $399* ⊠ *172 W.
Adams St., Loop* ☎ *312/332–1200, 877/822–0000* ⊕ *www.whotels.
com/citycenter* ↻ *358 rooms, 12 suites* ❂| *No meals* ⊹ *4:F2.*

$$ 🏨 **theWit.** The atmosphere at this sleek spot, topped by ROOF, one of
HOTEL the Loop's most happening bars around, is fun and youthful, and the
rooms are moderately sized and modern, with hanging wall art meant to
resemble puckered lips. **Pros:** bold and bright modern decor; dining and
drinking options are excellent; close to theaters, shopping, and public
transportation. **Cons:** may be too hip for some. **$** *Rooms from: $249*
⊠ *201 N. State St., Loop* ☎ *312/467–0200, 866/318–1514* ⊕ *www.
thewithotel.com* ↻ *310 room, 36 suites* ❂| *No meals* ⊹ *1:E6.*

SOUTH LOOP

$ 🏨 **Essex Inn.** Don't judge this hotel on appearance alone: the nonde-
HOTEL script, plain-brick tower is actually one of the city's most accessible
FAMILY and family-friendly hotels. **Pros:** good value; pool; free Wi-Fi. **Cons:**
Fodor'sChoice bathrooms on the small side; the Wi-Fi is free but slow. **$** *Rooms
★ from: $149* ⊠ *800 S. Michigan Ave., South Loop* ☎ *312/939–2800,
800/621–6909* ⊕ *www.essexinn.com* ↻ *231 rooms, 23 suites* ❂| *No
meals* ⊹ *4:G3.*

$$ 🏨 **Hilton Chicago.** On a busy day the lobby of this Hilton might be mis-
HOTEL taken for a terminal at O'Hare Airport; it's a bustling convention hotel,
but one that retains its distinguished 1920s heritage in a Renaissance-
inspired entrance hall and gold-and-gilt grand ballroom. **Pros:** close to
the museum district; well-appointed public spaces. **Cons:** a fee for use

Essex Inn

PUBLIC Chicago

Hotel Burnham

of the fitness area; steep parking fees. $ *Rooms from: $229* ⊠ *720 S. Michigan Ave., South Loop* ☎ *312/922–4400, 877/865–5320* ⊕ *www. hiltonchicagohotel.com* ⇆ *1,544 rooms, 49 suites* ⫶◯⫶ *Multiple meal plans* ✛ *4:G3.*

$ 🖼 **Holiday Inn & Suites Chicago-Downtown.** Thanks to its proximity to the
HOTEL financial district, this hotel welcomes hordes of business travelers; in
FAMILY summer months they and everyone else have an added incentive to visit:
the rooftop pool. **Pros:** staff goes out of their way to be helpful; convenient on-site washing machines and dryers. **Cons:** the lobby can get quite
crowded; bathrooms are on the small side. $ *Rooms from: $179* ⊠ *506
W. Harrison St., South Loop* ☎ *312/957–9100, 800/465–4329* ⊕ *www.
hidowntown.com* ⇆ *145 rooms, 27 suites* ⫶◯⫶ *No meals* ✛ *4:E3.*

$$$ 🖼 **Renaissance Blackstone Chicago Hotel.** The lobby of this classic hotel
HOTEL has gold-trimmed walls, a gold sofa, and modern flower arrangements
that make it an unusual mix of old and new; the guest rooms are simple
and elegant, with enough modern flair to feel updated yet still give a
sense of the past. **Pros:** great location; close to Museum Campus and
theater district. **Cons:** lobby can be a bit dark, and its decor a bit too
ornate. $ *Rooms from: $329* ⊠ *636 S. Michigan Ave., South Loop*
☎ *312/447–0955, 888/236–2427* ⊕ *www.blackstonerenaissance.com*
⇆ *328 rooms, 4 suites* ⫶◯⫶ *Multiple meal plans* ✛ *4:G3.*

$$ 🖼 **Wyndham Blake Chicago.** A multimillion renovation a few years back
HOTEL updated this spacious landmark in Chicago's historic Printers Row
neighborhood; the lobby is dark but welcoming, and the rooms, in
a mix of browns, reds, and creams, are very large, considering the
location. **Pros:** good South Loop location. **Cons:** the hotel spans three
connected buildings, so the layout can be tricky. $ *Rooms from: $289*
⊠ *500 S. Dearborn, South Loop* ☎ *312/344–4907, 888/999–3223*
⊕ *www.hotelblake.com* ⇆ *168 rooms, 4 suites* ⫶◯⫶ *No meals* ✛ *4:F3.*

BRIDGEPORT

$ 🖼 **Bridgeport Bed and Breakfast.** Located in the South Side neighborhood
B&B/INN that spawned both Mayor Daleys, this B&B inside a 1912 brownstone
FAMILY walk-up features two- and three-bedroom suites with flat-screen TVs,
Fodor'sChoice full-size refrigerators, and separate sitting areas. **Pros:** great for families
★ and groups; friendly staff; awesome food; free, gated parking. **Cons:**
may not be upscale enough for some, and the location won't suit everyone either. $ *Rooms from: $200* ⊠ *3322 S. Morgan St., Bridgeport*
☎ *773/927–1122* ⊕ *www.bridgeportbedandbreakfast.com* ⇆ *4 suites*
⫶◯⫶ *Breakfast* ✛ *4:D6.*

NEAR NORTH AND RIVER NORTH

With a cluster of accommodations around North Michigan Avenue (the
"Magnificent Mile"), the Near North neighborhood is where many
new hotels are springing up—or reinventing themselves, thanks to
multimillion-dollar renovations. Prices are at the high end, but there are
a few deals to be found if you're willing to forgo a pool or concierge service. Consider the area's proximity to great shopping part of the bargain.

In River North, aside from the concentration of independently owned
galleries, it's national chains that lead most of the commerce, including

some surprising boutique hotels that may be part of a chain but have nevertheless carved out a personality all their own.

WORD OF MOUTH

"I loved [the Conrad Chicago]! The room was super cool and modern. The bed was sooooo comfy. It was like sleeping in style. Rooms were equipped with . . . a plasma TV, dimming spot lights above your bed, plush robes and slippers."
—sophrn

NEAR NORTH

$ HOTEL **The Allerton Hotel Chicago.** Named a National Historic Landmark in 1999, this limestone building was a residential "club hotel" for men when it opened in 1924; a renovation restored the limestone facade and left it with a more contemporary, residential feel. **Pros:** lovely neighborhood; close to Mag Mile shopping, Rush Street nightlife, and Navy Pier; delightful concierge and doormen. **Cons:** guest rooms and bathrooms can be small. [$] *Rooms from: $199* ✉ *701 N. Michigan Ave., Near North* ☎ *312/440–1500* 🌐 *www.theallertonhotel.com* *443 rooms, 54 suites* 🍴 *No meals* ✣ *1:E3.*

$$ HOTEL FAMILY **Avenue Crowne Plaza Hotel and Suites Chicago Downtown.** Just yards away from Michigan Avenue, this kid-friendly, high-tech property has pullout leather couches in its suites and zebra-striped chairs in every room. **Pros:** the rooms are generously sized considering the location; the staff is accommodating; great concierge. **Cons:** elevators and pool are small; you might hear sirens, as the hotel is next to a hospital. [$] *Rooms from: $299* ✉ *160 E. Huron, Near North* ☎ *312/787–2900* 🌐 *www.avenuehotelchicago.com* *200 rooms, 150 suites* 🍴 *No meals* ✣ *1:C3.*

$$ HOTEL **Conrad Chicago.** This hotel's Art Deco–inspired lobby avoids feeling like a period piece through its clean-line furniture and creative floral arrangements, and the rooms here—featuring European duvets, oversize pillows, plush bathrobes, and slippers—aim to pamper. **Pros:** beautifully appointed lobby; free Wi-Fi in guest rooms. **Cons:** antiquated heating and cooling systems; it takes two elevators to reach some rooms. [$] *Rooms from: $279* ✉ *521 N. Rush St., Near North* ☎ *312/645–1500, 800/266–7237* 🌐 *www.conradchicago.com* *278 rooms, 33 suites* 🍴 *No meals* ✣ *1:E4.*

$$ HOTEL **The Drake.** Built in 1920, the grande dame of Chicago hotels stands tall where Michigan Avenue and Lake Shore Drive intersect in Chicago's swanky Gold Coast; the beautiful lobby was inspired by an Italian Renaissance palace, and the sounds of a fountain and harpist beckon at the Palm Court, a traditional setting for afternoon tea, especially appealing during the winter holidays. **Pros:** lovely, walkable neighborhood; steps from Oak Street Beach and high-end boutiques. **Cons:** no swimming pool; some rooms are tiny. [$] *Rooms from: $289* ✉ *140 E. Walton Pl., Near North* ☎ *312/787–2200, 800/553–7253* 🌐 *www.thedrakehotel.com* *535 rooms, 74 suites* 🍴 *No meals* ✣ *1:E2.*

$$ HOTEL FAMILY **Embassy Suites Chicago-Downtown/Lakefront.** Every room is spacious here, with a separate bedroom and living area, as well as a view of either Lake Michigan or the Chicago skyline. The sleek glass atrium bustles in the morning with the complimentary breakfast buffet and in the evening during the manager's reception, when free drinks and snacks are served. **Pros:** fitness center with a view of the city; heated indoor

10

CLOSE UP

Chicago Conventions

Travelers to Chicago take note: more than 1,000 conventions and trade shows are scheduled throughout the year. The National Restaurant Association show in May, the Manufacturing Technology show in September, the Radiological Society of America show in late November, and the National Housewares Manufacturing show in January are among the biggest. Hotel rooms may be hard to come by—and tables at popular restaurants even harder.

Proximity to McCormick Place, where most of Chicago's huge trade shows hunker down, is often a convention-eer's top priority, so most wind up staying in the Loop or South Loop, where hotels are just a five-minute cab ride away from the mammoth venue. In these neighborhoods accommodations tend to be older and somewhat less expensive—although there are certainly a few exceptions. Expect somewhat

quiet nights in these parts; although the Loop boasts a revitalized theater district, come sundown there's a lot more revelry north of the Chicago River in the neighborhoods surrounding the Mag Mile. Vibrant Rush Street is the site of many bars, and River North has a high concentration of restaurants and nightclubs.

A meeting or convention in Rosemont or a tight flight schedule should be the only reasons to consider an airport hotel. Prices at these properties are a bit lower, but the O'Hare area is drab. Plus, trips from there to downtown may take an hour during rush hour, bad weather, or periods of heavy construction on the Kennedy Expressway.

Contact the Chicago Convention and Tourism Bureau at ☎ 877/244–2246 for information on conventions, trade shows, and other travel concerns before you book your trip.

---

pool. **Cons:** long line for free wine. Ⓢ *Rooms from: $289* ✉ *511 N. Columbus Dr., Near North* ☎ *312/856–5900, 800/362–2779* ⊕ *www. chicagolakefront.embassysuites.com* ⮎ *455 suites* ⎮◎⎮ *Breakfast* ✛ *1:F4.*

$$
B&B/INN
Fodor's Choice
★

🄴 **Flemish House of Chicago.** This four-story bed-and-breakfast is a good value, considering the posh zip code; each of its eight suites has a slightly different decor, but all are roomy and well appointed, with an impressive collection of antique desks, lamps, and armoires. **Pros:** refrigerators stocked with healthy breakfast foods; complimentary use of laptops. **Cons:** the owners don't always rent rooms for a single night, though they try to be flexible. Ⓢ *Rooms from: $279* ✉ *68 E. Cedar St., Near North* ☎ *312/664–9981* ⊕ *www.innchicago.com* ⮎ *8 suites* ⎮◎⎮ *Breakfast* ✛ *1:E1.*

$$$$
HOTEL
Fodor's Choice
★

🄴 **Four Seasons Hotel Chicago.** At the refined Four Seasons, guest rooms begin on the 30th floor (the hotel sits atop the tony 900 North Michigan Shops), so there's a distinct feeling of seclusion—and there are great views to boot. **Pros:** in the middle of high-end shopping; well-appointed and generously sized rooms; outstanding room service and housekeeping. **Cons:** very expensive; being so high up means that rooms can get a little noisy on windy days. Ⓢ *Rooms from: $525* ✉ *120 E. Delaware Pl., Near North* ☎ *312/280–8800, 800/332–3442* ⊕ *www.fourseasons. com/chicagofs* ⮎ *175 rooms, 168 suites* ⎮◎⎮ *No meals* ✛ *1:E2.*

Flemish House of Chicago

Four Seasons Hotel

$$ ⊞ **Gold Coast Guest House Bed & Breakfast.** Set an enviable four blocks west
B&B/INN of the Magnificent Mile and the lakefront, this 1894 brick town home is
the ideal place to get a feel for Chicago's chichi side: it's near the Oak Street
boutiques and on a tree-lined street filled with similar houses. **Pros:** staff is
warm, welcoming, and very knowledgeable about surrounding bars and
restaurants. **Cons:** spiral stairs can be troublesome if you came with lots of
luggage. $ *Rooms from: $269* ⊠ *113 W. Elm St., Near North* ☎ *312/337–*
0361 ⊕ *www.bbchicago.com* ⤳ *4 rooms* ⦿ *Breakfast* ✛ *1:C1.*

$$ ⊞ **Homewood Suites by Hilton Chicago Downtown.** The suites here seem
HOTEL custom-designed for families, with sleeper sofas, separate bedrooms,
and fully equipped kitchens with full-sized refrigerators and granite
countertops. **Pros:** great view of skyline; heated pool; free, hot breakfast. **Cons:** bathrooms feel cramped. $ *Rooms from: $229* ⊠ *40 E.*
Grand Ave., Near North ☎ *312/644–2222, 800/225–5466* ⊕ *www.*
homewoodsuiteschicago.com ⤳ *233 suites* ⦿ *Breakfast* ✛ *1:E4.*

$ ⊞ **Hotel Indigo.** Even though this hotel caters to business travelers, there
HOTEL is something refreshingly noncorporate about its guest rooms and lobby,
which is dressed in plucky blues and greens. **Pros:** chic hotel; great value;
rooms are bright and uniquely designed. **Cons:** elevators seem noisy to
some guests. $ *Rooms from: $179* ⊠ *1244 N. Dearborn Pkwy., Near*
North ☎ *312/787–4980* ⊕ *www.goldcoastchicagohotel.com* ⤳ *165*
rooms, 2 suites ⦿ *No meals* ✛ *3:H4.*

$$ ⊞ **Hotel Palomar Chicago.** In the middle of one of Chicago's most vibrant
HOTEL neighborhoods and close to Rush Street nightlife, this trendy hot spot
delivers solid rooms and excellent cuisine. **Pros:** the hotel's bustling
vibe matches its surroundings; great for the young and hip; the restau-
rant Sable here is worth a visit. **Cons:** the lobby is on the small side.
$ *Rooms from: $249* ⊠ *505 N. State, Near North* ☎ *312/755–9703,*
877/731–0505 ⊕ *www.hotelpalomar-chicago.com* ⤳ *242 rooms, 19*
suites ⦿ *No meals* ✛ *1:D4.*

$$ ⊞ **InterContinental Chicago Magnificent Mile.** What we love about this for-
HOTEL mer club are the contemporary air of the guest rooms, which feature
mahogany furniture and rich red-and-gold fabrics, and the junior Olym-
pic swimming pool and fitness center. **Pros:** you are sure to be wowed by
the pool and the view of the Magnificent Mile. **Cons:** concierge service
is spotty; staff can be less than friendly. $ *Rooms from: $299* ⊠ *505 N.*
Michigan Ave., Near North ☎ *312/944–4100, 800/628–2112* ⊕ *www.*
icchicagohotel.com ⤳ *720 rooms, 72 suites* ⦿ *No meals* ✛ *1:E4.*

$ ⊞ **The James Chicago.** Sleek and contemporary, this boutique hotel has a
HOTEL prime location on Rush Street, the city's nightlife center, and offers com-
Fodor's Choice fortable rooms, many of them large, with platform beds and dark woods.
★ **Pros:** free Wi-Fi; steps from nightlife and close to many attractions. **Cons:**
some guests complain of noise; steep parking fees. $ *Rooms from: $199*
⊠ *55 E. Ontario St., Near North* ☎ *312/337–1000, 888/526–3778*
⊕ *www.jameshotels.com* ⤳ *297 rooms, 28 suites* ⦿ *No meals* ✛ *1:E4.*

$ ⊞ **Millennium Knickerbocker Hotel.** This 1927 hotel has had a number
HOTEL of identities—including a 1970s stint as the Playboy Hotel and Towers under owner Hugh Hefner; these days the guest rooms sport a
gold, beige, plum, and espresso color palette. **Pros:** location can't be
beat; generously sized rooms. **Cons:** service and quality of rooms are

inconsistent. $ *Rooms from: $189* ✉ *163 E. Walton Pl., Near North* ☎ *312/751–8100, 800/621–8140* ⊕ *www.knickerbockerchicago.com* ⌨ *306 rooms, 26 suites* ⭘⟊ *No meals* ✛ *1:F2.*

$$$
HOTEL
FAMILY

⊞ **Omni Chicago Hotel.** The only all-suites hotel on Michigan Avenue has other things going for it: every room is good-sized and has a plasma TV, and French doors separate the living room from the bedroom, helping make rooms feel like apartments. **Pros:** modern, comfortable rooms with spacious sitting area, desk, and bar. **Cons:** hotel can be too noisy for some. $ *Rooms from: $349* ✉ *676 N. Michigan Ave., Near North* ☎ *312/944–6664, 800/843–6664* ⊕ *www.omnichicago. com* ⌨ *347 suites* ⭘⟊ *No meals* ✛ *1:E3.*

$$$
HOTEL
Fodor'sChoice
★

⊞ **Park Hyatt Chicago.** This Gold Coast star dominates the skyline high above the old Water Tower, and the views are understandably spectacular from many of the oversize rooms, which are done in dark, understated tones. **Pros:** marble bath and soaking tub; free in-room Wi-Fi. **Cons:** some people complain of street noise and slow elevators. $ *Rooms from: $375* ✉ *800 N. Michigan Ave., Near North* ☎ *312/335–1234, 800/633–7313* ⊕ *www.parkchicago.hyatt.com* ⌨ *198 rooms, 13 suites* ⭘⟊ *No meals* ✛ *1:E3.*

$$$$
HOTEL
Fodor'sChoice
★

⊞ **The Peninsula Chicago.** On weekend nights the Peninsula's soaring lobby lounge becomes a sweet fantasia, centered on an overflowing chocolate buffet; guest rooms are lavish with plush pillow-top beds, Wi-Fi, and bedside consoles that control both the TV and the "do-not-disturb" light. **Pros:** top-notch bath products; separate shower and bath. **Cons:** in-house dining options are not the best for families with children; rates are sky-high. $ *Rooms from: $615* ✉ *108 E. Superior St., Near North* ☎ *312/337–2888, 866/288–8889* ⊕ *www.peninsula.com* ⌨ *339 rooms, 83 suites* ⭘⟊ *No meals* ✛ *1:E3.*

$
HOTEL
FAMILY
Fodor'sChoice
★

⊞ **Public Chicago.** With iMacs in the lobby, free Wi-Fi throughout, bikes for the borrowing at the front door, and generously sized, minimalist cream-and-white guest rooms, what was once the slightly faded Ambassador East is now hip and sleek; the location's as stellar as always. **Pros:** close to North Avenue Beach, nightlife, and downtown; friendly, jeans-clad staff; hotelier Ian Schrager's trademark glamour. **Cons:** smallish bathrooms; mocha-colored walls and ceilings and subtle lighting make the hallways dark. $ *Rooms from: $175* ✉ *1301 N. State Pkwy., Near North* ☎ *312/787–3700* ⊕ *www.publichotels.com* ⌨ *250 rooms, 35 suites* ⭘⟊ *No meals* ✛ *3:G4.*

$
HOTEL

⊞ **Raffaello Hotel.** Location is a big draw for visitors to this hotel near the many stores on the Magnificent Mile; inside, you'll find spacious and comfortable rooms in various neutral shades. **Pros:** rooms are comfortable and elegant. **Cons:** some guests have complained of long waits for elevators. $ *Rooms from: $199* ✉ *201 E. Delaware Pl., Near North* ☎ *312/943–5000, 800/898–7198* ⊕ *www.chicagoraffaello.com* ⌨ *170 rooms, 72 suites* ⭘⟊ *No meals* ✛ *1:F2.*

$$$$
FAMILY
Fodor'sChoice
★

⊞ **Ritz-Carlton Chicago.** Shoppers, get ready: the sophisticated and comfortable Ritz-Carlton has indoor access to the Water Tower Place shopping mall and is close to many high-end boutiques. **Pros:** guests feel pampered; great stay for families with children. **Cons:** expensive; some guests miss having in-room tea/coffeemakers. $ *Rooms from: $475*

10

The James Chicago

Park Hyatt Chicago

The Penninsula Chicago

✉ *160 E. Pearson St., Near North* ☎ *312/266–1000, 800/332–3442 outside Illinois* 🌐 *www.fourseasons.com/chicagorc* 🛏 *344 rooms, 91 suites* 🍴 *No meals* ✥ *1:F2.*

$$ HOTEL **Sheraton Chicago Hotel and Towers.** Enormous and ideally situated, this hotel calls out to families with its generously sized rooms and a large pool. **Pros:** a short walk from Michigan Avenue, Navy Pier, and Millennium Park. **Cons:** best for families and businesspeople, not those seeking a romantic escape. [$] *Rooms from: $229* ✉ *301 E. North Water St., Near North* ☎ *312/464–1000* 🌐 *www.sheratonchicago.com* 🛏 *1214 rooms* 🍴 *No meals* ✥ *1:G5.*

$$$ HOTEL Fodor's Choice ★ **Sofitel Chicago Water Tower.** A wonder of modern architecture, this French-owned gem is a prism-shaped structure that juts over the street and widens as it rises; design sensibility shines in guest rooms, too, with honey maple–wood furnishings, Barcelona chairs, and marble bathrooms. **Pros:** modern decor; great ambience. **Cons:** the place is so sleek that some guests have a hard time finding the light switches. [$] *Rooms from: $375* ✉ *20 E. Chestnut St., Near North* ☎ *312/324–4000, 877/813–7700* 🌐 *www.sofitel.com/Chicago* 🛏 *415 rooms, 33 suites* 🍴 *No meals* ✥ *1:E2.*

$$ HOTEL **The Talbott Hotel.** The Talbott is a European-style boutique hotel in a great location in Chicago's Gold Coast, with elegant guest rooms decorated in muted browns and creams, and a lobby that brings to mind an English manor house. **Pros:** hotel has an updated look; staff goes out of their way to please. **Cons:** a hike from Millennium Park and Museum Campus. [$] *Rooms from: $225* ✉ *20 E. Delaware Pl., River North* ☎ *312/944–4970* 🌐 *www.talbotthotel.com* 🛏 *149 rooms, 29 suites* 🍴 *No meals* ✥ *1:D2.*

$$ HOTEL **The Tremont Hotel Chicago at Magnificent Mile.** Just off North Michigan Avenue, this hotel's restaurant, Mike Ditka's, gets infinitely more attention than the rooms do, although its standard guest rooms offer all the essential amenities, including work desks and free Wi-Fi. **Pros:** great location; good value. **Cons:** some guests have complained of small rooms and slow elevators. [$] *Rooms from: $239* ✉ *100 E. Chestnut St., Near North* ☎ *312/751–1900, 800/621–8133* 🌐 *www.tremontchicago.com* 🛏 *130 rooms, 5 suites* 🍴 *No meals* ✥ *1:E2.*

$$$ HOTEL **W Chicago–Lakeshore.** Overlooking Lake Michigan and Navy Pier, this sleek, high-energy hotel has guest rooms with modern, clean design and an elegant neutral palette. **Pros:** cool, hip vibe; business center; right on the lake. **Cons:** service isn't as high as the price would lead you to expect. [$] *Rooms from: $369* ✉ *644 N. Lake Shore Dr., Near North* ☎ *312/943–9200, 877/946–8357* 🌐 *www.whotels.com/lakeshore* 🛏 *490 rooms, 30 suites* 🍴 *No meals* ✥ *1:G4.*

$$$$ HOTEL Fodor's Choice ★ **Waldorf Astoria Chicago.** Two large, Greek-inspired sculptures greet guests as they walk through the entrance of this exquisitely designed hotel, where rooms start at 632 square feet and double in size if you're willing to spend even more. **Pros:** you don't have to leave the hotel to enjoy a fabulous bar—theirs is packed on weekends. **Cons:** the high room bill; most guests say the staff is eager to please, but a few have complained about subpar service and long waits at the very popular bar/restaurant. [$] *Rooms from: $485* ✉ *111 E. Walton St., Near North* ☎ *312/646–1300, 888/370–1938* 🌐 *www.waldorfastoriachicagohotel.com* 🛏 *33 rooms, 155 suites* 🍴 *No meals* ✥ *1:E2.*

Ritz-Carlton Chicago

Sofitel Chicago Water Tower

$$ HOTEL **The Westin Michigan Avenue Chicago.** Location-wise, this hotel scores big, as major malls and flagship shops are within steps of the hotel's front door—and the rooms are restful. **Pros:** the "heavenly" beds; the proximity to area attractions; the ever-present cabs. **Cons:** guests have complained of poor water pressure; steep parking fees. [$] *Rooms from: $279* ✉ *909 N. Michigan Ave., Near North* ☎ *312/943–7200, 800/937–8461* 🌐 *www.westin.com/michiganavenue* 🛏 *752 rooms, 23 suites* 🍴 *No meals* ✥ *1:E2.*

$$$ HOTEL **The Whitehall Hotel.** An exclusive dining club for the city's elite in the 1920s, this Gold Coast boutique hotel that once hosted the likes of Katharine Hepburn and Mick Jagger has spacious, updated rooms in a stellar location close to Magnificent Mile shopping, Rush Street nightlife, and the Oak Street beach. **Pros:** terrific location; updated rooms; remarkably comfortable mattresses. **Cons:** small elevators and fitness center; expensive parking. [$] *Rooms from: $329* ✉ *105 E. Delaware Pl., Near North* ☎ *312/944–6300, 800/948–4255* 🌐 *www.thewhitehallhotel.com* 🛏 *214 rooms, 8 suites* 🍴 *No meals* ✥ *1:E2.*

RIVER NORTH

$$$ HOTEL **Amalfi Hotel Chicago.** With popular magazines on the desks and well-worn books on the shelves, this well-situated hot spot aims for a residential feel. **Pros:** Aveda products; close to nightlife. **Cons:** rooms can be small; some guests have complained of noisy plumbing and water pressure problems. [$] *Rooms from: $399* ✉ *20 W. Kinzie St., River North* ☎ *312/395–9000, 877/262–5341* 🌐 *www.amalfihotelchicago.com* 🛏 *215 rooms, 5 suites* 🍴 *Breakfast* ✥ *1:D5.*

$$$ HOTEL **Courtyard by Marriott Chicago/Magnificent Mile.** Visitors will love the location, the bustling lobby, and the stylish rooms with black granite and track lighting; the hotel is modern but not cold or pretentious. **Pros:** great location in the heart of the shopping district. **Cons:** pool is small; some guests complain of noise problems. [$] *Rooms from: $329* ✉ *165 E. Ontario St., River North* ☎ *312/573–0800, 800/321–2211* 🌐 *www.courtyardchicago.com* 🛏 *283 rooms, 23 suites* 🍴 *No meals* ✥ *1:F4.*

$$$ HOTEL **Dana Hotel and Spa.** Posh and comfy, this chic hot spot has crushed velvet couches, hardwood floors, elegant wood furniture, and floor-to-ceiling windows; head to the Vertigo Sky Lounge bar upstairs for incredible views and tasteful photos of tattooed beauties. **Pros:** the honor bar offers reasonably priced snacks and bottles of wine for under $20. **Cons:** rooms can be on the small side; some say the bathrooms don't allow for enough privacy. [$] *Rooms from: $359* ✉ *660 N. State St., River North* ☎ *312/202–6000, 888/301–3262* 🌐 *www.danahotelandspa.com* 🛏 *216 rooms, 22 suites* 🍴 *No meals* ✥ *1:D3.*

$$$ HOTEL **Embassy Suites Chicago Downtown.** The suites are arranged around an 11-story, plant-filled atrium lobby where bubbling fountains keep noise levels relatively high; bright rooms use the space efficiently, with separate living rooms with a pullout sofa, four-person dining table, and extra TV. **Pros:** great cocktail hour; hotel is just three blocks away from the Magnificent Mile. **Cons:** paid Internet ($9.95 a day or $44.95 for five days). [$] *Rooms from: $399* ✉ *600 N. State St., River North* ☎ *312/943–3800* 🌐 *www.embassysuiteschicago.com* 🛏 *369 suites* 🍴 *Breakfast* ✥ *1:D4.*

$ HOTEL **Hotel Cass, Holiday Inn Express.** With cheerful rooms and nicely designed public spaces, the Hotel Cass is a true boutique hotel that bears little resemblance to more generic branches in the Holiday Inn chain. **Pros:** stellar location; family-friendly; good value. **Cons:** some guests have complained of small rooms; crowded elevators. [$] *Rooms from: $149* ✉ *640 N. Wabash Ave., River North* ☎ *312/787–4030* 🌐 *www.hotelcass.com* 🛏 *172 rooms, 3 suites* 🍴 *Breakfast* ✣ *3:H6.*

$$ HOTEL **MileNorth, a Chicago Hotel.** In an often overlooked section of Chicago just east of Michigan Avenue, this hotel offers an outstanding 29th-floor outdoor bar with an enviable view of the city; the guest rooms are modern and homey. **Pros:** bars and restaurants steps away; excellent customer service. **Cons:** steep parking fees; might be a little too far to walk to Millennium Park and the theater district. [$] *Rooms from: $299* ✉ *166 E. Superior St., River North* ☎ *312/787–6000* 🌐 *www.milenorthhotel.com* 🛏 *126 rooms, 87 suites* 🍴 *No meals* ✣ *1:F3.*

$$$ HOTEL **Sax Chicago.** Visitors to Chicago would be hard-pressed to find a more chic or tech-savvy place than the Sax. **Pros:** no need to leave the hotel for nightlife, thanks to the popular Crimson Lounge; the House of Blues is right next door. **Cons:** the gym's small; no free Wi-Fi. [$] *Rooms from: $349* ✉ *333 N. Dearborn St., River North* ☎ *312/245–0333* 🌐 *www.hotelsaxchicago.com* 🛏 *334 rooms, 21 suites* 🍴 *No meals* ✣ *1:D5.*

$$$$ HOTEL Fodor's Choice ★ **Trump International Hotel & Tower Chicago.** With some of the best views in Chicago, the Trump International Hotel & Tower attracts a crowd of power brokers, women in fur coats, and anyone else who wants top-of-the-line luxury and is ready to pay for it. **Pros:** impeccable service; lavish amenities. **Cons:** the rates (and everything else) may be way too much; expensive drinks at the bar. [$] *Rooms from: $395* ✉ *401 N. Wabash Ave., River North* ☎ *312/588–8000, 866/891–2125* 🌐 *www.trumphotelcollection.com/chicago* 🛏 *218 rooms, 121 suites* 🍴 *No meals* ✣ *3:H6.*

$$$$ HOTEL **The Westin Chicago River North.** This elegant hotel is centrally located near the premier shopping destination, Michigan Avenue, as well as top Chicago attractions, which makes it an ideal stay for first-time visitors. **Pros:** polite staff; the "heavenly bed" lives up to its name. **Cons:** no pool; some say the decor is ready for an update. [$] *Rooms from: $799* ✉ *320 N. Dearborn St., River North* ☎ *312/744–1900, 887/866–9216* 🌐 *www.westinchicago.com* 🛏 *407 rooms, 17 suites* 🍴 *No meals* ✣ *1:D5.*

LINCOLN PARK AND WICKER PARK

Three miles of lakefront parkland draw people to the Lincoln Park neighborhood—and most hotels here are just blocks away. Room rates are decidedly lower than those downtown, the downside being that you'll invest more in transportation to hit top sites. Parking is easier, but never a snap; plan on using the valet. Bucktown and Wicker Park are both filled with top-notch bars and restaurants. Wicker Park attracts an artsy mix of young couples and singles who can't walk more than a yard without stumbling into a mom-and-pop-owned fast-food joint or a four-star restaurant. Bucktown is a mostly quiet, residential area, with its best restaurants on its far south and eastern edges.

A Beautiful Stay in the Neighborhood

Chicago is, famously, a city of neighborhoods. Chicagoans like to define themselves by where they hang their hat, with attendant pride, snobbery, or aspirations to street cred (of all kinds). For visitors, setting up a temporary base in one of the neighborhoods offers many advantages. This is especially true for leisure travelers. Without an expense account to ease downtown's hotel bills and menu shock, staying right in downtown can get very expensive very quickly.

When choosing accommodations, it pays to look beyond the Loop and the Magnificent Mile.

A walk up Clark Street or Lincoln Avenue in Lincoln Park opens up miles of reasonably priced dining possibilities. Along one short stretch of the former, you'll pass an excellent fusion restaurant, a take-out crepe place, a grocery store, and a couple of diners where the waitress might call you "hon." Remember that the next time you're called something else in the Loop.

There's also better and cheaper parking. Downtown you'll usually pay at least $30 a day. Rates at garages in outlying neighborhoods are less. There's even a chance, albeit rather remote, of finding street parking. Some days that's like saying there's a chance of a Republican mayor, but it happens.

The best reason to stay in a neighborhood is the chance to immerse yourself in the rhythms of the city. You get a chance to live as most Chicagoans live. In the neighborhoods you'll see the sky. You'll have countless distinctive restaurants and shops to browse in.

If you'd like to be somewhat near downtown, the happening Lincoln Park and Lakeview neighborhoods offer a handful of hotels. As a bonus, accommodations are relatively near the lakefront. Most also have relatively easy access to public transportation or routes well traveled by cabs. A determined walker can even get from Lincoln Park to the Magnificent Mile in a half hour.

Getting to downtown sights from farther afield may sound like too much trouble. But keep in mind that thousands upon thousands of Chicagoans make the trip every day. And, like them, you'll come home to something vital and intriguing at night. Much of the Loop, on the other hand, becomes relatively quiet after rush hour. In places like Lakeview the starting gun goes off at 7 pm.

The neighborhood experience isn't for everyone. Those determined to "see it all" may find the journey in from such outposts takes too much time. Also, small hotels and B&Bs cannot offer the same pampering and facilities that are typical at the luxury digs downtown.

It's a search for small moments, for random encounters, for something indefinable—the vibe, you might say—that most appeals to visitors who stay in outer neighborhoods. Each area's rhythm is different. And it's easier to hear the city's songs away from the hustle and bustle and the tall buildings.

10

Radisson Blu Aqua Chicago

Trump International Hotel & Tower

LINCOLN PARK

$$ HOTEL Fodor's Choice ★ **Hotel Lincoln.** Directly across from Lincoln Park, this historic property has a fresh, cool, kitschy vibe but feels authentic thanks to details like the original Hotel Lincoln sign in the lobby. **Pros:** pet-friendly; great residential neighborhood; authentic Chicago feel. **Cons:** a/c units are noisy; historic hotel means small bathrooms. [$] *Rooms from: $249* ✉ *1816 N. Clark St., Lincoln Park* ☎ *312/254–4700, 888/378–7994* 🌐 *www.hotellincolnchicago.com* 🛏 *127 guest rooms, 57 suites* 🍴 *No meals* ✣ *3:G2.*

$$ B&B/INN **Villa D'Citta Boutique Mansion.** This Tuscan-themed bed-and-breakfast—complete with a (shared) fully stocked gourmet kitchen—allows guests all the comforts of a top-notch hotel in a residential neighborhood where such rooms can be hard to find. **Pros:** meticulous innkeeper keeps the rooms well cared for; bustling neighborhood; steps away from dozens of boutique shops. **Cons:** some guests have complained of noise. [$] *Rooms from: $299* ✉ *2230 N. Halsted St., Lincoln Park* ☎ *312/771–0696, 800/228–6070* 🌐 *www.villadcitta.com* 🛏 *1 room, 5 suites* 🍴 *Breakfast* ✣ *3:E1.*

WICKER PARK

$ B&B/INN **Wicker Park Inn.** One of the condolike rooms in this small bed-and-breakfast is a great choice for anyone who wants to venture outside downtown Chicago for a taste of two of its most popular neighborhoods—Wicker Park and Bucktown. **Pros:** rooms are spacious, very well maintained, and homey; top-notch service; dozens of restaurants and bars located just blocks away. **Cons:** some complain of noise problems from the El or other guests. [$] *Rooms from: $139* ✉ *1329 N. Wicker Park Ave., Wicker Park* ☎ *773/486–2743* 🌐 *www.wickerparkinn.com* 🛏 *4 rooms, 3 suites* 🍴 *Breakfast* ✣ *3:B4.*

LAKEVIEW AND FAR NORTH SIDE

Seemingly light-years away from downtown, Lakeview hotels entice with their proximity to Wrigley Field and the summertime street festivals for which the neighborhood is known. As you venture farther north, accommodations tend to be quainter and spaces more intimate. But you'd be hard-pressed to find a better or more eclectic collection of shops and eateries. This is a vibrant neighborhood that buzzes well into the night; you're never too far from a cold Goose Island, a hole-in-the-wall sushi joint, or Lake Michigan itself.

LAKEVIEW

$ HOTEL **Best Western Plus Hawthorne Terrace Hotel.** This centrally located hotel in the city's Lakeview neighborhood offers all essential amenities at a reasonable price: a stay here includes free Continental breakfast and use of business facilities and a fitness center. **Pros:** close to Wrigley Field and popular bars and restaurants; helpful staff. **Cons:** parking is not ideal. [$] *Rooms from: $179* ✉ *3434 N. Broadway, Lakeview* ☎ *773/244–3434, 888/675–2378* 🌐 *www.hawthorneterrace.com* 🛏 *59 rooms, 24 suites* 🍴 *Breakfast* ✣ *1:F3.*

LODGING ALTERNATIVES

APARTMENT RENTALS

For your trip to Chicago, you may want a little more space than a hotel room provides. If you decide to book online, beware that apartment rental scams do exist. In some cases, travelers have lost their deposit money, or their prepaid rent (note: never wire money to an individual's account).

There are a few reputable providers of short-term rentals, such as **Vacation Rental By Owner** (⊕ www.vrbo.com), which offers a money-back guarantee. But many Fodorites have turned to suite hotels and B&Bs with apartmentlike accommodations to guard themselves from possible scams.

BED-AND-BREAKFASTS

For an intimate look at the city, some visitors like to stay at bed-and-breakfasts. For additional options, try the **Chicago Bed & Breakfast Association** (☎ 773/394–2000 or 800/375–7084 ⊕ www.chicago-bed-breakfast.com).

$ **City Suites Hotel.** European travelers love this hotel for its cozy, residential feel; two-thirds of the rooms have separate sitting areas and
HOTEL pullout couches. **Pros:** flat-screen TVs in all rooms; great neighborhood. **Cons:** rooms are on the small side; an underwhelming breakfast. $ *Rooms from: $139* ⊠ *933 W. Belmont Ave., Lakeview* ☎ *773/404–3400, 800/248–9108* ⊕ *www.chicagocitysuites.com* ↗ *16 rooms, 29 suites* ⦿| *Breakfast* ✛ *2:F4.*

$$$ **The Majestic Hotel.** It's no wonder lovey-dovey couples are a big part
HOTEL of this hotel's clientele; everything here—from the roaring fireplace in the lobby to the cozy rooms' Victorian-style furnishings—says romance. **Pros:** friendly staff; good for families as some rooms have pull-out couches; free Wi-Fi. **Cons:** furnishings are a bit dated; some have complained of issues with the heating. $ *Rooms from: $329* ⊠ *528 W. Brompton Ave., Lakeview* ☎ *773/404–3499, 800/727–5108* ⊕ *www.majestic-chicago.com* ↗ *28 rooms, 24 suites* ⦿| *Breakfast* ✛ *2:G3.*

$ **The Willows Hotel Chicago.** The lobby of this 1920s hotel, designed in
HOTEL 19th-century French Provincial style, opens onto a tree-lined street in Lakeview, just three blocks from the lake and central to stores, restaurants, and movie theaters; the hotel's prime location and proximity to the El make it a top choice. **Pros:** just steps away from bars, restaurants, and public transit. **Cons:** modestly decorated rooms. $ *Rooms from: $179* ⊠ *555 W. Surf St., Lakeview* ☎ *773/528–8400, 800/787–3108* ⊕ *www.willowshotelchicago.com* ↗ *51 rooms, 4 suites* ⦿| *Breakfast* ✛ *2:G5.*

EVANSTON

$ **Margarita European Inn.** While the varied room sizes and narrow corridors may bring to mind a college dormitory, you won't find a more
B&B/INN charming place to stay in Chicago's Near North suburbs. **Pros:** a fun, off-the-beaten-path place; close to Northwestern University. **Cons:** breakfast is merely adequate. $ *Rooms from: $189* ⊠ *1566 Oak Ave., Evanston* ☎ *847/869–2273* ⊕ *www.margaritainn.com* ↗ *46 rooms* ⦿| *Breakfast* ✛ *2:D1.*

SHOPPING

Updated
by Jessica
Herman

A potent concentration of famous retailers around Michigan Avenue and neighborhoods bursting with one-of-a-kind shops combine to make Chicago a shopper's city. Michigan Avenue's famous Magnificent Mile lures thousands of avid shoppers every week. How often can you find Neiman Marcus, Macy's, Nordstrom, Saks Fifth Avenue, Lord & Taylor, and Barneys New York within walking distance of one another? In recent years State Street has regained some of its former glory as well, with discount department stores sharing prime real estate with trendier clothing stores and the Block 37 retail development.

Neighborhood shopping areas, like fun-but-sophisticated Lincoln Park, eclectic Lakeview, and the hipster haven of Bucktown/Wicker Park, offer countless independent stores that cater to shoppers' every desire, whether Prairie Style furniture, cowboy boots, or outsider art. And there are countless smaller shopping enclaves within these neighborhoods that offer concentrated clusters of antiques stores, home-furnishings shops, high-end boutiques, and other specialty stores. Those averse to paying retail won't have to venture far to unearth bargains on everything from fine jewelry to business attire. When it comes to shopping, this is one city that has it all.

Be forewarned that a steep 9.5% sales tax is added to all purchases in the city except groceries and prescription drugs. Neighborhood shops on the North Side, especially those in Bucktown and Wicker Park, tend to open late—around 11 or noon. Most stores, particularly those on North Michigan Avenue and the North Side, are open on Sunday, although this varies by type of business (galleries, for example, are often closed on Monday); where applicable, more information is provided at the beginning of each category. With an open mind and an equally open wallet, you can find your own shopping paradise in Chi-town.

SHOPPING BY NEIGHBORHOOD

THE LOOP

Named for the elevated train tracks encircling it, the Loop is the city's business and financial hub. In recent years it has reclaimed some of its former glory as a thriving shopping destination as well.

The Loop's main thoroughfare, State Street, has had its share of ups and downs. After serving as Chicago's retail corridor for much of the 20th century, the street lost its stature for a time, but these days "that great street" is once again on the ascent, with a number of discount retailers like Old Navy and New York & Company dotted in between the two remaining department stores, Macy's (formerly Marshall Field's) and Sears. Branches of Urban Outfitters and the cosmetics store Sephora add to the mix. The opening of Block 37 in 2009 injected fresh excitement into the area. The glass-enclosed mall features major retail chains like Anthropologie and Zara alongside local independent shops. One block east, Wabash Street's "Jewelers Row" is a series of high-rises and street-level shops hawking serious bling.

ANTIQUES

Harlan J. Berk. Travel back to antiquity amid this wondrous trove of classical Greek, Roman, and Byzantine coins and artifacts. Don't miss the gallery rooms in the back. ⊠ *31 N. Clark St.* ☎ *312/609–0016* ⊕ *www. harlanjberk.com.*

BOOKS AND MUSIC

Accent Chicago. Pop into Accent Chicago in the John Hancock Center for a gift that's sure to inspire Chicago nostalgia, from a print of a vintage Chicago Transit Authority poster to a mug adorned with the city's iconic skyline. ⊠ *875 N. Michigan Ave.* ☎ *312/654–8125* ⊕ *www. accentchicagostore.com.*

Coulsons Music Matters. Musicians come here to find sheet music that suits their style—whether it's jazz, classical, pop, or just about anything else. You'll also find handy accessories like piano lights and metronomes. ⊠ *77 E. Van Buren St.* ☎ *312/461–1989.*

Selected Works Bookstore. This charming used bookstore relocated from a warrenlike basement in Wrigleyville to a bright, sunny shop on the second floor of the Fine Arts Building. Inside you'll find an intriguing, though somewhat chaotic, selection of used books and sheet music watched over by the proprietor's friendly cat. ⊠ *410 S. Michigan Ave., Suite 210* ☎ *312/447–0068* ⊕ *www.selworkschicago.com.*

BOUTIQUE

Florodora. The historic Monadnock Building location complements this boutique's selection of vintage-inspired clothing, accessories, and home decor items. Browse the well-edited selection at sister shop Florodora Shoes—with brands like Coclico and Chie Mihara—just down the hall at 348 S. Dearborn. ⊠ *330 S. Dearborn St.* ☎ *312/212–8860* ⊕ *florodora.com.*

CAMERAS AND ELECTRONICS

Fodor's Choice **Central Camera.** This century-old store is a Loop institution, stacked to
★ the rafters with cameras and darkroom equipment at competitive prices.
⊠ *230 S. Wabash Ave.* ☎ *312/427–5580* ⊕ *www.centralcamera.com.*

CLOTHING

Optimo Fine Hats. One of the last stores of its kind, Optimo makes high-
end custom straw and felt hats for men in an atmosphere that evokes
1930s and '40s haberdashery. The store, located in the Beverly neighborhood on the Far Southwest Side, also offers a complete line of hat
services, including cleaning, blocking, and repairs. ⊠ *10215 S. Western
Ave., Far Southwest Side* ☎ *773/238–2999* ⊕ *www.optimohats.com*
⊠ *320 S. Dearborn St.*

Syd Jerome. Board of Trade types who like special attention and snazzy
designers come to this legendary clothier for brands like Giorgio Armani
and Ermenegildo Zegna. Home and office consultations are available.
⊠ *2 N. LaSalle St.* ☎ *312/346–0333* ⊕ *www.sydjerome.com.*

FOOD AND TREATS

Garrett Popcorn. Bring home a tub of Chicago's famous popcorn instead
of a giant pencil or T-shirt, and you'll score major points. The lines can
be long, but trust us—this stuff is worth the wait. ⊠ *26 W. Randolph
St.* ☎ *888/476–7267* ⊕ *www.garrettpopcorn.com* ⊠ *4 E. Madison St.*
⊠ *27 W. Jackson Blvd.* ⊠ *500 W. Madison St., 2nd Floor* ⊠ *625 N.
Michigan Ave., Near North.*

Iwan Ries and Co. Iwan Ries did not just jump on the cigar bandwagon; the
family-owned store has been around since 1857. Cigar smokers are welcome to light up in the smoking area, which also displays antique pipes.
▉**TIP**→ **Almost 100 brands of cigars are available, as are 15,000 or so
pipes, deluxe Elie Bleu humidors, and many other smoking accessories.**
⊠ *19 S. Wabash Ave., 2nd fl.* ☎ *312/372–1306* ⊕ *www.iwanries.com.*

JEWELRY AND ACCESSORIES

Jewelers Center. The largest concentration of wholesale and retail jewelers in the Midwest has been housed in this building since 1921, and is
open to the general public. Roughly 190 retailers span 13 floors, offering all kinds of jewelry, watches, and related repairs and services. ⊠ *5
S. Wabash Ave.* ☎ *312/424–2664* ⊕ *www.jewelerscenter.com.*

Legend of Time. This family-owned business, the former Chicago Watch
Center, has one of the city's most outstanding inventories of used luxury
watches. ⊠ *3 S. Wabash Ave.* ☎ *312/609–0003* ⊕ *www.legendoftime.com.*

Wabash Jewelers Mall. Compare prices on engagement rings or tennis
bracelets at the Wabash Jewelers Mall, which houses more than a dozen
vendors under one roof. This is also one of the best places in the city
to shop for loose diamonds. ⊠ *21 N. Wabash Ave., at Washington St.*
☎ *312/263–1757.*

MUSEUM STORES

Fodor's Choice **Chicago Architecture Foundation ArchiCenter Shop & Tour Center.** Daniel
★ Burnham's 1904 Santa Fe Building is a fitting home for the Chicago
Architecture Foundation. Chock-full of architecture-related books,
home accessories, and everything and anything related to Frank Lloyd

Wright, the store is also the place to sign up for one of the foundation's acclaimed tours, which are conducted on foot or by bus, bicycle, and river cruise. ✉ *224 S. Michigan Ave.* ☎ *312/922–3432* ⊕ *caf. architecture.org.*

Illinois Artisans Shop. This store run by the Illinois State Museum culls the best jewelry, ceramics, glass, and dolls from craftspeople around the state and sells them at very reasonable prices. There are also exhibits on anything from quilting to Celtic design. ✉ *James R. Thompson Center, 100 W. Randolph St., Suite 2-200* ☎ *312/814–5321* ⊕ *www.museum. state.il.us/ismsites/chicago/index.html?IAS=* ☉ *Closed weekends.*

Museum Shop at the Art Institute of Chicago. Museum reproductions in the form of jewelry, posters, and Frank Lloyd Wright–inspired decorative accessories, as well as books and toys, fill the Art Institute's gift shop. If you're keen on one of the museum's current big exhibits, chances are you'll find some nifty souvenirs to take away. ✉ *111 S. Michigan Ave.* ☎ *312/443–3583* ⊕ *www.artinstituteshop.org.*

Spertus Shop. Come here for modern Jewish must-haves, like Moses action figures and Jonathan Adler yarmulkes. There's also more traditional holiday ware, books, and music. The shop's inside the Spertus Institute for Jewish Learning and Leadership. ✉ *610 S. Michigan Ave.* ☎ *312/322–1740* ⊕ *www.spertusshop.org.*

SHOES, HANDBAGS, AND LEATHER GOODS

Altman's Men's Shoes and Boots. Price tags are still written by hand at this family-owned institution that's been around since 1932. Its 27 stockrooms hold 50,000 pairs of men's shoes in sizes from 5 to 20 and in widths from AAA to EEEEEE. You can find anything from Timberland and Tony Lama boots to Allen Edmonds and Alden oxfords. ✉ *120 W. Monroe St.* ☎ *312/332–0667* ⊕ *www.altmansshoesandboots.com.*

SPAS

Valeo Spa. This isn't your typical spa, although you can get typical treatments if you like. Focused on wellness, the sprawling space includes a fitness center, pool, and elegant, understated locker and transition rooms, where you're offered a glass of wine at the end of your treatment. Men and women will feel comfortable in their separate spaces, but there's also a couples suite for those so inclined. In Valeo's "clarity chambers"—based on Turkish or Moroccan hammams—guests are warmed by a fireplace and heated stone benches and floors. At the center is an oval-shape "belly stone"—a slab of heated marble used for body treatments or just for relaxation. Among the options in the clarity chambers is an hour-long treatment to exfoliate and purify the skin with a clay compound from the Atlas Mountains of Morocco. Most treatments are priced based on length of time, so you can decide just how long a treatment will last. ✉ *JW Marriott, 151 W. Adams St.* ☎ *312/660–8250* ⊕ *www.valeochicago.com* ☉ *Daily 8–8* ☞ *$150 60-min massage, $125 90-min facial. Hair salon, sauna, steam room. Gym with: cardiovascular machines, free weights, weight-training equipment. Services: baths, body wraps, facials, massage, nail treatment, scrubs, waxing. Classes and programs: body sculpting, personal training, weight training.*

SOUTH LOOP

ANTIQUES

Susanin's Auctions. Live, usually themed, auctions occur on Saturday mornings about once a month. Preview items are also displayed on the floor for immediate sale at a set price. Preview hours are typically Monday through Saturday 10 am–5 pm the week before the auction. ⊠ *900 S. Clinton St.* ☎ *312/832–9800* ⊕ *www.susanins.com.*

WEST LOOP

ART GALLERIES

Douglas Dawson Gallery. Douglas Dawson has 5,000 square feet of space plus a sculpture garden in his West Loop space, which showcases ancient and historic art from Africa, Oceania, and the Americas. ⊠ *400 N. Morgan St.* ☎ *312/226–7975* ⊕ *www.douglasdawson.com.*

G.R. N'Namdi Gallery. This gallery represents contemporary painters and sculptors, with an emphasis on African-American and Latin-American artists. ⊠ *110 N. Peoria St.* ☎ *312/563–9240* ⊕ *www.grnnamdi.com.*

Mars Gallery. A neighborhood pioneer that showcases contemporary pop and outsider artwork, Mars Gallery shows work by Peter Mars and other well-known locals like Kevin Luthardt. ⊠ *1139 W. Fulton Market* ☎ *312/226–7808* ⊕ *www.marsgallery.com.*

Packer Schopf Gallery. Browse through an extensive collection of contemporary art with a special emphasis on folk and outsider pieces at this gallery, which is run by the well-known local owners Aron Packer and William Schopf. ⊠ *942 W. Lake St.* ☎ *312/226–8984* ⊕ *packergallery.com.*

Robert Wayner/Black Walnut Gallery. The gallery has a selection of beautiful handcrafted wood furniture, sculpture, and art as well as stunning and affordable contemporary art. ⊠ *220 N. Aberdeen* ☎ *312/286–2307* ⊕ *www.blackwalnutgallery.com.*

CAMERAS AND ELECTRONICS

Helix Camera & Video. Professional photographers buy and rent camera and darkroom equipment at this eight-story warehouse on Racine Avenue just west of Greektown (1½ mi west of the Loop). A good selection of used equipment is available. Underwater photography equipment is a specialty. ⊠ *310 S. Racine Ave.* ☎ *312/421–6000* ⊕ *www.helixcamera.com.*

FOOD AND TREATS

Terry's Toffee. This local fave hit the big time by becoming a staple in Academy Awards gift bags. Try exotic chai-infused, peppermint pistachio, or lavender-vanilla toffee—or stick with the irresistible almond-and-pecan McCall's Classic, named for owner Terry Opalek's grandmother, whose recipe inspired the entire operation. ⊠ *1117 W. Grand Ave.* ☎ *312/733–2700* ⊕ *www.terrystoffee.com* ⊠ *The Galleria, 5247 N. Clark St., 1st fl., Far North Side* ☎ *773/878–8570.*

MARKETS

Fodor's Choice
★
Chicago Antique Market. This indoor-outdoor flea market is similar to the ones you might find in London and Paris. More than 200 stalls fill the Plumber's Hall building and parking lot selling furniture, jewelry, books, and more. ■TIP→ The vibe is more funky fashions and vintage treasures than tube socks and refurbished vacuums. There's also an Indie Designer Fashion Market, showcasing one-of-a-kind wearables by up-and-coming local designers. Children under 12 get in free, and tickets are slightly cheaper if you buy them in advance. ⊠ *Plumbers Hall, 1340 W. Washington St.* ☎ *312/666–1200* ⊕ *www.randolphstreetmarket.com/chicagoantiquemarket* ⊠ *$10* ⊙ *March–Dec., usually runs last weekend of the month, 10–5.*

Maxwell Street Market. A legendary outdoor bazaar that is part of the cultural landscape of the city, the Maxwell Street Market was closed by the city of Chicago amid much controversy in the 1990s. Soon after, it reopened in its current location as the New Maxwell Street Market, where it remains a popular spot, particularly for Latino immigrants, to buy and sell wares. The finds aren't so fabulous, but the atmosphere sure is fun, with live blues and stalls selling Mexican street food. ⊠ *800 S. Desplaines St.* ☎ *312/745–4676* ⊠ *Free* ⊙ *Sun. 7 am–3 pm.*

SPAS

Spa Space. The warm, inviting spa is a favorite of stressed-out traders and other type A's who work nearby at the Chicago Board of Trade and other Loop office buildings. Serious pampering includes massages specifically geared to runners and golfers and a pedicure suite where bottles of wine are welcome. All facials are dermatologist approved, and body treatments include grape-seed scrubs, seaweed wraps, and waxing. The packages include the Space Stressbuster Express, with a 90-minute massage, facial, aromatherapy manicure, and peppermint pedicure. ⊠ *161 N. Canal St.* ☎ *312/466–9585* ⊕ *www.spaspace.com* ⊙ *Mon., Wed., Thurs. 10–8, Tues. 11–8, Fri. 9–7, Sat. 9–6, Sun. 11–5* ☞ *$95 60-min massage, $95 60-min facial, $160 3-treatment package. Steam room. Services: aromatherapy, body wraps, facials, massage, scrubs, waxing, nail treatment.*

NEAR NORTH AND THE MAGNIFICENT MILE

We've got news for shopaholics who consider the Midwest flyover country: if you haven't shopped Chicago's Magnificent Mile, you simply haven't shopped. With more than 450 stores along the stretch of Michigan Avenue that runs from the Chicago River to Oak Street, the Mag Mile is one of the best shopping strips the world over. Chanel, Hermès, and Gucci are just a few of the legendary fashion houses with fabulous boutiques here. Other notables such as Anne Fontaine, Kate Spade, and Prada also have Mag Mile outposts, recognizing the everybody-who's-anybody importance of the address. Shoppers with down-to-earth budgets will find there's plenty on the Mag Mile as well, with national chains making an extra effort at their multilevel megastores here. Cozying up against the Magnificent Mile is the Gold Coast, an area that's as moneyed as it sounds. The streets teem with luxury hotels, upscale restaurants, and snazzy boutiques, mainly concentrated on Oak and Rush streets. There's also a huge new Barneys New York on East Oak Street just off Rush. (Many consider swanky Oak Street part of the Mag Mile, though neighboring streets technically are not.)

ART GALLERIES

Colletti Gallery. Fine antique posters, a serious collection of European ceramics and glass, and an eclectic selection of furniture transport you to the late 19th century. ⊠ *49 E. Oak St.* ☎ *312/664–6767* ⊕ *www. collettigallery.com.*

Joel Oppenheimer, Inc. Established in 1969, this gallery in the Wrigley Building has an amazing collection of Audubon prints and specializes in antique natural-history pieces. ⊠ *410 N. Michigan Ave.* ☎ *312/642–5300* ⊕ *www.audubonart.com.*

Richard Gray Gallery. This gallery lures serious collectors with modern masters such as David Hockney and Roy Lichtenstein. ⊠ *John Hancock Center, 875 N. Michigan Ave., Suite 2503* ☎ *312/642–8877* ⊕ *www. richardgraygallery.com.*

R.S. Johnson Fine Art. More than 50 museums are among the clients of R.S. Johnson, a Mag Mile resident for more than 55 years. The family-run gallery sells old masters along with art by Picasso, Degas, and Goya to the public and to private collectors. ⊠ *645 N. Michigan Ave., 9th fl., entrance on Erie St.* ☎ *312/943–1661* ⊕ *www.rsjohnsonfineart.com.*

BEAUTY

Bravco Beauty Centre. Need a hard-to-find shampoo, an ionic hair dryer, or simply a jar of Vaseline? Bravco is the place for all this and more, with an expert staff and a huge inventory. Also check out B-Too upstairs for makeup and accessories. Cash or check only. ⊠ *43 E. Oak St.* ☎ *312/943–4305* ⊕ *www.bravcobeauty.com.*

BOOKS, MUSIC, AND SOUVENIRS

Accent Chicago. At this mini-chain, you can nab T-shirts, sweatshirts, mugs, puzzles, posters, shot glasses, and countless other items emblazoned with the city's iconic skyline or with local attractions, sports teams, and personalities. ⊠ *John Hancock Center, 875 N. Michigan Ave.* ☎ *312/654–8125* ⊕ *www.accentchicagostore.com* ⊠ *Water Tower Place, 835 N. Michigan Ave.* ☎ *312/944–1354* ⊠ *The Shops at North Bridge., 520 N. Michigan Ave.* ☎ *312/329–1130* ⊠ *150 N. Michigan Ave., Loop* ☎ *312/541–9155.*

SPOTLIGHT: NAVY PIER

Extending more than a half mile onto Lake Michigan from 600 East Grand Avenue, Navy Pier treats you to spectacular views of the skyline, especially from a jumbo Ferris wheel set in slow motion. Stores and carts gear their wares to families and tourists, and most don't merit a special trip. But if you're out there, check out **Oh Yes Chicago!** (☎ 312/321–0557) for souvenirs and the **Chicago Children's Museum Store** (☎ 312/527–4276) for educational kids' toys. Many stores are open late into the evening, especially in summer.

Jazz Record Mart. Billing itself as the world's largest jazz record store, this "mart" sells tens of thousands of new and used titles on CD, vinyl, and cassette. You'll also find a broad selection of world music. A vast, in-depth selection of jazz and blues and knowledgeable sales staff make the store a must for music lovers. ⊠ *27 E. Illinois St.* ☎ *312/222–1467* ⊕ *jazzmart.com.*

Space 519. Lost your luggage or need a gift in a hurry? Pop into this style-conscious Mag Mile general store for anything and everything you need—clothing, accessories, perfume and makeup, coffee-table books, vintage watches, and even vintage furniture. ⊠ *900 N. Michigan Shops, 900 N. Michigan Ave., Level 5* ☎ *312/751–1519* ⊕ *www.space519.com.*

CAMERAS AND ELECTRONICS

Apple Store. It's a multilevel fantasyland for fans of Apple's iPad, computers, and related accessories. There's also an Internet café where PC fans can get a glimpse of life on the other side. ⊠ *679 N. Michigan Ave.* ☎ *312/529–9500* ⊕ *apple.com* ⊠ *801 W. North Ave., Lincoln Park* ☎ *312/777–4200.*

CHILDREN'S CLOTHING

Madison and Friends. Mini Mag Mile shoppers get their own high-end shopping experience at this boutique, which stocks labels like Splendid and Les Tout Petits in newborn through junior sizes. They also carry top-of-the-line strollers and accessories. Adults can shop in the Denim Lounge downstairs, where the latest styles from J Brand, True Religion, and other of-the-moment brands are available. ⊠ *43 E. Oak St.* ☎ *312/642–6403* ⊕ *www.madisonandfriends.com.*

CLOTHING

Anne Fontaine Paris. The French designer's famous takes on the classic white shirt sport hefty price tags, though they also show a careful attention to detail. ⊠ *909 N. Michigan Ave.* ☎ *312/943–0401* ⊕ *www.annefontaine.com.*

Brooks Brothers. The bastion of conservative ready-to-wear fashion still sells boatloads of their classic 1837 navy blazer. But this one-stop shop for oxfords and khakis also sneaks in bold colors. ⊠ *713 N. Michigan Ave.* ☎ *312/915–0060* ⊕ *www.brooksbrothers.com.*

Burberry. The label once favored by the conservatively well dressed is now hot with lots of other people who can't get enough of the label's signature plaid on everything from bikinis to baby gear. Even the exterior of this stunning Mag Mile flagship features that tan-and-black plaid. ⊠ *633 N. Michigan Ave.* ☎ *312/787–2500* ⊕ *www.burberry.com.*

Chanel Boutique. Ensconced in the Drake Hotel, this shop carries the complete line of Chanel products, including ready-to-wear, fragrances, and cosmetics. ⊠ *935 N. Michigan Ave.* ☎ *312/787–5500* ⊕ *www.chanel.com.*

Ermenegildo Zegna. The sportswear, softly tailored business attire, and dress clothes of this Italian great are gathered all under one roof. ⊠ *645 N. Michigan Ave.* ☎ *312/587–9660* ⊕ *www.zegna.com/en/north-america.*

Giorgio Armani. An airy, two-floor space displays Armani's discreetly luxurious clothes and accessories. The store includes the top-priced Black Label line, considered a cut above the department store line. ⊠ *800 N. Michigan Ave.* ☎ *312/573–4220* ⊕ *www.armani.com.*

Gucci. Though the prices aren't for the faint of heart, there are some pieces here that will last a lifetime. ⊠ *900 North Michigan Shops, 900 N. Michigan Ave.* ☎ *312/664–5504* ⊕ *www.gucci.com.*

H&M. Bargain-savvy fashionistas around the world love the cheap-'n-chic styles on offer; the crowds at the Mag Mile store prove Chicagoans are no different. ⊠ *840 N. Michigan Ave.* ☎ *312/640–0060* ⊕ *www.hm.com* ⊠ *22 N. State St., Loop* ☎ *312/263–3614.*

Hermès of Paris. The well-heeled shop the Chicago flagship for suits, signature scarves, and leather accessories. ⊠ *25 E. Oak St.* ☎ *312/787–8175* ⊕ *www.hermes.com.*

Hugo BOSS. Men will find modern, well-cut suits with attention to tailoring, as well as other signature Boss clothing and accessories here. ⊠ *The Shops at North Bridge, 520 N. Michigan Ave.* ☎ *312/321–0700* ⊕ *www.hugoboss.com.*

Ikram. Best known for her role as informal stylist to Michelle Obama, fashion maven Ikram Goldman moved her eponymous boutique to a 16,000-square-foot mini-department store in 2011, effectively quadrupling her inventory—and her influence. The shop carries an assortment of new and old fashion icons, from Alexander McQueen and Jean Paul Gaultier to Narciso Rodriguez and Zac Posen, along with home furnishings and art. ⊠ *15 E. Huron St.* ☎ *312/587–1000* ⊕ *ikram.com.*

Jil Sander. This line has captured the devotion of the fashion crowd for its minimalist designs and impeccable tailoring. Prices are at the upper end of the designer range. ⊠ *48 E. Oak St.* ☎ *312/335–0006* ⊕ *www.jilsander.com.*

Karen Millen. The U.K. designer's first shop in the Midwest takes you from day to night with tailored skirts and cardigans to drapey tanks, skinny jeans, and leather jackets. There is a selection of sky-high heels featuring bold patterns and embellishments. ⊠ *900 N. Michigan Ave.* ☎ *312/867–1760* ⊕ *us.karenmillen.com.*

L.K. Bennett. A favorite of Kate Middleton, this London fashion house turns out tailored pieces for work and play. If your look leans toward modern but practical basics, sophisticated handbags, and chic wear-with-everything shoes, like the kitten heels the line is known for, you'll find plenty to fancy here. ⊠ *900 North Michigan Shops, 900 N. Michigan Ave.* ☎ *312/374–0958* ⊕ *www.lkbennett.com.*

Londo Mondo. A great selection of swimwear for buff beach-ready bodies is here. You can also find workout and yoga gear and men's and

---

FESTIVAL OF LIGHTS

Chicago's holiday season officially gets under way every year at the end of November with the Magnificent Mile Lights Festival, a weekend-long event consisting of family-friendly activities that pack the shopping strip to the gills. Music, ice-carving contests, and stage shows kick off the celebration, which culminates in a parade and the illumination of more than 1 million lights along Michigan Avenue. Neighborhood stores keep late hours to accommodate the crowds. For more information, check out ⊕ *www.themagnificentmile.com.*

women's in-line skates. ✉ *1100 N. Dearborn St.* ☎ *312/751–2794* ⊕ *www.londomondo.com* ✉ *2148 N. Halsted St., Lincoln Park* ☎ *773/327–2218.*

Marc Jacobs. Jacobs's high-end runway line is showcased in this glamorous boutique in the swanky Elysian Hotel. ✉ *11 E. Walton St.* ☎ *312/649–7260.*

Palazzo Bridal. Chic urban brides trust Jane and Saeed Hamidi for their clean-lined bridal collection. ✉ *49 E. Oak St.* ☎ *312/337–6940* ⊕ *palazzobridal.com.*

Polo/Ralph Lauren. Manor house meets mass marketing. The upper-crust chic covers men's, women's, and children's clothes and housewares. Fabrics are often enticing (suede, silk organza, cashmere), but expect to pay a pretty penny. ✉ *750 N. Michigan Ave.* ☎ *312/280–1655* ⊕ *www. ralphlauren.com.*

Prada. The store has a spare, cool look that matches its modern inventory of clothing, shoes, and bags. In fact, unless you're a Miuccia devotee, the three-story shop can seem almost bare. ✉ *30 E. Oak St.* ☎ *312/951–1113* ⊕ *www.prada.com.*

Saks Fifth Avenue Men's Store. Spread over 30,000 square feet and three levels, Saks is the city's leading retailer for menswear. With a swanky look that emulates a 1930s luxury ocean liner and clothes that range from conservative to avant-garde, this is one place that has it all. ✉ *717 N. Michigan Ave.* ☎ *312/944–6500, 312/944–6500* ⊕ *saksfifthavenue.com.*

Sarca. This Gold Coast boutique taps Europe for high-end clothing and accessories by established designers, including Issa, Markus Lupfer, and Sass & Bide. Adjacent boutique Odile caters to well-heeled tots (and those making purchases for them). ✉ *710 N. Wabash Ave.* ☎ *312/255–0900* ⊕ *shopsarca.com.*

Sofia. Named after Sophia Loren, this Gold Coast boutique channels the star's effortless glamour. Find women's clothing, shoes, and accessories from lines such as Winter Kate, House of Harlow 1960, Wren, and dozens of others. ✉ *100 E. Walton St.* ☎ *312/640–0878* ⊕ *www. sofialivelovely.com.*

Topshop. In 2011 this beloved British brand invaded a 30,000-square-foot space on the corner of Michigan Avenue and Pearson Street, bringing the latest U.K. fashions to the Mag Mile. Notable among the three floors of clothes, shoes, lingerie, and accessories are collections from Topman, the men's clothing branch, and cosmetics exclusive to Chicago. ✉ *830 N. Michigan Ave.* ☎ *312/280–6834* ⊕ *us.topshop.com.*

Zara. The Spanish chain's original Chicago outpost is sprawling with 34,000 square feet of cute, trendy clothing that usually won't bust your wallet. A second location opened in retail hub Block 37. ✉ *700 N. Michigan Ave.* ☎ *312/255–8123* ⊕ *www.zara.com* ✉ *Block 37, 1 W. Randolph St., Loop* ☎ *312/368–6178.*

MIGHTY VERTICAL MALLS

Forget all your preconceived notions about malls being suburban wastelands. Three decidedly upscale urban malls dot the Mag Mile, and one holds court on State Street. The toniest of the four is 900 North Michigan, with a dazzling list of tenants, plus live weekend piano serenades. A more casual but no less entertaining shopping mecca is just blocks away at Water Tower Place. The newest kids on the block are The Shops at North Bridge, which opened in 2000, and Block 37, which opened on State Street in late 2009 after much anticipation.

In the **900 North Michigan Shops** (⊠ *900 N. Michigan Ave.* ☎ *312/915–3916*) there's a ritzy feel to the mall that houses the Chicago branches of Bloomingdale's and L.K. Bennett along with dozens of boutiques and specialty stores, such as Gucci, Coach, L'Occitane, and Fogal.

The Ritz-Carlton Hotel sits atop **Water Tower Place** (⊠ *835 N. Michigan Ave.* ☎ *312/440–3165*), which contains branches of Macy's and Lord & Taylor, as well as seven floors of shops. The more unusual spots here include Teavana (a modern tea shop) and LittleMissMatched (children's wear). Foodlife, a step above usual mall food-court fare, is a fantastic spot for a quick bite.

The big draw at **The Shops at North Bridge** (⊠ *520 N. Michigan Ave.* ☎ *312/327–2300*) is Nordstrom. Chains such as Sephora and Ann Taylor Loft share space with specialty stores such as Vosges Haut-Chocolat, a local chocolatier with an international following.

Finally opening for business in late 2009 after numerous false starts and financial troubles halted its debut, the modern glass-enclosed mall known as **Block 37** (⊠ *108 N. State St.* ☎ *312/220–0037*) occupies a full city block—bordered by Randolph, Washington, Dearborn, and State streets (number 37 of the city's original 58 blocks). Big-name retail draws Zara, Anthropologie, and Puma are found alongside with local favorites Accent Chicago, Akira, and Alternatives Shoes.

DEPARTMENT STORES

Barneys New York. At 90,000 square feet, the massive six-level store boasts ample space for women's high-end designer threads, shoes, an expansive menswear department with on-site tailoring, and an in-house Co-Op, which carries clothes for young adults. After dropping a dime (or two) on fashion-forward finds, head up to the bright and airy sixth-floor eatery Fred's at Barneys for a chopped salad. ⊠ *15 E. Oak St.* ☎ *312/587–1700* ⊕ *www.barneys.com.*

Bloomingdale's. Chicago's Bloomie's is built in a clean, airy style that is part Prairie School, part postmodern (and quite unlike its New York City sibling), giving you plenty of elbow room to sift through its selection of designer labels. ⊠ *900 North Michigan Shops, 900 N. Michigan Ave.* ☎ *312/440–4460* ⊕ *bloomingdales.com.*

Macy's. In the fall of 2006 Marshall Field's, Chicago's most famous—and perpetually struggling—department store, became a Macy's. Some of the higher-end designers Field's carried are gone from the racks, but overall the store remains the same, still standing as a glorious reminder of how grand department stores used to be. Founder Marshall Field's motto was "Give the lady what she wants!" And for many years both ladies and gentlemen had been able to find everything from furs to personalized stationery on one of the store's nine levels. The ground floor and lower level are fashioned in the model of European department stores to include leased boutiques. These stores-within-the-store include national companies like Yahoo!, selling Internet service and computer equipment, and an Yves Saint Laurent accessories boutique, as well as local retailers like Barbara's Bookstore. You can still buy Field's famous Frango mints (some of which are still made locally), and the Walnut Room restaurant on the seventh floor is still a magical place to dine at Christmas. And, the famous Tiffany Dome—designed in 1907 by Louis Comfort Tiffany—is visible from the fifth floor. ⊠ *111 N. State St., Loop* ☎ *312/781–1000* ⊕ *macys.com* ⊠ *Water Tower Place, 835 N. Michigan Ave.* ☎ *312/335–7700.*

Neiman Marcus. Prices are high here, but they're usually matched by the outstanding and tasteful selection of designer clothing and accessories for men and women. The gourmet food area on the top floor tempts with hard-to-find delicacies and impeccable hostess gifts. ⊠ *737 N. Michigan Ave.* ☎ *312/642–5900* ⊕ *www.neimanmarcus.com.*

Nordstrom. This is a lovely department store with a killer shoe department, a vast BP juniors' section, great petites and menswear departments, and outstanding customer service. Note the Nordstrom Spa on the third floor (accessible via the main mall entrance) and Café Nordstrom on the fourth floor. ⊠ *The Shops at North Bridge, 520 N. Michigan Ave.* ☎ *312/327–2300* ⊕ *shop.nordstrom.com.*

Saks Fifth Avenue. The smaller, less crowded cousin of the New York flagship doesn't scrimp on its selection of designer clothes, though the primary draw might be the department store's noteworthy first-floor makeup and fragrance department. A men's specialty store is across the street. ⊠ *700 N. Michigan Ave.* ☎ *312/799–5211* ⊕ *saksfifthavenue. com* ⊠ *Men's Store, 717 N. Michigan Ave.* ☎ *312/944–6500.*

HOME DECOR

Fodor's Choice
★
Bloomingdale's Home Store. This former meeting space and concert hall, known as the Medinah Temple, was built for the Shriners in 1912. After it took over, Bloomie's kept the historically significant exterior intact but gutted the inside to create its first stand-alone furnishings store in Chicago. It's stocked to the rafters with everything you need to eat, sleep, and relax in your home in high style. ⊠ *600 N. Wabash Ave.* ☎ *312/324–7500* ⊕ *bloomingdales.com.*

Jonathan Adler. Design guru Adler's store is chock-full of his signature fun, funky pottery and home furnishings, all arranged in a series of small living spaces. ⊠ *676 Wabash Ave.* ☎ *312/274–9920* ⊕ *www. jonathanadler.com.*

Quatrine. The washable upholstered and slipcovered furniture for dining rooms, living rooms, and bedrooms here looks decidedly chic and not at all what you'd consider typically child- or pet-friendly. ⊠ *670 N. Wabash Ave.* ☎ *312/649–1700* ⊕ *www.quatrine.com.*

Floor upon floor upon floor of goodies

Room & Board. Straightforward yet stylish pieces with a modern sensibility blend quality craftsmanship and materials with relatively affordable pricing. ✉ *55 E. Ohio St.* ☎ *312/222–0970* ⊕ *www.roomandboard.com.*

LINGERIE

Intimacy. These bra-fit gurus specialize in a "holistic" fitting process that results in a more flattering shape; that's enough to make any customer, well, perk up. Schedule your fitting ahead of time if possible. ✉ *900 North Michigan Shops, 900 N. Michigan Ave.* ☎ *312/337–8366* ⊕ *myintimacy.com.*

MUSEUM STORES

Museum of Contemporary Art Chicago Store. This outstanding museum gift shop has out-of-the-ordinary decorative accessories, tableware, and jewelry, as well as a superb collection of books on modern and contemporary art. The shop has its own street-level entrance. ✉ *220 E. Chicago Ave.* ☎ *312/397–4000* ⊕ *www.mcachicagostore.org.*

SHOES, HANDBAGS, AND LEATHER GOODS

Adidas Originals Chicago. The main attractions here are old-school sneakers and hip urban fashions for a fresh generation of fans. ✉ *923 N. Rush St.* ☎ *312/932–0651* ⊕ *www.adidas.com.*

Allen Edmonds. Men's footwear essentials range from classic Italian leather wing-tips and slip-ons to casual moccasins and rugged boots. ✉ *541 N. Michigan Ave.* ☎ *312/755–9306* ⊕ *www.allenedmonds.com* ✉ *122 S. LaSalle St., Loop* ☎ *312/332–3210.*

Coach. Well-designed leather goods, in the form of purses, briefcases, and cell phone holders, are Coach's specialty. Smart shoes and other accessories have joined the inventory as well. Embossing is available on-site at this impressive location. ⊠ *625 N. Michigan Ave.* ☎ *312/587–3167* ⊕ *www.coach.com*. ⊠ *900 North Michigan Shops, 900 N. Michigan Ave.* ☎ *312/440–1777*.

Hanig's Footwear. This local, family-owned mini-chain stocks a well-chosen selection of stylish and comfortable European and U.S. brands, including Camper, Dansko, and Hunter. ⊠ *John Hancock Center, 875 N. Michigan Ave.* ☎ *312/787–6800* ⊕ *www.hanigs.com* ⊠ *1000 W. North Ave., Lincoln Park* ☎ *312/640–1234* ⊠ *847 W. Armitage Ave.,* ☎ *773/929–5568* ⊠ *Hanig's Slipper Box, 2754 N. Clark St., Lakeview* ☎ *773/248–1977*.

Jimmy Choo. These are the extremely expensive heels that keep celebs and stylish women the world over drooling. ⊠ *63 E. Oak St.* ☎ *312/255–1170* ⊕ *www.jimmychoo.com*.

Kate Spade. The goddess of handbags has filled her two-floor boutique in the heart of Oak Street with adorable shoes, pajamas, small leather goods and, of course, her to-die-for purses and totes. Head across the street for men's clothing and accessories at Jack Spade. ⊠ *56 E. Oak St.* ☎ *312/654–8853* ⊕ *www.katespade.com*.

Louis Vuitton. Louis Vuitton has it all under one roof—the coveted purses, leather goods, and luggage bearing the beloved logo, plus the designer's men's and women's shoes and jewelry lines. ⊠ *919 N. Michigan Ave.* ☎ *312/944–2010* ⊕ *www.louisvuitton.com*.

Nike Chicago. This is one of Chicago's top tourist attractions. Many visitors—including professional athletes—stop here to take in the sports memorabilia, road-test a pair of sneakers, or watch the inspirational videos. The shop now includes a Nike iD lab, where you can design your own kicks. ⊠ *669 N. Michigan Ave.* ☎ *312/642–6363* ⊕ *store.nike.com*.

Salvatore Ferragamo. The shoes have been the classic choice of the well-heeled for generations, but it's the designer's handbags, with a fresh, contemporary sensibility, that are generating excitement of late. ⊠ *444 N. Michigan Ave.* ☎ *312/397–0464* ⊕ *www.ferragamo.com*.

Tod's. Choose from a wide selection of the practical bags and driving moccasins that made Tod's famous, as well as newer additions to the line, including high heels. ⊠ *121 E. Oak St.* ☎ *312/943–0070, 800/457–8637* ⊕ *www.tods.com*.

SPAS

NoMi Spa at Park Hyatt. This simple and elegant spa offers big-time customer satisfaction by operating with the mantra "Eat well, live well, be well." NoMi, whose name is derived from its North Michigan location, has just two spa treatment rooms. One even comes with its own steam shower and bathroom, so there's no need for traipsing through the locker room to extend your indulgence. Spa-goers also have access to the hotel's swimming pool and fitness center, both with cityscape views. The products used include seasonal ingredients, French sunflower seeds, ground olive pits, and citrus. ⊠ *Park Hyatt, 800 N. Michigan Ave.* ☎ *312/239–4200* ⊕ *www.nomispa.com* ⊙ *Daily 8–8* ☞ *$160 60-min massage, $180 75-min facial. Hair salon, steam room. Gym with: cardiovascular machines, free weights, weight-training equipment. Services: aromatherapy, facials, light therapy, manicures, pedicures, massage, waxing.*

Spa at Four Seasons Hotel Chicago. Comfort and relaxation are taken seriously at this Four Seasons spa, where the private treatment rooms are soundproofed for maximum serenity; in the lounge guests can stretch out on daybeds and snack on fresh fruit and tea for as long as they like before and after services. A lovely, large pool and hot tub are also a part of the options here. Global influences include an herbal mud wrap from Hungary and a wrap that uses cane sugar and honey from Hawaii. There's a flip-flop pedicure—including a new pair of shoes—to get your feet ready for spring, and treatments that use bourbon in the spa and end with a drink of bourbon in the bar. If you're ready to splurge, go for the mini-spa escape package, which includes a manicure, mini-pedicure, 55-minute massage, and 25-minute facial. ⊠ *Four Seasons Hotel, 120 E. Delaware Pl.* ☎ *312/280–8800* ⊕ *www.fourseasons.com/chicagofs* ⊙ *Daily 8–8* ☞ *$150 55-min massage, $150 50-min facial, $290 4-treatment package. Lap pool, sauna, steam room. Gym with: cardiovascular machines, free weights, weight-lifting equipment. Services: body wraps, facials, massages, scrubs, waxing, tinting, nail treatment. Classes and programs: personal training.*

The Spa by Asha. It pays to be early at this spa on the lower level of the James Hotel so that you have time to take advantage of the complimentary preservice aromatherapy foot bath in the darkened lounge; a therapist will also tuck a heated pillow behind your neck and massage your feet and calves with a scrub of walnut, lavender, and herbal extracts. It may feel like a shame to leave for the actual treatments, but services that include Aveda plant-based facials, body wraps, and massages will only up your relaxation factor. Special services catering to moms-to-be include a hydrating belly treatment. There are massages and facials designed exclusively for men, and a Himalayan rejuvenation treatment claims to boost your immune system during the change of seasons. ⊠ *James Hotel, 55 E. Ontario St.* ☎ *312/664–0200* ⊕ *www.ashasalonspa.com* ⊙ *Weekdays 9–9, Sat. 8–7, Sun. 10–6* ☞ *$105 60-min massage, $115 60-min facial. Services: body wraps, facials, hair, makeup, massage, nail treatment, scrubs, waxing.*

TOYS

American Girl Place. American Girl attracts little girls from just about everywhere with their signature dolls in tow. There's easily a day's worth of activities here—shop at the boutique, take in a live musical revue, and have lunch or afternoon tea at the café, where dolls can partake in the meal from their own "sassy seats." ■TIP➜ Brace yourself for long lines just to get into the store during high shopping seasons. ⊠ *835 N. Michigan Ave.* ☎ *877/247–5223* ⊕ *www.americangirl.com.*

The Disney Store. At this Mouse emporium, there's everything little Disney disciples need for a fix: a plethora of plush toys, DVDs, games, and other goodies. ⊠ *717 N. Michigan Ave.* ☎ *312/654–9208* ⊕ *www. disneystore.com* ⊠ *Block 37, 108 N. State St., Loop* ☎ *312/269–4776.*

WINE

The House of Glunz. Don't let the upper-crust vibe dissuade you from setting foot inside. The folks at this family-owned wine shop know their stuff but aren't in the least snobbish or pretentious about helping you find a bottle that suits your needs, whether you're building your cellar with rare vintages or in the market for a $15 bottle for dinner. ⊠ *1206 N. Wells St.* ☎ *312/642–3000* ⊕ *thehouseofglunz.com.*

RIVER NORTH

This area between the buzzy Gold Coast and the Chicago River has a less frenetic vibe in most of its stores, which consist mainly of galleries and home-furnishings stores. Somewhat surprisingly, there are also some touristy mega-restaurants here—including Ed Debevic's, Rainforest Café, and a humongous flagship McDonald's. Two noteworthy buildings here are the Moorish Revival–style Medinah Temple, today occupied by a Bloomingdale's Home & Furniture Store, and the adjacent Tree Studios, a former artists' colony that now houses a cluster of shops.

ANTIQUES

Antiquarians Building. Four floors of dealers in Asian and European antiques display their wares; some examples of modernism and Art Deco are thrown in for good measure. ⊠ *159 W. Kinzie St.* ☎ *312/527–0533.*

Christa's, Ltd. Chests, cabinets, tables, and bureaus are stacked three and four high, creating narrow aisles that are precarious to negotiate but make for adventurous exploring. Look in, over, and under each and every piece to assess the gems stashed in every possible crevice. ⊠ *217 W. Illinois St.* ☎ *312/222–2520* ⊕ *www.christasltd.com.*

The Golden Triangle. In a block-long, 23,000-square-foot space, Asian furnishings and artifacts are arranged in vignettes depicting various eras and regions, from a British Colonial reception hall to a Chinese scholar's courtyard. The vast collection includes a line of custom-designed modern furnishings made from reclaimed wood. ⊠ *330 N. Clark St.* ☎ *312/755–1266* ⊕ *www.goldentriangle.biz.*

JRoberts Antiques. The sprawling, 50,000-square-foot showroom once known as Jay Robert's Antique Warehouse holds 17th- to 21st-century European furniture—ranging from French Empire to Art Deco—as well as objets d'art. ⊠ *149 W. Kinzie St.* ☎ *312/222–0167* ⊕ *www. jayroberts.com.*

P.O.S.H. It's hard to resist the charming displays of piled-up, never-been-used, vintage hotel and restaurant china here. There's also an impressive selection of silver gravy boats, creamers, and flatware that bear the marks of ocean liners and private clubs. ⊠ *613 N. State St.* ☎ *312/280–1602* ⊕ *www.poshchicago.com.*

Rita Bucheit, Ltd. Devoted to the streamlined Biedermeier aesthetic, this shop carries choice furniture and accessories from the period along with Art Deco and modern pieces that are perfect complements to the style. ⊠ *449 N. Wells St.* ☎ *312/527–4080* ⊕ *www.ritabucheit.com.*

A gem-studded horse statue for the living room, perhaps?

ART GALLERIES

Alan Koppel Gallery. An eclectic mix of works by modern masters and contemporary artists is balanced by a selection of French and Italian Modernist furniture from the 1920s to 1950s. ⊠ *806 N. Dearborn Ave., Near North* ☎ *312/640–0730* ⊕ *alankoppel.com.*

Ann Nathan Gallery. The specialty here is contemporary paintings, but the gallery also showcases sculpture and singular artist-made furniture. ⊠ *212 W. Superior St.* ☎ *312/664–6622* ⊕ *www.annnathangallery.com.*

Carl Hammer Gallery. Lee Godie and Henry Darger are among the outsider and self-taught artists whose work is shown at this gallery. ⊠ *740 N. Wells St.* ☎ *312/266–8512* ⊕ *www.hammergallery.com.*

Catherine Edelman Gallery. This gallery of contemporary photography explores the work of emerging, mixed-media, photo-based artists such as Carlos Diaz and Jack Spencer. ⊠ *300 W. Superior St.* ☎ *312/266–2350* ⊕ *www.edelmangallery.com.*

Echt Gallery. Collectors of fine studio art glass are drawn here by such luminaries as Dale Chihuly. ⊠ *222 W. Superior St.* ☎ *312/440–0288* ⊕ *www.echtgallery.com.*

Primitive. Find ethnic and tribal art, including textiles, furniture, and jewelry, at this longtime Chicago favorite gallery. ⊠ *130 N. Jefferson St., Near West Side* ☎ *312/575–9600* ⊕ *www.beprimitive.com.*

Stephen Daiter Gallery. This space showcases stunning 20th-century European and American photography, particularly avant-garde photojournalism. ⊠ *230 W. Superior St., 4th fl.* ☎ *312/787–3350* ⊕ *www. stephendaitergallery.com.*

BOOKS, SOUVENIRS, AND STATIONERY

Abraham Lincoln Book Shop. The shop owner here buys, sells, and appraises books, paintings, documents, and other paraphernalia associated with American military and political history. It's been around since 1938. ⊠ *357 W. Chicago Ave.* ☎ *312/944–3085* ⊕ *www.alincolnbookshop.com.*

Flight 001. In a space with curved walls designed to mimic the inside of an airplane, Flight 001 has all the essentials for the frequent traveler, including tiny portable luggage scales, funky patterned eye masks, and cool retro luggage tags and document holders. ⊠ *1133 N. State St., at Washington St.* ☎ *312/944–1001* ⊕ *www.flight001.com.*

Paper Source. Reams and reams of different types of paper are sold here; much of it is unusual and expensive. Check out the custom invitation department and good selection of rubber stamps and bookbinding supplies. Classes are also offered. ⊠ *232 W. Chicago Ave.* ☎ *312/337–0798* ⊕ *www.paper-source.com* ⊠ *919 W. Armitage Ave., Lincoln Park* ☎ *773/525–7300* ⊕ *www.paper-source.com.*

CLOTHING

Blake. A no-nonsense boutique without pomp, circumstance, or even signage, Blake displays clean-lined clothes in a pristine setting. You'll find designers like Dries van Noten and Balenciaga, and shoes and accessories of a similar subtle elegance. ⊠ *212 W. Chicago Ave.* ☎ *312/202–0047.*

DEPARTMENT STORES

Merchandise Mart. This massive marketplace between Wells and North Orleans streets just north of the Chicago River is more notable for its Art Deco design than its shopping. Much of the building's stores are only for the design trade, meaning that you have to be an interior designer to access their wares. However, the first two floors have been turned into retail with the unveiling of LuxeHome, the world's largest collection of high-end kitchen, bath, and building showrooms that are open to the public. Tenants include de Giulio kitchen design and Waterworks, and the Chopping Block, a local culinary school with a loyal fan base, has a spacious location here. ⊠ *222 W. Merchandise Mart Plaza* ☎ *800/677–6278* ⊕ *www.merchandisemart.com.*

FOOD AND TREATS

Blommer Chocolate Outlet Store. "Why do parts of River North smell like freshly baked brownies?" is a question you hear fairly often. The oh-so-sweet reason: it's near the Blommer Chocolate Factory, which has been making wholesale chocolates here since 1939. More important, the retail outlet store is also here, so you can snap up your Blommer chocolates and candies at a discount—a handy tip to know when those smells give you a case of the munchies. ⊠ *600 W. Kinzie St., at N. Jefferson St.* ☎ *312/492–1336* ⊕ *www.blommerstore.com.*

HOME DECOR

The Chopping Block. New and seasoned chefs appreciate the expertly chosen selection of pots and pans, bakeware, gadgets, and ingredients here. The intimate cooking classes are hugely popular and taught by a fun, knowledgeable staff. (Students get 10% off store merchandise.) The Lincoln Square location has a wine shop. ⊠ *The Merchandise Mart, 222 Merchandise Mart Plaza, Suite 107* ☎ *312/644–6360* ⊕ *www.*

thechoppingblock.net ✉ *4747 N. Lincoln Ave., Lincoln Square* ☎ *773/472–6700.*

Lightology. This 20,000-square-foot showroom of modern light designs is an essential stop for designers and architects, not to mention passersby drawn to the striking designs visible from the windows. It's the brain-child of Greg Kay, who started out as a roller-disco lighting designer in the 1970s and made a name for himself in Chicago with Tech Lighting, a contemporary design gallery. ✉ *215 W. Chicago Ave.* ☎ *312/944–1000* ⊕ *www.lightology.com.*

GALLERY TOURS

Every Saturday morning at 11, Chicago Gallery News offers complimentary gallery tours. Groups meet at the Starbucks at 750 North Franklin Street and are guided each week by a different gallery owner or director from the River North area. For more information, and to check holiday weekend schedules, call ☎ *312/649–0064* or go to ⊕ *www.chicagogallerynews.com.*

Luminaire. The international contemporary furniture in this 21,000-square-foot showroom includes pieces by Philippe Starck, Antonio Citterio, and Jeffrey Bernett. Sleek kitchen designs and tabletop pieces are from Zaha Hadid, Joseph Joseph, Damian Evans, KnIndustrie, and many more edgy designers from around the globe. ✉ *301 W. Superior St.* ☎ *312/664–9582* ⊕ *luminaire.com.*

Manifesto. In a huge, street-level space lies one of the largest design ateliers in the city; look for work by furniture designer (and owner) Richard Gorman and a smattering of home accessories. ✉ *755 N. Wells St.* ☎ *312/664–0733* ⊕ *www.manifestofurniture.com.*

Orange Skin. The go-to resource for modern furniture, lighting, and accessories in Chicago carries pieces by Minotti, Philippe Starck, and Piero Lissoni in a bi-level industrial space. ✉ *223 W. Erie St., Suite 1NW* ☎ *312/335–1033* ⊕ *www.orangeskin.com.*

SPAS

Sir Spa. There's nothing pretty or poufy about Sir Spa, and that's the way the clients who come to this men's spa—awash in black leather, exposed brick, and marble—like it. The space is well appointed, including a Grooming Club Lounge with armchairs, a plasma TV, and beer-stocked fridge. With services like a back buff and detoxifying mud wrap, treatments are just as focused on cleaning and revitalizing from the inside out as they are on purely relaxing. ✉ *5151 N. Clark St., Andersonville* ☎ *773/271–7000* ⊕ *www.sirspa.com* ⊙ *Weekdays 11–9, Sat. 10–8, Sun. noon–8* ⌕ *$90 60-min massage, $195 3-treatment packages, $150 couple packages. Hair salon, steam room. Services: Botox, facials, reflexology, sports and deep-tissue massages, tanning.*

Spa at Trump. The one thing most Trump hotel spas have in common is that they're likely the swankiest places in their respective towns to relax and rejuvenate, with luxe locker rooms tricked out with multijet showers, signature gemstone massages with the essences of rubies, diamonds, emeralds, and sapphires (you can see the tiny stones in the oil bottles), and your every need addressed. What makes each location unique, though, are its seasonal offerings, such as a hot-chocolate pedicure or body scrub, very welcome in the middle of a brutal Chicago winter. ⊠ *Trump International Hotel & Tower Chicago, 401 N. Wabash Ave.* ☎ *312/588–8000* ⊕ *www.trumpchicagohotel.com* ☉ *Daily 8–9* ☞ *$150 60-min massage, $185 60-min facial. Lap pool, sauna, steam room. Gym with: cardiovascular machines, free weights, weight-lifting equipment. Services: body wraps, facials, massages, tinting, waxing, nail treatment, scrubs. Classes and programs: body sculpting, kickboxing, personal training, Pilates, Spinning, weight training, yoga.*

WINE

Pops for Champagne. Select from well-chosen group of bubbly plus assorted accoutrements at the retail shop of a popular champagne bar. ⊠ *601 N. State St.* ☎ *312/266–7676* ⊕ *popsforchampagne.com.*

LINCOLN PARK

Upscale Lincoln Park features a mix of distinctive boutiques and national chain stores. It was an established shopping destination way back when rents were low and the vibe was still gritty in nearby Bucktown and Wicker Park. Start your visit on Armitage Avenue, where you'll find boutiques selling everything from of-the-moment clothing and shoes to bath products and goods for pampered pooches. Around the corner on Halsted Street, independent shops are dotted in among big-name clothing stores. Hit North and Clybourn avenues for housewares from the flagship Crate&Barrel, Restoration Hardware, and other chains.

BARGAIN SHOPPING

Fox's. Snap up canceled and overstocked designer clothes from the likes of Tahari and ABS at 40% to 70% discounts. New shipments come in several times a week, so there's always something new to try on. (Modest shoppers take note: the dressing room is communal.) ⊠ *2150 N. Halsted St.* ☎ *773/281–0700* ⊕ *foxs.com.*

BEAUTY

Aroma Workshop. Customize lotions, massage oils, and bath salts with more than 150 essential and fragrance oils in this beauty boutique. The workshop makes its own line of facial-care products, too. ⊠ *2050 N. Halsted St.* ☎ *773/871–1985* ⊕ *www.aromaworkshop.com.*

BOOKS AND MUSIC

Old Town School of Music Store. A sibling to the Old Town School of Music Store in Lincoln Square, this shop within the Old Town School of Folk Music has a good selection of kids' instruments, plus all manner of instruments for rent. ⊠ *909 W. Armitage Ave.* ☎ *773/751–3410* ⊕ *www.oldtownschool.org/musicstore* ⊠ *4544 N. Lincoln Ave., Lincoln Square* ☎ *773/751–3398.*

Gramaphone Records. Local DJs and club kids go to Gramaphone to find vintage and cutting-edge dance, house, and hip-hop releases, and hear them on the spot at one of the store's listening stations. The store also stocks DJ gear. ⊠ *2843 N. Clark St.* ☎ *773/472–3683* ⊕ *gramaphonerecords.com.*

Powell's Bookstore. This is one of the oldest and most reliable independent bookshops around; the strength here is the section featuring art, architecture, and photography. Also check out the impressive collection of rare books. ✉ *2850 N. Lincoln Ave.* ☎ *773/248–1444* ⊕ *powellschicago. com* ✉ *1501 E. 57th St., Hyde Park* ☎ *773/955–7780.*

CHILDREN'S CLOTHING

Camelot Children's Kingdom. This brightly colored boutique carries American and European clothing lines for babies and boys up to age 12, girls to size 14. Some of the brands you'll find are Little Mass and IKKS. Also on offer are cute Room Seven diaper bags and gifts. ✉ *854 W. Armitage Ave.* ☎ *773/525–7706.*

Giggle. This style-focused children's boutique proves that having a baby doesn't have to mean sacrificing your modern aesthetic. Contemporary nursery furniture, strollers, and gear share space with well-designed activity mats, clothes, and keepsakes. ✉ *2116 N. Halsted St.* ☎ *773/296–6228* ⊕ *www.giggle.com.*

Piggy Toes. This store stocks a good (though pricey) selection of European footwear for children with well-heeled parents. ✉ *2205 N. Halsted St.* ☎ *773/281–5583* ⊕ *www.ptoes.com* ✉ *4548 N. Western Ave., Lincoln Square* ☎ *773/878–1122.*

CLOTHING

Art Effect. This modern-day general store stocks trendy clothes and accessories at approachable prices. Sharing the space with the Ella Moss tanks, Rich and Skinny jeans, fedoras, and Alexis Bittar necklaces, there are also gifts and home furnishings, ranging from candles and bath products to mortar-and-pestle sets and juicers. ✉ *934 W. Armitage Ave.* ☎ *773/929–3600* ⊕ *www.shoparteffect.com.*

The Green Goddess Boutique. This expansive boutique, whose motto is "sustainably chic," sells "upcycled," cruelty-free, and fair-trade clothing, jewelry, and home accessories from around the globe—think vintage jewelry, handmade knits, and more. There are unique products at every price point. ✉ *1009 W. Armitage Ave.* ☎ *773/281–5600* ⊕ *thegreengoddessboutique.com.*

Haberdash. Owner Adam Beltzman ditched his job as a lawyer to launch this men's shop. The tailored clothes from designers like Barbour and Gitman Bros, the Wolverine boots, and wood shelving make this store decidedly masculine. Its sister—or, rather, brother—store, EDC (for "every day carry"), focuses on apothecary items, accessories, and footwear. ✉ *607 N. State St.* ☎ *312/624–8551* ⊕ *haberdashmen.com* ✉ *611 N. State St., River North* ☎ *312/646–7870.*

Mint Julep. This Southport store is not afraid of color. Find a cheery selection of statement necklaces, pastel denims, bright printed dresses, and much more for reasonable prices. ✉ *3432 N. Southport Ave., Lakeview* ☎ *773/472–6717.*

FOOD AND TREATS

Vosges Haut-Chocolat. Local chocolatier Katrina Markoff's exotic truffles, flavored with spices like curry and ancho chili, have fans across the globe. Her ever-expanding line of goodies now includes caramels, ice cream, chocolate tortilla chips, and even yoga wear and dresses. ✉ *951 W. Armitage Ave.* ☎ *773/296–9866* ⊕ *www.vosgeschocolate. com* ✉ *The Shops at North Bridge, 520 N. Michigan Ave., Near North* ☎ *312/644–9450.*

HOME DECOR

Bedside Manor. Dreamland is even more inviting with these handcrafted beds and lush designer linens, many of which come in interesting jacquard weaves or are nicely trimmed and finished. ✉ *2056 N. Halsted St.* ☎ *773/404–2020* ⊕ *www.shopbedside.com.*

Fodor's Choice ★ **CB2.** A concept store by furniture giant Crate&Barrel, CB2 got its start right here in Chicago. The idea is stylish, bold basics for trendy urban abodes, all sans big-ticket price tags. ✉ *800 W. North Ave.* ☎ *312/787–8329* ⊕ *www.cb2.com.*

Crate&Barrel. There are plenty of "oohs" and "aahs" throughout the three floors of stylish home furnishings and kitchenware at Crate&Barrel's flagship location. There's plenty of free parking as well. ✉ *850 W. North Ave.* ☎ *312/573–9800* ⊕ *www.crateandbarrel.com.*

Crate&Barrel Outlet. Around the corner from Crate&Barrel's massive flagship, the outlet carries odds and ends from the company's housewares and kitchen lines. Look for discounts of up to 75% on out-of-season items. ✉ *1864 N. Clybourn Ave.* ☎ *312/787–4775* ⊕ *www. crateandbarrel.com.*

Jayson Home & Garden. Loaded with new and vintage European and American furnishings, this decor store carries the Mitchell Gold + Bob Williams line. Look for oversize cupboards and armoires and decorative accessories, plus stylish garden furniture and a bevy of beautiful floral arrangements. ✉ *1885 N. Clybourn Ave.* ☎ *800/472–1885* ⊕ *www. jaysonhome.com.*

The Land of Nod. Crate&Barrel is a next-door neighbor (and business partner) to this quirky-cool children's furniture store. There are plenty of parent-pleasing designs, plus loads of fun accessories, toys, and a great music section, too. ✉ *900 W. North Ave.* ☎ *312/475–9903* ⊕ *www.landofnod.com.*

A New Leaf. You'll find one of the best selections of fresh flowers in town here. The breathtaking Wells Street space, designed by architect Cynthia Weese, is also stocked with singular antique and vintage furnishings and accessories as well as a mind-boggling selection of candles, vases, tiles, and pots. ✉ *1818 N. Wells St.* ☎ *312/642–8553* ⊕ *www. anewleafchicago.com* ✉ *1645 N. Wells St.* ☎ *312/642–1576* ✉ *312 S. Dearborn St., South Loop* ☎ *312/427–9097.*

CLOSE UP

Unpacking Crate&Barrel

11

Gordon and Carole Segal saw a void in the Chicago retail market in 1962, and they set out to fill it by opening the first Crate&Barrel store in an abandoned elevator factory in the then-questionable Old Town neighborhood.

"I was doing the dishes—classic Arzberg dishes we had picked up on our Caribbean honeymoon—and I said to Carole, 'How come nobody is selling this dinnerware in Chicago?,'" Gordon Segal recalls. "I think we should open a store." And, as they say, the rest is history. With "more taste than money," the Segals displayed their unique housewares en masse on the crates and barrels they were shipped in, and found a niche and a name.

At a time when gas-station give-away glasses were common kitchen table fixtures, shoppers were immediately drawn to the grocery store–style displays of contemporary merchandise at reasonable prices. As the business grew, store displays became more sophisticated and the inventory more diverse.

Before the age of home-improvement cable television shows, the Segals brought accessible design into the American home. They added the Finnish fabric line Marimekko to their inventory in the late 1960s, and the bold, colorful prints became a signature style of the era.

Carole retired to raise their family, but Gordon Segal still runs the Chicago-based company they founded together about 50 years ago, now a dominant home-furnishings chain with more than 100 stores across the United States. Always keeping his motto, "Stay humble, stay nervous," in the back of his mind, Segal has continued to fine-tune Crate&Barrel throughout its history, creating shopping environments that engage the senses. He pays close attention to the exteriors, too, focusing on building stores with architectural merit. Stores in Illinois, Pennsylvania, and Chicago have received awards for their outstanding architectural design.

The home-furnishings industry has exploded since Crate&Barrel's humble beginnings, and Segal has kept a keen eye on what interests the buying public. In 2000 Crate&Barrel launched CB2, a new concept store aimed at a young urban market with—again—a single store on Chicago's North Side. And, so that no one in the family feels left out, in 2001 Crate&Barrel formed a partnership with Land of Nod, a quirky children's furniture catalog company. They opened one store—guess where?—on Chicago's North Side to start, and have since expanded to several locations. The Segal empire just keeps growing.

Quiltology. Colette Cogley's Lincoln Park shop and design studio stocks everything that funky DIY-ers need to keep a quilting habit going, including classes and workshops. ✉ *1221 W. Diversey Pkwy.* ☎ *773/549–6628* ⊕ *www.quiltology.com.*

Tabula Tua. The colorful, contemporary, mix-and-match dishes and table-top accessories here are worlds away from standard formal china. Other offerings include breathtaking mosaic tables handmade to order, rustic furniture crafted from old barn wood, and sleek, polished pewter pieces. ⊠ *1015 W. Armitage Ave.* ☏ *773/525–3500* ⊕ *www.tabulatua.com.*

JEWELRY AND ACCESSORIES

The Left Bank. An eclectic mix of antique-style French jewelry brings a touch of Paris chic to Chicago. There's also a beautiful selection of French-themed jewelry boxes, perfume bottles, and other accessories. Owner Susan Jablonski has become known for her large assortment of bridal headpieces and tiaras, and she's a wedding planner too. ⊠ *1155 W. Webster Ave.* ☏ *773/929–7422* ⊕ *www.leftbankjewelry.com.*

Sequin. Sisters Kim and Linda Renk's love of travel and history provides inspiration for their trendsetting jewelry label, available in their tiny jewelbox of a shop. ⊠ *845 W. Armitage Ave.* ☏ *312/224–4859* ⊕ *www.sequin-nyc.com.*

LINGERIE

Underthings. At this small but well-stocked shop, you can augment your collection of everyday bras, panties, and pajamas or splurge on sexy lingerie. Lines range from Hanky Panky to high-end designers such as Dolce & Gabbana. ⊠ *804 W. Webster Ave.* ☏ *773/472–9291.*

PET STORES

Barker & Meowsky. This "paw firm" carries great gifts for dogs, cats, and humans. There are beautiful bowls, plush beds, picture frames, treats, and even pet massage and grooming services—just the things to get tails wagging. ⊠ *1003 W. Armitage Ave.* ☏ *773/868–0200* ⊕ *www. barkerandmeowsky.com.*

SHOES, HANDBAGS, AND LEATHER GOODS

1154 Lill Studio. Creative types design their own handbags (from chic clutches to diaper totes) from tons of fabric and shape options at this superpopular shop housed in a pretty brownstone. Some limited-edition, ready-made bags are available, too. ⊠ *904 W. Armitage Ave.* ☏ *773/477–5455* ⊕ *www.1154lill.com.*

Fleet Feet Sports. Serious runners rely on this store for expert running-shoe fittings, which entail foot measurement and a thorough gait analysis. Athletic wear and sports gear round out the offerings. ⊠ *1620 N. Wells St.* ☏ *312/587–3338* ⊕ *www.fleetfeetchicago.com* ⊠ *4762 N. Lincoln Ave., Lincoln Square* ☏ *773/271–3338* ⊕ *www.fleetfeetchicago.com.*

Fodor'sChoice ★ **Lori's Designer Shoes.** Owner Lori Andre's obsession with shoes takes her on biannual trips to Europe to scour for styles you won't likely see at department stores. The result is an inventory that many fine-footed women consider to be the best in Chicago. Shoes by designers like Jeffrey Campbell, Frye, and Sam Edelman are sold in a self-serve atmosphere. Terrific handbags, jewelry, bridal shoes, and other accessories are also available. ⊠ *824 W. Armitage Ave.* ☏ *773/281–5655* ⊕ *www.lorisshoes.com.*

Running Away Multisport. Whatever sports gear you need, this expansive store likely has it in stock: wet suits, running shoes and apparel, sunglasses, hydration gear, and more. ⊠ *2219 N. Clybourn Ave.* ☏ *773/395–2929* ⊕ *www.runningawaymultisport.com.*

11

TOYS

Rotofugi. A toy store for grown-up kids, Rotofugi specializes in artist-created, limited-edition toys. You'll find dozens of specialty lines from the United States, China, and Japan, like Shawnimals and Tinder Toys. The store also hosts revolving gallery exhibitions. ⌧ *2780 N. Lincoln Ave.* ☎ *773/868–3308* ⊕ *rotofugi.com.*

WICKER PARK

Former artists' enclaves Wicker Park and Bucktown were long ago taken over by trendy shops, bars, restaurants, and the hip-seekers who inhabit them. Today the ever-more-gentrified areas are clogged with hip clothing stores, trendy restaurants, and galleries, mostly centered on the intersection of North, Damen, and Milwaukee avenues and along Division Street. Recently large retailers such as Urban Outfitters, American Apparel, and Marc by Marc Jacobs have moved into the area, to the chagrin of local hipsters.

ANTIQUES

Salvage One. An enormous warehouse chock-full of stained leaded glass, garden ornaments, fireplace mantels, bathtubs, bars, and other architectural artifacts draws creative home remodelers and restaurant designers from around the country. ■ TIP➜ This is the place to hunt for all kinds of treasures, from vintage dental chairs to Paris street lamps. ⌧ *1840 W. Hubbard St., Near West Side* ☎ *312/733–0098* ⊕ *salvageone.com.*

BEAUTY

RR#1 Chicago. A wood-paneled 1930s pharmacy is the setting for this charming gift shop, which stocks eclectic wares for everyone on your list, plus a tempting selection of bath and beauty products. ⌧ *814 N. Ashland Ave., West Town* ☎ *312/421–9079* ⊕ *www.rr1chicago.com.*

Ruby Room. This Wicker Park spa–boutique sells a mix of bath, body, and beauty products from brands like Weleda Bare Escentuals, and Arcona. The spa services are an interesting mix, too, with everything from intuitive astrology to brow waxing and facials. ⌧ *1743–45 W. Division St.* ☎ *773/235–2323* ⊕ *rubyroom.com.*

BOOKS, MUSIC, AND STATIONERY

Dusty Groove. The retail outlet of a massive online business, Dusty Groove stocks an enormous collection of older jazz, funk, soul, and blues in both LP and CD formats. They also buy used records. ⌧ *1120 N. Ashland Ave.* ☎ *773/342–5800* ⊕ *www.dustygroove.com.*

Myopic Books. One of Chicago's largest used-book dealers stocks more than 80,000 titles and buys books from the public on Friday evenings and all day Saturday. ■ TIP➜ This community mainstay also hosts regular music and poetry events. ⌧ *1564 N. Milwaukee Ave.* ☎ *773/862–4882* ⊕ *www.myopicbookstore.com.*

Paper Doll. Doll up your gift with an unusual card and handmade wrapping paper from this Wicker Park shop. Finger puppets, candles, and other gift items are also stocked here. ⌧ *2027 W. Division St.* ☎ *773/227–6950* ⊕ *paperdollchicago.com.*

This old-fashioned apothecary stocks a great selection of newfangled products.

CHILDREN'S CLOTHING

The Boring Store. Outfit your aspiring sleuth with the necessary spy paraphernalia and secret agent supplies—such as mirror glasses, fake mustaches, and voice amplifiers—at this shop run by the writer Dave Eggers's nonprofit group 826CHI. Proceeds help fund the group's after-school tutoring and writing programs for kids. ⊠ *1331 N. Milwaukee Ave.* ☎ *773/772–8108* ⊕ *www.826chi.org/shop.*

CLOTHING

Akira. Young trendsetters flock to this mini-empire for fashion-forward threads at easy-to-swallow prices. The flagship women's boutique shares a stretch of North Avenue with offshoot men's clothing and women's shoe stores. ⊠ *1814 W. North Ave.* ☎ *773/489–0818* ⊕ *www. akirachicago.com* ⊠ *1910 W. North Ave.* ☎ *312/423–6693* ⊠ *1849 W. North Ave.* ☎ *773/342–8684* ⊠ *2357 N. Clark St., Lincoln Park* ☎ *773/404–5826* ⊠ *122 S. State St., Loop* ☎ *312/346–3034.*

Alcala's Western Wear. Alcala stocks more than 10,000 pairs of cowboy boots—many in exotic skins—for men, women, and children. Since it's in Ukrainian Village, it's a bit out of the way if you're staying downtown, but the amazing array of Stetson hats and rodeo gear makes this a must-see for cowboys, caballeros, and country-and-western dancers. ⊠ *1733 W. Chicago Ave., Ukrainian Village* ☎ *312/226–0152* ⊕ *www.alcalas.com.*

Mulberry & Me. Snag work-appropriate blouses, cute dresses, glitzy jackets, and accessories in this boutique with a New York feel. ⊠ *2019 W. Division St.* ☎ *773/952–7551* ⊕ *mulberryandme.com.*

Penelope's. Step inside this spacious shop for flirty dresses from Sessun, Mink Pink, and Dolce Vita, as well as funky accessories such as Cheap

Monday sunglasses. Menswear by the likes of APC and Gitman Bros. and a selection of housewares and gift items round out the collection. ✉ *1913 W. Division St.* ☎ *773/395–2351* ⊕ *shoppenelopes.com.*

Una Mae's. This Wicker Park favorite is bursting at the seams with affordable styles for guys and girls. The accessories here, often even more fun than the clothing, may include vintage bow ties, Mexican blankets, backpacks, and incredibly colorful jewelry. ✉ *1528 N. Milwaukee Ave.* ☎ *773/276–7002* ⊕ *www.unamaeschicago.com.*

HOME DECOR
Asrai Garden. Although you'd be hard-pressed to find fresher blooms or more carefully constructed bouquets, this quirky boutique is more than a flower shop. It also houses a thoughtful collection of terrariums, jewelry, soaps, scented candles, ornate tableware, scrimshaw, stationery, and other gifts. ✉ *1935 W. North Ave., at Winchester Ave., Wicker Park* ☎ *773/782–0680* ⊕ *www.asraigarden.com.*

Sprout Home. If your taste runs toward the modern, you'll drool over every nook and cranny of this home-furnishings store, which sells items like terrariums, planters, and bud vases for your indoor life, plus unusual plants and gardening products for your outdoor one. ✉ *745 N. Damen Ave., Ukrainian Village* ☎ *312/226–5950* ⊕ *www.sprouthome.com.*

JEWELRY AND ACCESSORIES
Red Eye. This boutique stocks a wide array of specs from the likes of Anne Klein alongside stylish newcomers such as Jai Kudo and Gant. There's also an in-house optometrist to make sure your glasses not only look good but help you look better. ✉ *1869 N. Damen Ave.* ☎ *773/782–1660* ⊕ *www.redeyeoptical.com.*

SHOES, HANDBAGS, AND LEATHER GOODS
John Fluevog Boots & Shoes. Canadian designer Fluevog's chunky platforms and bold designs have graced the famous feet of Madonna and throngs of other loyal devotees, and they can house your toes, too, if you shop here. ✉ *1539 N. Milwaukee Ave.* ☎ *773/772–1983* ⊕ *www.fluevog.com.*

BUCKTOWN

ANTIQUES
Pagoda Red. Exceptionally well-priced Asian furnishings from owner Betsy Nathan's frequent overseas trips pack this open loft space. Among the treasures, you'll find Chinese deco chairs, Nepalese rugs, antique lanterns, and a rare collection of 20th-century Chinese advertising posters. ✉ *1714 N. Damen Ave.* ☎ *773/235–1188* ⊕ *www.pagodared.com.*

Pavilion. The specialty here is French, Italian, and Scandinavian antiques, but you'll be lured in by the altogether uncommon mix of industrial and decorative furnishings, accessories, and fixtures. The selection reflects the collecting acumen of its two idiosyncratic owners, who scour Europe and the Midwest for items in the perfect state of intriguing decay. ✉ *2055 N. Damen Ave.* ☎ *773/645–0924* ⊕ *pavilionantiques.com.*

CHILDREN'S CLOTHING

Psychobaby. The best-dressed urban tykes send their parents to this shop to spend a pretty penny on funky duds by lines like Levi's, Sourpuss, and Appaman. There's also a great selection of shoes, toys, and books, plus a story hour every Wednesday for parents brave enough to tote their tykes along. ⊠ *1630 N. Damen Ave.* ☎ *773/772–2815* ⊕ *www.psychobabyonline.com.*

> **WORD OF MOUTH**
>
> "Definitely hit Bucktown and Wicker Park (my neighborhood) for some unique, funky boutiques and designers who aren't as well known."
>
> —Vittrad

The Red Balloon. A good selection of children's clothing, books, and toys are on offer at these stores. ⊠ *1940 N. Damen Ave.* ☎ *773/489–9800* ⊕ *www.theredballoon.com* ⊠ *5407 N. Clark St., Andersonville, Far North* ☎ *773/989–8500.*

CLOTHING

apartment number 9. Siblings Amy and Sarah Blessing offer sisterly advice to guys on what styles best suit them. Their store, named for the Tammy Wynette song, carries classic lines like Paul Smith and Jack Spade as well as a wall full of Warby Parker specs. ⊠ *1804 N. Damen Ave.* ☎ *773/395–2999* ⊕ *www.apartmentnumber9.com.*

Belly Dance Maternity. The hippest moms-to-be shop here for up-to-the-minute maternity fashions by Japanese Weekend, Seraphine, and Citizens of Humanity. ⊠ *1647 N. Damen Ave.* ☎ *773/862–1133* ⊕ *www.bellydancematernity.com.*

Cynthia Rowley. Cynthia Rowley is a Chicago-area native, and she fills her Bucktown store with the exuberant, well-priced dresses, separates, and accessories that have made her so popular. ⊠ *1653 N. Damen Ave., Bucktown* ☎ *773/276–9209* ⊕ *www.cynthiarowley.com.*

Helen Yi. This loftlike, minimalist boutique stocks sophisticated styles from up-and-coming designers. ⊠ *1725 N. Damen Ave.* ☎ *773/252–3838* ⊕ *www.helenyi.com.*

Intermix. Label hunters were thrilled when branches of this New York boutique opened in Lincoln Park and the Gold Coast. The third outpost offers the same mix of designer lines, which might include Rag & Bone, Elizabeth & James, Helmut Lang, and Missoni. ⊠ *1633 N. Damen Ave.* ☎ *773/292–0894* ⊕ *www.intermixonline.com* ⊠ *40 E. Delaware Pl., Gold Coast* ☎ *312/640–2922* ⊠ *841 W. Armitage Ave., Lincoln Park* ☎ *773/404–8766.*

Marc by Marc Jacobs. Neighborhood style mavens rejoiced when this store opened in Bucktown. It's a fitting locale for the fashion icon, whose whimsical, slightly offbeat designs make trend-followers drool. ⊠ *1714 N. Damen Ave.* ☎ *773/276–2998* ⊕ *www.marcjacobs.com.*

Michelle Tan. Local indie design star Michelle Tan's shop also serves as a working studio where she creates clothes with an emphasis on interesting textures. You'll also find pieces by other local designers. ⊠ *1872 N. Damen Ave.* ☎ *773/252–1888* ⊕ *michelletan.com.*

p.45. This store is a must-hit for its fashion-forward collection by a cadre of hip designers like MiH, Rachel Comey, and Ulla Johnson. Customers from all over the city and well beyond come here for adventurous to elegant styles and prices that don't get out of hand. ✉ *1643 N. Damen Ave.* ☎ *773/862–4523* ⊕ *p45.com.*

Riley. Put together a polished urban look at this clean, modern space. Men's lines include Penguin and Ben Sherman, and women can pick up cute wardrobe staples from Akiko, Michael Stars, LA Made, and more. ✉ *1659 N. Damen Ave.* ☎ *773/489–0101* ⊕ *www.shopriley.com.*

Robin Richman. Robin Richman showcases her famous knitwear alongside designs from lesser-known European labels and local clothes designers. The eclectic displays never disappoint. ✉ *2108 N. Damen Ave.* ☎ *773/278–6150* ⊕ *robinrichman.com.*

Silver Moon Chicago. Vintage wedding gowns and tuxedos are a specialty here, but you can also find less-formal vintage clothing and even Vivienne Westwood accessories. ✉ *1721 W. North Ave.* ☎ *773/235–5797* ⊕ *www.silvermoonvintage.com.*

Sir and Madame. Displayed among the leather suitcases and vintage furniture are of-the-moment denim, tops, Ts, and dresses from the likes of Cheap Monday, Boxing Kitten, and Funktional, along with the equally hip in-house label—for men and women, naturally. Vintage eyewear keeps you looking just as sharp from the neck up. ✉ *938 N. Damen Ave.* ☎ *773/489–6660* ⊕ *www.sirandmadame.com.*

Tangerine. Popular designers such as Tibi and Plenty provide the fun, feminine clothes and accessories here. There's also a good denim selection, including styles by Genetic Denim and J Brand. ✉ *1719 N. Damen Ave.* ☎ *773/772–0505* ⊕ *www.shopattangerine.com.*

The T-Shirt Deli. Order up a customized T-shirt with iron-on letters or throwback '70s decals. Your creation will be served to you on the spot, wrapped in paper like a sandwich, and packed with a bag of chips for good measure. ✉ *1739 N. Damen Ave.* ☎ *773/276–6266* ⊕ *www.tshirtdeli.com.*

vive la femme. The motto is "style beyond size," and the specialty is sexy, exciting clothes for women in sizes 12 to 24, from lines that include Gayla Bentley, Kristin Miles, and Elsa Dee. ✉ *2048 N. Damen Ave.* ☎ *773/772–7429* ⊕ *vivelafemme.com.*

HOME DECOR

Alan Design Studio. The offerings at this design atelier, owned by a former feature-film set decorator, range from Victorian to mid-20th-century modern. There's always a healthy assortment of sofas and chairs recovered in eclectic fabrics, plus pillows made of unusual textiles and refurbished vintage lamps with marvelous shades. ✉ *2134 N. Damen Ave.* ☎ *773/278–2345* ⊕ *www.alandesignstudio.com.*

LINGERIE

G Boutique. Here's an all-in-one stop for women planning for a little romance. There's beautiful lingerie from brands such as Eberjey and Cosabella, plus massage oils, books, videos, and toys. Looking for some education? Check out the workshops, which are listed online. ✉ *2131 N. Damen Ave.* ☎ *773/235–1234* ⊕ *www.boutiqueg.com.*

Browse through colorful rows of jewelry, accessories, and pajamas.

SHOES, HANDBAGS, AND LEATHER GOODS

City Soles. This on-trend shoe shop is like mecca for shoe lovers. There's a vast selection of edgy men's and women's shoes from designers like Coclico, Chie Mihara, Sorel, and others. ⊠ *2001 W. North Ave.* ☎ *773/489–2001* ⊕ *www.citysoles.com.*

Soutache. French for "braid," Soutache is all about the extras that make life so much more interesting: high-end trimmings and embellishments like tortoise shell–and–bamboo belt buckles and purse handles; exotic ostrich plumes; suede tassels; and reams and reams of ribbon. It's up to you how to get creative with all this fun stuff. ⊠ *2125 N. Damen Ave.* ☎ *773/292–9110* ⊕ *soutacheribbons.com.*

Stitch. Leather goods of every ilk—purses, travel bags, desk accessories—are the main attraction here, but you also find minimalist furniture, tabletop goods, and jewelry. ⊠ *1723 N. Damen Ave.* ☎ *773/782–1570* ⊕ *stitchchicago.com.*

LAKEVIEW

Home to Wrigley Field, the North Side neighborhood Lakeview is broken into several smaller shopping areas, each with a distinct flavor and each making for a fun afternoon out. Clark Street, between Diversey Avenue and Addison Street, is Cubs central, with shops hawking sports-centric paraphernalia. A slew of upscale boutiques draw trend seekers to Southport Avenue between Belmont Avenue and Grace Street. Antiquers and bargain hunters should head straight for the intersection of Lincoln Avenue and Diversey Parkway and meander north on Lincoln.

ANTIQUES

Antique Resources. Choice antiques from Europe and elsewhere are sold at fair prices here. This is an excellent source for stately desks and dignified dining sets, but the true find is a huge trove—numbering more than 1,000—of antique crystal and gilt chandeliers from France. ⊠ *1741 W. Belmont Ave.* ☎ *773/871–4242* ⊕ *www.antiqueresourcesinc.com.*

Chicago Antique Centre. Open seven days a week, this one-stop, bi-level spot houses about 30 dealers selling art, jewelry, furniture, and many other items. ⊠ *3036 N. Lincoln Ave.* ☎ *773/929–0200* ⊕ *chicagoantiquecentre.com.*

Father Time Antiques. Father Time bills itself as the Midwest's largest retailer of vintage timepieces. In addition to the pocket watches and clocks, there are also accessories available, such as watch holders and display cases. ⊠ *2108 W. Belmont Ave.* ☎ *773/880–5599* ⊕ *www.fathertimeantiques.com.*

Modlife. The emphasis here is on mid-20th-century finds from Paul McCobb, Eames, Eero Saarinen, and other well-known designers. You'll also find original paintings and sculptures at overall affordable price points. ⊠ *3061 N. Lincoln Ave.* ☎ *773/868–0844* ⊕ *modlifehome.com.*

Smythson Yeats Antiques. An always-changing selection here includes plenty of Art Deco and Art Nouveau treasures, with an impressive selection of lamps, chandeliers, and ceramics. There are plenty of fabulous larger pieces, too—dark-wood sideboards, bookcases, and plush leather chairs. Lamp-repair service is available. ⊠ *3851 N. Lincoln Ave.* ☎ *773/244–6365* ⊕ *www.smythsonyeats.com.*

Urban Artifacts. The superb selection of furniture, lighting, and decorative accessories from the 1940s to the '70s here emphasizes industrial designs. ⊠ *2928 N. Lincoln Ave.* ☎ *773/404–1008.*

BEAUTY

City Olive. This cute shop sells olive oil in every imaginable form, from beautiful bottles of the extra-virgin variety to bath and body products made with the stuff. ⊠ *2236 W. Roscoe St.* ☎ *773/687–9980* ⊕ *www.cityolive.com.*

BOOKS AND MUSIC

Bookworks. The stock here includes thousands of titles, many of them used or rare. There's an emphasis on sports (for Cubs fans strolling by from nearby Wrigley Field) and contemporary fiction. Check out the vinyl-record section. The store buys used books in good condition, too. ⊠ *3444 N. Clark St.* ☎ *773/871–5318* ⊕ *www.thebookworks.com.*

Reckless Records. Reckless Records ranks as one of the city's leading alternative and secondhand record stores. Besides the indie offerings, you can flip through jazz, classical, and soul recordings, or catch a live appearance by an up-and-comer passing through town. ⊠ *3126 N. Broadway St.* ☎ *773/404–5080* ⊕ *www.reckless.com* ⊠ *1532 N. Milwaukee Ave., Wicker Park* ☎ *773/235–3727* ⊠ *26 E. Madison St., Loop* ☎ *312/795–0878.*

Unabridged Bookstore. Since 1980 this independent bookshop has maintained a loyal clientele who loves its vast selection and dedicated staff. Known for having one of the most extensive gay and lesbian selections in the city, it also has an impressive children's section and great magazines, too. ✉ *3251 N. Broadway* ☎ *773/883–9119* ⊕ *www. unabridgedbookstore.com.*

CHILDREN'S CLOTHING

Little Threads. Trumpette, Wes & Willy, and Petunia Picklebottom are just some of the funky kids' labels at this cute neighborhood shop. There's also a fun selection of children's reading material. ✉ *2033 W. Roscoe St.* ☎ *773/327–9310* ⊕ *www.shoplittlethreads.com.*

CLOTHING

Belmont Army. Here, Converse, Dr. Martens and other funky brands get mixed in with fatigues, flak jackets, skate gear, and faux-fur coats. The Lakeview veteran—open since 1975—occupies an entire building just down the street from its original home adjacent to the Belmont L station. ✉ *855 W. Belmont Ave.* ☎ *773/549–1038* ⊕ *thebelmontstop.com.*

Cerato Boutique. Highlighting local designers and a handful of favorites from outside the city, this boutique showcases eco-friendly pieces by Lara Miller, blouses by Kate Boggiano, jewelry by jules, and more. ✉ *3451 N. Southport Ave.* ☎ *773/248–8604* ⊕ *ceratoboutique.com.*

Hubba-Hubba. Flowy, feminine clothes with a retro flavor mix with vintage and modern jewelry and accessories at this packed-to-the-gills shop that feels like rummaging through your best friend's closet. ✉ *2040 W. Roscoe St.* ☎ *773/477–1414* ⊕ *hubbahubbachicago.com.*

Kickin'. Hip, urban women snap up their maternity wear at this shop. There's an emphasis on workout and yoga gear. ✉ *2142 W. Roscoe St.* ☎ *773/281–6577* ⊕ *www.kickinmaternity.com* ✉ *2120 N. Halsted St., Lincoln Park* ☎ *773/525–2120.*

Krista K Boutique. An inventory of must-haves for women from designers like Citizens of Humanity, Theory, and Splendid reflects the style of the neighborhood. The shop has become the go-to spot for the latest denim, too. ✉ *3458 N. Southport Ave.* ☎ *773/248–1967* ⊕ *www.kristak.com.*

Uncle Dan's. This is the place to go for camping, skiing, and general outdoorsy gear by brands like Marmot and the North Face. There's a good kids' selection, too. ✉ *3551 N. Southport Ave.* ☎ *773/348–5800* ⊕ *www.udans.com.*

HOME DECOR

J. Toguri Mercantile Company. This warehouse-style store carries all things Asian, including tea sets, lacquerware, kimonos, hard-to-find pots, and Japanese music. ✉ *851 W. Belmont Ave.* ☎ *773/929–3500.*

Waxman Candles. The candles sold here are made on the premises and come in countless shapes, colors, and scents. There's an incredible selection of holders for votives and pillars, and incense, too. ✉ *3044 N. Lincoln Ave.* ☎ *773/929–3000* ⊕ *www.waxmancandles.com.*

JEWELRY AND ACCESSORIES

Bourdage Pearls. Sherry Bourdage sells Chinese freshwater pearls in a staggering array of colors and styles that range from simple and inexpensive to elaborate custom designs. ✉ *4039A N. Ravenswood* ☎ *773/244–1126* ⊕ *www.bourdagepearls.com.*

Combine holiday shopping with fantastic eye candy at the Magnificent Mile Lights Festival.

Glam to Go. The lotions and potions found here will help you stay soft and smelling good. There's also clothing by Language, Talla, Scrapbook, and others for getting glammed up, along with handbags, accessories, toys, and baby clothes. ✉ *2002 W. Roscoe St.* ☏ *773/525–7004* ⊕ *glamtogo.com.*

MARKETS
Dose Market. This hip monthly market, which opened in 2011, unites food, fashion, and other goods from local artisans and designers in a contemporary, loftlike space. Browse the edible and eclectic merchandise; past markets have included Samantha Sleeper's eco-conscious clothing, elegant Greer stationery, Cheap Tart baked goods, and blends from Rare Tea Cellar. Check the website for tickets and dates. ✉ *River East Art Center, 435 E. Illinois St., River North* ☏ *312/321–1001* ⊕ *dosemarket. com* ✉ *$8 online or $10 at the door.* ☉ *Once a month on Sun., 10–4.*

PET STORES
Wigglyville. Everything you need for your furry friend (leashes, collars, bedding, carriers, pet shampoo, food dishes, and more), along with pet-themed artwork, is carefully arranged in this clean and inviting pet boutique. Another branch is at 1137 W. Madison Street, in the West Loop. ✉ *3337 N. Broadway Ave.* ☏ *773/528–3337* ⊕ *www.wigglyville.com.*

SHOES, HANDBAGS, AND LEATHER GOODS
Spare Parts. The selection of fine leather goods here draws from many sources, including Village Tannery, Jack Spade, and Brynn Capella. Jewelry. Bath and body products, baby gear, and home accessories round out the selection. ✉ *2947 N. Broadway St.* ☏ *773/525–4242* ⊕ *www. shopspareparts.com.*

TOYS

Building Blocks. Shop here for classic toys designed to appeal to kids' natural curiosity and imagination, from cars and train sets to puzzles and musical instruments. Complimentary gift wrapping is available with purchase. ✉ *3306 N. Lincoln Ave.* ☎ *773/525–6200* ⊕ *www.buildingblockstoys. com* ✉ *2130 W. Division St., Wicker Park* ☎ *773/235–1888.*

WINE

Lush Wine and Spirits. This full-service liquor store specializes in wine, microbrews, and obscure spirits from small-batch distilleries. Attend one of the frequently held wine tastings to try before you buy. ✉ *2232 W. Roscoe St.* ☎ *773/281–8888* ⊕ *www.lushwineandspirits.com* ✉ *1412 W. Chicago Ave., West Town, Wicker Park* ☎ *312/666–6900* ✉ *1257 S. Halsted St., University Village* ☎ *312/738–1900.*

FAR NORTH AND FAR NORTHWEST SIDES

On the Far North, Swedish-settled Andersonville specializes in antiques and home furnishings, along with funky coffee shops and casual restaurants.

ANTIQUES

Architectural Artifacts. The selection matches the warehouse proportions here. The mammoth two-story space houses oversize garden ornaments (arbors, benches), statuary, iron grills, fixtures, and decorative tiles. Architectural fragments—marble, metal, wood, terra-cotta—hail from American and European historic buildings. ✉ *4325 N. Ravenswood Ave., Ravenswood, Far Northwest Side* ☎ *773/348–0622* ⊕ *architecturalartifacts.com.*

Broadway Antique Market. More than 75 hand-picked dealers, plus quality that is more carefully monitored than at most malls, make it worth the trek to the Broadway Antique Market, called BAM by its loyal fans. Mid-20th century is the primary emphasis, but items range from Arts and Crafts and Art Deco to Heywood-Wakefield. Display is the market's strong suit—the furniture, jewelry, and other items are wonderfully presented. The building itself is a prime example of Deco architecture. ✉ *6130 N. Broadway St.* ☎ *773/743–5444.*

Edgewater Antique Mall. A couple of blocks north of the Broadway Antique Market, this mall specializes in 20th-century goods. ✉ *6314 N. Broadway St.* ☎ *773/262–2525* ⊕ *www.edgewaterantiquemall.com.*

Lincoln Antique Mall. Dozens of dealers carrying antiques and collectibles share this large space. There's a good selection of French and mid-20th-century modern furniture, plus estate jewelry, oil paintings, and photographs, but you can find virtually anything and everything here. ✉ *3115 W. Irving Park Rd., Far Northwest Side* ☎ *773/604–4700* ⊕ *www.lincolnantiquemall.com.*

BEAUTY

Merz Apothecary. In addition to being a normal pharmacy, this old-fashioned druggist also stocks all manner of homeopathic and herbal remedies, as well as a great selection of hard-to-find European toiletries, cosmetics, candles, and natural laundry products. It's closed Sunday.

✉ *4716 N. Lincoln Ave., Lincoln Square* ☎ *773/989–0900* ⊕ *www. merzapothecary.com* ✉ *Palmer House Hilton, 17 E. Monroe St., Loop* ☎ *312/781–6900.*

BOOKS, SOUVENIRS, AND STATIONERY

The Book Cellar. In addition to a well-edited selection of books ranging from local interest to popular fiction, the bright, inviting space houses a small wine bar/coffee shop where customers can linger with their purchases over a glass of cabernet. Readings and other literary events are held here frequently. ✉ *4736 N. Lincoln Ave., Far Northwest Side* ☎ *773/293–2665* ⊕ *www.bookcellarinc.com.*

Enjoy. Calling itself an "urban general store," this bright and inviting Lincoln Square shop stocks a wide selection of greeting cards, cute clothes and toys for kids and babies, and gift items such as a high heel-shaped cake server and bacon-flavored toothpicks. ✉ *4723 N. Lincoln Ave., Far Northwest Side* ☎ *773/334–8626* ⊕ *www.urbangeneralstore.com.*

Gallimaufry Gallery. Browse the tightly packed selection of wood carvings, jewelry, incense, and greeting cards in this little shop. ✉ *4712 N. Lincoln Ave., Lincoln Square* ☎ *773/728–3600* ⊕ *www.gallimaufry.net.*

Women & Children First. This feminist bookstore stocks fiction and nonfiction, periodicals, journals, small-press publications, and a strong selection of gay and lesbian titles. The children's section has a great array of books, all politically correct. ✉ *5233 N. Clark St., Andersonville* ☎ *773/769–9299* ⊕ *womenandchildrenfirst.com.*

CLOTHING

Bellybum Boutique. A one-stop shop for eco-minded expectant moms, this boutique carries organic maternity wear and transitional clothing, cloth diapers and diapering accessories, baby slings, and toxin-free toys and bath products for baby. ✉ *4347 N. Lincoln Ave., Lincoln Square* ☎ *773/868–0944* ⊕ *bellybumboutique.com.*

TOYS

Timeless Toys. This old-timey toy shop has a Santa's-workshop feel. Inside you'll find plenty of classic wooden toys alongside fanciful dress-up costumes, plush puppets, cuddly stuffed animals, board games, puzzles, and books. ✉ *4749 N. Lincoln Ave., Lincoln Square* ☎ *773/334–4445* ⊕ *timelesstoyschicago.com.*

NIGHTLIFE AND THE ARTS

Updated by
Heidi Moore

Despite their hardworking Midwestern image, Chicagoans know how to let loose. And, unlike that big city on the East Coast (ahem), the city that plays as hard as it works is refreshingly devoid of attitude. Sure, some nightclubs trot out the velvet ropes or feature exclusive, members-only VIP rooms, but for the most part Chicago's nightlife scene reflects the same qualities that make the city itself great: it's lively, diverse, and completely unpretentious.

Entertainment options abound every night of the week. The challenge won't be finding something that suits your mood and budget, but rather narrowing down the seemingly endless array of choices. Should you hit the theater for a Broadway-in-Chicago spectacle followed by a post-performance cocktail? Or explore the city's dynamic fringe theater scene? Catch some first-rate improv? Or get your dance on at a trendy nightclub?

Music lovers will find much to adore in Chicago. The city is justifiably famous for its blues scene, which still thrives in clubs from the South Side to the North Side, but it's equally fertile ground for classical, folk, rock, alt-country, or whatever genre captures your fancy. The summer's free concert series in Grant Park and Millennium Park—from the jam-packed blues and jazz festivals to low-key weeknight concerts—consistently draw top-tier performers.

If your idea of the perfect evening means kicking back with a local brew or a glass of wine, there are bars and lounges catering to every taste—from neighborhood dives to sports bars to swanky spots where patrons dress to the nines. Some of these locales also feature entertainment in the form of karaoke, trivia competitions, readings, and poetry slams.

In the summer, Chicagoans thankful for an end to the long winter head out in droves to the city's many rooftop bars and patios. The hotel bar scene has exploded, and now features some of the city's trendiest nightspots, including a number of rooftop lounges with bird's-eye views of the city.

There's only one thing you won't find in Chicago: the urge to hole up in your hotel room at night.

FESTIVALS

Chicago Blues Festival. The Chicago Blues Festival leaves no doubt about it: Chicago still loves to sing the blues. Each June, the city pulses with sounds from the largest free blues festival in the world, which takes place over three days and on four stages in both Grant Park and Millennium Park. The always-packed open-air festival has been headlined by blues legends such as B.B. King, Koko Taylor, and Buddy Guy. ☎ *312/744–3315* ⊕ *www.cityofchicago.org/city/en/depts/dca/supp_info/chicago_blues_festival.html.*

Chicago Improv Festival. The springtime Chicago Improv Festival, the nation's largest festival for improvisers, has stages devoted to group, pair, and single improv; sketch comedy; and more. ☎ *773/875–6616* ⊕ *www.chicagoimprovfestival.org.*

GET TICKETS

You can save money on seats at **Hot Tix** (⊕ *www.hottix.org*), where unsold tickets are available, usually at half price (plus a service charge) on the day of performance; you won't know what's available until that day. On Friday, however, you can buy tickets for Saturday and Sunday. Hot Tix booths are at the Chicago Tourism Center at 72 East Randolph Street and at the Chicago Water Works Visitor Center at the southeast corner of Michigan Avenue and Pearson Street. Both Hot Tix booths are closed Monday. Hot Tix also functions as a Ticketmaster outlet, selling advance, full-price, cash-only tickets.

Ticketmaster. You can charge full-price tickets over the phone or online at Ticketmaster.com. ☎ *800/745–3000* ⊕ *www.ticketmaster.com.*

For a cheaper, more intimate, and—arguably—equally rewarding theater experience, Chicago has a lively fringe theater scene. You'll find smaller storefront theater spaces scattered across the city (but concentrated on the North Side), where you can catch everything from dramatic classics mounted on tiny stages to edgy works by emerging writers. Best of all, tickets often go for $20 or less and are usually available at the box office on the day of performance.

For hot, sold-out shows, such as performances by the Chicago Symphony Orchestra or the Lyric Opera of Chicago, call a day or two before the show to see if there are any subscriber returns. Another option is to show up at the box office on concert day—a surprising number of people strike it lucky with on-the-spot tickets because of cancellations.

Small fees can have big payoffs! Many of the smaller neighborhood street festivals (there are hundreds in summer) request $5 to $10 donations upon entry, but it's often worth the expense: big-name bands are known to take the stage of even the most under-publicized festivals. For moment-to-moment festival coverage, check out ⊕ *chicago.metromix.com* or ⊕ *timeoutchicago.com.*

RESOURCES

To find out what's happening in the Windy City, the *Chicago Tribune*'s Metromix Chicago (⊕ *chicago.metromix.com*) is a good resource. Read *TimeOut Chicago* for club listings, rotating parties, and DJ appearances. *The Chicago Reader* and Metromix also dish on the hottest bars and clubs. (You'll find theater and music listings in all these publications as well.) Centerstage Chicago (⊕ *www.centerstagechicago.com*) has a calendar of music and theater events.

TIMING

Live music starts around 9 pm at bars around town. If you want to guarantee a seat, arrive well before the band's scheduled start and stake out a spot. Most bars close at 2 am Sunday through Friday and 3 am Saturday. A few dance clubs and late-night bars remain open until 4 am or 5 am (Berlin, Transit, and Enclave are very popular). Outdoor beer gardens such as Sheffield's and John Barleycorn are the exception; these close at 11 pm on weeknights and midnight on weekends. Some bars are not open seven days a week, so call before you go. Curtain calls for performances are usually at 7:30 or 8 pm.

GETTING THERE

Parking in North Side neighborhoods—particularly Lincoln Park, Lakeview, and Wicker Park/Bucktown—is increasingly scarce, even on weeknights. If you're going out in these areas, take a cab or the El. The Red, Brown, and Blue lines will get you within a few blocks of most major entertainment destinations downtown and on the North and Near Northwest sides. If you do decide to drive, use the curbside valet service available at many restaurants and clubs for about $7 to $10. If you're headed to the South Side, be cautious about public transportation late at night. It's best to drive or cab it here.

NIGHTLIFE

Chicago's entertainment varies from loud and loose to sophisticated and sedate. You'll find classic Chicago corner bars in most neighborhoods, along with trendier alternatives like wine bars and lounges. The strains of blues and jazz provide much of the backbeat to the city's groove, and an alternative country scene is flourishing. As far as dancing is concerned, take your pick from cavernous clubs to smaller spots with DJs spinning dance tunes; there's everything from hip-hop to swing. Wicker Park/Bucktown and River North have the hottest nightlife, but prime spots are spread throughout the city.

Shows usually begin at 9 pm; cover charges generally range from $3 to $20, depending on the day of the week (Friday and Saturday nights are the most expensive). The list of blues and jazz clubs includes several South Side locations: be cautious about transportation here late at night, because some of these neighborhoods can be unsafe. Drive your own car or ask the bartender to call you a cab.

THE LOOP, SOUTH LOOP, AND WEST LOOP

12

Sleek and sexy wine bars and lounges such as Encore and ROOF on theWit Hotel light up Chicago's core business district after work. On weekends and late nights the action shifts to the West Loop—centered on Fulton, Lake, and Randolph streets—which is home to a diverse array of nightspots, from megaclubs like Transit to of-the-minute drinking establishments like the Aviary. ■**TIP→ If you're sticking to downtown and North Side bars, it's relatively safe to patronize public transportation. But if you're planning on staying out past midnight, we suggest taking a cab home.**

BARS

The Aviary. Chef Grant Achatz applies his cutting-edge culinary style to cocktails at this West Loop bar, adjacent to his high-concept restaurant Next. Your newfangled old-fashioned might arrive injected into an egg of ice, or your drink's flavor might change subtly as its flavored ice melts. Inventive bar bites are on offer as well. Be prepared for a wait. ✉ *955 W Fulton Market, West Loop* ☎ *312/226–0868* ⊕ *www.theaviary.com.*

Encore. Encore is a jazzed-up hotel lounge sandwiched between the Cadillac Palace Theatre and the Hotel Allegro. Clubby seating and a classic cocktail menu make it an appealing downtown destination for post-dinner or -theater drinks, a light bite, and conversation. ✉ *171 W. Randolph St., Loop* ☎ *312/338–3788* ⊕ *www.encorechicago.com.*

Kitty O'Shea's. Kitty O'Shea's, a handsome room in the Chicago Hilton and Towers, is an authentic Emerald Isle pub with all things Irish, including live music seven nights a week, beer, food, and bar staff. ✉ *Chicago Hilton and Towers, 720 S. Michigan Ave., South Loop* ☎ *312/922–4400.*

Lumen. Lumen is worth the difficulty getting here—it's in a former meat-packing plant in the out-of-the-way warehouse district. Once inside, you'll find a clean-lined space with low-slung modular seating, sleek bamboo tables, and a stainless-steel bar. The white walls are lighted by thousands of tiny lights that pulse with the music—mostly cool electronica and trip-hop beats. ✉ *839 W. Fulton Market, West Loop* ☎ *312/733–2222* ⊕ *www.lumen-chicago.com.*

Red Kiva. Red Kiva serves up cocktails, martinis, and draft beers—along with house-made flat-bread pizzas—in a cozy, candlelit lounge space centered on a sunken circular area (the titular kiva). DJs spin tunes, or musical guests heat up the grand piano. ✉ *1108 W. Randolph St., West Loop* ☎ *312/226–5577* ⊕ *www.redkiva.com.*

ROOF on theWit. One of the city's hottest perches, ROOF occupies the 27th floor of theWit Hotel. The outdoor space entices with fire pits and panoramic city views, and the indoor lounge is equally breathtaking, with floor-to-ceiling glass windows. DJs spinning eclectic beats and a menu of pricey cocktails and small plates complete the scene. ✉ *201 N. State St., Loop* ☎ *312/239–9501* ⊕ *www.roofonthewit.com.*

The Tasting Room. The Tasting Room makes the short list of nightspots where Chicagoans take guests they want to impress. This two-story wine bar has a casual, loft-chic look and sweeping skyline views. More than 100 wines are poured by the glass or flight, and more than 300 by the bottle. Cheese, caviar, and other light bites are the perfect complement. If you love the vintage you taste here, buy a bottle to take home at the adjacent wine shop, Randolph Wine Cellars. ⊠ *1415 W. Randolph St., West Loop* ☎ *312/942–1313* ⊕ *www.thetastingroomchicago.com.*

> **WORD OF MOUTH**
>
> "[We went] to Buddy Guy's Legends to have dinner and hear some blues and it was so much fun! All the acts we saw were good . . . but best of all was the fact that Buddy Guy was there and got up and did a few numbers too. The joint was jumpin'."
> —goddesstogo

DANCE CLUBS

Transit. Transit, despite being hidden away underneath the El tracks in a spooky stretch west of downtown, is wildly popular with young clubgoers. Inside, the multiroom space has a crisp design and sumptuous VIP area. Don't miss the glowing black-and-white bar between the oval and chandelier rooms, or the mezzanine with its minimalist furniture and oversize mahogany table. ⊠ *1431 W. Lake St., West Loop* ☎ *312/836–7000, 312/491–9729* ⊕ *www.transitnightclubchicago.com.*

MUSIC VENUES

BLUES

Blues Heaven Foundation. For a walk into history, stop by the Blues Heaven Foundation, which occupies the former home of the legendary Chess Records. Breathe the same rarefied air as blues (and rock-and-roll) legends Muddy Waters, Howlin' Wolf, Chuck Berry, and the Rolling Stones, all of whom recorded here. Check out the Chess brothers' private offices, the recording studio, and the back stairway used only by signed musicians. Don't miss the eerie "Life Cast Portraits" wall showcasing the plaster heads of the Chess recording artists. Tour hours are 11 to 4 Monday to Friday and noon to 2 Saturday. ⊠ *2120 S. Michigan Ave., South Loop* ☎ *312/808–1286* ⊕ *www.bluesheaven.com.*

Fodor's Choice ★ **Buddy Guy's Legends.** Relocated from its original location a few doors down, Buddy Guy's Legends has a superb sound system, excellent sightlines, and more space to showcase Grammy Award–winning blues performer/owner Buddy Guy's collection of blues memorabilia. Look for local blues acts during the week and larger-scale touring acts on weekends. Don't miss Buddy Guy in January, when he performs a monthlong home stand of shows (tickets go on sale one month in advance). There's also a substantial menu of Cajun and Creole favorites. ⊠ *700 S. Wabash Ave., South Loop* ☎ *312/427–1190* ⊕ *www.buddyguy.com.*

Continued on page 287

CHICAGO SINGS THE BLUES

Cool, electric, urban blues are the soundtrack of the Windy City. The blues traveled up the Mississippi River with the Delta sharecroppers during the Great Migration, settled down on Maxwell Street and South Side clubs, and gave birth to such big-name talent as Muddy Waters, Howlin' Wolf, Willie Dixon, and, later, Koko Taylor. Today, you can still hear the blues in a few South Side clubs where it all began, or check out the current scene on the North Side. *Check the listings in the chapter for specifics.*

Clockwise from top left: Chicago Jazz & Blues at the Chicago History Museum; Chicago Blues Festival; Chicago Blues Festival; Carlos Johnson performing at Rosa's Lounge

THE BIRTH OF THE CHICAGO BLUES

CHESS RECORDS

Founded by Philip and Leonard Chess, Polish immigrant brothers, in 1947. For the first two years, the label was called Aristocrat. Its famous address, 2120 S. Michigan Avenue, was the nucleus of the blues scene. Up-and-comers performed on the sidewalk out front in hopes of being discovered. Even today, locals and visitors peek through the windows of the restored studio (now the Blues Heaven Foundation) looking for glimpses of past glory.

The label's first hit record was Muddy Waters' *I Can't Be Satisfied*.

The brothers were criticized for having a paternalistic relationship with their artists. They reportedly bought Muddy Waters a car off the lot when he wasn't able to finance it himself.

The company was immortalized in the excellent 2008 film *Cadillac Records*, which starred Adrian Brody.

Did you know? When the Rolling Stones recorded the track "2120 South Michigan Avenue" (off the *12 x 5* album) at the Chess Records studio in June 1964, the young Brits were reportedly so nervous about singing in front of Willie Dixon (Buddy Guy and Muddy Waters were also hanging around the studio that day) that they literally became tongue-tied. As a result, the song is purely instrumental.

WILLIE DIXON (July 1, 1915–Jan. 29, 1992) Chess Records' leading A & R (artist and repertoire) man, bass player, and composer. Founded the Blues Heaven Foundation, Chess Records' restored office and studio. *See Blues Heaven Foundation review next page.*

Famous compositions: "Hoochie Coochie Man" (recorded by Muddy Waters), "My Babe" (recorded by Little Walter), and "Wang Dang Doodle" (recorded by Koko Taylor)

MUDDY WATERS: KING OF ELECTRIC BLUES (4/1915–4/1983)

When Muddy Waters gave his guitar an electric jolt, he didn't just revolutionize the blues. His electric guitar became a magic wand: Its jive talk (and cry) turned country-blues into city-blues, and it gave birth to rock and roll. Waters's signature sound has been firmly imprinted on nearly all subsequent musical genres.

Best known for: Riveting vocals, a swooping pompadour, and, of course, plugging in the guitar

Biggest break: Leonard Chess, one of the Chess brothers of Chess Records, let Waters record two of his own songs. The record sold out in two days, and stores issued a dictum of "one per customer."

Biggest song: "Hoochie Coochie Man"

Lyrics: *Y'know I'm here / Everybody knows I'm here / And I'm the hoochie-coochie man*

Awards: 3 Grammies, Lifetime Achievement induction into the Rock and Roll Hall of Fame

Local honor: A strip of 43rd Street in Chicago is renamed Muddy Waters Drive.

HOWLIN' WOLF (June 10, 1910–Jan. 10, 1976)

In 1951, at the age of 41, Wolf recorded with Sun Studios in Memphis, TN. Shortly thereafter, Sun sold Wolf's only two songs, "Moanin' At Midnight" and "How Many More Years," to Chess Records, kicking off his prolific recording career with Chess.

Most popular songs: "Backdoor Man" and "Little Red Rooster"

Instruments: Electric guitar and harmonica

Dedication to his craft: Wolf was still taking guitar lessons even a year before his death, even though he was long recognized as one of the two greatest blues musicians in the world.

Fodor's Choice ★ **Lee's Unleaded Blues.** Lee's Unleaded Blues has been a South Side favorite since it opened in the early 1970s. Locals come decked out in their showiest threads and University of Chicago students often pop in for a round. The cramped, triangular bar may inhibit free movement, but that doesn't seem to bother the crowd that comes for powerhouse blues and jazz. Note: the club can be difficult to find if you don't know the area, so be sure to take a cab or study a map before making the trip. ✉ *7401 S. Chicago Ave., Grand Crossing* ☎ *773/493–3477* ⊕ *www. leesunleadedblues.com.*

NEAR NORTH AND RIVER NORTH

Rush Street may have lost its former glory, but the bars lining Division Street still attract rowdy singles. Reprieve from the bustling Division Street scene is only a few blocks south, in the Near North and River North neighborhoods. Hunker down in a low-key lounge or sip a hearty pint of Guinness at an authentic Irish pub. At the southern edge of River North, waterfront lounges popular with the after-work crowd line the Chicago Riverwalk.

BARS

3rd Coast Cafe & Wine Bar. Third Coast Café, the oldest coffeehouse in the Gold Coast, pleases just about everyone with a full menu served until midnight seven nights a week. The inviting space combines warm woods, etched glass, and funky local art. A diverse clientele—from students and twentysomethings to retirees living nearby—comes for coffee, Sunday brunch, or late-night jazz sessions. ✉ *1260 N. Dearborn St., Near North* ☎ *312/649–0730* ⊕ *www.3rdcoastcafe.com.*

Bridge House Tavern. With an enormous patio overlooking the Chicago River, this bar attracts both the after-work crowd and tourists searching for the quintessential city view. Order a burger or po'boy and watch the boats docking barside. Off-season visitors can take refuge inside the cozy lounge with stone walls and wood paneling. ✉ *321 N. Clark St., River North* ☎ *312/644–0283* ⊕ *www.bridgehousetavern.com.*

Bull & Bear. Bull & Bear amps up the testosterone, with a dual focus on sports—the bar's name references two Chicago sports teams—and the stock market. Reserve one of five booths with built-in beer taps (pay by the ounce), or grab a seat at the bar and catch the game on one of several flat-screen TVs. ✉ *431 N. Wells St., River North* ☎ *312/527–5973* ⊕ *www.bullbearbar.com.*

Castaways. Castaways puts you so close to Lake Michigan, you might consider wearing a swimsuit. Perched atop the North Avenue Beach Boathouse, the breezy, casual bar and grill creates the perfect setup for lazy, summertime sipping. ✉ *1603 N. Lake Shore Dr., River North* ☎ *773/281–1200* ⊕ *www.castawayschicago.com.*

Citizen Bar. Everyone's welcome at Citizen Bar, a sleek space with exposed brick walls and traditional bar fare. But the real draw is the huge, multilevel outdoor area, one of the city's most coveted spots come summer. ✉ *364 W. Erie St., River North* ☎ *312/640–1156* ⊕ *www.citizenbar.com.*

Coq d'Or. A dark, wood-paneled room in the Drake Hotel, Coq d'Or has red-leather booths where Chicago legend Buddy Charles held court before retiring. Fine music and cocktails served in blown-glass goblets draw hotel guests as well as neighborhood regulars. ✉ *140 E. Walton St., Near North* ☎ *312/932–4623* ⊕ *www.thedrakehotel. com/dine/coq-dor.*

Crimson Lounge. Crimson Lounge, in the Hotel Sax, delivers on its name—red leather couches, red satin perches, and plush red rugs break up the wood-dominated interior. Every detail adds to the swanky atmosphere, from the ornate furnishings to the exotic scent created for the room. ✉ *333 N. Dearborn St., River North* ☎ *312/923–2453* ⊕ *www. crimsonchicago.com.*

Division Street. For the vestiges of the old Rush Street, continue north to Division Street, between Clark and State streets. The crowd here consists mostly of suburbanites and out-of-towners on the make. The bars are crowded and noisy. Among the better-known singles' bars are Butch McGuire's, the Lodge, and Original Mother's.

The Drawing Room. Adjacent to private lounge Privet (only guests with personal connections to staff and owners are admitted), "culinary cocktail lounge" The Drawing Room puts the focus on top-flight wines, expertly crafted cocktails, and small plates in a plush, intimate atmosphere. ✉ *937 N. Rush St., Near North* ☎ *312/266–2694* ⊕ *www. thedrchicago.com.*

Fado. Fado uses imported wood, stone, and glass to create its Irish look. The second floor—with a bar imported from Dublin—feels more like the real thing than the first. There's expertly drawn Guinness, a fine selection of whiskeys, live music on weekends, and a menu of traditional dishes. ✉ *100 W. Grand Ave., River North* ☎ *312/836–0066* ⊕ *www. fadoirishpub.com.*

Gilt Bar. Cocktails like the Bee's Knees (gin, lemon, and honey) set the scene—1920s speakeasy—at this low-lighted lounge with vintage furnishings. The food is a major draw here; get in the spirit of indulgence with the foie gras and pork liver mousse on toast. Downstairs is the handsome book-lined bar **The Library** with cocktails and lighter bites; cash only. ✉ *230 W. Kinzie St., River North* ☎ *312/464–9544* ⊕ *www. giltbarchicago.com.*

Howl at the Moon. The dueling pianists at Howl at the Moon attract a rowdy crowd that delights in belting out popular tunes. Reservations aren't accepted, but party packages are available if you're willing to shell out beaucoup bucks (around $150). ✉ *26 W. Hubbard St., Near North* ☎ *312/863–7427* ⊕ *www.howlatthemoon.com.*

Hub 51. Hub 51 features a vaulted, loftlike industrial space. Sip cocktails with the after-work crowd and then linger for inventive light bites or more substantial fare. Downstairs lounge space **Sub 51** serves up DJ-driven beats, but get there early or reserve a table. ✉ *51 W. Hubbard St., River North* ☎ *312/828–0051* ⊕ *www.hub51chicago.com.*

Hubbard Inn. Billing itself as a "Continental tavern," this two-story River North hot spot pays homage to Ernest Hemingway's travels with classic cocktails and eclectic, globetrotting decor—think Moroccan tiled walls, vintage books, dramatic oil paintings, brass light fixtures, and tables made from reclaimed wood. Small plates are designed with communal dining in mind, though you may want to keep your perfectly balanced Sazerac all to yourself. ✉ *110 W. Hubbard St., River North* ☎ *312/222–1331* ⊕ *www.hubbardinn.com.*

The Motel Bar. The Motel Bar has all the comforts of a real, honest-to-goodness motel bar (TVs tuned to sports, classic cocktails, and a retro color scheme), but the atmosphere is amped-up with sexy, low-rise furniture and a "room service" menu of upscale bites. ✉ *600 W. Chicago Ave., River North* ☎ *312/822–2900* ⊕ *www.themotelbar.com.*

Old Town Ale House. Old Town Ale House, just a stone's throw from Second City, has attracted a diverse cast of characters since it opened in 1958, including comedy legends John Belushi and Bill Murray. With eclectic artwork, a mural of bar denizens painted in the '70s, and a lending library on-site, it's a dingy neighborhood bar unlike any other in the city—perhaps the country. ✉ *219 W. North Ave., Near North* ☎ *312/944–7020* ⊕ *www.theoldtownalehouse.com.*

Original Mother's. Since the 1960s, Original Mother's has been a local favorite for cutting-edge music and dance-'til-you-drop partying. The subterranean singles' destination was immortalized by Demi Moore, Jim Belushi, and Rob Lowe in the film *About Last Night.* ✉ *26 W. Division St., Near North* ☎ *312/642–7251.*

Pump Room. Ian Schrager revamped the historic Ambassador East Hotel as the affordably chic Public Chicago. In keeping with the democratic pricing, he opened up the restaurant naming to locals, who voted to keep it the Pump Room. In the sleek bar area, complete with gold-leaf ceiling, celebrity spotting still reigns supreme—as it did in the storied restaurant's heydey, when the likes of Humphrey Bogart and Lauren Bacall occupied Booth One. A separate Library Bar off the lobby offers coffee and pastries by day and cocktails at night. ✉ *1301 N. State Pkwy., Old Town* ☎ *312/787–3700* ⊕ *www.pumproom.com.*

Rockit Bar & Grill. Designer Nate Berkus assembled Rockit's hunter-lodge look: wood-plank-framed plasma TVs, antler chandeliers, and brown-leather booths. The crowd, much like the beer list, is diverse and tasteful, and despite the masculine vibe, there's a good mix of men and women. Dress to impress. ✉ *22 W. Hubbard St., River North* ☎ *312/645–6000* ⊕ *www.rockitbarandgrill.com.*

Rush Street. The famous Chicago bar scene known as Rush Street has faded into the mists of time, although the street has found resurgent energy with the opening of a string of upscale restaurants and outdoor cafés.

Signature Lounge. The Signature Lounge has no competition when it comes to views. Perched on the 96th floor of the John Hancock Center—above even the tower's observation deck—the bar offers stunning vistas of the skyline and lake for only the cost of a pricey drink. The ladies' room has an incredible south-facing view through floor-to-ceiling windows. ✉ *875 N. Michigan Ave., Near North* ☎ *312/787–9596* ⊕ *www.signatureroom.com/Signature-Lounge/.*

12

The Violet Hour serves a perfectly executed Red Moon Fizz for your drinking pleasure.

Vertigo Sky Lounge. Trendsetters hit the scene on the 26th floor of the Dana Hotel and Spa for cocktails with penthouse views or gravitate toward the fire pit on the patio. In winter, chill at the outdoor ice bar. ⊠ *2 W. Erie St., Near North* ☎ *312/202–6060* ⊕ *www.danahotelandspa. com/vertigo-lounge.aspx.*

Zebra Lounge. Zebra Lounge, small and funky with zebra-stripe lamps and other kitsch, attracts an interesting crowd of dressed-up and dressed-down regulars who come to sing along with the pianist on duty. ⊠ *1220 N. State St., Near North* ☎ *312/642–5140.*

COMEDY AND IMPROV CLUBS

Fodor's Choice ★ **Second City.** Second City, an institution since 1959, has served as a launching pad for some of the hottest comedians around. Alumni include Dan Aykroyd, Tina Fey, Amy Poehler, and the late John Belushi. It's the anchor of Chicago improv. The revues on the company's main stage and in its smaller e.t.c. space next door are actually sketch comedy shows, but the scripts in these pre-rehearsed scenes have been developed through improvisation and there's usually a little time set aside in each show for the performers to demonstrate their quick wit. Most nights there is a free improv set after the late show, featuring cast members and invited guests (sometimes famous, sometimes not, never announced in advance). It's in **Donny's Skybox** upstairs that you're more likely to see one of Chicago's many fledgling improv comedy troupes making their first appearance working together on freshly penned material in public. ⊠ *1616 N. Wells St., Near North* ☎ *312/337–3992* ⊕ *www.secondcity.com.*

Zanies Comedy Night Club. Zanies books outstanding national talent and is Chicago's best stand-up comedy spot. Jay Leno, Jerry Seinfeld, and Jackie Mason have all performed at this intimate venue. ✉ *1548 N. Wells St., Near North* ☎ *312/337–4027* ⊕ *chicago.zanies.com.*

DANCE CLUBS

Castle. Castle won't win any prizes for breaking new ground, but this River North nightclub complex, carved out of the Romanesque fortress that was the original home of the Chicago Historical Society, has been going strong for years (previously as Excalibur) with its mix of dancing, dining, and posing. ✉ *632 N. Dearborn St., River North* ☎ *312/266–1944* ⊕ *www.excaliburchicago.com.*

Enclave. Enclave has a loftlike feel and three bars spread out on two floors. Sip a snazzy cocktail and groove to remixed tunes in a grown-up nightclub complete with hardwood floors, exposed brick, and a timber-beam ceiling. ✉ *220 W. Chicago Ave., River North* ☎ *312/654–0234* ⊕ *www.enclavechicago.com.*

Funky Buddha Lounge. Funky is the operative word for the Funky Buddha Lounge, with its diverse crowd, seductive dance music, and a big metal Buddha guarding the front door. It has an intimate bar and dark dance floor, where patrons groove as DJs spin dance hall, hip-hop, R&B, funk, and old-school house. ✉ *728 W. Grand Ave., Near North* ☎ *312/666–1695* ⊕ *www.funkybuddha.com.*

Sound-Bar. Sound-Bar is a labyrinth of nine bars, each with a unique design and color scheme (some even serve matching colored cocktails). Feel like dancing? Join the pulse of Chicago's best-dressed on the huge dance floor. ✉ *226 W. Ontario St., River North* ☎ *312/787–4480* ⊕ *sound-bar.com.*

Spy Bar. Spy Bar pulls some smooth moves. Image is everything at this subterranean spot with a brushed stainless-steel bar and exposed-brick walls. The slick, stylish crowd hits the tight dance floor for house, underground, and DJ remixes. ✉ *646 N. Franklin St., River North* ☎ *312/337–2191* ⊕ *www.spybarchicago.com.*

The Underground. Unmarked entrances, military outfit–clad servers, and artillery case cocktail tables create the illusion of an underground military bunker. Sounds strange, but it works—at least according to the celebs and international DJs who make appearances at this subterranean dance club. ✉ *56 W. Illinois St., River North* ☎ *312/644–7600* ⊕ *www.theundergroundchicago.com.*

MUSIC VENUES

BLUES

Blue Chicago. In an upscale part of downtown, Blue Chicago has none of the trademark grit or edginess of the older South Side blues clubs. What is does offer is a good sound system, a packed calendar that regularly features female vocalists, and a cosmopolitan audience that's a tad more diverse than some of the baseball-capped crowds at Lincoln Park blues clubs. ✉ *536 N. Clark St., River North* ☎ *312/661–0100* ⊕ *www.bluechicago.com.*

ECLECTIC

Baton Show Lounge. At Baton Show Lounge, boys will be girls. The lip-synching revues with female impersonators have catered to curious out-of-towners and bachelorette parties since 1969. Some of the regular performers, such as Chili Pepper and Mimi Marks, have become Chicago cult figures. The more the audience tips, the better the show gets, so bring your bills. ⊠ *436 N. Clark St., River North* ☏ *312/644–5269* ⊕ *www.thebatonshowlounge.com.*

Fodor's Choice
★

House of Blues. House of Blues, though its name implies otherwise, attracts big-name performers of all genres, from jazz, roots, blues, and gospel to alternative rock, hip-hop, world, and R&B. The interior is an elaborate cross between blues bar and ornate opera house. Its restaurant has live blues every night on a "second stage," as well as a satisfying Sunday gospel brunch. Part of the Marina City complex, the entrance is on State Street. ⊠ *329 N. Dearborn St., River North* ☏ *312/923–2000* ⊕ *www.houseofblues.com/venues/clubvenues/chicago.*

JAZZ

Andy's Jazz Club. Andy's Jazz Club, a favorite after-work watering hole with a substantial bar menu, has live music ranging from swing jazz to bebop. The early-bird 5 pm set is a boon for music lovers who aren't night owls. ⊠ *11 E. Hubbard St., River North* ☏ *312/642–6805* ⊕ *www.andysjazzclub.com.*

Pops for Champagne. Pops for Champagne can be found in trendy River North. The bi-level space is gloriously turned out with a champagne bar, raw bar, sidewalk café, and even a retail space called Pops Shop. The former basement jazz lounge is now home to Watershed, a cozy spot with limestone walls focused on Great Lakes regional craft beers and spirits, along with cheese and charcuterie plates. ⊠ *601 N. State St., River North* ☏ *312/266–7677* ⊕ *www.popsforchampagne.com.*

WICKER PARK, BUCKTOWN, AND LOGAN SQUARE

Hepcats, artists, and yuppies converge on the famed six corners of North, Milwaukee, and Damen avenues, where the cast of Real World Chicago once resided. Previously scruffy and edgy, the area is now dotted with pricey, upscale bars, though the occasional honky-tonk still survives. Those looking for a dance party tend to head to Funky Buddha Lounge or Debonair Social Club, and cocktail connoisseurs brave the wait at the Violet Hour.

BARS

The California Clipper Lounge. In Humboldt Park, just to the west of Wicker Park, California Clipper has a 1940s vintage look, including a curving 60-foot-long Brunswick bar and tiny booths lining the long room back-to-back like seats on a train. Alternative country acts and soul-gospel DJs are part of the eccentric musical lineup. ⊠ *1002 N. California Ave., Wicker Park* ☎ *773/384–2547* ⊕ *www. californiaclipper.com.*

Davenport's Piano Bar & Cabaret. Davenport's, a sophisticated cabaret booking both local and touring acts, brings a grown-up presence to the Wicker Park club scene. The piano lounge is set up for casual listening, while the cabaret room is a no-chat zone that requires your full attention—as well as reservations and a two-drink minimum. ⊠ *1383 N. Milwaukee Ave., Wicker Park* ☎ *773/278–1830* ⊕ *www. davenportspianobar.com.*

Debonair Social Club. Debonair Social Club, in the historic Flat Iron Building, combines visual arts, music, and late-night dining. Upstairs, curated video installations line the walls surrounding the stage-cum–dance floor, while the dimly lighted downstairs has a more clandestine feel. ⊠ *1575 N. Milwaukee Ave., Bucktown* ☎ *773/227–7990* ⊕ *www. debonairsocialclub.com.*

The Map Room. The Map Room might help you find your way around Chicago, if not the world. Guidebooks decorate the walls of this self-described "travelers' tavern," and the beers represent much of the world. Tuesday is international buffet night; each week brings a different country's cuisine. ⊠ *1949 N. Hoyne, Bucktown* ☎ *773/252–7636* ⊕ *www.maproom.com.*

The Matchbox. In West Town near Wicker Park, the Matchbox isn't much bigger than a you-know-what, but the hodgepodge of regulars don't seem to mind. In fact, many claim it's the dark, cramped quarters (we're talking 3 feet wide at its narrowest) that keep them coming back. The crowd spills outside in summer, when wrought-iron tables dot the sidewalk. ⊠ *770 N. Milwaukee Ave., Wicker Park* ☎ *312/666–9292.*

Nick's Beer Garden. Nick's Beer Garden is a neighborhood favorite, especially in the wee hours (it's open until 4 am; 5 am Sunday). Kitschy tropical decor—think palm trees, flamingos, and a surfboard—adds to the appeal. ⊠ *1516 N. Milwaukee Ave., Wicker Park* ☎ *773/252–1155* ⊕ *www.nicksbeergarden.com.*

Northside Bar & Grill. Northside Bar & Grill was one of the first anchors of the now-teeming Wicker Park nightlife scene. Locals come to drink, eat, shoot pool, and see and be seen. The enclosed indoor-outdoor patio lets you get the best out of the chancy Chicago weather. ⊠ *1635 N. Damen Ave., Wicker Park* ☎ *773/384–3555* ⊕ *www. northsidechicago.com.*

Rainbo Club. Rainbo Club is the unofficial meeting place for Chicago hipsters and indie rockers. Apart from the working photo booth wedged into a corner, the stripped-down hangout is pretty barren, but drinks are dirt cheap and the bartenders are upbeat—and willing—conversationalists. ⊠ *1150 N. Damen Ave., Wicker Park* ☎ *773/ 489–5999.*

Rodan. The highly stylized Rodan is a restaurant and lounge that caters mostly to the young neighborhood hipsters who arrive at dinnertime (served until 11 pm) and stay put until closing. The narrow space often feels cramped, but if you can snag a spot at the bar or on a blue-suede banquette, an evening of major-league people-watching is in store. Snacks are served all night, so refuel with a pile of wasabi-tempura fries. ✉ *1530 North Milwaukee Ave., Wicker Park* ☎ *773/276–7036* ⊕ *www.rodanchicago.com.*

Silver Cloud Bar & Grill. Silver Cloud Bar & Grill might be the only place in the city where you can order a champagne cocktail alongside sloppy joes and tater tots and not open yourself up to a citizen's arrest. For us, that's reason enough to go. Spacious red-leather booths, retro fringed lamps, friendly service, and an upbeat neighborhood crowd round out the good points. ✉ *1700 N. Damen Ave., Bucktown* ☎ *773/489–6212* ⊕ *www.silvercloudchicago.com.*

The Violet Hour. The Violet Hour channels a Prohibition-era speakeasy—an unmarked door in the boarded-up facade leads to a mysterious, curtained hallway. Inside, twinkling crystal chandeliers cast a glow on cornflower-blue walls, and extremely high-backed blue leather chairs encourage intimate conversations. Add to that pricey but flawlessly executed cocktails and a sign discouraging cell-phone use, and it's our idea of nightlife heaven. ✉ *1520 N. Damen Ave., Wicker Park* ☎ *773/252–1500* ⊕ *www.thevioSlethour.com.*

MUSIC VENUES
BLUES

Fodor'sChoice ★ **Rosa's Lounge.** On a given night at Rosa's Lounge, near Bucktown, you'll find Tony, the owner, working the crowd, and his mother, Rosa, behind the bar. What makes the club special is that the duo moved here from Italy out of a pure love for the blues. Stop by and partake in Rosa's winning mixture of big-name and local talent, stiff drinks, and friendly service—the same since it opened in 1984. ✉ *3420 W. Armitage Ave., Logan Square* ☎ *773/342–0452* ⊕ *www.rosaslounge.com.*

COUNTRY

The Hideout. The Hideout, which is literally hidden away in a North Side industrial zone, has managed to make country music hip in Chicago. Players on the city's alternative country scene have adopted the friendly hole-in-the-wall, and bands ranging from the obscure to the semi-famous take the stage. ✉ *1354 W. Wabansia, Bucktown* ☎ *773/227–4433* ⊕ *www.hideoutchicago.com.*

ECLECTIC

The Empty Bottle. Empty Bottle, in the Ukrainian Village near Wicker Park, may have toys and knickknacks around the bar (including a case of macabre baby-doll heads), but when it comes to booking rock, punk, and jazz bands from the indie scene, it's a serious place with no pretensions. ✉ *1035 N. Western Ave., Wicker Park* ☎ *773/276–3600* ⊕ *www. emptybottle.com.*

OFF THE
BEATEN
PATH

FitzGerald's Nightclub. FitzGerald's, though a 30-minute schlep west of Chicago, draws crowds from all over the city and suburbs with its mix of folk, jazz, blues, zydeco, and rock. This early 1900s roadhouse has great sound and sight lines for its roots music. ✉ *6615 W. Roosevelt Rd., Berwyn* ☎ *708/788–2118* ⊕ *www.fitzgeraldsnightclub.com.*

12

Logan Square Auditorium. The second-floor ballroom hosts all-ages rock shows put on by the team at the Empty Bottle, and other live shows and special events. The acoustics aren't the best, but the younger, hipster crowd doesn't seem to mind. For those 21 and over, there's a full bar. ✉ *2539 N. Kedzie Blvd., Logan Square* ☎ *773/252–6179* ⊕ *www. logansquareauditorium.com.*

ROCK

Double Door. Double Door is a hotbed for music in hip Wicker Park. The large bar books up-and-coming local and national acts from rock to acid jazz. Unannounced Rolling Stones shows have been held here. The entrance is on Damen Avenue. ✉ *1572 N. Milwaukee Ave., Wicker Park* ☎ *773/489–3160* ⊕ *www.doubledoor.com.*

LINCOLN PARK

One of the most beautiful (and bustling) neighborhoods on the north side of Chicago, Lincoln Park is largely defined by the DePaul students who inhabit the area. Irish pubs and sports bars line the streets, but chic wine bars attract an older, more sophisticated set. Bonus: the constant crowds make this one of the city's safest nightlife destinations.

BARS

Delilah's. Delilah's is a rare dive bar amid Lincoln Park's tonier establishments. Dark and a bit grungy, the bar has a friendly, unpretentious vibe and a standout whiskey selection (more than 300 types on offer). DJs spin punk and rockabilly. ✉ *2771 N. Lincoln Ave., Lincoln Park* ☎ *773/472–2771* ⊕ *www.delilahschicago.com.*

Faith & Whiskey. Faith & Whiskey stands out among Lincoln Park bars with its hard-rock focus. Silver-framed replicas of famous guitars line the wall, along with black-and-white photos of rock stars, antler chandeliers, steer skulls, and, suspended above the restrooms, twin motorcycles. ✉ *1365 W. Fullerton Ave., Lincoln Park* ☎ *773/248–9119* ⊕ *www. faithandwhiskey.com.*

Gamekeepers. Gamekeepers is full of sports fans and former frat boys. With more than 40 TVs, three projection screens, and complete satellite sports coverage, there's barely a game Gamekeepers doesn't get. ✉ *345 W. Armitage Ave., Lincoln Park* ☎ *773/549–0400* ⊕ *www. gamekeeperschicago.com.*

Hi-Tops. Hi-Tops, relocated a bit south of its original Wrigleyville location, may be the ultimate sports bar. Multiple flat-screen TVs, a lively crowd, and solid bar food keep sports fans coming. ✉ *2462 N. Lincoln Ave., Lincoln Park* ☎ *773/549–3232* ⊕ *www.hi-topschicago.com.*

Bluesman Jimmy Burns singing at

John Barleycorn. A historic pub with a long wooden bar, John Barleycorn can get somewhat rowdy despite the classical music (played until 8 pm) and the art slides shown on video screens. It has a spacious summer beer garden, a good pub menu, and a wide selection of beers. ⊠ *658 W. Belden Ave., Lincoln Park* ☎ *773/348–8899* ⊕ *www.johnbarleycorn.com* ⊠ *3524 N. Clark St., Wrigleyville* ☎ *773/549–6000* ⊕ *www.johnbarleycorn.com.*

Kincade's. This spot packs 'em in on two levels with a 10-foot-wide video monitor, several plasma screens, and a bar menu that invites patrons to linger for a game—or three. The popular bar scores bonus points with an outdoor beer garden, two pool tables, and French doors that prop open on warm summer days. ⊠ *950 W. Armitage Ave., Lincoln Park* ☎ *773/348–0010* ⊕ *www.kincadesbar.com.*

Webster's Wine Bar. A romantic place for a date, Webster's stocks more than 500 bottles of wine—with at least 30 by the glass—as well as ports, sherries, single-malt Scotches, a few microbrews, and a menu of small tasting entrées at reasonable prices. ⊠ *1480 W. Webster Ave., Lincoln Park* ☎ *773/868–0608* ⊕ *www.websterwinebar.com.*

MUSIC VENUES
BLUES

Fodor'sChoice ★ **B.L.U.E.S.** The best part about B.L.U.E.S. is that there isn't a bad seat in the joint. The worst part? The crowds—arrive early if you want to score a seat. Narrow and intimate, the jam-packed North Side club has attracted the best in local talent since it opened in 1979. Big names such as Son Seals, Otis Rush, Jimmy Johnson, and Magic Slim have all played here. ⊠ *2519 N. Halsted St., Lincoln Park* ☎ *773/528–1012* ⊕ *www.chicagobluesbar.com.*

Kingston Mines. In 1968, Kingston Mines went down in Chicago history as the first blues club to open on the North Side. Though it's since moved to bigger digs, it still offers the same traditional sounds and late-night hours as the original club. Swarms of blues lovers and partying singles take in the good blues and tasty barbecue. ✉ *2548 N. Halsted St., Lincoln Park* ☎ *773/477–4646* ⊕ *www.kingstonmines.com.*

12

ROCK

Lincoln Hall. The owners of Lincoln Hall transformed a former movie theater into an intimate concert space with great sight lines, an excellent sound system, and a wraparound balcony with seating. There's a separate bar and dining area up front for preshow dining. ✉ *2424 N. Lincoln Ave., Lincoln Park* ☎ *773/525–2501* ⊕ *www.lincolnhallchicago.com.*

LAKEVIEW AND FAR NORTH SIDE

Lakeview, Uptown, and Andersonville, all on the Far North Side, have one thing in common: affordability. Unbelievable as it sounds, there are places in the city where $20 stretches beyond the price of admission and a martini. Drink deals are frequently offered at many bars. If you're heading out early, take the El or a bus, but you'll probably want to cab it back to your hotel.

BARS

Blokes & Birds. A departure from the typical Wrigleyville sports bar, this modern public house draws Anglophiles thirsty for a well-poured pint and contemporary takes on classic English pub fare, such as a shepherd's pie with stout-braised lamb and fish-and-chips with malt vinegar aioli. (The bar's name is British slang for "guys and girls.") ✉ *3343 N. Clark St., Wrigleyville* ☎ *773/472–5252* ⊕ *www.blokesandbirdschicago.com.*

Cubby Bear Lounge. Diagonally across the street from Wrigley Field stands the Cubby Bear, a Chicago institution since 1953. It is the place where Cub fans come to drown their sorrows in beer or lift one to celebrate. There are plenty of TVs for game watching, live music, and a bar food menu featuring burgers and other bar food. ✉ *1059 W. Addison St., Wrigleyville* ☎ *773/327–1662* ⊕ *www.cubbybear.com.*

404 Wine Bar. Enter through rowdy Jack's Bar & Grill to find the serene 404 Wine Bar, a romantic spot filled with cozy nooks. The librarylike back room has ornate chandeliers, shelves lined with books, and dramatic oxblood walls. You can grab a spot on the patio or near one of two fireplaces and enjoy a glass, flight, or bottle of wine accompanied by a cheese plate. ✉ *2856 N. Southport Ave., Lakeview* ☎ *773/404–5886* ⊕ *www.404winebarchicago.com.*

Gingerman Tavern. Up the street from Wrigley Field, Gingerman Tavern deftly manages to avoid being pigeonholed as a sports bar. Folks here take their beer and billiards seriously, with three pool tables and—our favorite part—a list of more than 100 bottles of beer. New and vintage tunes crank out of the jukebox all night long. ✉ *3740 N. Clark St., Lakeview* ☎ *773/549–2050.*

Holiday Club. Holiday Club bills itself as the "Swinger's mecca." Rat Pack aficionados will appreciate the 1950s decor and well-stocked CD juke-box, which has selections ranging from Dean Martin and Frank Sinatra to early punk. Down a pint of good beer (or even bad beer in cans) and scan the typical (but tasty) bar menu. ⊠ *4000 N. Sheridan Rd., Far North Side* ☎ *773/348–9600* ⊕ *www.holidayclubchicago.com.*

Hopleaf. Hopleaf, an anchor in the Andersonville corridor, continues the tradition of the classic Chicago bar hospitable to conversation (not a TV in sight). Pick one of the too-many-to-choose-from beers on the menu, with an emphasis on Belgian beers and regional microbrews. A menu of Belgian bar fare far surpasses typical bar food options. Don't miss the ale-steamed mussels and delectable skinny fries served with aioli. ⊠ *5148 N. Clark St., Far North Side* ☎ *773/334–9851* ⊕ *www. hopleaf.com.*

Joie de Vine. Joie de Vine started as a wine bar catering to a lesbian cli-entele but has expanded its focused to include craft beer and cocktails. The space itself remains cozy, though good design (and sidewalk tables in summer months) keeps things from feeling claustrophobic. Sit at the long wooden bar or opposing banquette and enjoy the real focal point of the room, a glass-brick wall lighted up in multiple colors. Try stopping by on a weeknight when the neighborhood regulars are least likely to crowd the slender bar. ⊠ *1744 W. Balmoral Ave., Far North Side* ☎ *773/989–6846.*

Sheffield's. Sheffield's spans the seasons with a shaded beer garden in summer and a roaring fireplace in winter. This laid-back neighborhood pub has billiards and more than 100 kinds of bottled beer that change seasonally, including regional microbrews, the bartender's "bad beer of the month"—a cheap can of beer (think PBR)—as well as 18 brands on tap. ⊠ *3258 N. Sheffield Ave., Lakeview* ☎ *773/281–4989* ⊕ *www. sheffieldschicago.com.*

Sluggers. Sluggers is packed after Cubs games in the nearby stadium, and the ballplayers make occasional appearances in summer. Check out the fast- and slow-pitch batting cages on the second floor, as well as the pool tables, air hockey tables, and electronic basketball. ⊠ *3540 N. Clark St., Lakeview* ☎ *773/248–0055* ⊕ *www.sluggersbar.com.*

GAY AND LESBIAN

Big Chicks. In the Uptown area of the Far North Side, Big Chicks is a striking alternative to the Halsted strip, with a funky crowd that appreciates the owner's art collection hanging on the walls. The fun-loving staff and their self-selected eclectic music are the payoffs for the hike to get here. Special attractions include weekend dancing and free Sunday-afternoon buffets. ⊠ *5024 N. Sheridan Rd., Far North Side* ☎ *773/728–5511* ⊕ *www.bigchicks.com.*

Charlie's. A country-and-western dance club, Charlie's lets you two-step nightly to achy-breaky tunes, though dance music is played every night from about 2 am to 4 am. It's mostly a boots-and-denim crowd on weekends. ⊠ *3726 N. Broadway, Lakeview* ☎ *773/871–8887* ⊕ *www. charlieschicago.com.*

Circuit. The biggest dance club in Boystown, Circuit is a stripped-down dance hall energized by flashing lights, booming sounds, and a partying crowd. Take a break in the up-front martini bar. ✉ *3641 N. Halsted St., Lakeview* ☎ *773/325–2233* ⊕ *www.circuitclub.com.*

The Closet. The Closet is a basic dive bar with a gay twist. This compact bar—one of the few that caters to lesbians, though it draws gay men, too—can be especially lively after 2 am when most other bars close. Stop by Sunday afternoons when bartenders serve up what are hailed as the best Bloody Marys in town. ✉ *3325 N. Broadway, Lakeview* ☎ *773/477–8533* ⊕ *www.theclosetchicago.com.*

Hydrate. Hydrate combines a relaxed front lounge with a late-night, high-energy dance floor in the back. Weekly events include drag shows. ✉ *3458 N. Halsted St., Lakeview* ☎ *773/975–9244* ⊕ *www. hydratechicago.com.*

North End. A gay sports bar, the North End is a favorite spot to watch the big game or play some pool. Later at night, it has more of a typical gay bar atmosphere. ✉ *3733 N. Halsted St., Lakeview* ☎ *773/477–7999* ⊕ *www.northendchicago.com.*

Roscoe's Tavern and Cafe. Roscoe's Tavern, in the heart of Boystown, is a longtime favorite with a mix of amenities sure to please its peppy patrons, including a jam-packed front bar, a dance floor, a pool table, an outdoor garden, and lively music. The sidewalk café serves May through September. ✉ *3356 N. Halsted St., Lakeview* ☎ *773/281–3355* ⊕ *www.roscoes.com.*

Sidetrack. The video bar Sidetrack is tuned into a different theme every night of the week, from show tunes on Monday to comedy on Thursday—all broadcast on TV screens that never leave your sight. The sprawling stand-and-pose bar and rooftop deck are always busy with a good-looking, professional crowd, and the vodka slushies are a house specialty. ✉ *3349 N. Halsted St., Lakeview* ☎ *773/477–9189* ⊕ *www. sidetrackchicago.com.*

CAFÉS

Intelligentsia. Intelligentsia was named to invoke the pre-chain days when cafés were forums for discussion, but the long, broad farmer's tables and handsome couches are usually occupied by students and other serious types who treat the café like their office. The store does all of its own coffee roasting and sells its house blends to local restaurants. ✉ *3123 N. Broadway, Lakeview* ☎ *773/348–8058* ⊕ *www.intelligentsiacoffee. com* ✉ *Monadnock Building, 53 W. Jackson Blvd., Loop* ☎ *312/253–0594* ⊕ *www.intelligentsiacoffee.com* ✉ *53 E. Randolph St., Loop* ☎ *312/920–9332.*

Kopi, a Traveler's Cafe. Kopi, a Traveler's Cafe is a study in opposites, with healthy vegetarian options as well as decadent desserts. In the Andersonville neighborhood, a 20-minute cab ride from downtown, this café has a selection of travel books, global gifts, and artfully painted tables. Now it also offers a full bar. ✉ *5317 N. Clark St., Far North Side* ☎ *773/989–5674.*

Chicago is the undisputed capital of improv comedy.

Pick Me Up Café. The Pick Me Up Café combines the charm of a quirky, neighborhood café with the late-night hours of those chain diners. The thrift-store treasures hanging on the walls are as eclectic as the crowd that comes at all hours of the day and night to drink bottomless cups of coffee or dine on sandwiches, appetizers, and desserts. ⊠ *3408 N. Clark St., Lakeview* ☎ *773/248–6613.*

Uncommon Ground. The original location of Uncommon Ground is roomy and inviting, with a hand-carved bar and large street-facing windows offering views of passersby. Patrons brave the wait for bowls of coffee and hot chocolate. There's also a full bar and a hearty menu. Perks include two fireplaces, a sidewalk café, and a steady lineup of acoustic musical acts. A second location on the Far Northwest Side gets bonus points for eco-friendliness, with a green roof, solar panels, and tables made from reclaimed wood. ⊠ *3800 N. Clark St., Lakeview* ☎ *773/929–3680* ⊕ *www.uncommonground.com* ⊠ *1401 W. Devon Ave., Edgewater* ☎ *773/465–9801.*

COMEDY AND IMPROV CLUBS

The Annoyance Theatre & Bar. The Annoyance Theatre is home base for Annoyance Productions, an irreverent group best known for hits like *Coed Prison Sluts* and *Splatter Theatre.* ⊠ *4830 N. Broadway Ave., Far North* ☎ *773/561–4665* ⊕ *www.annoyanceproductions.com.*

ComedySportz. ComedySportz specializes in "competitive improv," in which two teams vie for the audience's favor. Book a family-friendly early performance or a late-night show rife with raunchy humor. The space features cabaret-style seating and a full bar. ⊠ *929 W. Belmont Ave., Lakeview* ☎ *773/549–8080* ⊕ *www.comedysportzchicago.com.*

I.O. Formerly called ImprovOlympic, I.O. is the city's home to long-form improvisation. The signature piece is "The Harold," in which a team of improvisers explores a single audience suggestion throughout a series of stories and characters until they all eventually weave back together to fit with the original audience idea. No drink or age minimum. ⊠ *3541 N. Clark St., Lakeview* ☎ *773/880–0199* ⊕ *chicago.ioimprov.com.*

DANCE CLUBS

Fodor's Choice
★
Berlin Nightclub. Berlin, a multicultural, pansexual dance club near the Belmont El station, has progressive electronic dance music and fun themed nights—Madonna and Prince are celebrated on the first and last Sunday of the month, and one Wednesday a month is devoted to disco. The crowd tends to be predominantly gay on weeknights, mixed on weekends. ⊠ *954 W. Belmont Ave., Lakeview* ☎ *773/348–4975* ⊕ *www.berlinchicago.com.*

MUSIC VENUES

COUNTRY

Carol's Pub. Carol's Pub, in the Uptown area of the Far North Side, showcased country before it was ever cool. The house band at this urban honky-tonk plays country and country-rock tunes on weekends, and the popular Thursday and Sunday karaoke nights draw all walks of life, from preppie to punk. ⊠ *4659 N. Clark St., Far North Side* ☎ *773/334–2402.*

Horseshoe. Horseshoe brings a slice of Texas to the Midwest, along with barbecue brisket and pulled pork (and some surprisingly good vegetarian versions). Live bluegrass bands or honky-tonk jukebox tunes draw displaced Southerners, whose nostalgia is drowned out by the down-home decor—think chicken-wire, scruffy floors, and horseshoe-shaped booths—and rounds of ice-cold Lone Star beer. ⊠ *4115 N. Lincoln Ave., Far Northwest Side* ☎ *773/334–2402.*

ECLECTIC

Beat Kitchen. North Side stalwart Beat Kitchen brings in the crowds because of its good sound system and local and touring rock, alternative-rock, country, and rockabilly acts. It also serves soups, salads, sandwiches, pizzas, and desserts. ⊠ *2100 W. Belmont Ave., Lakeview* ☎ *773/281–4444* ⊕ *www.beatkitchen.com.*

Elbo Room. Elbo Room, a multilevel space in an elbow-shaped corner building, has a basement rec-room feel. The bar plays host to talented live bands seven days a week, with a strong dose of nu-jazz, funk, soul, pop, and rock. ⊠ *2871 N. Lincoln Ave., Lakeview* ☎ *773/549–5549.*

FOLK

Old Town School of Folk Music. Old Town School of Folk Music, Chicago's first and oldest folk-music school, has served as folk central in the city since it opened in 1957. This welcoming spot in Lincoln Square hosts outstanding performances by national and local acts in an intimate-feeling 420-seat concert hall boasting excellent acoustics. A major expansion in 2012 added a new, environmentally friendly facility across the street, with a 150-seat performance hall and acoustically engineered classrooms. ⊠ *4544 N. Lincoln Ave., Far Northwest Side* ☎ *773/728–6000* ⊕ *www.oldtownschool.org.*

12

JAZZ

Green Mill Cocktail Lounge. Green Mill, a Chicago institution off the beaten track in not-so-trendy Uptown, has been around since 1907. Deep leather banquettes and ornate wood paneling line the walls, and a photo of Al Capone occupies a place of honor on the piano behind the bar. The jazz entertainment is both excellent and contemporary—the club launched the careers of Kurt Elling and Patricia Barber—and the Uptown Poetry Slam, a competitive poetry reading, takes center stage on Sunday. ⊠ *4802 N. Broadway Ave., Far North Side* ☎ *773/878–5552* ⊕ *www.greenmilljazz.com.*

> ## WORD OF MOUTH
>
> Jazz thrives all around town. For a recorded listing of upcoming live performances, call the Jazz Institute Hot Line (press "0" when voicemail picks up to reach the event listings). ☎ *312/427–3300.*

ROCK

The Abbey Pub. The Abbey Pub, about 15 minutes northwest of downtown in the Irving Park neighborhood, showcases rock, as well as some Irish, Celtic, and country music, in a large concert hall with a separate, busy pub. By day the hall is used to show soccer and rugby games from the United Kingdom and Ireland. ⊠ *3420 W. Grace St., Far Northwest Side* ☎ *773/478–4408* ⊕ *www.abbeypub.com.*

Martyrs'. Martyrs' brings local and major-label rock bands to this small, North Side neighborhood sandwiched between Lincoln Square and Roscoe Village. Music fans can see the stage from just about any corner of the bar, while the more rhythmically inclined gyrate in the large standing-room area. A mural opposite the stage memorializes late rock greats. ⊠ *3855 N. Lincoln Ave., Far Northwest Side* ☎ *773/404–9494* ⊕ *www.martyrslive.com.*

Metro. Metro brings in progressive, nationally known artists and the cream of the local crop. A former movie palace, it's an excellent place to see live bands, whether you're moshing on the main floor or above the fray in the balcony. In the basement is **Smart Bar,** a late-night dance club that starts hopping after midnight. ⊠ *3730 N. Clark St., Lakeview* ☎ *773/549–4140* ⊕ *metrochicago.com.*

Schubas Tavern. Schubas Tavern favors local and national power pop, indie rock, and folk musicians. The wood-paneled back room has a laid-back atmosphere and good seating. The bar was built in 1903 by the Schlitz Brewing Company, and it still sells Schlitz beer on draft. For pre-concert dining, **Harmony Grill** serves up regional American comfort food. ⊠ *3159 N. Southport Ave., Lakeview* ☎ *773/525–2508* ⊕ *www.schubas.com.*

The Chicago-based Rosedales headlining at the Metro

THE PERFORMING ARTS

If you're even mildly interested in the performing arts, Chicago has the means to put you in your seat—be it floor, mezzanine, or balcony. Just pick your preference (theater, dance, or symphony orchestra), and let Chicago's impressive body of artists do the rest. From critically acclaimed big names to fringe groups that specialize in experimental work, there truly is a performance art for everyone.

Ticket prices vary wildly, depending on whether you're seeing a high-profile group or venturing into more obscure territory. Chicago Symphony tickets range from $15 to $200, the Lyric Opera from $30 to $180 (if you can get them). Smaller choruses and orchestras charge from $10 to $30; watch the listings for free performances. Commercial theater ranges from $15 to $75; smaller experimental ensembles might charge $5, $10, or pay-what-you-can. Movie prices range from $11 for first-run houses to as low as $1.50 at some suburban second-run houses.

PERFORMING ART VENUES

Athenaeum Theatre. The 1,000-seat Athenaeum Theatre adjacent to St. Alphonsus Church hosts comedy, dance, children's theater performances, and more. ⊠ *2936 N Southport Ave., Lakeview* ☎ *773/935–6860* ⊕ *www.athenaeumtheatre.com.*

Auditorium Theatre of Roosevelt University. Designed by notable architects Louis Sullivan and Dankmar Adler, the 4,300-seat, Romanesque Revival–style Auditorium Theatre of Roosevelt University opened in 1889 as an opera house and later became a National Historic Landmark. Known for its perfect acoustics and excellent sight lines, the ornate theater features marble mosaics, dramatic gilded ceiling arches, and intricate murals. (Also of note: The theater was one of the first public buildings to have electric lighting and air-conditioning.) ⊠ *50 E. Congress Parkway, South Loop* ☎ *312/922–2110* ⊕ *www.auditoriumtheatre.org.*

Bank of America Theatre. After its 1906 debut as the Majestic Theatre, the 1,800-seat Bank of America Theatre became a major stop on the vaudeville circuit, only to close for a 15-year period following the Great Depression. Today, after a series of name changes (from the Shubert Theatre to the LaSalle Bank Theatre to its current incarnation), the plush, red-and-gold theater hosts Broadway in Chicago performances such as *Jersey Boys* and Monty Python's *Spamalot.* ⊠ *18 W. Monroe St., Loop* ☎ *312/977–1700, 800/775–2000* ⊕ *www.broadwayinchicago.com.*

Broadway Playhouse at Water Tower Place. Formerly known as Drury Lane, this 550-seat theater in Water Tower Place was taken over in 2010 by the Broadway in Chicago group, which modernized the space and reopened it as Broadway Playhouse. The inaugural season included a new production of hometown scribe Studs Terkel's *Working.* ⊠ *175 E. Chestnut St., Near North* ☎ *312/642–2000* ⊕ *www.broadwayinchicago.com.*

Cadillac Palace Theatre. Designed by famed theater architects the Rapp Brothers, Cadillac Palace Theatre opened as the Palace Theatre in 1926 to much fanfare; the ornate, gilded interior was inspired by the palaces of Versailles and Fontainebleau. This impressive, 2,500-seat space was restored to its original opulence in 1999. ⊠ *151 W. Randolph St., Loop* ☎ *312/977–1700, 800/775–2000* ⊕ *www.broadwayinchicago.com.*

Chicago Cultural Center. Chicago Cultural Center is a block-long landmark building that houses several performance spaces. The most magnificent is the top-floor Preston Bradley Hall, with its Tiffany glass dome and ornately detailed white marble walls. ⊠ *78 E. Washington St., Loop* ☎ *312/346–3278, 312/744–6630* ⊕ *www.chicagoculturalcenter.org.*

The Chicago Theatre. Since 1921, visitors to the Chicago Theatre, which began as a Balaban and Katz movie palace, have marveled at its stunning Baroque interior; the 3,600-seat auditorium features crystal chandeliers, bronze light fixtures, and murals on the wall and ceiling. Lately it has hosted big-name music acts like Indigo Girls and Arcade Fire. ⊠ *175 N. State St., Loop* ☎ *212/465–6225* ⊕ *www.thechicagotheatre.com.*

Ford Center for the Performing Arts/Oriental Theatre. Ford Center for the Performing Arts/Oriental Theatre opened in 1926 as a movie palace with grand, over-the-top Far Eastern decor (think Buddha statues and huge mosaics of an Indian prince and princess). After a period of disrepair, it reopened in 1998 to stage big-name Broadway hits—for several years it served as the Chicago home for *Wicked.* ⊠ *24 W. Randolph St., Loop* ☎ *312/977–1700, 800/775–2000* ⊕ *www.broadwayinchicago.com.*

12

Goodman Theatre. Goodman Theatre presents an exceptional repertoire of plays each year featuring local and national performers. Plays by August Wilson and David Mamet have premiered here, and the Goodman's annual holiday staging of *A Christmas Carol* is a Chicago tradition. ⊠ *170 N. Dearborn St., Loop* ☎ *312/443–3800* ⊕ *www.goodmantheatre.org.*

Joan W. and Irving B. Harris Theater for Music and Dance. Located on the northwest corner of Millennium Park, the 1,500-seat, mostly below-ground Joan W. and Irving B. Harris Theater for Music and Dance is a sleek, contemporary space where you can catch music and dance performances by the likes of Laurie Anderson, Magnetic Fields, and Chicago-based Luna Negra Dance Theater. ⊠ *205 E. Randolph Dr., Loop* ☎ *312/334–7777* ⊕ *www.harristheaterchicago.org.*

Royal George Theatre Center. Royal George Theatre Center is actually a complex of three theaters: a spacious main stage, a smaller studio theater, and a cabaret space. Popular plays and long-running musical comedies are the draw here. ⊠ *1641 N. Halsted. St., Lincoln Park* ☎ *312/988–9000* ⊕ *www.theroyalgeorgetheatre.com.*

Stage 773. Formerly the Theatre Building, Stage 773 showcases new works by up-and-coming playwrights and musical theater talent on three small stages. ⊠ *1225 W. Belmont, Lakeview* ☎ *773/327–5252* ⊕ *www.stage773.org.*

Storefront Theater. This storefront theater, operated by the Chicago Department of Cultural Affairs and Special Events, is an intimate, black-box venue for a diverse array of performances by local theater ensembles. ⊠ *66 E. Randolph St., Loop* ☎ *312/742–8497* ⊕ *www.cityofchicago.org/city/en/depts/dca/supp_info/chicago_culturalcenterpresents.html.*

Theatre on the Lake. Each summer a rotating roster of local off-Loop ensembles takes over the open-air stage Theatre on the Lake, located within spitting distance of Lake Michigan. ⊠ *2401 N. Lake Shore Dr., Lincoln Park* ☎ *312/742–7994* ⊕ *www.chicagoparkdistrict.com.*

DANCE

Hubbard Street Dance Chicago. Chicago's most notable success story in dance, Hubbard Street Dance Chicago exudes a jazzy vitality that has made it extremely popular. The style mixes classical-ballet techniques, theatrical jazz, and contemporary dance. Most performances take place at the Harris Theater in Millennium Park. ☎ *312/850–9744* ⊕ *www.hubbardstreetdance.com.*

Joffrey Ballet. Joffrey Ballet's fine-tuned performances, such as the glittering production of *The Nutcracker,* make this Chicago's premier classical-dance company. Treat yourself to one of several annual performances at the Auditorium Theatre and help celebrate more than 50 seasons of superb ballet. Performances take place at the Auditorium Theatre of Roosevelt University. ☎ *312/386–8905* ⊕ *www.joffrey.org.*

THEATER

About Face Theatre. The city's best-known gay, lesbian, bisexual, and transgender performing group, About Face Theatre in its short history has garnered awards for original works, world premieres, and

Back in the day, Ford Center (née the Oriental Theatre) hosted performances by Bing Crosby, Ella Fitzgerald, Danny Kaye, and Billie Holiday.

adaptations presented in larger theaters like Steppenwolf and the Goodman. ⊠ *1222 W. Wilson, 2W, Far North* ☎ *773/784–8565* ⊕ *www.aboutfacetheatre.com.*

Bailiwick Chicago. Bailiwick Chicago stages new and classical material at various locations throughout the city. Its Pride Performance series, held every summer, focuses on plays by gays and lesbians. ☎ *773/969–6201* ⊕ *www.bailiwickchicago.com.*

PERFORMING ARTS BY CATEGORY

CHOIR

Apollo Chorus of Chicago. Apollo Chorus of Chicago, formed in 1872, is one of the country's oldest oratorio societies. Don't miss the annual Handel's *Messiah* if you're here in December. Otherwise, the group performs various choral classics throughout the year at area churches. ☎ *312/427–5620* ⊕ *www.apollochorus.org.*

Bella Voce. Bella Voce —"beautiful voices," indeed. Formerly known as His Majestie's Clerkes, the 20-person a cappella group performs a variety of sacred and secular music, including everything from early music to works by living composers. Concerts are often held in churches throughout the city, providing a powerful acoustical and visual accompaniment to the music. ☎ *312/479–1096* ⊕ *www.bellavoce.org.*

FAMILY **Chicago Children's Choir.** A performance by the Chicago Children's Choir is the closest thing we can imagine to hearing angels sing. Its members— ages 8 to 18—are culled from a broad spectrum of racial, ethnic, and economic groups. Performances, selected from an international music base, take place during the holiday season and in May. Other concerts are scheduled periodically, sometimes in the Chicago Cultural Center's Preston Bradley Hall. ☎ *312/849–8300* ⊕ *www.ccchoir.org.*

Oriana Singers. The small but mighty Oriana Singers are an outstanding a cappella sextet with an eclectic early, classical, and jazz repertoire. The close-knit traveling group performs from September to June, periodically in conjunction with the Joffrey Ballet and other Chicago-area groups. ☎ *773/262–4558* ⊕ *www.oriana.org.*

12

CLASSICAL MUSIC

FAMILY **Chicago Symphony Orchestra.** Chicago Symphony Orchestra, with internationally celebrated conductor Riccardo Muti at the helm as music director, is a musical tour de force. They have two in-house award-winning composers and more than 150 magnificent performances a year. The impressive annual roster offers regular concerts and special themed series including classical, chamber, and children's concerts. Performances are held September through June. Tickets are sometimes scarce, but they do become available; call or check the website for status updates. If you buy your tickets online, click on the "Know Your Seats" section, where you can see photos of the views of the stage from different seats. ⊠ *Symphony Center, 220 S Michigan Ave., Loop* ☎ *312/294–3000, 800/223–7114* ⊕ *www.cso.org.*

Mandel Hall at the University of Chicago. Mandel Hall at the University of Chicago hosts an annual classical concert series featuring a wide range of composers and ensembles. ⊠ *5720 S. Woodlawn Ave., Hyde Park* ☎ *773/702–7300, 773/702–8068* ⊕ *chicagopresents.uchicago.edu.*

Music of the Baroque. Take a step back in time with Music of the Baroque, one of the Midwest's leading music ensembles specializing in Baroque and early classical music. See one of eight or so yearly programs at either Millennium Park's Harris Theater or one of several beautiful Chicago-area churches. ☎ *312/551–1414* ⊕ *www.baroque.org.*

The Newberry Library. Head to the stately Newberry Library for performances by the Newberry Consort, an early-music chamber group, and other ensembles in Ruggles Hall. ⊠ *60 West Walton St., Near North* ☎ *312/943–9090* ⊕ *www.newberry.org.*

DANCE

Dance Center of Columbia College Chicago. Dance Center of Columbia College Chicago presents thought-provoking fare with leading national and international contemporary-dance artists. ⊠ *1306 S. Michigan Ave., South Loop* ☎ *312/369–8300* ⊕ *www.colum.edu/dancecenter.*

Lookingglass Theatre Company. At the Lookingglass Theatre Company, marvel at offbeat and fantastically acrobatic performances inside the belly of the historic Chicago Water Works building. The company's physically and artistically daring works incorporate theater, dance, music, and circus arts. ⊠ *821 N. Michigan Ave., Near North* ☎ *312/337–0665* ⊕ *www.lookingglasstheatre.org.*

Luna Negra Dance Theater. Luna Negra Dance Theater has rapidly become one of Chicago's standout dance troupes, staging highly original performances by Latino choreographers, including its Cuban-born founder

Eduardo Vilaro. Performances take place at the Harris Theater in Millennium Park. ☎ *312/337–6882* ⊕ *www.lunanegra.org.*

Muntu Dance Theatre of Chicago. Muntu Dance Theatre of Chicago showcases dynamic interpretations of contemporary and traditional African and African-American dance. Artistic director Amaniyea Payne travels to Africa to learn traditional dances and adapts them for the stage. Performances take place at various venues across the city. ☎ *773/241–6080* ⊕ *www.muntu.com.*

Trinity Academy of Irish Dance. Trinity Irish Dance Co., founded long before *Riverdance*, promotes traditional and progressive Irish dancing. Performances take place at various venues in the city and suburbs. In addition to the world-champion professional group, you can also catch performances by younger dancers enrolled in the Trinity Academy of Irish Dance. ☎ *773/529–4822* ⊕ *www.trinity-dancers.com.*

FILM

Brew and View. The rowdy crowd at Brew and View comes for cheap flicks—both newer releases and cult faves—and beer specials. ✉ *Vic Theatre, 3145 N. Sheffield Ave., Lakeview* ☎ *773/929–6713* ⊕ *www. brewview.com.*

Facets. Facets Cinematheque shows independent and art films in its cinema and video theater. ✉ *1517 W. Fullerton Ave., Lincoln Park* ☎ *800/331–6197* ⊕ *www.facets.org.*

Gene Siskel Film Center. Gene Siskel Film Center screens new releases from around the globe and revivals of cinematic classics; the best part is that filmmakers often make appearances at screenings. ✉ *164 N. State St., Loop* ☎ *312/846–2600, 312/846–2800* ⊕ *www. siskelfilmcenter.org.*

IMAX and OMNIMAX Theaters. For IMAX and OMNIMAX theaters, go to Navy Pier or the Museum of Science and Industry. ⊕ *www.imax. com/oo/navy-pier-imax, www.msichicago.org.*

Movies in the Parks. For a change of scenery, watch current and classic films in neighborhood parks throughout the city during the Chicago Park District's Movies in the Parks series, which runs on various evenings June through September. ☎ *312/742–7529* ⊕ *www. chicagoparkdistrict.com.*

Music Box Theatre. If you love old theaters, old movies, and ghosts (rumor has it the theater is haunted by the spirit of its original manager), don't miss a trip to the Music Box Theatre. ✉ *3733 N. Southport Ave., Lakeview* ☎ *773/871–6604* ⊕ *www.musicboxtheatre.com.*

OPERA

Chicago Opera Theater. Chicago Opera Theater shrugs off esoteric notions of opera, preferring to make productions that are accessible to aficionados and novices alike. The production of *Nixon in China*, a contemporary American opera detailing conversations between the former U.S. President and Henry Kissinger (among others), is a shining example of the company's open-mindedness toward the operatic canon. From innovative versions of traditional favorites to important lesser-known works, the emphasis is on both theatrical and musical aspects. Fear not—performances are sung in English, or in Italian with English supertitles projected above the stage. They're held at the Harris Theater for Music and Dance in Millennium Park. ☎ *312/704–8414* ⊕ *www. chicagooperatheater.org.*

Light Opera Works. Light Opera Works favors the satirical tones of the distinctly British Gilbert and Sullivan operettas, but takes on frothy Viennese, French, and other light operettas and American musicals from June to early January. Performances take place in Evanston, just north of the city and easily accessible by train or El. ✉ *Ticket office, 516 4th St., Wilmette* ☎ *847/920–5360* ⊕ *www.light-opera-works.org.*

Lyric Opera of Chicago. At the Lyric Opera of Chicago, the big voices of the opera world star in top-flight productions September through March. This is one of the top two opera companies in America today. Don't worry about understanding German or Italian; English translations are projected above the stage. All of the superb performances have sold out for more than a dozen years, and close to 90% of all Lyric tickets go to subscribers. The key to getting in is to call the Lyric in early August, when individual tickets first go on sale. ✉ *20 N. Wacker Dr., Loop* ☎ *312/332–2244* ⊕ *www.lyricopera.org.*

THEATER

Black Ensemble Theater. Black Ensemble Theater has a penchant for long-running musicals based on popular African-American icons. Founder and executive producer Jackie Taylor has written and directed such hits as *The Jackie Wilson Story* and *The Other Cinderella.* ✉ *4450 N. Clark St., Far North Side* ☎ *773/769–4451* ⊕ *www.blackensembletheater.org.*

Briar Street Theatre. Originally built as a horse stable for Marshall Field, Briar Street Theatre is the spot to catch the long-running hit *Blue Man Group.* ✉ *3133 N. Halsted St., Lakeview* ☎ *773/348–4000, 800/258–3626* ⊕ *www.blueman.com/tickets/chicago.*

Chicago Shakespeare Theater. Chicago Shakespeare Theater devotes its considerable talents to keeping the Bard's flame alive in the Chicago area, with at least three plays a year. The best part? The Courtyard Theater, on Navy Pier, has sparkling views of the city, and seats are never farther than 30 feet from the thrust stage. ✉ *800 E. Grand Ave., Near North* ☎ *312/595–5600* ⊕ *www.chicagoshakes.com.*

City Lit Theatre. City Lit Theatre produces notable staged readings and full productions of famous literary works—by the likes of Henry James, Alice Walker, and Raymond Carver—as well as original material with a literary bent. ✉ *1020 W. Bryn Mawr Ave., Edgewater* ☎ *773/293–3682* ⊕ *www.citylit.org.*

Get out of your chair and shake your booty like a Chicagoan!

Collaboraction. Collaboraction lets actors, artists, and musicians share the stage together in an experimental free-for-all that puts the "fun" in dysfunctional. Of its several performances a year, we recommend Sketchbook—a series of 15 to 20 seven-minute-long plays—for its color and energy. ⊠ *1579 N. Milwaukee, 3rd Floor, Wicker Park* ☎ *312/226–9633* ⊕ *www.collaboraction.org.*

ETA Creative Arts Foundation. ETA Creative Arts Foundation, a South Side performing-arts center, has established a strong presence for African-American theater. In addition to showcasing new works by black playwrights, the space is home to an art gallery and a library. The best way to get here is by taxi. ⊠ *7558 S. Chicago Ave., Grand Crossing* ☎ *773/752–3955* ⊕ *www.etacreativearts.org.*

Neo-Futurists. Neo-Futurists perform their long-running, late-night hit *Too Much Light Makes the Baby Go Blind* in a space—oddly enough—above a funeral home. The piece is a series of 30 ever-changing plays performed in 60 minutes; the order of the plays is chosen by the audience. In keeping with the spirit of randomness, the admission price is set by the roll of a die, plus $9. ⊠ *5153 N. Ashland Ave., Far North* ☎ *773/275–5255* ⊕ *www.neofuturists.org.*

Fodor'sChoice
★

Redmoon Theater. Redmoon Theater tells imaginative, almost magical stories that weave together puppetry and live action. The company's annual outdoor spectacle series stages madcap theater in unlikely places, from community parks to a lagoon. The series usually takes place in fall, but experimental theater would be nothing if not unpredictable, so be sure to check the website or call for confirmation. Other performances are held in a warehouse space called Spectacle Hall in Pilsen. ⊠ *2120 S. Jefferson St., Pilsen* ☎ *312/850–8440* ⊕ *www.redmoon.org.*

Fodor's Choice
★

Steppenwolf. Steppenwolf's alumni roster speaks for itself: John Malkovich, Gary Sinise, Joan Allen, and Laurie Metcalf all honed their chops with this troupe. The company's trademark cutting-edge acting style and consistently successful productions have won national acclaim. ⊠ *1650 N. Halsted St., Lincoln Park* ☎ *312/335–1650* ⊕ *www. steppenwolf.org.*

Victory Gardens Theater. Victory Gardens Theater is known for its workshop productions and Chicago premieres. After buying the landmark Biograph Theater (site of John Dillinger's infamous demise) in 2006, the company stages all its productions in the impressive 299-seat proscenium-thrust house. Victory Gardens' original theater, now called the Greenhouse, hosts plays by local production companies on four stages. ⊠ *2433 N. Lincoln Ave., Lincoln Park* ☎ *773/871–3000* ⊕ *www.victorygardens.org.*

TRAVEL SMART
CHICAGO

GETTING HERE AND AROUND

Chicago is famously known as a city of neighborhoods. The Loop is Chicago's epicenter of business, finance, and government. Neighborhoods surrounding the Loop are River North (an area populated by art galleries and high-end boutiques), Near North (bordered by Lake Michigan and Navy Pier), and West Loop and South Loop, both up-and-coming areas with trendy residential areas and hip dining and shopping options.

Moving north, you'll encounter the Magnificent Mile (North Michigan Avenue), which gives way to the Gold Coast, so named for its luxurious mansions, stately museums, and deluxe entertainment venues. Lincoln Park, Lakeview, Wrigleyville, Lincoln Square, and Andersonville all lie north of these areas, and each has considerable charms to explore.

Neighborhoods west of the Loop are River West, Ukrainian Village, Wicker Park, and Bucktown, where of-the-moment art, shopping, dining, and nightlife venues line the streets.

Beyond South Loop lie Chinatown; Pilsen, where long-standing Mexican murals and taquerias intermingle with a burgeoning arts scene; and Hyde Park, home to the University of Chicago and the Museum of Science and Industry.

Traveling between neighborhoods is a relatively sane experience, thanks to the matrix of bus and train routes managed by the Chicago Transit Authority. Driving can be harried, but taxis are normally plentiful in most parts of town.

Chicago streets generally follow a grid pattern, running north–south or east–west and radiating from a center point at State and Madison streets in the Loop. East and west street numbers go up as you move away from State Street; north and south street numbers rise as you move away from Madison Street. Each block is represented by a hundred number (so the 12th block north of Madison will be the 1200 block).

∎TIP→ Ask the Chicago Office of Tourism about hotel and local transportation packages that include tickets to major museum exhibits, theater productions, or other special events.

∎ AIR TRAVEL

To Chicago: from New York, 2 hours; from San Francisco, 4 hours; from Los Angeles, 4 hours; from Dallas, 2½ hours; from London, 7 hours; from Sydney, 17 hours (not including layovers).

In Chicago the general rule is to arrive at the airport two hours before an international flight; for a domestic flight, plan to arrive 90 minutes early if you're checking luggage and 60 minutes if you're not.

Airline Security Issues Transportation Security Administration. Transportation Security Administration has answers for almost every question that might come up. ☎ 866/289–9673 ⊕ www.tsa.gov.

AIRPORTS

The major gateway to Chicago is **O'Hare International Airport** (ORD). Because it's one of the world's busiest airports, all major airlines pass through O'Hare. The sprawling structure is 19 miles from downtown, in the far northwest corner of the city. It can take anywhere from 30 to 90 minutes to travel between downtown and O'Hare, based on time of day, weather conditions, and construction on the Kennedy Expressway (Interstate 90). The Blue Line El train offers a reliable 40-minute trip between the Loop and O'Hare.

Got some time to spend before your flight? Plenty of dining and shopping options are scattered throughout O'Hare's four terminals. Chicago favorites such as the Berghoff Café, Billy Goat Tavern, Goose Island Brewing Company, Pizzeria Uno, Garrett Popcorn, and Gold Coast Dogs can be found among the usual chain restaurants. Grab that last-minute souvenir or in-flight necessity at an array of shops, including the Field Museum Gift Shop and Vosges Haut-Chocolat. Take young travelers to visit the Chicago Children's Muscum's "Kids on the Fly" exhibit. Or spring for a mini-massage from the Back Rub Hub. Wi-Fi is also available throughout the building.

TIP→ If you're stuck at O'Hare longer than you expected, the Hilton Chicago O'Hare (☎773/686–8000) is within walking distance of all terminals.

Midway Airport (MDW) is about 11 miles southwest from downtown. Midway Airport serves Southwest, Delta, AirTran, and Frontier. Driving between Midway and downtown can take 30 to 60 minutes, depending on traffic conditions on the Stevenson Expressway (Interstate 55). The Orange Line El train runs from the Loop to Midway in about 30 minutes.

Some say the more recently renovated Midway has better dining options than O'Hare. With downtown standouts such as Harry Caray's, Manny's Deli, Pegasus On the Fly, and Lalo's Mexican Restaurant all on-site, it's a good point. The Midway Boulevard area in the center of the building features cute shops such as Discover Chicago and Kids Works. Wi-Fi is available throughout the airport.

An extended stay near Midway Airport can be spent at a number of nearby hotels, including Chicago Marriott Midway (☎800/228–9290), Hampton Inn Midway (☎708/496–1900), and Hilton Garden Inn Midway (☎708/496–2700).

Security screenings at both airports can be fairly quick during off-peak travel times or long and arduous during the holidays; it's best to arrive a minimum of two hours before your flight during the busiest time periods.

TIP→ Long layovers don't have to be only about sitting around or shopping. These days they can be about burning off vacation calories. Check out ⊕ www.airportgyms.com for lists of health clubs that are in or near many U.S. and Canadian airports.

Airport Information Chicago Midway Airport ☎773/838–0600 ⊕ www.flychicago.com/midway/en/home/Pages/default.aspx. **O'Hare International Airport** ☎773/686–2200, 800/832–6352 ⊕ www.flychicago.com/ohare/en/home/Pages/default.aspx.

GROUND TRANSPORTATION

If you're traveling to or from the airport by bus or car during morning or afternoon rush hours, factor in some extra time—ground transport to or from both O'Hare and Midway airports can be slow.

BUS TRAVEL

Shuttle buses run between O'Hare and Midway airports and to and from either airport and various points in the city. When taking an airport shuttle bus to O'Hare or Midway to catch a departing flight, be sure to allow at least 1½ hours. When going to either airport, it's a good idea to make a reservation 24 hours in advance. Though some shuttles make regular stops at the major hotels and don't require reservations, it's best to check. Reservations are not necessary from the airports. Omega Airport Shuttle runs an hourly shuttle between the two airports for approximately $45 per person. Travel time is approximately one hour. Omega Airport Shuttle also provides an hourly service from the two airports and Hyde Park. The fare is $35 from O'Hare to Hyde Park and $19 from Midway to Hyde Park. GO Airport Express coaches provide service from both airports to major downtown and Near North locations and most suburbs. The trip downtown from O'Hare takes at least 45 minutes, depending on traffic conditions; the fare is $29, $53 round-trip. The trip downtown from Midway takes at least a half hour; the fare is $24, $44 round-trip. Call to find out times and prices for other destinations.

CAR TRAVEL

Depending on traffic and the time of day, driving to and from O'Hare takes about an hour, and driving to and from Midway takes at least 45 minutes. From O'Hare, follow the signs to Interstate 90 east (Kennedy Expressway), which merges with Interstate 94 (Edens Expressway). Take the eastbound exit at Ohio Street for Near North locations, the Washington or Monroe Street exit for downtown. After you exit, continue east about a mile to get to Michigan Avenue. From Midway, follow the signs to Interstate 55 east, which leads to Interstate 90.

TAXI TRAVEL

Metered taxicab service is available at both O'Hare and Midway airports. Trips to and from O'Hare may incur a $1 surcharge to compensate for changing fuel costs. Expect to pay about $40 to $45 plus tip from O'Hare to Near North and downtown locations, about $30 to $35 plus tip from Midway. Some cabs, such as Checker Taxi and Yellow Cab, participate in a shared-ride program in which each cab carries up to four individual passengers going from the airport to downtown. The cost per person—a flat fee that varies according to destination—is substantially lower than the full rate. Or use the Hailo app to hail the nearest taxi using your smartphone.

TRAIN TRAVEL

Chicago Transit Authority (CTA) trains, called elevated or El trains (locals often refer to it simply as "the El"), are the cheapest way to and from the airports; they can also be the most convenient transfer. "Trains to city" signs will guide you to the subway or elevated train line. In O'Hare Airport the Blue Line station is in the underground concourse between terminals. Travel time to the city is about

45 minutes. Get off at the station closest to your hotel; or, from the first stop in the Loop (Washington and Dearborn streets), you can take a taxi to your hotel or change to other transit lines. At Midway Airport the Orange Line El runs to the Loop. The stop at Adams Street and Wabash Avenue is the closest to the hotels on South Michigan Avenue; for others, the simplest strategy is to get off anywhere in the Loop and hail a cab to your final destination. Train fare is $2.25, and you'll need to pay by transit card. Transit card vending machines are in every train station. They do not give change, so add only as much as you'd like to put on your card. Pick up train brochures and system maps outside the entrances to the platforms; the "Downtown Transit Sightseeing Guide" is also helpful.

TRANSFERS BETWEEN AIRPORTS

O'Hare and Midway airports are on opposite ends of the city, so moving between them can be a time-consuming and arduous task. Your best and cheapest move is hopping on the El. You will travel the Blue Line to the Orange Line, transferring at the Clark Street stop to get from O'Hare to Midway, reversing the trip to go from Midway to O'Hare. The entire journey should take you less than two hours.

Taxis and Shuttles American United Cab Co. ☎ 773/248-7600. **Checker Taxi** ☎ 312/243-2537 ⊕ www.checkertaxichicago. com. **Flash Cab** ☎ 773/561-4444 ⊕ www.flashcab.com. **GO Airport Express** ☎ 888/284-3826 ⊕ www.airportexpress.com. **Hailo** ⊕ www.hailocab.com/chicago. **Omega Airport Shuttle** ☎ 773/734-6688 ⊕ www. omegashuttle.com. **Yellow Cab** ☎ 312/829-4222 ⊕ www.yellowcabchicago.com.

Public Transit Information CTA ☎ 888/968-7282 ⊕ www.transitchicago.com.

▌BIKE TRAVEL

Mayor Richard Daley worked to establish Chicago as one of the most bike-friendly cities in the United States, and it remains that way today. More than 120 miles of designated bike routes run throughout the city, through historic areas, beautiful parks, and along city streets (look for the words "bike lane"). Bicycling on busy city streets can be a challenge and is not for the faint of heart—cars come within inches of riders, and the doors of parked cars can swing open at any time. The best bet for a scenic ride is the lakefront, which has a traffic-free 18-mile asphalt trail with scenic views of the skyline. When your bike is unattended, always lock it; there are bike racks throughout the city.

In Millennium Park at Michigan Avenue and Randolph Street there are 300 free indoor bike spaces (⊕ *www.chicagobikestation.com*) plus showers, lockers, and bike-rental facilities offering beach cruisers, mountain and road bikes, hybrid/comfort models, tandem styles, and add-ons for kids (wagon, baby seat, and so on). Bike rentals are also readily available at Bike and Roll Chicago, which has five locations, one at Millennium Park, one at Navy Pier, two at the Riverwalk (one at river level at Wacker Drive and Columbus and one at Wacker and Wabash Avenue), and one at the 53rd Street Bike Center in Hyde Park. Bike and Roll Chicago carries a good selection of mountain and cross bikes. Rates start at $10 per hour. The Chicago Department of Transportation publishes free route maps. Active Transportation Alliance maps cost $10. Maps are updated every few years. From April through October, Bobby's Bike Hike takes guests on cycling tours of Chicago. The three-hour tours begin at the Water Tower on the Magnificent Mile and cycle through historic neighborhoods, shopping areas, and the lakefront. A $35 to $60 fee includes bikes, helmets, and guides; book online for a 10% discount.

Information Active Transportation Alliance ☎ 312/427–3325 ⊕ www.activetrans.org. **Bike and Roll Chicago** ☎ 773/404–2500 ⊕ www.bikechicago.com. **Bobby's Bike Hike** ☎ 312/915–0995 ⊕ www.bobbysbikehike.com. **The City of Chicago Department of Transportation (CDOT)** ☎ 312/742–2453 ⊕ www.chicagobikes.org/bikemap.

▌BOAT TRAVEL

Water taxis are an economical and in-the-know way to cruise parts of the Chicago River and Lake Michigan. A combination of working stiffs and tourists boards these boats daily. You won't get the in-depth narrative of an architecture tour, but the views of Chicago's waterways are just as good.

Wendella Boats operates Chicago Water Taxis, which use four downtown docks (Madison Street, LaSalle Street, Michigan Avenue, and Chinatown) along the Chicago River. The entire ride takes about a half hour, and you'll get to see a good portion of the downtown part of the river. The boats operate seven days a week, April through October. You can purchase tickets at any dock or on the company's website.

Shoreline Sightseeing's water taxis run two routes: the River Taxi cruises between the Willis (formerly Sears) Tower and Navy Pier, and the Harbor Taxi navigates Lake Michigan between Navy Pier and the Museum Campus. Water taxis run 10 am to 6 pm late May to early September. You can purchase tickets at any dock or in advance on the company's website.

Information Shoreline Sightseeing ✉ 474 N. Lake Shore Dr., Suite 3511 ☎ 312/222–9328 ⊕ www.shorelinesightseeing.com. **Wendella Boats** ✉ 400 N. Michigan Ave. (main dock) ☎ 312/337–1446 ⊕ www.wendellaboats.com.

■ CAR TRAVEL

Chicago's network of buses and rapid-transit rail is extensive, and taxis and limousines are readily available (the latter often priced competitively with metered cabs), so rent a car *only* to visit the outlying suburbs that are not accessible by public transportation. Chicago traffic is often heavy, on-street parking is nearly impossible to find, parking lots are expensive, congestion creates frustrating delays, and other drivers may be impatient with those who are unfamiliar with the city and its roads. Expect snarled traffic during rush hours. In these circumstances you may find a car to be a liability rather than an asset. The Illinois Department of Transportation gives information on expressway congestion, travel times, and lane closures and directions on state roadways.

The Illinois tollways snake around the outskirts of the city. Interstate 294 runs north and south between Wisconsin and Indiana. Interstate 90 runs northwest to western Wisconsin, including Madison and Wisconsin Dells. Interstate 88 runs east–west and goes from Eisenhower to Interstate 55. Traffic on all is sometimes just as congested as on the regular expressways. Most tollgates are unmanned, so bring lots of change if you don't have an I-Pass, which is sometimes included with rental cars. Even though tolls are double without the I-Pass, it's not cost-effective to purchase one for a couple of days.

If you decide to rent a car, you'll have plenty of options, from the big rental chains to luxury options. The common rental agencies regularly stock new models, many with modern amenities (navigation systems, satellite radio).

Rates in Chicago begin at around $50 a day, $200 a week, or $75 a weekend for an economy car with air-conditioning, automatic transmission, and unlimited mileage. This does not include the car-rental tax and other taxes totaling 18% plus a $2.75 surcharge per rental. If you rent from the airport, it's slightly more expensive because of airport taxes.

GASOLINE

Gas stations are less numerous in downtown Chicago than in the outlying neighborhoods and suburbs. Filling up is about 50¢ higher per gallon downtown, when you can find a station. Expect to pay anywhere between $3 and $4 per gallon of gas (prices at time of writing). Major credit cards are accepted at all gas stations, and the majority of stations are completely self-serve.

PARKING

Most of Chicago's streets have metered parking, but during peak hours it's hard to find a spot. Most parking pay boxes accept quarters and credit cards in increments as small as five minutes in high-traffic areas, up to an hour in less crowded neighborhoods. Prices average $2–$6.50 an hour. Parking lots and garages are plentiful downtown, but they're expensive. You could pay anywhere from $13 for the day in a municipal lot to $25 for three hours in a private lot. Some neighborhoods, such as the area of Lakeview known as Wrigleyville, enforce restricted parking (especially strict on Cubs' game nights) and will tow cars without permits. You won't find many public parking lots in the neighborhoods. Many major thoroughfares restrict parking during peak travel hours, generally from 7 to 9 am heading toward downtown and from 4 to 6 pm heading away. Read street signs carefully to determine whether a parking spot is legal. On snow days in winter cars parked in designated "snow route areas" will be towed. There's a $30 fine plus the cost of towing the car. In sum, Chicago isn't the most car-friendly place for visitors. Unless it's a necessity, it's best to forget renting a car and use public transportation.

ROAD CONDITIONS

Chicago drivers can be reckless, zipping through red lights and breaking posted speed limits. The Loop and some residential neighborhoods such as Lincoln Park, Lakeview, and Bucktown are made up of mostly one-way streets, so be sure to read signs carefully. Check both ways after a light turns green to make sure that the cross traffic has stopped.

Rush hours are 6:30 to 9:30 am and 4 to 7 pm, but don't be surprised if the rush starts earlier or ends later, depending on weather conditions, big events, and holiday weekends. There are always bottlenecks on the expressways, particularly where the Edens and Kennedy merge, and downtown on the Dan Ryan from 22nd Street into the Loop. Sometimes anything around the airport is rough. There are electronic signs on the expressways that post updates on the congestion. Additionally, summertime is high time for construction on highways and inner-city roads. Drive with patience.

ROADSIDE EMERGENCIES

Dial 911 in an emergency to reach police, fire, or ambulance services. AAA Chicago provides roadside assistance to members. Mr. Locks Security Systems will unlock your vehicle 24 hours a day.

Emergency Services AAA Chicago
☎ 800/222–4357 (AAA–HELP) ⊕ www.aaa.com.
Mr. Locks Security Systems ☎ 866/675–6257
⊕ www.mr-locks.com.

RULES OF THE ROAD

Speed limits in Chicago vary, but on most city roads it's 30 mph. Most interstate highways, except in congested areas, have a speed limit of 55 mph. In Chicago you may turn right at a red light after stopping if there's no oncoming traffic and no restrictions are posted. When in doubt, wait for the green. Cameras have been installed at many major intersections in the city to catch drivers who run red lights and commit other infractions. There are many one-way streets in Chicago, particularly in and around the Loop, so be alert to signs and

NAVIGATING CHICAGO

Chicago is a surprisingly well-ordered and manageable city. There are a few city-planning quirks, however, and streets that run on a diagonal, such as Milwaukee, Elston, and Lincoln avenues. These passageways are actually old Indian trails that followed the Chicago River. Chicago also has a proliferation of double- and even triple-decker streets, Wacker Drive being the best-known example. The uppermost level is generally used for street traffic, and the lower levels serve as thoroughfares for cutting through the city rather quickly.

The most helpful landmark to help you navigate Chicago is Lake Michigan. It will always lie on the east, as it serves as the city's only eastern border. Also, look for the Willis (formerly Sears) Tower and John Hancock Center, which reach up far enough into the sky to serve as beacons. The Willis Tower is in the Loop, and the John Hancock Center is on northern Michigan Avenue.

Chicago's public transit system blankets the city well and is fairly intuitive. Major bus lines include the 151–Sheridan, which runs along the Lakefront; the 36–Broadway, which cuts through the Gold Coast, Lincoln Park, and Lakeview; and the 125–Water Tower Express, which takes a meandering route from Union Station to Water Tower. The train system (referred to as the El, short for "elevated") is a comprehensive network, with eight train lines crisscrossing the city and nearby suburbs. The busiest routes are the Blue Line, which runs from O'Hare Airport into the city through Bucktown and back out again through the Loop; the Red Line, which cuts a north–south swath through the city, crossing through Edgewater, Lakeview, Lincoln Park, the Gold Coast, the Loop, and the South Side; and the Brown Line, which travels from the Far Northwest Side through Lakeview and Lincoln Park, into the Loop, and back up north.

other cars. Illinois drunk-driving laws are quite strict. Anyone caught driving with a blood-alcohol content of .08 or more will automatically have his or her license seized and be issued a ticket, and authorities in home states will be notified. Those with Illinois driver's licenses can have their licenses suspended for three months on the first offense.

Passengers are required to wear seat belts. Always strap children under age eight into approved child-safety seats.

It's illegal to use handheld cellular phones while driving in the city, and the restrictions vary in the suburbs. Headlights are compulsory if you're using windshield wipers. Radar detectors are legal in Illinois.

▌ PUBLIC TRANSPORTATION

Chicago's extensive public transportation network includes rapid-transit trains, buses, and a commuter-rail network. The Chicago Transit Authority, or CTA, operates the rapid-transit trains (the El), city buses, and suburban buses (Pace). Metra runs the commuter rail.

The Regional Transportation Authority (RTA) for northeastern Illinois oversees and coordinates the activities of the CTA and Metra. The RTA's website can be a useful first stop if you are planning to combine suburban and city public transit while in Chicago.

Information Pace ☎ 847/364–7223 ⊕ www.pacebus.com. **Regional Transportation Authority** ☎ 312/913–3110 ⊕ www.rtachicago.com.

CTA: THE EL AND BUSES

The Chicago Transit Authority (CTA) operates rapid-transit trains and buses. Chicago's rapid-transit train system is known as the El. Each of the eight lines has a color name as well as a route name: Blue (O'Hare–Congress–Douglas), Brown (Ravenswood), Green (Lake–Englewood–Jackson Park), Orange (Midway), Purple (Evanston), Red (Howard–Dan Ryan),

Yellow (Skokie Swift), and Pink (Cermak). In general, the route names indicate the first and last stop on the train. Chicagoans refer to trains both by the color and the route name. Most, but not all, rapid-transit lines operate 24 hours; some stations are closed at night. The El, though very crowded during rush hours, is the quickest way to get around (unless you're coming from the suburbs, in which case the Metra is quicker but doesn't run as often). Trains run every 15 minutes, though during rush hour they run about every 10 minutes, and on weekends every 30 minutes. Pick up the brochure "Downtown Transit Sightseeing Guide" for hours, fares, and other pertinent information. (You can also download it at ⊕ *www.transitchicago.com/assets/1/ brochures/*13JD_002_Downtown_Transit_Sightseeing_Guide.pdf.) In general, late-night CTA travel is not recommended. Note that many of the Red and Blue line stations are subways; the rest are elevated. This means if you're heading to O'Hare and looking for the Blue Line, you may have to look for a stairway down, not up.

Fares must be paid by transit card on trains; buses accept both transit cards and cash (dollar bills or coins; no change given). Transit cards can be purchased from machines at CTA train stations as well as at Jewel and Dominick's grocery stores and currency exchanges. These easy-to-use cards are inserted into the turnstiles at CTA train stations and into machines as you board CTA buses; directions are clearly posted. Use them to transfer between CTA vehicles. To transfer between the Loop's elevated lines and the subway or between rapid-transit trains and buses, you must either use a transit card with at least 25¢ stored on it, or, if you're not using a transit card, buy a transfer when you first board. If two CTA train lines meet, you can transfer for free. You can also obtain free train-to-train transfers from specially marked turnstiles at the Washington/State subway station or the State/Lake El station, or ask for a transfer card, good on downtown trains, at the ticket booth.

Buses generally stop on every other corner northbound and southbound (on State Street they stop at every corner). Eastbound and westbound buses generally stop on every corner. Buses from the Loop generally run north–south. Principal transfer points are on Michigan Avenue at the north side of Randolph Street for northbound buses, Adams Street and Wabash Avenue for westbound buses and the El, and State and Lake streets for southbound buses.

Bus schedules vary depending on the time of day and route, and run every 8 to 15 minutes, though service is less frequent on weekends, very early in the morning, and late at night. Schedules are available online at ⊕ *www.transitchicago.com.*

The CTA fare structure is as follows: the basic fare for rapid-transit trains is $2.25 by transit card. The basic fare for buses is $2.25 when paying cash and $2 when using a transit card. Transfers are 25¢ when using a transit card; no transfers are issued when paying cash. Transit cards can be purchased in preset denominations of $10 or $20 at many local grocery stores, currency exchanges, and stations. You can also purchase a transit card of any denomination over $2 at any CTA stop. Transfers can be used twice within a two-hour time period. Transfers between CTA train lines are free—no transfer card is needed. Transit cards may be shared.

For $10 a one-day Visitor Pass offers 24 hours of unlimited CTA riding from the time you first use it. Visitor Passes are sold at hotels, museums, and other places tourists frequent, plus all transit-card booths. A three-day pass is $20, and a seven-day pass is $28.

Information CTA ⊠ *Merchandise Mart, 567 W. Lake St.* ☎ *888/968–7282* ⊕ *www.transitchicago.com.*

METRA: COMMUTER TRAINS

Metra commuter trains serve the city and suburbs. The Metra Electric railroad has a line close to Lake Michigan; its trains stop in Hyde Park. The Metra commuter rail system has 11 lines to suburbs and surrounding cities, including Aurora, Elgin, Joliet, and Waukegan; one line serves the North Shore suburbs, and another has a stop at McCormick Place. Trains leave from several downtown terminals.

Metra trains use a fare structure based on distance. A Metra weekend pass costs $7 and is valid for rides on any of the eight operating lines all day on weekends, except for the South Shore line.

Information Metra information line ☎ *312/322–6777* ⊕ *www.metrarail.com.*

▋ TAXI TRAVEL

You can hail a cab on just about any busy street in Chicago. Hotel doormen will hail a cab for you as well. Cabs aren't all yellow anymore, but look for standard-size sedans or, in some cases, minivans. Available taxis are sometimes indicated by an illuminated rooftop light. Chicago taxis are metered, with fares beginning at $3.25 (including a $1 fuel surcharge) upon entering the cab and 20¢ for each additional 1/9 mile or 36 seconds of wait time. A charge of $1 is made for the first additional passenger and 50¢ for each additional passenger. There's no extra baggage or credit-card charge. Taxi drivers expect a 15% tip.

Taxi Companies American United Cab Co. ☎ *773/248–7600* ⊕ *www.americanunitedtaxiaffiliation.com.* **Checker Taxi** ☎ *312/243–2537* ⊕ *www.checkertaxichicago.com.* **Flash Cab** ☎ *773/561–4444* ⊕ *www.flashcab.com.* **Yellow Cab** ☎ *312/829–4222* ⊕ *www.yellowcabchicago.com.*

▋ TRAIN TRAVEL

Amtrak offers nationwide service to Chicago's Union Station, at 225 South Canal Street.

Information Amtrak ☎ *800/872-7245* ⊕ *www.amtrak.com.*

ESSENTIALS

■ COMMUNICATIONS

INTERNET

Chicago is for the most part a wireless city, with most hotels and coffee shops offering high-speed wireless access. Some hotels have a nominal fee (usually less than $10) that gets you online for 24 hours. You can also duck into places like FedEx Kinko's to check your email, either on your own laptop or the available computers, but charges there can run high if you're online longer than a few minutes.

Contacts Cybercafes. Cybercafes lists more than 4,000 Internet cafés worldwide. ⊕ *www. cybercafes.com.* **FedEx Kinko's** ⊠ *444 N. Wells St.* ☎ *312/670–4460* ⊕ *www.fedexkinkos.com.*

■ DAY TOURS AND GUIDES

Chicago Tours. A comprehensive collection of Chicago sightseeing tours by air, water, and land can be found through Chicago Tours, a travel-reservation company offering more than 75 tours, cruises, events, and activities. ☎ *888/881–3284* ⊕ *www. chicagotours.us.*

BOAT TOURS

Get a fresh perspective on Chicago by taking a water tour or cruise. Boat tour schedules vary by season; be sure to call for exact times and fares. The season usually runs from May 1 through mid-November. One cruise in particular stands out, though it's a *bit* more expensive than the rest: the Chicago Architecture Foundation river cruise aboard *Chicago's First Lady, Chicago's Little Lady,* or *Chicago's Fair Lady.* The CAF tour highlights more than 50 architecturally significant sights. The cost is $38 ($35 if reserved online, and $30 for select Tuesdays and Wednesdays); reservations are recommended. Shoreline Sightseeing also runs architecture-themed boat tours.

If you're looking for a maritime adventure, you can get a blast from the past on the tall ship *Windy,* a 148-foot ship modeled on old-time commercial vessels. Passengers may help the crew or take a turn at the wheel during several different themed sailing cruises of Lake Michigan. The cost is $25 to $45.

Boat Tours Chicago Architecture Foundation River Cruise ☎ *312/922–3432 information, 312/922–3432 tickets* ⊕ *caf.architecture. org.* **Mercury Chicago Skyline Cruiseline** ☎ *312/332–1353 recorded information* ⊕ *www.mercuryskylinecruiseline.com.* **Shoreline Sightseeing** ☎ *312/222–9328* ⊕ *www. shorelinesightseeing.com.* **Wendella** ⊠ *400 N. Michigan Ave.* ☎ *312/337–1446* ⊕ *www. wendellaboats.com.* **Windy of Chicago Ltd.** ☎ *312/451–2700* ⊕ *www.tallshipwindy.com.*

BUS AND TROLLEY TOURS

A narrated bus or trolley tour can be a good way to orient yourself among Chicago's main sights. Tour costs start at roughly $20 and can last from two hours to a full day. American Sightseeing offers about 30 routes, from classic sightseeing outings to pizza- and blues-themed tours. The double-decker buses of Chicago Trolley & Double Decker Co. vehicles stop at all the downtown attractions. You can get on and off the open-air trolleys as you like; these tours vary in price, so call for details. The Chicago Architecture Foundation's bus tours often go farther afield, exploring everything from cemeteries to movie palaces.

Bus and Trolley Tours American Sightseeing Tours Chicago Gray Line Prairie Trailways ☎ *312/251–3100* ⊕ *www.prairietrailways.com.* **Chicago Architecture Foundation** ⊠ *Tour Center, Santa Fe Bldg., 224 S. Michigan Ave.* ☎ *312/922–3432* ⊕ *www.architecture.org.* **Chicago Trolley & Double Decker Co.** ☎ *773/648–5000* ⊕ *www.chicagotrolley.com.*

FOREIGN-LANGUAGE TOURS
Chicago Tour Guides Institute, Inc. ☎ *773/276–6683* ⊕ *www.chicagoguide.net.*

SPECIAL-INTEREST TOURS
African-American Black Coutours ☎ *773/233–8907* ⊕ *www.blackcoutours.com.*

Architecture ⇨ *Walking Tours.*

Chocolate Accenting Chicago Events & Tours, Inc. ☎ *312/819–5363* ⊕ *www.accentingchicago.com.* **Chicago Chocolate Tours** ☎ *312/929–2939* ⊕ *www.chicagochocolatetours.com.*

Gangsters Untouchable Tours ☎ *773/881–1195* ⊕ *www.gangstertour.com.*

Ghosts Chicago Supernatural Tours ☎ *708/499–0300* ⊕ *www.ghosttours.com.*

Historic Neighborhoods Bronzeville Visitor Information Center ☎ *773/819–5170* ⊕ *www.explorechicago.org/city/en/things_see_ do/attractions/tourism/bronzeville_visitor.html.*

Horse-and-Carriage Rides Antique Coach and Carriage Company ☎ *773/735–9400* ⊕ *www.antiquecoach-carriage.com.* **Chicago Horse & Carriage Ltd.** ☎ *312/988–9090* ⊕ *www.chicagocarriage.com.* **Noble Horse** ☎ *312/266–7878* ⊕ *www.noblehorsechicago.com.*

WALKING TOURS
The Chicago Architecture Foundation has by far the largest selection of guided tours, with more than 50 itineraries covering everything from department stores to Frank Lloyd Wright's Oak Park buildings. Especially popular walking tours of the Loop are given daily throughout the year. Chicago Greeter and InstaGreeter (for last-minute weekend visits) are two free city services that match knowledgeable Chicagoans with visitors for tours of various sights and neighborhoods.

Information Chicago Architecture Foundation ⊠ *Tour Centers, Santa Fe Bldg., 224 S. Michigan Ave.* ☎ *312/922–3432* ⊕ *www.architecture.org.* **Chicago Greeter** ⊠ *Chicago Office of Tourism, 78 E. Washington St.* ☎ *312/945–4231* ⊕ *www.chicagogreeter.com.*

▌ HOURS OF OPERATION

Neighborhood business hours are generally 9 to 6 Sunday through Wednesday, with later hours Thursday through Saturday. When holidays fall on a weekend, businesses usually close around 4 on the preceding Friday. On a Monday after a weekend holiday, retail businesses are rarely closed but regular businesses often are. Most stores close for Christmas, New Year's, and Easter Sunday.

Chicago museums are generally open daily 9–5, closing only on major holidays; some larger attractions keep later hours (until about 8 pm) one weeknight per week. A number of smaller museums keep limited hours; it's always advisable to phone ahead for details.

Most pharmacies are open regular business hours, starting as early as 8 am. Some close as early as 5 pm, but many stay open later, anywhere from 6 to 10 pm. Major chains have outposts that are open 24 hours.

▌MONEY

Costs in Chicago are quite reasonable compared with other large cities such as San Francisco and New York, though the sales tax here, at 9.25%, is one of the highest of any U.S. city. Restaurants, events, and parking costs are markedly higher in the Loop than in any other area of the city.

ATMs are plentiful. You can find them in banks, grocery stores, and hotels, as well as at some drugstores, gas stations, and convenience stores.

Prices throughout this guide are given for adults. Substantially reduced fees are almost always available for children, students, and senior citizens.

▌SAFETY

The most common crimes in public places are pickpocketing, purse snatching, jewelry theft, and gambling scams. Keep your wallet in a front coat or pants pocket. Close your bag or purse securely and keep it close to you. Also beware of someone jostling you and of loud arguments; these could be ploys to distract your attention while another person grabs your wallet. Leave unnecessary credit cards at home, and hide valuables and jewelry from view.

Although crime on CTA buses and trains in general has declined, recently robbers have been targeting El travelers with smartphones; keep your phone and other portable electronic devices out of sight on train platforms. Several additional precautions can reduce the chance of your becoming a victim: look alert and purposeful; know your route ahead of time; have your fare ready before boarding; and keep an eye on your purse or packages during the ride. Avoid taking public transit late at night.

▌**TIP➜** Distribute your cash, credit cards, IDs, and other valuables between a deep front pocket, an inside jacket or vest pocket, and a hidden money pouch. Don't reach for the money pouch once you're in public.

TIPS TO REMEMBER

Chicago cityPASS. To save money on sightseeing, buy a Chicago cityPASS, which costs $94. The passes are good for nine days from the day of first use and include admission to Shedd Aquarium, The Field Museum, Skydeck Chicago at Willis (Sears) Tower, either Museum of Science and Industry or John Hancock Observatory, and either Adler Planetarium or Art Institute of Chicago. ☎ 888/330–5008 ⊕ www.citypass.com/chicago.

Go Chicago Card. The Go Chicago Card is good for more than 25 attractions and various discounts. The card can be purchased as a one-day or a multiday pass, starting at $75. ☎ 866/628–9031 ⊕ www.gochicagocard.com.

▌TAXES

At restaurants you'll pay approximately 10% meal tax (thanks to special taxing initiatives, some parts of town are higher than others).

The hotel tax in Chicago is 16.4%, and slightly less in suburban hotels.

In Chicago a steep 9.25% state and county sales tax is added to all purchases except groceries, which have a 2.25% tax. Sales tax is already added into the initial price of prescription drugs.

▌TIME

Chicago is in the central time zone. It's 1 hour behind New York, 2 hours ahead of Los Angeles, 6 hours behind London, and 16 hours behind Sydney.

Time Zones Timeanddate.com. Timeanddate.com can help you figure out the correct time anywhere in the world. ⊕ www.timeanddate.com/worldclock.

▌TIPPING

You should tip 15% for adequate service in restaurants and up to 20% if you feel you've been treated well. At higher-end restaurants, where there are more service personnel per table who must divide the tip, up these measures by a few percentage points. An especially helpful wine steward should be acknowledged with $2 or $3. It's not necessary to tip the maître d' unless you've been done a very special favor and you intend to visit again. Tip $1 per checked coat.

Taxi drivers, bartenders, and hairdressers expect about 15%. Bellhops and porters should get about $1 per bag; valet-parking attendants $1 or $2 (but only after they bring your car to you, not when they park it); and hotel maids about $1 to $2 per room per day of your stay. On package tours, conductors and drivers usually get about $2 to $3 per day from each group member. Concierges should get tips of $5 to $10 for special service.

▌VISITOR INFORMATION

The Chicago Convention and Tourism Bureau is a great place to start planning your visit to the Windy City. The organization's website is a veritable gold mine of information, from hotel packages to sample itineraries, event calendars, and maps. You can also call the toll-free number to speak with a travel consultant. The Illinois Bureau of Tourism (⊕ *enjoyillinois.com*) offers detailed information about what to do and see in Chicago and is especially helpful if your travel plans will take you outside of the downtown area. Once you're here, you can count on the visitor centers at the Chicago Cultural Center, Chicago Water Works, and Navy Pier. They are stocked with free maps, local publications, and knowledgeable staff to help you out.

Contacts Chicago Convention and Tourism Bureau ✉ *2301 S. Lake Shore Dr.* ☎ *312/567–8500, 877/244–2246* ⊕ *www.choosechicago.com.* **Chicago Cultural Center** ✉ *78 E. Washington St.* ☎ *312/744–6630* ⊕ *www.chicagoculturalcenter.org.* **Chicago Water Works** ✉ *163 E. Pearson* ☎ *312/742–8811* ⊕ *www.choosechicago.com.* **Illinois Bureau of Tourism** ☎ *800/226–6632* ⊕ *www.enjoyillinois.com.* **Navy Pier Welcome Center** ✉ *600 E. Grand Ave.* ☎ *800/595–7437, 312/595–7437* ⊕ *www.navypier.com.*

ONLINE TRAVEL TOOLS
ART
For a preview of the Art Institute of Chicago, check out ⊕ *www.artic.edu.*

NEWSPAPERS AND MAGAZINES
The websites of the city's daily newspapers, the *Chicago Tribune* and the *Chicago Sun-Times*, are great sources for reviews and events listings. The *Chicago Reader's* site is rich in arts, entertainment, and dining reviews. *Chicago* magazine's site carries a few web-exclusive features along with articles from the monthly. *Metromix Chicago and Time Out Chicago* thoroughly cover Chicago's dining and entertainment scenes.

Contacts *Chicago* magazine ☎ *312/222–8999* ⊕ *www.chicagomag. com.* ***Chicago Reader*** ☎ *312/828–0350* ⊕ *www.chireader.com.* ***Chicago Sun-Times*** ☎ *312/321–3000* ⊕ *www.suntimes.com.* ***Chicago Tribune*** ☎ *800/874–2863* ⊕ *www.chicagotribune.com.* ***Metromix Chicago*** ⊕ *chicago.metromix.com.* ***Time Out Chicago*** ☎ *312/924–9555* ⊕ *www.timeoutchicago.com.*

INDEX

PHOTO CREDITS

Front cover: Universal Images Group/SuperStock [Description: "The Bean" (Anish Kapoor's "Cloud Gate"), Millennium Park]. 1, Michael Ventura/Alamy. 2–3, Stuart Pernick, Fodors.com member. 5, Rosa's Lounge. Chapter 1: Experience Chicago: 8-9, Alan Copson/age fotostock. 10, Chicago Park District. 11 (left), City of Chicago/GRC. 11 (right), Laurie Proffitt. 12, City of Chicago/GRC. 14 (left), wikipedia.org. 14 (top right), Doreen Miller, Fodors.com member. 14 (bottom right), Luke McGuff/Flickr. 16 (left), joevare/Flickr. 16 (top center), Alexandre Moreau Photography/Flickr. 16 (bottom center), City of Chicago/GRC. 16 (right), John Caruso. 17 (left), Kim Karpeles/Alamy. 17 (top center), Jason Lindsey/City of Chicago. 17 (bottom right), CuriousCarm, Fodors.com member. 17 (top right), LouKellenberger, Fodors.com member. 18, BetsyKellenberger, Fodors.com member. 19, Anne Evans for the Chicago Architecture Foundation. 20, City of Chicago/GRC. 21 (left), City of Chicago/GRC. 21 (right), Adler Planetarium & Astronomy Museum. 22, Marina S, Fodors.com member. 23, Robert Koss/Shutterstock. 24, Chicago Children's Museum. 25, Chicago Air & Water Show. 26 (bottom), Library of Congress Prints and Photographs Division. 26 (top), Master Sgt. Cecilio Ricardo, U.S. Air Force/wikipedia.org. 27 (bottom), Library of Congress Prints and Photographs Division. 27 (top left), Ingorrr/Flickr. 27 (top right), Jim Hitch, Fodors.com member. 28, rpongsaj/Flickr. 29 (left), b.jelonek/Flickr. 29 (right), Brood_wich/Flickr. 30, Mike Boehmer/Flickr. 34, Bernt Rostad. 39 (left), City of Chicago/GRC. 39 (right), City of Chicago/GRC. 40, Sun Chan/iStockphoto. Chapter 2: The Loop: 41, BJenk, Fodors.com member. 43, City of Chicago/GRC. 44, amdeda/Flickr. 46, Kim Karpeles/age fotostock. 48-49, Kim Karpeles/Alamy. 50, City of Chicago/GRC. 53, TC, Fodors.com member. 54, Kim Karpeles/Alamy. 56 (top), Kord.com/age fotostock. 56 (bottom), The Art Institute of Chicago. 57 (top), Danny Hernandez, Fodors.com member. 57 (bottom), Bruno Perousse/age fotostock. 58 (top), The Art Institute of Chicago: Friends of American Art Collection, 1930.934. All rights reserved by The Art Institute of Chicago and VAGA, New York, NY 1930.934. 58 (second from top), The Art Institute of Chicago, Friends of the American Art Collection, 1942.51. 58 (third from top), The Art Institute of Chicago, Robert A. Waller Fund, 1910.2. 58 (bottom), The Art Institute, Gift of Arthur M. Wood in memory of Pauline Palmer Wood 1985.1103. 59 (top), Charles G. Young, Interactive Design Architects. 59 (second from top), Dave Jordano Photography, Inc. 59 (3rd from top), Charles G. Young, Interactive Design Architects. 59 (bottom), Dave Jordano Photography, Inc. 60, Raga/age fotostock. 63, Adler Planetarium & Astronomy Museum. 64, City of Chicago/GRC. 65, Ed Lines Jr. and Patrice Ceisel/Shedd Aquarium. 69, chihuly glass In pond by Ben Collins Sussman http//www.flickr.com/photos/bcollsuss/4240587225/Attribution-NonCommercial License. Chapter 3: Near North and River North: 71, SuperStock/age fotostock. 73, rpongsaj /Flickr. 74, City of Chicago/GRC. 76-77, Kim Karpeles/age fotostock. 78, Chicago Children's Museum. 79, jaaasper/fl ickr. 80, John Caruso. 83, Jeremy Edwards/iStockphoto. 84 (left), Stephen Finn/Shutterstock. 84 (center), Steve Geer/iStockphoto. 84 (right), Therese McKeon/iStockphoto. 85 (left), Henryk Sadura/iStockphoto. 85 (center), LauraEisenberg/iStockphoto. 85 (right), Chris Pritchard/iStockphoto. 86, Todd Bannor / age fotostock. 89, NJCoop, Fodors.com member. Chapter 4: Lincoln Park, Wicker Park, and Bucktown: 91, Cathy Melloan/Alamy. 93, City of Chicago/Willy Schmidt. 94, Jeremy Atherton/wikipedia.org. 96, Thomas Barrat/Shutterstock. 98-99, Heeb Christian/age fotostock. Chapter 5: Lakeview and the Far North Side: 103, Kim Karpeles/age footstock. 105, Zagalejo/wikipedia.org. 106, ttarasiuk/Flickr. 108, Steve Geer/iStockphoto. 110, Kim Karpeles/age fotostock. Chapter 6: Pilsen, Little Italy, and Chinatown: 111, FRI-LET Patrick/age fotostock. 113, Kenneth Sponsler/Shutterstock. 114, City of Chicago/ Cheryl Tadin. 117, Danita Delimont / Alamy. 118, Glessner House Museum. 121, City of Chicago/ Cathy Bazzoni. Chapter 7: Hyde Park: 123, Kim Karpeles/age fotostock. 125, Chicago Neighborhood Tours. 126, JOE MARINARO/Flickr. 128, Andre Jenny/Alamy. 129, Scott Brownell, Museum of Science and Industry. 130, Lykantrop/wikipedia.org. Chapter 8: Getting Out of the City: 133, Robin J. Carlson. 135, Flickr. 136, Cantigny Park. 138, Wildgruber/age fotostock. 139 (top), Library of Congress Prints and Photographs Division. 139 (bottom), Kim Karpeles/age fotostock. 140, Carol M. Highsmith/Library of Congress Prints and Photographs Division. 141 (bottom), PETER COOK/age fotostock. 141 (top), Library of Congress Prints & Photographs Division. 142 (top), wrightplus.org. 142 (bottom), Martyn Goddard/Alamy. 143, Jim Jurica/iStockphoto. 144, Kim Karpeles/Alamy. 147, Chuck Eckert/Alamy. 148, Robin J. Carlson. 150, Lisa Andres/Flickr. Chapter 9: Where to Eat: 151, The Peninsula Chicago. 152, Mike Abrahams / Alamy. 158, Kimpton Hotels. 159 (top), chirapbogdan/Shutterstock. 159 (bottom), scaredy_kat/flickr. 161, City of Chicago/GRC. 164, Battman Studios. 167, Kimpton Hotels. 169, Eno. 171, Grant Kessler. 175, The Peninsula Chicago. 178, daveyurek, Fodors.com member. 186, Alinea. 188, Neil Burger. 190, North Pond Restaurant. 192, JOE MARINARO/flickr. 195, Yasmina Cadiz. 197, David Hilowitz/flickr. 200, chadmagiera/flickr. Chapter 10: Where to Stay: 215-16, Sofitel Chicago Water Tower. 223 (top), Essex Inn. 223 (bottom left), Courtesy of PUBLIC Chicago. 223

NOTES

NOTES

ABOUT OUR WRITERS

Carly Fisher is a food writer and editor in Chicago, where she has lived for most of her life. She can be found praising eats in *Food & Wine, Saveur, The Atlantic, MSNBC, McSweeney's, Time Out Chicago, Tasting Table, Serious Eats,* and NBC. She always has room for dessert and worships her grandmother's cooking.

Terri Colby is a Chicagoan by birth and by choice. She has toured the world as a travel writer, but there's nowhere else she would ever call home. She has written for the *Chicago Tribune, Chicago Sun-Times,* and *Los Angeles Times,* among others. She has a soft spot for hotels with on-site spas and windows that open.

Jessica Herman, a Chicago writer and freelancer, updated our Shopping section.

Heidi Moore is a fifth-generation Chicagoan who loves exploring the city's neighborhoods, though she always comes back to the Northwest Side. A freelance writer, editor, and children's book author, Heidi has written for the *Chicago Tribune, Time Out Chicago,* and *Alaska Airlines Magazine,* among other publications.

Roberta Sotonoff, an award-winning travel junkie, writes to support her habit. Her family often complains that she spends more time with gate agents than with them. Her work has been published in dozens of domestic and international newspapers, magazines, websites, and guidebooks. She never tires of exploring her hometown of Chicago.